Palgrave Studies in Agricultural Economics and Food Policy

# Palgrave Textbooks in Agricultural Economics and Food Policy

**Series Editor**

Christopher Barrett, Cornell University, Ithaca, NY, USA

This book series provides instructors and students with cutting-edge textbooks in agricultural economics and food policy.

More information about this subseries at http://www.palgrave.com/gp/series/16444

Michael K. Wohlgenant

# Market Interrelationships and Applied Demand Analysis

## Bridging the Gap Between Theory and Empirics in Commodities Markets

palgrave
macmillan

Michael K. Wohlgenant
North Carolina State University
Raleigh, NC, USA

ISSN 2662-3889 ISSN 2662-3897 (electronic)
Palgrave Studies in Agricultural Economics and Food Policy
ISSN 2662-5474 ISSN 2662-5482 (electronic)
Palgrave Textbooks in Agricultural Economics and Food Policy
ISBN 978-3-030-73143-4 ISBN 978-3-030-73144-1 (eBook)
https://doi.org/10.1007/978-3-030-73144-1



This Palgrave Macmillan imprint is published by the registered company Springer Nature Switzerland AG
The registered company address is: Gewerbestrasse 11, 6330 Cham, Switzerland

*To Peggy*

# Contents

# About the Author

**Dr. Michael K. Wohlgenant** is William Neal Reynolds Distinguished Professor Emeritus of Agricultural & Resource Economics at North Carolina State University (NCSU). He was Assistant Professor at NCSU from 1978 to 1982; Associate Professor at Texas A&M University from 1983 to 1986; Associate Professor at NCSU from 1986 to 1988; Full Professor at NCSU from 1988 until 2018; and William Neal Reynolds Distinguished Professor from 1996 to 2018 until retirement. He received a Ph.D. in Agricultural Economics from the University of California at Davis in 1978, an M.S. degree in Agricultural Economics, and a B.S. degree in Economics from Montana State University in 1973 and 1972, respectively. His specialty is development of economic models of agricultural marketing, policy, demand, and price analysis problems. He has developed economic models to understand farm to retail price linkages, consumer demand, market supply/demand, and the effects of advertising, among other applications. Dr. Wohlgenant has had extensive commodity experience, including work on applied price and marketing problems for cotton, dairy, beef, pork, grapes, sugar, tobacco, wine, and horticultural crops. His work has been published in professional journals, including the *American Journal of Agricultural Economics*, *Review of Economics and Statistics*, *Empirical Economics*, *Australian Journal of Agricultural and Resource Economics*, *Journal of Agricultural and Resource Economics*, and the *European Review of Agricultural Economics*. His contributions to agricultural economics are numerous and his research is widely cited and recognized by awards, with Best Article awards in four journals including the *American Journal of Agricultural Economics*. He is also a recipient of the Publication of Enduring Quality Award by the American Agricultural Economics Association. His H-index from Google Scholar is 34 and i-10 index is 71.

Dr. Wohlgenant is past editor of the *American Journal of Agricultural Economics*. He also served as an associate editor of the *American Journal of Agricultural Economics*, the *European Review of Agricultural Economics*, the *Journal of Agricultural and Resource Economics*, and the *Australian Journal of Agricultural and Resource Economics*. He has served as an economic consultant for the Research Triangle Institute, the Food and Agriculture Organization of the United Nations, for various law firms in expert witness testimony (including expert witness testimony before the U.S. International Trade Commission). He is an academic affiliate of Analysis Group. Dr. Wohlgenant has been called upon to be a consultant to the North Carolina legislature on economic issues related to the N.C. swine industry, the U.S. Department of Agriculture's Economic Research Service, and the U.S. Government Accountability Office. He also has served as an external reviewer of outside research programs. Dr. Wohlgenant taught both undergraduate and graduate courses in economics and agricultural economics at NCSU. He served as chair or co-chair for thirty PhD students, many of whom hold prestigious positions in academics, government, and industry. For his scholarly and research contributions, he was awarded a William Neal Reynolds Distinguished Professorship in 1996. Dr. Wohlgenant was elected a Fellow of the Agricultural and Applied Economics Association in 2001.

# List of Tables

# Chapter 1
# Introduction

## 1.1 Background

This book is based on a set of class notes I used in a graduate course in economics and agricultural economics at North Carolina State for over thirty years. The course, entitled "Consumption, Demand, and Market Interdependencies," addresses the core issues facing economists concerning price determination in commodity markets, especially food and agricultural commodities. The focus is on the conceptual basis of the various relationships, with special emphasis on market interrelationships, both horizontally and vertically. Many problems exist when moving from the theoretical or conceptual models to the empirical applications, and considerable attempt is undertaken to bridge this gap.

Bridging the gap between theory and empirical analysis is a hallmark of this book. Going from theory to empirics requires that we have data—time-series or cross section—that match the theoretical constructs. Often the data match is not perfect, either by definition or how the data are computed. For example, the USDA Economic Research Service publishes per capita consumption by food commodity, although the per capita consumption values are based on assumptions about how food is transformed into the final consumer good, which may or may not be true for industry practice. While these data have useful purposes for policy purposes, they may not be appropriate for demand estimation, or may require further care when used for econometric analysis. In addition to problems of matching data with theoretical constructs, the researcher needs to know how to specify, estimate, and interpret results within the context of imperfect and often incomplete data. A prime example here is how to handle missing values for purchases with cross-section data. It is for these reasons that I use several data sets in this book to illustrate how one might address the problems and help bridge the gap between theory and empirics.

 
M. K. Wohlgenant, *Market Interrelationships and Applied Demand Analysis*,
Palgrave Studies in Agricultural Economics and Food Policy,
https://doi.org/10.1007/978-3-030-73144-1_1

## 1.2 Organization of Chapters

Chapter 2 lays out the basic consumer demand model and determinants of the various demand relationships one encounters in empirical work. The focus is on the comparative static results and quantitative restrictions resulting from the analysis. I use the primal approach, based on the direct utility function, to develop these results because it is the most comprehensive, allowing for quantitative analysis of shifts in preferences. For completeness, the major duality results are presented, and comparative static results for inverse demand functions are reported.

In the spirit of Brandow (1961) and George and King (1971), attention is directed toward demand interrelationships at the retail level and derived demand interrelationships for raw materials producing the final retail products. Separability in preferences plays a central role in deriving these relationships. Much confusion has surrounded the application of separability in two-stage budgeting. In Chapter 3, considerable effort is made to clarify application of these concepts in estimation of demand interrelationships.

Chapter 4 is a review of alternative functional forms used in estimating systems of demand functions. The focus is on empirical tractability. Particular attention is given to the Rotterdam Model (RM) and the Almost Ideal Demand System (AIDS), because of their common and extensive use. Discussion focuses on critique of these models and relative advantages/disadvantages compared to other modeling approaches in the literature. Generalizations of the RM and AIDS model, including the recent EASI demand system, are also presented.

A notable feature of this book is original empirical applications to different data sets constructed from published data. In Chapter 5, a data set on meats is developed and applied to estimation of consumer demand using two common functional forms: RM and the AIDS. Both conditional and unconditional demand models are estimated and major hypotheses of consumer demand are tested.

Consumption, income, and prices are also spatially interrelated. In Chapter 6, cross-sectional and panel demand models are presented and evaluated. As with time-series applications, the focus is on models with demand interrelationships. Special attention is given to quality variation, caused by product heterogeneity, which leads to estimation complications, particularly for consumption-income relationships. Models of product heterogeneity, including linear utility and hedonic distance modeling approaches, are presented and critiqued. Specification and estimation of panel data and pseudo-panel data models are discussed. A major issue is how to model zero values of consumption, especially in a system of demand equations. Although empirically tractable approaches exist and are discussed, problems still exist and knowledge of sources of zero observations is needed to avoid estimation problems.

Consistent with Gardner (1975) and Wohlgenant (1989), theoretically consistent retail-to-farm price linkage models are developed and presented in Chapter 7. The validity and usefulness of the approach is illustrated through empirical application to meats. The data set in Chapter 5 is extended to include meats at the farm level. A large part of the chapter is on the empirical analysis, showing how to implement the theoretical framework in the absence of data for final consumption. Model testing and sensitivity of the results to errors in data are highlights of this chapter.

In Chapter 8, the theory of derived demand is extended to general systems of derived demand functions. The results of Theorem 3 are used to evaluate the retail-to-farm demand linkages in an interrelated framework, extending the earlier work of Wohlgenant (1989). The framework allows one to consistently estimate the effects of exogenous changes in retail demand, marketing input prices, and raw material (farm output) supplies on retail and raw material prices. This chapter also discusses the modification of the models of market intermediary behavior to the degree of competitiveness in food industries, with a focus on meat industries.

In the short run, inventories can play a prominent role in price determination. In Chapter 8, I discuss theoretical foundations for lags between retail and producer prices using a model developed by Wohlgenant (1985). The model is applied to monthly data for beef showing how implicit inventory costs can explain a negative relationship between farm-to-retail price spreads and farm prices, a widely proclaimed empirical puzzle. Causes of, and testing for, asymmetry in price response are also discussed.

In Chapter 9, dynamic models of consumer behavior are presented and discussed. Habit formation is the main cause of dynamic consumer behavior and significant models in the literature developed for this purpose are discussed. Special attention is devoted to intertemporal behavior. As in the static analysis, I present empirical results to illustrate how to go from theory to empirics. I present and evaluate econometric results for alcoholic beverages using a data set constructed from published data.

In Chapter 10, formulation and estimation of dynamic factor demand relationships is the subject. Adjustment costs and product demand and supply uncertainty interact to affect firms' investment decisions in capital. Single capital adjustment models as well as multivariate models of factor adjustment costs are presented. Particular focus of the chapter is on inventory models of the firm to describe food processor behavior. As in past chapters, different modeling approaches are discussed, with emphasis on empirical tractability.

Over thirty-plus years of teaching this course, topics covered in the course have come and gone. An attempt has been made to update the material to current applications in the literature. Moreover, I have added new results to many of existing topics and have added significantly to the empirical illustrations. While the topics addressed do not exhaust all the topics and models presented in the literature, I believe the major topics of concern to demand analysts are addressed. My approach has been to be selective, but rigorous and comprehensive, on the topics addressed. The reader will find an emphasis on price-taking, competitive behavior in the book, although reference is made to some of the main ways one can modify the models to account for imperfectly competitive behavior. In addition, some topics are not covered. Specifically, spatial equilibrium and spatial economic modeling are not covered in this book because excellent work can already be found elsewhere (e.g., Fackler and Goodwin 2001).

## References

Brandow, G.E. *Interrelations Among Demands for Farm Products and Implications for Control of Market Supply.* Pennsylvania Agric. Exp. Sta. Bul. 680, University Park, PA, 1961.

Fackler, P.F., and B.K. Goodwin. "Spatial Price Analysis." In B.L. Gardner and G.C. Rausser (eds.) *Handbook of Agricultural Economics,* Vol. 1b, , pp. 971–1026. Amsterdam: Elsevier Science B.V., 2001, Chapter 17.

Gardner, B. "The Farm-Retail Price Spread in a Competitive Food Industry." *American Journal of Agricultural Economics* 57(1975): 399–409.

George, P.S., and G.A. King. *Consumer Demand for Food Commodities in the United State with Projections for 1980.* Giannini Foundation Monograph No. 26, California Agricultural Experiment Station, Berkeley, CA, 1971.

Wohlgenant, Michael K. "Competitive Storage, Rational Expectations, and Short-Run Food Price Determination." *American Journal of Agricultural Economics* 67(1985): 739–748.

Wohlgenant, Michael K. "Demand for Farm Output in a Complete System of Demand Functions." *American Journal of Agricultural Economics* 71 (1989): 241–252.

# Chapter 2
# Consumer Demand—Theory

## 2.1 Introduction

The neoclassical theory of consumer behavior constitutes the conceptual basis for the demand analysis framework formulated in this book. In this chapter, I develop the general results using the primal approach in order to account for all factors affecting consumer behavior. The main result is the Fundamental Demand Matrix of Consumer Demand (Barten 1964). Additional topics include duality theory and inverse demand functions. Comprehensive treatments of the topics covered here can be found elsewhere (e.g., Phlips 1983; Deaton and Muellbauer 1980b; Theil 1975/1976).

## 2.2 Consumer's Choice Problem

The theory of consumer behavior is that the individual makes rational decisions that satisfy a given set of axioms. These axioms are: (1) reflexivity, (2) completeness, (3) transitivity, and (4) continuity. These four axioms imply that we can represent the consumer's preferences with a single-valued utility function. With the additional axioms of (5) non-satiation and (6) convexity, the utility function will be quasi-concave with indifference curves exhibiting diminishing marginal rates of substitution (Varian 1992).

The consumer's choice problem is as follows:

$$\max_{\boldsymbol{q}} u = v(\boldsymbol{q})$$

subject to:



M. K. Wohlgenant, *Market Interrelationships and Applied Demand Analysis*,
Palgrave Studies in Agricultural Economics and Food Policy,
https://doi.org/10.1007/978-3-030-73144-1_2

$$\boldsymbol{p}'\boldsymbol{q} \le y$$

$$\boldsymbol{q} \ge 0$$

where $\boldsymbol{q}$ is an $nx1$ vector of quantities of commodities consumed, $\boldsymbol{p}$ is the corresponding price vector, $y$ is total expenditures or income, and $v(\boldsymbol{q})$ is the utility function. The two sets of constraints are the budget constraint and the non-negativity requirement of quantities purchased and consumed.

### 2.2.1 *First-Order Conditions: Application of the Kuhn-Tucker Theorem*

Consider the Lagrangian function:

$$L = v(\boldsymbol{q}) + \lambda(y - \boldsymbol{p}'\boldsymbol{q}) + \sum_{i=1}^{n} \mu_i q_i$$

where $\lambda$ and $\mu_i$ are Lagrange multipliers associated with the budget and non-negativity constraints, respectively. By the Kuhn-Tucker Theorem

$$\frac{\partial L}{\partial q_i} = \frac{\partial v(\boldsymbol{q})}{\partial q_i} - \lambda p_i + \mu_i = 0, \ \forall i$$

subject to the budget constraint and non-negativity constraints on the quantities and the Lagrange multipliers. In addition, there are complementary slackness conditions:

$$\lambda(y - \boldsymbol{p}'\boldsymbol{q}) = 0$$

$$\mu_i q_i = 0, \ \forall i$$

By the Envelope Theorem we know that $\lambda$ is the marginal utility of income, and it is positive according to axioms 5 and 6[1]. Thus, taking account of the complementary conditions, the first-order conditions for utility maximization are:

$$\frac{\partial v(\boldsymbol{q})}{\partial q_i} - \lambda p_i \le 0, \ \forall i$$

[1]The Envelope Theorem states that the derivative of the optimum value of the function (in this case the Lagrangian function) with respect to an exogenous parameter equals the partial derivative of the function with respect to the specific exogenous parameter (Silberberg 1990). In this case, the optimized value is maximum utility and the partial derivative of the Lagrangian function with respect to y is $\lambda$; hence, $\lambda$ is the marginal utility of income.

$$p'q = y$$

The first set of first-order conditions indicate that corner solutions are possible if zero quantities are purchased. This means there are additional factors to consider when estimating models with data, such as cross-sectional data, where zero purchases are frequent. On the other hand, if interior solutions exist, $q_i > 0$ and $\mu_i = 0$ according to the complementary slackness conditions. Therefore, the first-order conditions can be expressed as follows:

$$\frac{\partial v(\boldsymbol{q})}{\partial q_i} - \lambda p_i = 0, \ \forall i$$

$$\boldsymbol{p}'\boldsymbol{q} = y$$

### 2.2.2 *Demand Functions*

Because the utility function is quasi-concave, these first-order conditions are both necessary and sufficient for utility maximization. Moreover, if the utility function is strictly quasi-concave, unique solutions of $\boldsymbol{q}$ and $\lambda$ exist for given prices and income:

$$\boldsymbol{q} = \boldsymbol{g}(y, \boldsymbol{p})$$

$$\lambda = \lambda(y, \boldsymbol{p})$$

## 2.3 Comparative Statics of Income and Price Changes

In anticipation of the ensuing empirical specification, a vector of exogenous shift variables $\boldsymbol{s}$ is introduced into the utility function. Both the first-order conditions and solutions to the first-order conditions depend on this $r x 1$ vector of parameters:

$$\frac{\partial v(\boldsymbol{q}, \boldsymbol{s})}{\partial q_i} - \lambda p_i = 0, \ \forall i \tag{2.1}$$

$$\boldsymbol{p}'\boldsymbol{q} = y \tag{2.2}$$

$$\boldsymbol{q} = \boldsymbol{g}(y, \boldsymbol{p}, \boldsymbol{s}) \tag{2.3}$$

$$\lambda = \lambda(y, \boldsymbol{p}, \boldsymbol{s}) \tag{2.4}$$

### 2.3.1 Fundamental Matrix Equation of Consumer Demand

Comparative statics of the effects of changes in prices, income, and taste change parameters on demand can be quantified through totally differentiating (2.1) and (2.2). Define $\boldsymbol{U} = \left[\frac{\partial^2 v}{\partial q_i \partial q_j}\right]$, $\boldsymbol{V} = \left[\frac{\partial^2 v}{\partial q_i \partial s_j}\right]$, $\boldsymbol{Q}_p = \left[\frac{\partial q_i}{\partial p_j}\right]$, $\boldsymbol{q}_y = \left(\frac{\partial q_1}{\partial y}, \frac{\partial q_2}{\partial y}, \ldots, \frac{\partial q_n}{\partial y}\right)'$, $\lambda_p = \left(\frac{\partial \lambda}{\partial p_1}, \frac{\partial \lambda}{\partial p_2}, \ldots, \frac{\partial \lambda}{\partial p_n}\right)'$, $\lambda_s = \left(\frac{\partial \lambda}{\partial s_1}, \frac{\partial \lambda}{\partial s_2}, \ldots, \frac{\partial \lambda}{\partial s_r}\right)'$, $d\boldsymbol{q} = (dq_1, dq_2, \ldots, dq_n)'$, $d\boldsymbol{p} = (dp_1, dp_2, \ldots, dp_n)'$, $d\boldsymbol{s} = (ds_1, ds_2, \ldots, ds_r)'$, and $\lambda_y = \frac{\partial \lambda}{\partial y}$. Then the comparative static results can be expressed as follows:

$$\begin{bmatrix} \boldsymbol{U} & \boldsymbol{p} \\ \boldsymbol{p}' & o \end{bmatrix} \begin{bmatrix} d\boldsymbol{q} \\ -d\lambda \end{bmatrix} = \begin{bmatrix} \boldsymbol{o} & \lambda \boldsymbol{I} & -V \\ 1 & -\boldsymbol{q}' & 0 \end{bmatrix} \begin{bmatrix} dy \\ d\boldsymbol{p} \\ d\boldsymbol{s} \end{bmatrix} \tag{2.5}$$

The total differentials of Eqs. (2.3) and (2.4) are as follows:

$$\begin{bmatrix} d\boldsymbol{q} \\ -d\lambda \end{bmatrix} = \begin{bmatrix} \boldsymbol{q}_y & \boldsymbol{Q}_p & \boldsymbol{Q}_s \\ -\lambda_y & -\lambda_p' & -\lambda_s' \end{bmatrix} \begin{bmatrix} dy \\ d\boldsymbol{p} \\ d\boldsymbol{s} \end{bmatrix} \tag{2.6}$$

Therefore, at the initial equilibrium point, equating (2.5) with (2.6) yields:

$$\begin{bmatrix} \boldsymbol{U} & \boldsymbol{p} \\ \boldsymbol{p}' & o \end{bmatrix} \begin{bmatrix} \boldsymbol{q}_y & \boldsymbol{Q}_p & \boldsymbol{Q}_s \\ -\lambda_y & -\lambda_p' & -\lambda_s' \end{bmatrix} = \begin{bmatrix} \boldsymbol{o} & \lambda \boldsymbol{I} & -V \\ 1 & -\boldsymbol{q}' & 0 \end{bmatrix} \tag{2.7}$$

Equation (2.7) is the *Fundamental Matrix Equation of Consumer Demand* (Barten 1964; Phlips 1983)[2]. This matrix provides a concise summary of all the comparative static effects of the static theory of consumer behavior. We can derive the specific comparative static results through solving for the $(n + 1)x(n + r + 1)$ second matrix on the left-hand side of (2.7), provided the first matrix is non-singular. But we know that it is non-singular because of the assumption that the utility function is strictly quasi-concave in $\boldsymbol{q}$, which implies that this matrix is non-singular and in fact is strictly negative semi-definite. This also implies that the matrix

[2]Note that this is really the augmented Fundamental Matrix Equation of consumer demand because it includes the comparative static results for preference parameter shift variables, whereas the original result did not include the preference shift variables.

$$\begin{bmatrix} \boldsymbol{U} & \boldsymbol{p} \\ \boldsymbol{p}' & o \end{bmatrix}^{-1} = \begin{bmatrix} \boldsymbol{Z} & z \\ z' & z \end{bmatrix}$$

exists and is strictly negative semi-definite. Using this result in (2.7) yields the specific comparative static results:

$$\begin{bmatrix} \boldsymbol{q}_y & \boldsymbol{Q}_p & \boldsymbol{Q}_s \\ -\lambda_y & -\lambda_p^{'} & -\lambda_s^{'} \end{bmatrix} = \begin{bmatrix} \boldsymbol{Z} & z \\ z' & z \end{bmatrix} \begin{bmatrix} o & \lambda \boldsymbol{I} & -V \\ 1 & -\boldsymbol{q}' & 0 \end{bmatrix} \tag{2.8}$$

Writing out the solutions for the partial derivatives of the demand functions and marginal utility of income gives:

$$\boldsymbol{q}_y = z \tag{2.9}$$

$$\boldsymbol{Q}_p = \lambda \boldsymbol{Z} - z\boldsymbol{q}' \tag{2.10}$$

$$\boldsymbol{Q}_s = -\boldsymbol{Z}\boldsymbol{V} \tag{2.11}$$

$$-\lambda_y = z \tag{2.12}$$

$$-\lambda_p^{'} = -\lambda z^{'} - z\boldsymbol{q}' \tag{2.13}$$

$$-\lambda_s^{'} = -z^{'}\boldsymbol{V} \tag{2.14}$$

## 2.3.2 Slutsky Substitution Matrix

Substituting (2.9) into (2.10) and defining $\lambda \boldsymbol{Z} = \boldsymbol{K}$ we obtain the *matrix of generalized Slutsky equations*:

$$\boldsymbol{Q}_p = \boldsymbol{K} - \boldsymbol{q}_y\boldsymbol{q}^{'} \tag{2.15}$$

The matrix $\boldsymbol{K}$ is the substitution matrix and $-\boldsymbol{q}_y\boldsymbol{q}^{'}$ is the matrix of income effects. To show that $\boldsymbol{K}$ is indeed the substitution matrix, note that utility held constant means $du = v_q^{'}d\boldsymbol{q} = 0$. From the first-order conditions (2.1), $du = v_q^{'}d\boldsymbol{q} = \lambda \boldsymbol{p}'d\boldsymbol{q} = 0$. Substituting into the differential form of the budget constraint (2.5), holding $\boldsymbol{s}$ constant, gives: $dy|_{ds=0} = \boldsymbol{q}'d\boldsymbol{p}$. Substitution into the differential of the demand functions (2.6) (holding $\boldsymbol{s}$ constant) gives $d\boldsymbol{q}|_{ds=0} = \boldsymbol{Q}_p d\boldsymbol{p} + \boldsymbol{q}_y dy =$

$\boldsymbol{Q}_p d\boldsymbol{p} + \boldsymbol{q}_y \boldsymbol{q}' d\boldsymbol{p} = (\boldsymbol{Q}_p + \boldsymbol{q}_y \boldsymbol{q}')d\boldsymbol{p} = \boldsymbol{K}d\boldsymbol{p}$. Therefore, the matrix $\boldsymbol{K}$ is the matrix of income-compensated price changes to maintain the original utility level.

The Slutsky substitution matrix has the following properties: (1) negative semi-definite, (2) non-positive own-price effects, (3) symmetric price effects, and (4) rank $\leq n-1$. The matrix $\boldsymbol{K}$ is negative semi-definite because $\boldsymbol{Z} = \lambda^{-1}\boldsymbol{K}$ is the principal $n-1$ submatrix of $\begin{bmatrix} \boldsymbol{U} & \boldsymbol{p} \\ \boldsymbol{p}' & o \end{bmatrix}^{-1}$ which we already know is strictly negative semi-definite. Because any principal submatrix of any negative semi-definite matrix must also be negative semi-definite, $\boldsymbol{K}$ is negative semi-definite because $\lambda^{-1} > 0$. This immediately implies all diagonal elements of $\boldsymbol{K}$ are non-positive. This matrix is also symmetric because it is proportional to the principal submatrix of $\begin{bmatrix} \boldsymbol{U} & \boldsymbol{p} \\ \boldsymbol{p}' & o \end{bmatrix}^{-1}$, which is symmetric. Therefore, $k_{ij} = k_{ji} \forall i \neq j$, or all cross-compensated price effects are equal. Finally, the matrix $\boldsymbol{K}$ has less than full rank because the columns of $\boldsymbol{K}$ are linearly dependent. To see this, post-multiplying $\boldsymbol{K}$ by the price vector, we have $\boldsymbol{K}\boldsymbol{p} = (\boldsymbol{Q}_p + \boldsymbol{q}_y \boldsymbol{q}')\boldsymbol{p} = \boldsymbol{Q}_p \boldsymbol{p} + \boldsymbol{q}_y \boldsymbol{q}' \boldsymbol{p} = \boldsymbol{Q}_p \boldsymbol{p} + \boldsymbol{q}_y y$, upon substituting for the budget constraint. This vector is a zero vector for the simple reason that the uncompensated (Marshallian) demand functions (2.3) are homogeneous of degree zero in all prices and income. This is easy to see because the proportional price and income changes only affect the budget constraint since preferences are independent of prices and income. The expression $\boldsymbol{Q}_p \boldsymbol{p} + \boldsymbol{q}_y y$ is then a zero vector because it is the set of Euler equations for functions homogeneous of degree zero in prices and income. Therefore, $\boldsymbol{K}\boldsymbol{p} = 0$ or the Slutsky substitution matrix has at most rank equal to $n-1$.

In addition to the properties of the Slutsky equation, we also know that the demand functions, as just shown, are homogeneous of degree zero in prices and income, known as the Homogeneity Condition. In addition, the demand functions must satisfy the adding-up property, which states that the sum of the demand functions, weighted by their respective prices, must exactly equal income. There are two important derivative properties of the adding-up condition.

The first is the Engel Aggregation Condition: $\sum_{i=1}^{n} p_i \frac{\partial g_i}{\partial y} = 1$. The second derivative property is the Cournot Aggregation Condition: $-q_i = \sum_{j=1}^{n} p_j \frac{\partial g_j}{\partial p_i} \forall i$.

### 2.3.3 General Restrictions of Consumer Behavior

In general, there are two types of demand functions: (1) Marshallian or nominal-income constant demand functions (2.3), and (2) Hicksian or real income constant demand functions:

$$\boldsymbol{q} = \boldsymbol{h}(u, \boldsymbol{p}, \boldsymbol{s}) \tag{2.16}$$

The Homogeneity requirement for this set of demand functions is that they be homogeneous of degree zero in $\boldsymbol{p}$, implying $\boldsymbol{Kp} = 0$. There are no adding-up requirements on this set of demand functions and the conditions on the substitution matrix are as indicated above.

The general restrictions of consumer behavior are summarized below for both the Marshallian and Hicksian demand functions in elasticity form. Define $e_{ij} = \frac{\partial g_i}{\partial p_j}\frac{p_j}{q_i}$, $e_i = \frac{\partial g_i}{\partial y}\frac{y}{q_i}$, $e^*_{ij} = \frac{\partial h_i}{\partial p_j}\frac{p_j}{q_i}$, and $w_i = \frac{p_i q_i}{y}$. Then the conditions are as follows:

Engel aggregation:

$$\sum_{i=1}^{n} w_i e_i = 1 \tag{2.17}$$

Cournot aggregation:

$$-w_i = \sum_{j=1}^{n} w_j e_{ji} \forall i \tag{2.18}$$

Homogeneity condition: $e_i + \sum_{j=1}^{n} e_{ij} = 0$;

$$\sum_{j=1}^{n} e^*_{ij} = 0 \tag{2.19}$$

Symmetry condition: $e_{ij} + w_j e_i = e_{ji} + w_i e_j$;

$$w_i e^*_{ij} = w_j e^*_{ji} \tag{2.20}$$

Negative semi-definiteness: $\left[w_i e^*_{ij}\right]$ is negative semi-definite with

$$\text{rank} \leq n - 1 \tag{2.21}$$

$$\text{Negativity: } e_{ii} + w_i e_i \leq 0,\ e^*_{ii} \leq 0 \forall i \tag{2.22}$$

## 2.4 Comparative Statics of Exogenous Preference Shift Variables

The effects of preference shift parameters from (2.11) are

$$\boldsymbol{Q}_s = -\boldsymbol{Z}\boldsymbol{V} = -\lambda^{-1}\boldsymbol{K}\boldsymbol{V} \tag{2.23}$$

These effects are proportional to the Slutsky substitution effects. This means there is an intrinsic relationship to price effects in the Marshallian demand functions. Consider the set of total differentials of the Marshallian demand functions (2.6). Substituting (2.15) and (2.23) into (2.6) and collecting terms gives:

$$d\boldsymbol{q} = \boldsymbol{K}\left(d\boldsymbol{p} - \lambda^{-1}\boldsymbol{V}d\boldsymbol{s}\right) + \boldsymbol{q}_y\left(dy - \boldsymbol{q}'d\boldsymbol{p}\right) \tag{2.24}$$

This specification shows, as before, that demand can be decomposed into substitution and income effects. This decomposition also shows that effects of exogenous preference changes can be quantified as adjustments to price changes. If, for example, $\boldsymbol{s}$ represents quality characteristics, then the relevant price changes are quality-adjusted prices. One can envision following a two-step process, in such an instance, where one first estimates hedonic price equations and then uses these residuals to obtain the quality-adjusted prices in the demand model. Such an approach has been taken by Cowling and Raynor (1970) in the context of tractor prices, and Cox and Wohlgenant (1986) in the context of demand for foods. To the author's knowledge, this is the first time a theoretical justification has been provided for this specification. In general, the decomposition of price changes shows that specific restrictions are imposed on the demand structure from introducing exogenous shift parameters into the utility function, whatever they may be.

## 2.5 Comparative Statics with Strictly Concave Utility Function

We can relate changes in marginal utilities to changes in demand by assuming further that the utility function is strictly concave in $\boldsymbol{q}$. This assumption, although more restrictive than quasi-concavity, is allowable because strict quasi-concavity is an increasing, monotonic transformation of strict concavity; therefore, the preference ordering is preserved and one obtains the same solutions for $\boldsymbol{q}$ and $\lambda$. When the utility function is strictly concave, we know that $\boldsymbol{U}$ is non-singular so that $\boldsymbol{U}^{-1}$ exists. By the rule for partitioned inverse (e.g., Hadley 1961):

$$\begin{bmatrix} \boldsymbol{U} & \boldsymbol{p} \\ \boldsymbol{p}' & o \end{bmatrix}^{-1} = \begin{bmatrix} \boldsymbol{U}^{-1} - \boldsymbol{U}^{-1}\boldsymbol{p}\left(\boldsymbol{p}'\boldsymbol{U}^{-1}\boldsymbol{p}\right)^{-1}\boldsymbol{p}'\boldsymbol{U}^{-1} & \boldsymbol{U}^{-1}\boldsymbol{p}\left(\boldsymbol{p}'\boldsymbol{U}^{-1}\boldsymbol{p}\right)^{-1} \\ \left(\boldsymbol{p}'\boldsymbol{U}^{-1}\boldsymbol{p}\right)^{-1}\boldsymbol{p}'\boldsymbol{U}^{-1} & -\left(\boldsymbol{p}'\boldsymbol{U}^{-1}\boldsymbol{p}\right)^{-1} \end{bmatrix}$$

Replacing $\begin{bmatrix} \boldsymbol{Z} & z \\ z' & z \end{bmatrix}$ on the right-hand side of (2.8) with the above partitioned solution, we obtain the comparative static results:

$$\boldsymbol{K} = \lambda \boldsymbol{Z} = \lambda \boldsymbol{U}^{-1} - \left(\lambda/_{\lambda_y}\right)\boldsymbol{q}_y\boldsymbol{q}_y^{'} \tag{2.25}$$

$$-\lambda_p^{'} = -\lambda \boldsymbol{q}_y^{'} - \lambda_y \boldsymbol{q}' \tag{2.26}$$

$$\boldsymbol{q}_y = \boldsymbol{U}^{-1}\boldsymbol{p}\left(\boldsymbol{p}'\boldsymbol{U}^{-1}\boldsymbol{p}\right)^{-1} \tag{2.27}$$

$$-\lambda_y = -\left(\boldsymbol{p}'\boldsymbol{U}^{-1}\boldsymbol{p}\right)^{-1} \tag{2.28}$$

Equation (2.25) shows that the substitution matrix can be decomposed into two effects: the matrix $\lambda \boldsymbol{U}^{-1}$ and $-\left(\lambda/_{\lambda_y}\right)\boldsymbol{q}_y\boldsymbol{q}_y^{'}$. With $U^{ij}$ referring to the $(i, j)$ th element of the inverse matrix $\boldsymbol{U}^{-1}$, the $(i, j)$ th element of $\boldsymbol{K}$ is:

$$k_{ij} = \lambda U^{ij} - \left(\lambda/_{\lambda_y}\right)\frac{\partial q_i}{\partial y}\frac{\partial q_j}{\partial y} \tag{2.29}$$

Houthakker (1960) refers to $\lambda U^{ij}$ as the *specific substitution effect* of the total substitution effect because it gives the income-compensated price change to hold the marginal utility of income, $\lambda_y$, constant. It follows that $-\left(\lambda/_{\lambda_y}\right)\frac{\partial q_i}{\partial y}\frac{\partial q_j}{\partial y}$ is the *general substitution effect*, because it shows the overall effect on demand from an income-compensated price change. As will be shown later, this decomposition will prove very important when it comes to imposing restrictions on preferences to aggregate price effects. As an example, suppose that all goods are independent in the sense that the marginal utility of good $i$ only depends on consumption of good $i$. Then it is easy to show that $k_{ij} = -\left(\lambda/_{\lambda_y}\right)\frac{\partial q_i}{\partial y}\frac{\partial q_j}{\partial y}\forall i \neq j$. In this case, all cross-compensated price effects are proportional to income effects. As we shall see, weaker restrictions than this can produce desired aggregation effects.

It is useful to express (2.29) in elasticity form:

$$e_{ij}^{*} = e_{ij}^{f} - \phi e_i w_j e_j \forall i, j \tag{2.30}$$

The decomposition of the Hicksian price elasticities is into Frisch-compensated elasticities, $e_{ij}^{f} = \lambda U^{ij}\frac{p_j}{q_i}$, which is named after the renowned econometrician, Ragnar Frisch (Frisch 1959). It is the income-compensated price elasticity to keep the marginal utility of income constant, thereby reflecting specific substitution between goods. The scalar, $\phi$, is the so-called "money flexibility," or the reciprocal of the elasticity of marginal utility of income with respect to income.

## 2.6 Duality Theory: Relationships Between Marshallian, Hicksian, and Frischian Demands

In addition to Marshallian demand functions, (2.2), and Hicksian demand functions, (2.16), there are also Frischian demand functions:

$$\boldsymbol{q} = \boldsymbol{f}(y, r, \boldsymbol{p}, \boldsymbol{s}) \tag{2.31}$$

where $r = \lambda^{-1}$ is the price of utility. These sets of demand functions are related to, and can be derived from, the indirect utility function, the expenditure function, and the (consumer) profit function, respectively[3].

First, with respect to the Marshallian demand functions we have:

$$\boldsymbol{q} = \boldsymbol{g}(y, \boldsymbol{p}, \boldsymbol{s}) = \arg\max_{\boldsymbol{q}} \left\{ v(\boldsymbol{q}, \boldsymbol{s}) | \boldsymbol{p}'\boldsymbol{q} = y \right\} \tag{2.32}$$

$$\varphi(y, \boldsymbol{p}, \boldsymbol{s}) = \max_{\boldsymbol{q}} \left\{ v(\boldsymbol{q}, \boldsymbol{s}) | \boldsymbol{p}'\boldsymbol{q} = y \right\} \tag{2.33}$$

The indirect utility function, $\varphi(y, \boldsymbol{p}, \boldsymbol{s})$, is increasing in income, decreasing in prices, convex in prices, and homogenous of degree zero in income and prices. Roy's identity can be applied to the indirect utility function to obtain Marshallian demand functions[4]:

$$q_i = -\frac{-\frac{\partial \varphi(y, \boldsymbol{p}, \boldsymbol{s})}{\partial p_i}}{\frac{\partial \varphi(y, \boldsymbol{p}, \boldsymbol{s})}{\partial y}} \tag{2.34}$$

The relationships associated with the Hicksian demand functions are as follows:

$$\boldsymbol{q} = \boldsymbol{h}(u, \boldsymbol{p}, \boldsymbol{s}) = \arg\min_{\boldsymbol{q}} \left\{ \boldsymbol{p}'\boldsymbol{q} = y \middle| u = v(\boldsymbol{q}, \boldsymbol{s})| \right\} \tag{2.35}$$

$$C(u, \boldsymbol{p}, \boldsymbol{s}) = \min_{\boldsymbol{q}} \left\{ \boldsymbol{p}'\boldsymbol{q} = y \middle| u = v(\boldsymbol{q}, \boldsymbol{s})| \right\} \tag{2.36}$$

The expenditure or cost function,$C(u, \boldsymbol{p}, \boldsymbol{s})$, is increasing in prices and utility, concave in prices, and homogeneous of degree one in prices. Shephard's lemma can be applied to the cost function to obtain Hicksian demand functions[5]:

---

[3]See, e.g., Sproule (2013) for a concise discussion on the relationship between these various relationships. See Cornes (1992) for a comprehensive approach to duality.

[4]Roy's identity can be derived from the Envelope Theorem through differentiation of the maximized value of the Lagrangian function associated with the constrained maximization problem (2.33) with respect to both $y$ and $p_i$.

[5]Shephard's lemma can be derived from the Envelope Theorem through differentiation of the maximized value of the Lagrangian function associated with the constrained minimization problem (2.36) with respect to $p_i$.

$$q_i = \frac{\partial C(u, \boldsymbol{p}, \boldsymbol{s})}{\partial p_i} \tag{2.37}$$

Finally, we have the relationships corresponding to the Frischian demand functions:

$$\boldsymbol{q} = \boldsymbol{f}(r, \boldsymbol{p}, \boldsymbol{s}) = \arg\max_{q}\{rv(\boldsymbol{q}, \boldsymbol{s}) - \boldsymbol{p}'\boldsymbol{q}\} \tag{2.38}$$

$$\pi(r, \boldsymbol{p}, \boldsymbol{s}) = \max_{q}\{rv(\boldsymbol{q}, \boldsymbol{s}) - \boldsymbol{p}'\boldsymbol{q}\} \tag{2.39}$$

The profit function, $\pi(r, \boldsymbol{p}, \boldsymbol{s})$, is increasing in the price of utility, decreasing in prices, homogenous of degree one in $r$ and $\boldsymbol{p}$, and convex in $r$ and $\boldsymbol{p}$. Hotelling's theorem applied directly to the profit function yields the Frischian demand functions[6]:

$$q_i = -\frac{\partial \pi(r, \boldsymbol{p}, \boldsymbol{s})}{\partial p_i} \tag{2.40}$$

At the same initial equilibrium point, it can be shown that all three demand functions are equal, i.e.,:

$$\boldsymbol{q} = \boldsymbol{g}(y, \boldsymbol{p}, \boldsymbol{s}) = \boldsymbol{h}(u, \boldsymbol{p}, \boldsymbol{s}) = \boldsymbol{f}(r, \boldsymbol{p}, \boldsymbol{s}) \tag{2.41}$$

To see this, note first that because $r = \lambda^{-1}, \boldsymbol{q} = \boldsymbol{f}(r, \boldsymbol{p}, \boldsymbol{s}) = \boldsymbol{f}\left(\frac{\partial C(u, \boldsymbol{p}, \boldsymbol{s})}{\partial u}, \boldsymbol{p}, \boldsymbol{s}\right) = \boldsymbol{h}(u, \boldsymbol{p}, \boldsymbol{s})$. Second, $\boldsymbol{q} = \boldsymbol{f}(r, \boldsymbol{p}, \boldsymbol{s}) = \boldsymbol{f}\left(\left[\frac{\partial \varphi(y, \boldsymbol{p}, \boldsymbol{s})}{\partial y}\right]^{-1}, \boldsymbol{p}, \boldsymbol{s}\right) = \boldsymbol{g}(y, \boldsymbol{p}, \boldsymbol{s})$. Equating the two leads to (2.41).

## 2.7 Inverse Demand Functions

It is sometimes the case that we want demand functions, expressed in terms of prices, as functions of quantities and income. For example, if supplies of goods are predetermined, such as quantities of different varieties of fresh fish, market prices will adjust to clear the market in response to changes in fixed supplies of goods offered for sale. The following discussion parallels Barten and Betandorf (1989). A distance function approach to specification of inverse demand functions can be found in Anderson (1980).

---

[6]By the Envelope Theorem, partial differentiation of the maximized value of the profit function, (2.39), with respect to $p_i$ equals the negative of the Frischian demand function.

### 2.7.1 Wold-Hotelling Identity

Recall the system of Marshallian demand functions, $\boldsymbol{q} = g(y, \boldsymbol{p})$, where we have suppressed preference shift variables, $\boldsymbol{s}$, for convenience. These demand functions, which are homogeneous of degree zero in income and prices can be expressed as $\boldsymbol{q} = g(\boldsymbol{\pi})$, $\boldsymbol{\pi} = \left(\frac{1}{y}\right)\boldsymbol{p}$. We can solve for normalized prices to obtain

$$\boldsymbol{\pi} = g^{-1}(\boldsymbol{q}) = b(\boldsymbol{q}) \tag{2.42}$$

which is the vector of uncompensated inverse demand functions. The first-order conditions for utility maximization are

$$\boldsymbol{v}_q = \mu\boldsymbol{\pi} \tag{2.43}$$

$$1 = \boldsymbol{\pi}'\boldsymbol{q} \tag{2.44}$$

where $\mu = y\lambda$. Multiplying (2.43) by $\boldsymbol{q}'$ and using (2.44) yields the so-called Wold-Hotelling identity:

$$\boldsymbol{\pi} = \left(\frac{1}{\boldsymbol{q}'\boldsymbol{v}_q}\right)\boldsymbol{v}_q = \boldsymbol{b}(\boldsymbol{q}) \tag{2.45}$$

The Wold-Hotelling identity delivers directly the *uncompensated inverse demand functions*, which we see express normalized prices (i.e., prices deflated by total expenditures) as functions of all $n$ commodity quantities.

### 2.7.2 Comparative Statics

In order to determine the properties of uncompensated inverse demand functions, totally differentiate (2.45) to obtain:

$$d\boldsymbol{\pi} = \left(\frac{1}{\boldsymbol{q}'\boldsymbol{v}_q}\right)\left[-\boldsymbol{\pi}'\boldsymbol{v}_q d\boldsymbol{q} + \left(\boldsymbol{I} - \boldsymbol{\pi}'\boldsymbol{v}_q\right)d\boldsymbol{v}_q\right]$$

$$= -\boldsymbol{\pi}\boldsymbol{\pi}'d\boldsymbol{q} + \left(\boldsymbol{I} - \boldsymbol{\pi}'\boldsymbol{v}_q\right)\boldsymbol{U}^* d\boldsymbol{q}$$

where $\boldsymbol{U}^* = \left(\frac{1}{\boldsymbol{q}'\boldsymbol{v}_q}\right)\boldsymbol{U}$, with $\boldsymbol{U} = \left[\frac{\partial^2 v}{\partial q_i \partial q_j}\right]$ as defined previously. We can rearrange this last term to obtain:

$$d\boldsymbol{\pi} = \boldsymbol{g}\boldsymbol{\pi}'d\boldsymbol{q} + \boldsymbol{G}d\boldsymbol{q} \tag{2.46}$$

where

$$\boldsymbol{g} = -\left[\boldsymbol{\pi} - \left(\boldsymbol{I} - \boldsymbol{q}\boldsymbol{\pi}'\right)\boldsymbol{U}^*\boldsymbol{q}\right] \tag{2.47}$$

$$\boldsymbol{G} = \left(\boldsymbol{I} - \boldsymbol{q}\boldsymbol{\pi}'\right)'\boldsymbol{U}^*\left(\boldsymbol{I} - \boldsymbol{q}\boldsymbol{\pi}'\right) \tag{2.48}$$

The form of (2.46) shows that the total change in inverse demand can be decomposed into two effects given by (2.47) and (2.48). The first is a scale effect (Anderson, 1980). Define a proportionate increase in the components of $\boldsymbol{q}$ as $d\boldsymbol{q} = \kappa\boldsymbol{q}$, $\kappa$ a positive scalar. It follows that $\boldsymbol{\pi}'d\boldsymbol{q} = \kappa\boldsymbol{\pi}'\boldsymbol{q} = \kappa$. Note using (2.48) that $\boldsymbol{G}\boldsymbol{q} = 0$. Therefore, the scale effect only works through the first term in (2.46). The change in scale is monotonously related to change in utility. Note that $du = \boldsymbol{v}_{\boldsymbol{q}}'d\boldsymbol{q} = \mu\boldsymbol{\pi}'d\boldsymbol{q} = \mu\kappa$. This means $\boldsymbol{G}d\boldsymbol{q}$ is the utility or real income-compensated effect of quantity changes. The matrix $\boldsymbol{G}$, called the *Antonelli substitution matrix*, is the counterpart to the Slutsky substitution matrix.

The scale measure, $\boldsymbol{\pi}'d\boldsymbol{q}$, can be represented as the Divisia volume index, $d\log Q$. This follows from the fact that $\boldsymbol{\pi}'d\boldsymbol{q} = \sum_j \pi_j dq_j = \sum_j \pi_j q_j d\log q_j = \sum_j w_j d\log q_j = d\log Q$. Therefore, we can rewrite (2.46) as

$$d\boldsymbol{\pi} = \boldsymbol{g}d\log Q + \boldsymbol{G}d\boldsymbol{q} \tag{2.49}$$

Totally differentiating the budget constraint gives $\boldsymbol{\pi}'d\boldsymbol{q} + \boldsymbol{q}'d\boldsymbol{\pi} = 0$, which implies $\boldsymbol{q}'d\boldsymbol{\pi} = -\boldsymbol{\pi}'d\boldsymbol{q} = -d\log Q$. Premultiplying both sides of (2.49) by $\boldsymbol{q}'$ gives $\boldsymbol{q}'d\boldsymbol{\pi} = -d\log Q$, provided $\boldsymbol{q}'\boldsymbol{g} = -1$ and

$$\boldsymbol{q}'\boldsymbol{G} = 0 \tag{2.50}$$

which are adding-up properties. We also have the result

$$\boldsymbol{G}\boldsymbol{q} = 0 \tag{2.51}$$

or the homogeneity restriction. Finally, we have the result that $\boldsymbol{G}$ is a negative semi-definite matrix with rank $\leq n - 1$. This follows from Eq. (2.48), showing $\boldsymbol{G}$ is a quadratic function of $\boldsymbol{U}^*$ which is negative semi-definite, and from (2.51), showing the $n$ columns of $\boldsymbol{G}$ are linearly dependent.

The *compensated inverse demand functions*, $\boldsymbol{\pi} = \boldsymbol{a}(\boldsymbol{q}, u)$, are negative semi-definite in quantities, implying all own-quantity changes are non-positive. Commodities whose cross-quantity effects are negative are called q-substitutes and cross-quantity effects that are positive are called q-complements. The counterpart to the Slutsky equation can be derived from the relationship between compensated and uncompensated inverse demand functions:

$$\boldsymbol{\pi} = \boldsymbol{a}(\boldsymbol{q}, u) = \boldsymbol{a}\big[\boldsymbol{q}, v(\boldsymbol{q})\big] = \boldsymbol{b}(\boldsymbol{q}) \tag{2.52}$$

For the $i$th good, $\frac{\partial \pi_i}{\partial q_j} = \frac{\partial a_i}{\partial q_j}\Big|_u + \frac{\partial a_i}{\partial u}\frac{\partial v}{\partial q_j} = \frac{\partial b_i}{\partial q_j}$. In light of (2.49), this expression becomes

$$\frac{\partial \pi_i}{\partial q_j} = g_{ij} + g_i \pi_j = \frac{\partial b_i}{\partial q_j} \tag{2.53}$$

The total effect of a change in quantity of good $j$ on normalized price $i$ is the sum of the Antonelli substitution effect and the scale effect. These functions are subject to the adding-up, homogeneity, symmetry, and negativity restrictions discussed above.

## Problems

2.1 Using the Kuhn-Tucker Theorem, derive the Marshallian demand functions for the linear utility function, $u = v(q_1, q_2) = \alpha_1 q_1 + \alpha_2 q_2$.

2.2 Verify the elasticity form of the general restrictions, Eqs. (2.17)–(2.18).

2.3 Show in the two good case that diminishing MRS does not imply diminishing MU, and vice versa. (Hint: note that the indifference curve in this case is $u_0 \equiv v[q_1, \phi(q_1)], q_2 = \phi(q_1)$. The MRS is $-\frac{dq_2}{dq_1}\Big|_{u=u_0} = \frac{v_1}{v_2}$. Diminishing MRS means $\frac{dMRS}{dq_1} < 0$.)

2.4 Prove that the matrix $\lambda U^{ij}$ is the specific substitution matrix obtained by income-compensating price changes holding the marginal utility of income constant.

2.5 Using the Envelope Theorem, derive: (a) Roy's Identity, Eq. (2.34); (b) Shephard's lemma, Eq. (2.37); and (c) Hotelling's Theorem, Eq. (2.40).

2.6 Consider the Cobb-Douglas utility function, $u = v(\boldsymbol{q}) = \prod_{j=1}^{n} q_j^{\beta_j}$.

   (a) Derive Marshallian, Hicksian, and Frischian demand functions using the duality relationships in Eqs. (2.31)–(2.40). Specifically, verify that condition (2.41) holds.

   (b) Show that the same results would be obtained if the utility function had either the form (i) $u = v(\boldsymbol{q}) = \sum_{j=1}^{n} \beta_j \log q_j$ or (ii) $u = v(\boldsymbol{q}) = \prod_{j=1}^{n} q_j^{\beta_j / \sum_{k=1}^{n} \beta_j}$. Why is it the case that the resulting demand functions are the same with these two utility functions?

2.7 Show that the elasticity form of the Antonelli equation is $f_{ij} = f_{ij}^* + f_i w_j$, where $f_{ij}$ is the elasticity of the $i$th normalized price with respect to the $j$th quantity (flexibility of $i$th price with respect to $j$th quantity), $f_{ij}^*$ is the compensated price flexibility, $f_i$ is the scale flexibility (i.e.,, relative change in price to an equal proportional change in all quantities), and $w_j$ is the budget share as defined before. Compare and contrast this form with the Slutsky equation, $e_{ij} = e_{ij}^{*} - e_i w_j$.

## References


Anderson, R.W. "Some Theory of Inverse Demand for Applied Demand Analysis." *European Economic Review* 14(1980): 281–290.

Barten, A.P. "Consumer Demand Functions under Conditions of Almost Additive Preferences." *Econometrica* 32(1964): 1–38.

Barten, A.P., and L.J. Bettendorf. "Price Formation of Fish: An Application of an Inverse Demand System." *European Economic Review* 33(1989): 1509–1515.

Cornes, R. *Duality and Modern Economics*. New York, NY: Cambridge University Press, 1992.

Cowling, K., and A.J. Raynor. "Price, Quality, and Market Share." *Journal of Political Economy* 78(1970): 1292–1309.

Cox, T., and M.K. Wohlgenant. "Prices and Quality Effects in Cross-Sectional Demand Analysis." *American Journal of Agricultural Economics* 68(1986): 908–919.

Deaton, A.S., and J. Muellbauer. *Economics and Consumer Behavior*. Cambridge: Cambridge University Press, 1980b.

Frisch, R.A. "A Complete Scheme for Computing All Direct and Cross Demand Elasticities." *Econometrica* 27(1959): 177–196.

Hadley, G. *Linear Algebra*. Reading, MA: Addison-Wesley Publishing Company, Inc., 1961.

Houthakker, H.S. "Additive Preferences." *Econometrica* 28(1960): 244-257.

Phlips, L. *Applied Consumption Analysis*. Amsterdam: North-Holland Publishing Co., 1983.

Silberberg, E. *The Structure of Economics: A Mathematical Analysis*. New York: McGraw Hill Publishing Co., 1990.

Sproule, R. "A Systematic Analysis of the Links Amongst the Marshallian, Hicksian, and Frischian Demand Functions: A Note." *Economics Letters* 121(2013): 555–557.

Theil, H. *Theory and Measurement of Consumer Demand*, Vol. I. Chicago: University of Chicago Press, 1975/1976.

Varian, H.R. *Microeconomic Analysis*. New York: W.W. Norton & Co., 1992.

# Chapter 3
# Consumer Demand—Separability and Commodity Aggregation

## 3.1 Introduction

A significant problem to address prior to empirical implementation of the theory of consumer demand is the problem of degrees of freedom. In particular, because of the large number of goods purchased by the consumer, there are literally thousands of individual goods and, therefore prices of related goods, one would need to include in the analysis to make it complete. To see why this is a problem, there are $n + n^2$ income and price elasticities to estimate. The general restrictions provide a total of $1 + n + \frac{1}{2}n(n-1)$ restrictions, leaving a net total of $\frac{1}{2}\left(n^2 + n-2\right)$ elasticities to estimate. Even for a modest number of commodities, there are still a relatively large number of elasticities to estimate requiring a relatively large data sample[1].

## 3.2 Restrictions on Price Movements

The traditional and most common approach to commodity aggregation has been Hicks Composite Commodity Theorem, which says that for a group of commodities whose prices move together we can aggregate them into a single composite group with a single price index. In the case of proportional price changes within the group, the composite good for quantity of, say, group $G$ is $\sum_{i \in G} p_i^* q_i$ (Deaton and Muellbauer, 1980b, Chapt. 5), where $p_i^*$ denotes price for some base period. The group price index would be obtained by dividing group expenditures, $y_G = \sum_{i \in G} p_i q_i$, by the composite quantity to obtain the Paasche price index, $\frac{\sum_{i \in G} p_i q_i}{\sum_{i \in G} p_i^* q_i}$. A less known form of the Composite Commodity Theorem is when price differences of goods within the composite move together. The composite quantity in this case is the simple

[1] As an example, if the number of goods is 10, then we still have 54 income and price elasticities to estimate. This is clearly too large for most time-series data sets as well as many panel data sets.

 
M. K. Wohlgenant, *Market Interrelationships and Applied Demand Analysis*, Palgrave Studies in Agricultural Economics and Food Policy,
https://doi.org/10.1007/978-3-030-73144-1_3

sum aggregate of goods within the group, $\sum_{i \in G} q_i$ (Weiss and Sharir 1978). The appropriate price index would then be the unit value index, $\frac{\sum_{i \in G} p_i q_i}{\sum_{i \in G} q_i}$.

Although both forms of the Composite Commodity Theorem (CCT) are used (particularly for very disaggregated goods), it's use is quite limited due to the fact that it requires exact price proportionality (respectively, price difference proportionality). Lewbel (1996) has relaxed the assumption of the price proportionality version of the CCT by allowing for deviations in price proportionality so that on average price proportionality occurs. This method is called the Generalized Composite Commodity Theorem (GCCT). While this approach shows some promise, it is still somewhat restrictive in its restrictions on price movements. Moreover, empirical applications of the GCCT to date are limited[2].

This chapter focuses on the widely applicable approach based on imposing restrictions on preferences rather than movements of relative prices within commodity aggregates. Major separability approaches are reviewed and the implications of weak separability and two-stage budgeting are discussed. An attempt is made to make a difficult and complex subject clearer with an emphasis placed on empirical tractability.

## 3.3 Separability Concepts

There are two main concepts of separability: weak and strong. Weak separability states that preferences may be partitioned into $N < n$ partitions such that

$$u = F\left[v_1(\boldsymbol{q}_1), v_2(\boldsymbol{q}_2), \ldots, v_N(\boldsymbol{q}_N)\right] \tag{3.1}$$

where $\boldsymbol{q}_G = (q_1, q_2, \ldots, q_{n_G})'$ for $\sum_{G=1}^{N} n_G = n$. Weak separability implies the following:

$$\frac{\partial\left(\frac{\frac{\partial v}{\partial q_i}}{\frac{\partial v}{\partial q_k}}\right)}{\partial q_j} = 0 \quad i, k \in G; \; j \in H; \; H \neq G \tag{3.2}$$

And

$$k_{ij} = \mu_{GH} \frac{\partial q_i}{\partial y} \frac{\partial q_j}{\partial y} \quad i \in G; \; j \in H; \; H \neq G \tag{3.3}$$

The last restriction on compensated cross-price effects is both a necessary and sufficient condition for weak separability (Goldman and Uzawa 1964).

---

[2]Notable applications to date, aside from Lewbel (1996), include Davis et al. (2000) and Reed et al. (2005).

Strong separability states that preferences may be partitioned into $N < n$ partitions such that

$$u = F\left[\sum_{j=1}^{N} v_j(\mathbf{q}_j)\right] \tag{3.4}$$

where $\mathbf{q}_G = (q_1, q_2, \ldots, q_{n_G})'$ for $\sum_{G=1}^{N} n_G = n$. Strong separability implies the following:

$$\frac{\partial\left(\frac{\frac{\partial v}{\partial q_i}}{\frac{\partial v}{\partial q_k}}\right)}{\partial q_j} = 0 \quad i \in H; k \in I; j \in G; H, I \neq G \tag{3.5}$$

And

$$k_{ij} = \mu \frac{\partial q_i}{\partial y}\frac{\partial q_j}{\partial y} \quad i \in G; j \in H; H \neq G \tag{3.6}$$

The last restriction on compensated cross-price effects is both a necessary and sufficient condition for strong separability (Goldman and Uzawa 1964). Also note that with $F$ a monotonic, increasing function, an equivalent representation of preferences for strong separability is $u = \sum_{j=1}^{N} v_j(\mathbf{q}_j)$.

Additional concepts of separability are developed and discussed in Blackorby, Primont, and Russell (1978). For use in this book, we will also make use of homogeneous separability. *Homogeneous separability* is weak separability plus the requirement that each group utility function be homogeneous of degree one.

## 3.4 Implications of Weak Separability

### *3.4.1 Theorem 1: Conditional Demand Functions*

One implication of weak separability is that we may formulate conditional demand functions. That is, weak separability implies:

*Theorem 1* (Pollack 1970)

$$q_i = g_i^G(y_G, \mathbf{p}_G) \ \forall i \in G \tag{3.7}$$

where $\mathbf{p}_G = (p_1, p_2, \ldots, p_{n_G})'$ is the price vector of commodities only in group $G$. This system of demand functions can be treated in all respects as a system of Marshallian Demand functions with all the properties inherent in the theory.

Proof:

Under weak separability, the first-order conditions for utility maximization are:

$$\frac{\partial u}{\partial q_i} = \frac{\partial F}{\partial v_G}\frac{\partial v_G}{\partial q_i} - \lambda p_i = 0 \quad \forall i \in G$$

$$y = \sum\nolimits_{i \in G} p_i q_i + \sum\nolimits_{\substack{j \in H \\ H \neq G}} p_j q_j$$

Eliminating λ we obtain

$$\frac{\frac{\partial F}{\partial v_G}\frac{\partial v_G}{\partial q_i}}{\frac{\partial F}{\partial v_G}\frac{\partial v_G}{\partial q_k}} = \frac{\frac{\partial v_G}{\partial q_i}}{\frac{\partial v_G}{\partial q_k}} = \frac{p_i}{p_k} \quad \forall i, k \in G$$

$$y = \sum\nolimits_{i \in G} p_i q_i + \sum\nolimits_{\substack{j \in H \\ H \neq G}} p_j q_j$$

These conditions give us demand functions:

$$q_i = m_i\left(y - \sum\nolimits_{\substack{j \in H \\ H \neq G}} p_j q_j, \boldsymbol{p}_G\right) \forall i \in G$$

If $q_j = g_j(y, \boldsymbol{p}) \; \forall j \in H, H \neq G$,
then $q_i = m_i\left[y - \sum\nolimits_{\substack{j \in H \\ H \neq G}} p_j q_j(y, \boldsymbol{p}), \boldsymbol{p}_G\right] = g_i^G(y_G, \boldsymbol{p}_G)$. QED

### 3.4.2 *Total Differential of First-Stage Allocation Equations*

Another implication of weak separability concerns the total differential of group expenditure:

$$\boldsymbol{p}'_G d\boldsymbol{q}_G = b_G(dy - \boldsymbol{q}'d\boldsymbol{p}) + \sum\nolimits_{H=1}^{N} \varphi_{GH} d\pi_H \tag{3.8}$$

where $\boldsymbol{p}'_G d\boldsymbol{q}_G$ is the change in real expenditure on group G, $b_G = \boldsymbol{p}'_G \boldsymbol{q}_{yG}$, $\boldsymbol{q}_{yG} = \left(\frac{\partial q_1^G}{\partial y_G}, \frac{\partial q_2^G}{\partial y_G}, \ldots, \frac{\partial q_{n_G}^G}{\partial y_G}\right)'$, $\varphi_{GH} = b_G b_H \mu_{GH}$, $\varphi_{GG} = -\sum_{H \neq G} \varphi_{GH}$ and $d\pi_H = \sum_{j \in H} \frac{\partial q_j^H}{\partial y_G} dp_j$ is an index of prices associated with group $H$ (Barten 1977). It would appear that this result can be used directly with the total differential of the conditional demand functions (3.7) to obtain comparative statics of the total effect of changes in prices on demand. The total differential of (3.7) can be written as follows:

$$dq_i = \frac{\partial g_i^G}{\partial y_G}(dy_G - q'dp_G) + \sum\nolimits_{j \in G} k_{ij}^G dp_k = \frac{\partial g_i^G}{\partial y_G}(p'_G dq_G) + \sum\nolimits_{j \in G} k_{ij}^G dp_j$$

where $k_{ij}^G$ is the compensated price effect associated with the Slutsky submatrix for group $G$.

Substituting from (3.8) then gives:

$$dq_i = \frac{\partial g_i^G}{\partial y_G}\left[b_G(dy - \boldsymbol{q}'d\boldsymbol{p}) + \sum_{H=1}^N \varphi_{GH} d\pi_H\right] + \sum_{j \in G} k_{ij}^G dp_j \tag{3.9}$$

Therefore, we have as comparative effects for total changes in prices and income:

$$k_{ij} = \frac{\partial g_i^G}{\partial y_G}\frac{\partial g_j^G}{\partial y_G}\varphi_{GG} + k_{ij}^G \quad \forall i, j \in G \tag{3.10}$$

$$k_{ij} = \frac{\partial g_i^G}{\partial y_G}\frac{\partial g_j^H}{\partial y_H}\varphi_{GH} \quad \forall i \in G, j \in H, H \neq G \tag{3.11}$$

$$\frac{\partial q_i}{\partial y} = \frac{\partial g_i^G}{\partial y_G} b_G \quad \forall i \in G \tag{3.12}$$

Uncompensated price effects can be calculated directly using the Slutsky equation: $\frac{\partial q_i}{\partial p_j} = k_{ij} - q_j \frac{\partial q_i}{\partial y}$.

Consider the log differential of Eq. (3.8). After dividing both sides by $y$, it can be written as (see, e.g., Deaton and Muellbauer 1980b, Chapt. 5):

$$w_G dlog\bar{y}_G = b_G(dlogy - \boldsymbol{w}'dlogp) + \sum_{H=1}^N \overset{*}{\varphi}_{GH} dlog\pi_H \tag{3.13}$$

where $w_G = \sum_{i \in G} w_i$, $dlog P = \boldsymbol{w}'dlog\,\boldsymbol{p} = \sum_{j=1}^n w_j dlogp_j$ is the relative change in real expenditure of group $G$, $\boldsymbol{w} = (w_1, w_2, \ldots, w_n)'$, $\overset{*}{\varphi}_{GH} = \varphi_{GH}/y$, and the two price indexes are:

$$dlog P = \boldsymbol{w}'dlog\,\boldsymbol{p} = \sum_{j=1}^n w_j d\log p_j \tag{3.14}$$

$$dlog\pi_H = \sum_{j \in \boldsymbol{H}} b_j^H dlogp_j \tag{3.15}$$

where $b_j^H = p_j \frac{\partial g_i^H}{\partial y_H}$ is the marginal expenditure value of the $jth$ good from changing expenditure on group $H$ and $b_G = \sum_{j \in G} p_j \frac{\partial g_j}{\partial y}$ is the marginal expenditure value of group $G$. In general, we do not have numerical estimates of these price indices because they depend on the unknown functions $b_j^H$ One might use conditional expenditure shares, $w_i^G = \frac{p_i q_i}{y_G}$, in place of the conditional marginal expenditure values in (3.15). Barten and Turnovsky (1966) argue that such an approximation need only have minor effects on the estimated parameters.

## 3.5 Two-Stage Budgeting

### 3.5.1 Theorem 2 and Consistency Requirement

What one would like to do, of course, is use price indices such as the widely published Laspeyres or Paasche type indices. An important question then is: under what condition will two-stage budgeting yield the same solution as single-stage budgeting? That is, when will the following conditions occur?

$$q_i = g_i^G(y_G, \boldsymbol{p}_G) = g_i^G\left[y_G(y, P^1, P^2, \ldots, P^N), \boldsymbol{p}_G\right] = g_i(y, \boldsymbol{p}) \tag{3.16}$$

where $P^G, G = 1, 2, \ldots, N$ are price indices. This condition is called the *Consistency Requirement* for aggregation. For local price indices of the form $dP^H = \sum_{i \in H} a_i^H(y, \boldsymbol{p})dp_i$ to exist, it must be true that

$$\frac{\frac{\partial q_i}{\partial p_s}}{\frac{\partial q_i}{\partial p_t}} = \frac{\frac{\partial g_i^G}{\partial y_G}\frac{\partial y_G}{\partial P^H}\frac{\partial P^H}{\partial p_s}}{\frac{\partial g_i^G}{\partial y_G}\frac{\partial y_G}{\partial P^H}\frac{\partial P^H}{\partial p_t}} = \frac{\frac{\partial P^H}{\partial p_s}}{\frac{\partial P^H}{\partial p_t}}$$

is independent of $G$ (Strotz 1957, Gorman 1959). The following theorem gives the necessary and sufficient conditions for aggregation (Gorman, 1959 Green 1964):

*Theorem 2*

The Consistency Requirement (3.16) holds if and only if the utility function is weakly separable and:

(i) there are only two groups; or
(ii) each group utility function is homogeneous of degree one; or
(iii) the quantity indices for all groups but one (say the first) are homogeneous and the utility function may be written as a function of the one non-homogeneous group and a function of the remaining homogeneous functions, $H(v_{d+1}, v_{d+2}, \ldots, v_N)$; or
(iv) the quantity indices beyond the $dth$ are homogeneous and the utility function may be written as $u = F\left[\sum_{j=1}^{d} v_j(\boldsymbol{q}_j), H(v_{d+1}, v_{d+2}, \ldots, v_N)\right]$.

Proof:

The proof is long and difficult to reproduce all the details. I will outline the significant aspects of it. See Strotz (1957), Gorman (1959), and Green (1964, Chapt. 3) for additional details.

Consider the first-stage problem which for simplicity, but still generality, can be written as follows:

$$\max_{\{Q_G, Q_H, Q_I\}} u = v(Q^G, Q^H, Q^I)$$

subject to:

$$y = y_G + y_H + y_I$$

This maximization problem is equivalent to the problem:

$$\max_{\{y_G, y_H, y_I\}} \quad u = V(\varphi_G, \varphi_H, \varphi_I)$$

subject to:

$$y = y_G + y_H + y_I$$

where $\varphi_G = \max_{q_G}\{v_G(q_G)|\boldsymbol{p}'_G q_G = y_G\}$. The first-order conditions for utility maximization are:

$$V_G\varphi'_G - V_I\varphi'_I = 0$$

$$V_H\varphi'_H - V_I\varphi'_I = 0$$

$$y = y_G + y_H + y_I$$

where $V_G = \frac{\partial V}{\partial \varphi_G}$, $\varphi'_G = \frac{\partial \varphi_G}{\partial y_G}$, etc. Solutions to these first-order conditions are:
$y_G = y_G(p_s, p_t)$, $y_H = y_H(p_s, p_t)$, $y_I = y_I(p_s, p_t)$ $\forall s, t \in I; I \neq G, I \neq H$

where I have suppressed notation for all other prices and income. These solutions are substituted into the above first-order conditions and then differentiated with respect to both $p_s$ and $p_t$. The algebra is tedious, but one can show that:

$$\left(\frac{\varphi'_{Is}}{\varphi_{Is}} - \frac{\varphi'_{It}}{\varphi_{It}}\right)(V_{GI}\varphi'_G - V_{HI}\varphi'_H) = 0$$

So either (a) $\left(\frac{\varphi'_{Is}}{\varphi_{Is}} - \frac{\varphi'_{It}}{\varphi_{It}}\right) = 0$ or
(b) $(V_{GI}\varphi'_G - V_{HI}\varphi'_H) = 0$.

For case (a), $\varphi'_{Is} = \frac{\partial\left(\frac{\partial \varphi_I}{\partial y_I}\right)}{\partial p_s}$,

$\varphi_{Is} = \frac{\partial \varphi_I}{\partial p_s}$, etc., which implies $\frac{\frac{\partial\left(\frac{\partial \varphi_I}{\partial y_I}\right)}{\partial p_s}}{\frac{\partial \varphi_I}{\partial p_s}} = \frac{\frac{\partial\left(\frac{\partial \varphi_I}{\partial y_I}\right)}{\partial p_t}}{\frac{\partial \varphi_I}{\partial p_t}}$. Let $\lambda_I = \frac{\partial \varphi_I}{\partial y_I}$ so that condition (a) can be written as $\frac{\frac{\partial \lambda_I}{\partial p_s}}{\frac{\partial \varphi_I}{\partial p_s}} = \frac{\frac{\partial \lambda_I}{\partial p_t}}{\frac{\partial \varphi_I}{\partial p_t}}$. By Roy's identity (2.34), $\frac{\partial \varphi_I}{\partial p_s} = -q_s\lambda_I$ and likewise for $\frac{\partial \varphi_I}{\partial p_t}$. Substituting in the above expression and rearranging terms gives: $\frac{q_s}{q_t} = \frac{\frac{\partial \lambda_I}{\partial p_s}}{\frac{\partial \lambda_I}{\partial p_t}}$. From Eq. (2.26), we infer that $\frac{\partial \lambda_I}{\partial p_s} = \lambda_I \frac{\partial p_s}{\partial y_I} + \frac{\partial \lambda_I}{\partial y_I} q_s$; similarly for $\frac{\partial \lambda_I}{\partial p_t}$. Upon substituting for the numerator and denominator above and rearranging terms: $\frac{q_s}{q_t} = \frac{\frac{\partial q_s}{\partial y_I}}{\frac{\partial q_t}{\partial y_I}}$. Therefore, we find that condition (a) is that all income- consumption curves must be straight lines through the origin. This means preferences for each group must be homothetic, which in turn, implies homogeneous preferences.

Condition (b) can be shown to mean preferences are strongly separable. Strong separability means that: $\frac{\partial\left(\frac{\frac{\partial u}{\partial v_G}}{\frac{\partial u}{\partial v_H}}\right)}{\partial v_I} = 0$. Carrying out the differentiation we find: $\frac{V_{GI}V_H - V_{HI}V_G}{V_H^2} = 0$, which implies $V_{GI}V_H - V_{HI}V_G = 0$. From the first-order conditions,

$V_G\varphi'_G - V_H\varphi'_H = 0$, or $\frac{V_G}{V_H} = \frac{\varphi'_H}{\varphi'_G}$. Substituting into the equation, $V_{GI}V_H - V_{HI}V_G = 0$, we obtain: $(V_{GI}\varphi'_G - V_{HI}\varphi'_H) = 0$, which is precisely condition (b). QED Homogeneous separability is the least attractive of the two requirements. In particular, because homogeneous separability implies all conditional demand functions have unitary income elasticities, it is usually rejected empirically as too restrictive[3]. Typically, the least restrictive condition is strong separability, which has formed the basis of much empirical work.

### 3.5.2 *Form of Price Indices*

Theorem 2 gives the consistent criteria for local price indices. For global price indices, $P^H = P^H(\boldsymbol{p}_H)$, the conditions are more stringent. As proved by Gorman (1959), global price indices exist if there is strong separability plus the requirement that each group have the *Gorman Polar Form*:

$$C_G(u_G, \boldsymbol{p}_G) = a_G(\boldsymbol{p}_G) + u_G b_G(\boldsymbol{p}_G) \tag{3.17}$$

This functional form implies all Engel curves are linear, but does not require the curves to go through the origin as in homogeneous preferences. Indeed, homogeneous preferences are a special case of (3.17) when $a_G(\boldsymbol{p}_G) = 0$. However, the quasi-linear nature of (3.17) leads to quite stringent conditions on conditional demand functions.

Sometimes one would like price and quantity indices such that the product of the two equals total expenditure on the group in question. If one requires that the price indices depend only on prices within the group and the quantity indices depend only on quantities within the group, then group preferences must be homogeneous (Green 1964, Chapt. 4). Fortunately, for two-stage budgeting only existence of local price indices is required, leading us back to Theorem 2.

[3]Note from part (a) of Theorem 2 that the condition $\frac{q_s}{q_t} = \frac{\frac{\partial q_s}{\partial y_I}}{\frac{\partial q_t}{\partial y_I}}$ is equivalent to assuming each second stage income elasticity equals one.

## 3.6 Implications of Strong Separability

### 3.6.1 General Form of Composite Demand Function

As indicated above, strong separability is the least restrictive of the requirements to attain the Consistency Requirement for two-stage budgeting. Theil (1980, Chapt. 2) shows that the composite demand function for the first-stage utility maximization problem with strong separability can be written as

$$w_G dlog Q^G = b_G(dlogy - \boldsymbol{w}\prime dlog\boldsymbol{p}) + \phi b_G(dlog\pi_G - dlog\pi) \quad (3.18)$$

where $Q^G = \sum_{i\in G}\frac{w_i}{w_G}dlogq_i$, $dlog\pi_G$ as defined in (3.15), $\phi$ is the "money flexibility" as defined in Chapter 2, and $dlog\pi = \sum_H b_H dlog\pi_H = \sum_{j=1}^n b_j dlogp_j$. The functions $b_G = \sum_{j\in G} b_j$ are group marginal expenditure values, with $b_j = p_j\frac{\partial g_j}{\partial y}$. The empirical counterpart of this specification is called the "relative price version of the Rotterdam Model" because the price index for group $G$ is deflated by the general price index, $\pi$, known as the "Frisch price index."

In Chapter 2, we showed that substitution effects could be decomposed into specific and general effects. The total differential of demand in the case of strong separability can be written as

$$w_i dlogq_i = b_i(dlogy - \boldsymbol{w}\prime dlog\boldsymbol{p}) + \sum_{j=1}^n (v_{ij} - \phi b_i b_j)dlogp_j$$

where, using (2.30), we have that $c_{ij} = w_i e^*_{ij} = v_{ij} - \phi b_i b_j$, where $v_{ij} = w_i e^f_{ij}$, and $w_i e_i = b_i$ so that the last term becomes $\phi w_i e_i w_j e_j = \phi b_i b_j$. Because $\sum_{j=1}^n b_j = 1$ from adding-up, $\sum_{j=1}^n v_{ij} = \phi b_i$. Therefore, the above log differential can be expressed as

$$w_i dlogq_i = b_i(dlogy - \boldsymbol{w}\prime dlog\boldsymbol{p}) + \sum_{j=1}^n v_{ij}dlogp_j - \sum_{j=1}^n v_{ij}\sum_{k=1}^n b_k dlogp_k$$

$$= b_i(dlogy - \boldsymbol{w}\prime dlog\boldsymbol{p}) + \sum_{k=1}^n v_{ik}\left(dlogp_k - \sum_{j=1}^n b_j dlogp_j\right) \text{ or}$$

$$w_i dlogq_i = b_i(dlogy - \boldsymbol{w}\prime dlog\boldsymbol{p}) + \sum_{k=1}^n v_{ik}(dlogp_k - dlog\pi) \quad (3.19)$$

Noting that for block additivity, $\sum_{i=1}^n v_{ij} = \sum_{i\in G} v_{ij}$ and $v_{ik} = v_{ki}$, upon summing over both sides we get

$$\sum_{i\in G} w_i dlogq_i = b_G(dlogy - \boldsymbol{w}\prime dlog\boldsymbol{p}) + \sum_{i\in G}\sum_{k=1}^n v_{ki}(dlogp_k - dlog\pi)$$

$$= b_G(dlogy - \boldsymbol{w}\prime dlog\boldsymbol{p}) + \sum_{i\in G}\phi b_i(dlogp_k - dlog\pi) \text{ or}$$

$$\sum_{i \in G} w_i dlogq_i = b_G(dlogy - \boldsymbol{w}\prime dlog\,\boldsymbol{p}) + \phi b_G(dlogp_k - dlog\pi)$$

Multiplying and dividing $\sum_{i \in G} w_i dlogq_i$ by $w_G$ then gives (3.18).

### 3.6.2 Unconditional Demand Elasticities

The first-stage composite demand function (3.18) and the conditional demand functions can be combined to produce unconditional demand responses as in the case of weak separability shown above. The total differential of the conditional demand functions can be written as

$$w_i dlogq_i = b_i^G\left(w_G dlog\,Q^G\right) + \sum_{i \in G} c_{ik}^G dlogp_k \tag{3.20}$$

where $c_{ij}^G = w_i k_{ij}^G$. The unconditional demand responses under strong separability are obtained upon substituting (3.18) into (3.20):

$$w_i dlogq_i = b_i^G\left[b_G(dlogy - \boldsymbol{w}\prime dlog\,\boldsymbol{p}) + \phi b_G(dlog\pi_G - dlog\pi)\right] + \sum_{j \in G} c_{ik}^G dlogp_k \tag{3.21}$$

The unconditional demand elasticities under strong separability are therefore

$$e_{ij}^* = \frac{\phi b_i^G b_j^G b_G(1 - b_G) + c_{ij}^G}{w_i} \quad \forall i, j \in G \tag{3.22}$$

$$e_{ij}^* = \frac{-\phi b_i^G b_j^H b_G b_H}{w_i} \quad \forall i \in G, j \in H, H \neq G \tag{3.23}$$

$$e_i = \frac{b_i^G b_G}{w_i} \tag{3.24}$$

These comparative statics, in contrast to those in (3.10), (3.11) and (3.12), indicate additional information on the money flexibility, $\phi$, and group expenditure values, $b_G$, is required, in addition to the conditional demand parameters, to estimate unconditional elasticities. To see this more clearly, we can express Eqs. (3.10), (3.11) and (3.12) in elasticities as follows:

$$e_{ij}^* = \frac{b_i^G b_j^G \varphi_{GG}^* + c_{ij}^G}{w_i} \quad \forall i, j \in G \tag{3.25}$$

$$e_{ij}^* = \frac{b_i^G b_j^H \varphi_{GH}^*}{w_i} \quad \forall i \in G, j \in H, H \neq G \tag{3.26}$$

$$e_i = \frac{b_i^G b_G}{w_i} \tag{3.27}$$

As can be seen, the two sets of elasticities will be identical when

$$\varphi_{GG}^* = \phi b_G(1-b_G)\ \forall i, j \in G$$

$$\varphi_{GH}^* = -\phi b_G b_H\ \forall i \in G, j \in H, H \neq G$$

When the compensated price elasticity of group demand exists, the two expressions for this elasticity can be written as (see 3.13 and 3.18):

$$e_{GG}^* = \frac{\varphi_{GG}^*}{w_G} = \frac{\phi b_G(1-b_G)}{w_G}\ \forall i, j \in G \tag{3.28}$$

$$e_{GH}^* = \frac{\varphi_{GH}^*}{w_G} = \frac{-\phi b_G b_H}{w_G}\ \forall i \in G, j \in H, H \neq G \tag{3.29}$$

## 3.7 Weak Separability Alone Insufficient to Estimate Unconditional Demand Elasticities

Thus, clearly strong separability imposes more restrictions on the first-stage income allocation problem than weak separability alone[4]. The question becomes: Why not just assume weak separability and ignore the much stronger restrictions imposed by strong separability? The answer is that Theorem 2 says such an approach leads to inconsistency in two-stage budgeting. It is hard to see this because of the finding earlier, Eq. (3.13), that weak separability alone yields direct allocation equations of the form: $w_G dlog\bar{y}_G = b_G(dlogy - \boldsymbol{w}\prime dlog\boldsymbol{p}) + \sum_{H=1}^{N} \varphi_{GH}^* dlog\pi_H$ Checking the adding-up requirement we find that it is satisfied so long as $\sum_{G=1}^{N}\sum_{H=1}^{N} \varphi_{GH}^* dlog\pi_H$, which it does because $\sum_{G=1}^{N} \varphi_{GH}^* = \sum_{G=1}^{N} \varphi_{HG}^* = 0$. Also, symmetry can be shown to hold as well. So we must dig deeper to see why strong separability must hold as well (save for the case of homogeneous separability). As shown above in the proof for strong separability, condition (b), strong separability exactly satisfies the first-order condition, $V_{GI}V_H - V_{HI}V_G = 0$. This was shown to be the case because strong separability occurs when $\frac{\partial\left(\frac{\frac{\partial u}{\partial v_G}}{\frac{\partial u}{\partial v_H}}\right)}{\partial v_I} = 0$ In the case

[4]As a reminder, we are talking here about the case where the number of groups is three or larger because two groups is necessary and sufficient for weak separability alone to satisfy the Consistency Requirement (see Theorem 2).

of weak separability alone, $\frac{\frac{\partial u}{\partial v_G}}{\frac{\partial u}{\partial v_H}}$ will depend upon $v_G$, $v_H$, and $v_I$. As first shown by Leontief (1947; see also Green 1964, Chapt. 3), $\frac{\frac{\partial u}{\partial v_G}}{\frac{\partial u}{\partial v_H}}$, will depend only on $v_G$ and $v_H$ so that $\frac{\partial\left(\frac{\frac{\partial u}{\partial v_G}}{\frac{\partial u}{\partial v_H}}\right)}{\partial v_I} = 0$ only if the function $u$ is additive in $v_G$, $v_H$, and $v_I$, which is the definition of strong separability. Thus, weak separability alone leads to violation of the first-order condition for income allocation across broad groups and we must add the additional requirement of strong separability.

We can see these shortcomings of weak separability by observing the total differential of the composite demand equation, Eq. (3.9). Partial differentiation with respect to $p_s$ of good $i$ in group $H$ $(H \neq G)$ and partial differentiation of good $i$ with respect to $p_t$ in group $H$ implies that the price ratio of price indices with weak separability alone is: $\frac{\frac{\partial p^H}{\partial p_s}}{\frac{\partial p^H}{\partial p_t}} = \frac{b_G\left(-q_s + \mu_{GH}\frac{\partial g_s}{\partial y}\right)}{b_G\left(-q_t + \mu_{GH}\frac{\partial g_t}{\partial y}\right)} = \frac{q_s - \mu_{GH}\frac{\partial g_s}{\partial y}}{q_t - \mu_{GH}\frac{\partial g_t}{\partial y}}$, which is not independent of $G$, so it fails to satisfy the Consistency Requirement (Bieri and deJanvry 1972). On the other hand, with strong separability, $\mu = \mu_{GH}$, and the price ratio becomes: $\frac{\frac{\partial p^H}{\partial p_s}}{\frac{\partial p^H}{\partial p_t}} = \frac{q_s - \mu\frac{\partial g_s}{\partial y}}{q_t - \mu\frac{\partial g_t}{\partial y}}$, which does satisfy the Consistency Requirement. Finally, with the homogeneity requirement, $\frac{\frac{\partial p^H}{\partial p_s}}{\frac{\partial p^H}{\partial p_t}} = \frac{q_s - \mu_{GH}\frac{\partial g_s}{\partial y}}{q_t - \mu_{GH}\frac{\partial g_t}{\partial y}} = \frac{q_s - \mu_{GH} b_H \frac{\partial g_s^H}{\partial y_H}}{q_t - \mu_{GH} b_H \frac{\partial g_t^H}{\partial y_H}} = \frac{q_s - \mu_{GH} b_H \frac{q_s}{y_H}}{q_t - \mu_{GH} b_H \frac{q_t}{y_H}} = \frac{q_s\left(1 - \mu_{GH} b_H \frac{1}{y_H}\right)}{q_t\left(1 - \mu_{GH} b_H \frac{1}{y_H}\right)} = \frac{q_s}{q_t}$, which is also independent of $G$ as required for consistency. So we see that weak separability by itself is not sufficient to satisfy the Consistency Requirement, but that strong separability or homogeneous separability produce the desired result.

In light of this finding, it should be clear that weak separability alone should not be used to specify and estimate first-stage income allocation equations. The assumption of approximation of true price indices by Paasche price indices (Carpentier and Guyomard 2001) is insufficient to guarantee conditions for two-stage budgeting will be met. Whether group price indices are approximated by published price indices, the elasticities calculated from the first-stage must be constrained to equal the expressions shown in (3.28) and (3.29), which as we have shown results from the additional requirement of strong separability.

## 3.8 Empirical Implications

Much empirical work has been done (mainly by Theil and co-workers) using the weak separability plus strong separability preference restrictions. An example of this approach is Clement and Johnson (1983) in estimation of Australian demand for alcoholic beverages. They use the Rotterdam Model (to be discussed in Chapter 4), which essentially consists of the time-discrete versions of (3.18) and (4.8). Conditional demand parameter estimates are obtained using Eq. (4.8) in its discrete time form, and these estimates are used in constructing the within group price functions used in estimating the income allocation Eq. (3.18). They assume for empirical application that price indices for groups other than alcohol can be approximated by using average budget shares rather than marginal expenditure values for approximation to weights. This is similar to the approach of Barten and Turnovsky (1966), although the assumption of strong separability is maintained here.

Another empirical approach in the literature is to use cross-sectional data to estimate the marginal expenditure values from which estimates of both within group and composite marginal expenditure values can be obtained. With an extraneous estimate of the money flexibility, one can then calculate elasticities in (3.22), (3.23) and (3.24) with within group price and income parameter estimates obtained from estimation of conditional demand functions with time-series data (see, e.g., Bieri and de Janvry 1972).

A general approach to the problem is recommended here. First, estimate within group parameters for conditional demand functions using time-series data. For all $N$ groups we have all the information we need to compute the marginal expenditure values for the price indices to be used in the first-stage income allocation equations. In turn, we can then estimate all $N$ first-stage equations jointly to estimate the money flexibility parameter that is internally consistent with all demand functions. Other less data intensive approaches can be considered, such as using cross-sectional data to estimate marginal expenditure values and price indices for the first-stage income allocation equations. Such approaches would yield internally consistent estimates of the elasticities in (3.22), (3.23) and (3.24).

Questions still exist on how to empirically determine what the separable groups are for a given data set. Cluster analysis has been widely used with many variants available for testing for different separability structures (see, e.g., Bieri and de Janvry 1972; Pudney 1981). Because these are mainly statistical approaches, they will not be discussed further.

A more theoretical approach has been proposed by Moschini et al. (1994). Separable groups are specified a priori, and then the Slutsky restrictions imposed by weak separability (3.3) are used to test for appropriate groupings. Consider two goods $i, j$ from group $G$, and two goods $l, m$ from group $H$, $H \neq G$. Dividing the two Slutsky terms $k_{il}$ and $k_{jm}$ by one another we obtain $\frac{k_{il}}{k_{jm}} = \frac{\frac{\partial q_i}{\partial y}\frac{\partial q_l}{\partial y}}{\frac{\partial q_j}{\partial y}\frac{\partial q_m}{\partial y}}$. Using the definitions of compensated elasticities and income elasticities, we can show

$$\frac{e^*_{il}/w_l}{e^*_{jm}/w_m} = \frac{e_i e_l}{e_j e_m} i, j \in G; l, m \in H; H \neq G \tag{3.30}$$

In general, there are $0.5\left[n(n-1) - \sum_{G=1}^{N} n_G(n_G - 1) - N(N-1)\right]$ number of non-redundant restrictions. While the set of restrictions in (3.30) will only hold locally for most functional forms, these restrictions hold globally for the absolute version of the Rotterdam Model to be discussed in the next chapter.

This discussion has focused mainly on the requirement of strong separability. For completeness, weak separability plus homogeneous group utility functions would imply the compensated unconditional elasticities in order to satisfy the consistency requirement should equal[5]:

$$e_{ij}^{*} = \frac{\left(\frac{w_i}{w_G}\right)\left(\frac{w_j}{w_G}\right)\varphi_{GG}^{*} + c_{ij}^{G}}{w_i} \forall i, j \in G \tag{3.31}$$

$$e_{ij}^{*} = \frac{\left(\frac{w_i}{w_G}\right)\left(\frac{w_j}{w_H}\right)\varphi_{GH}^{*}}{w_i} \forall i \in G, j \in H, H \neq G \tag{3.32}$$

$$e_i = \frac{\left(\frac{w_i}{w_G}\right) b_G}{w_i} \tag{3.33}$$

## Problems

3.1 Show that if preferences are homothetic then homogeneous preferences (utility function homogeneous of degree 1) preserve the same rank ordering of preferences. Also, show that the expenditure elasticities are all unity with homothetic preferences.

3.2 Why is the Consistency Requirement for two-stage budgeting important? If it doesn't hold, what can we say about the resulting system of demand functions?

3.3 Discuss the differences between first-stage and second-stage demand elasticities. Why would we expect the compensated conditional demand elasticities to be more meaningful than the uncompensated conditional demand elasticities?

3.4 Verify that Eq. (3.30) is true starting from the definition as the ratio of Slutsky substitution effects. What will the restrictions be if preferences are homothetic? What does this imply about the relationship among compensated cross-price elasticities between groups for a given commodity?

3.5 Show that point-wise strong separability (i.e., utility function additive in individual commodities) yields the so-called Frisch Relations: $e_{ij} = -e_i w_j (1 + \phi e_j), \forall i \neq j$ and $e_{ii} = \phi e_i - e_i w_i (1 + \phi e_i)$. Discuss how these conditions can generate an entire matrix of price elasticities with knowledge only of budget shares, income elasticities, and the money flexibility. What can we say about these elasticities as the number of commodities increases?

3.6 Suppose there are three commodities: food consumed at home (FAH), food consumed away from home (FAFH), and non-food (NF). Suppose also that

[5]We use the result that homogeneous of degree one implies $b_i^G = e_i^G \left(\frac{w_i}{w_G}\right) = \left(\frac{w_i}{w_G}\right)$ because all second stage income elasticities equal one. Imposing this restriction on (3.25), (3.26) and (3.27) leads to the results in (3.31), (3.32) and (3.33).

you are interested in testing whether FAH and FAFH can be treated as weakly separable from NF, i.e., whether the utility function has the structure, $u = v[v_1(q_{fah}, q_{fafh}), v_2(q_{nf})]$.

a. If you were to reject the null hypothesis of weak separability, what does this mean from an economic point of view? Does this make sense? (Hint: see Eq. 3.2).
b. Suppose that you found that the above commodity partition was indeed weakly separable. Is this restriction enough by itself for consistency of the two-stage maximization procedure?

## References

Barten, A.P. “The Systems of Demand Functions Approach: A Review.” *Econometrica* 45(1977): 23–51.

Barten, A.P., and S.J. Turnovsky. “Some Aspects of the Aggregation Problem for Aggregate Demand Systems.” *International Economic Review* 7(1966): 231–259.

Bieri, J., and Alain de Janvry. *Empirical Analysis of Demand under Consumer Budgeting*. University of California, Giannini Foundation Monograph No. 30, Calif. Agric. Exp. Sta., Berkeley, CA, 1972.

Blackorby, C., D. Primont, and B.R. Russell. *Duality, Separability, and Functional Structure*. New York: North Holland Publishing Co., 1978.

Carpentier, Alan, and Herve’ Guyomard. “Unconditional Elasticities in Two-Stage Demand Systems: An Approximate Solution.” *American Journal of Agricultural Economics* 83(2001): 222–229.

Clements, K.W., and L.W. Johnson. “The Demand for Beer, Wine, and Spirits: A Systemwide Analysis.” *Journal of Business* 56(1983): 273–304.

Davis, G.C., N. Lin, and C.R. Shumway. “Aggregation Without Separability: Tests of the American and Mexican Agricultural Data.” *American Journal of Agricultural Economics* 82(2000): 214–230.

Deaton, A.S., and J. Muellbauer. *Economics and Consumer Behavior*. Cambridge: Cambridge University Press, 1980b.

Goldman, S.M., and H. Uzawa. “A Note on Separability in Demand Analysis.” *Econometrica* 32(1964): 1–38.

Gorman, W.M. “Separable Utility and Aggregation.” *Econometrica* 27(1959): 469–481.

Green, H.A.J. *Aggregation in Economics Analysis: An Introductory Survey*. Princeton, NJ: Princeton University Press, 1964.

Lewbel, A. “Aggregation Without Separability: A Generalized Composite Commodity Theorem.” *The American Economic Review* 86(1996): 524–543.

Leontief, W. “Introduction to a Theory of the Internal Structure of Functional Forms.” *Econometrica* 15(1947): 361–373.

Moschini, G., D. Moro, and R.D. Green. “Maintaining and Testing Separability in Demand Systems.” *American Journal of Agricultural Economics* 76(1994): 61–73.

Pollack, R.A. “Conditional Demand Functions and the Implications of Separable Utility.” *Southern Economic Journal* 37(1970): 423–433.

Pudney, S.E. “An Empirical Model of Approximating the Separable Structure of Consumer Preferences.” *Review of Economic Studies* 48(1981): 561–577.

Reed, A.J., and J.W. Levedahl, and C. Hallahn. “The Generalized Composite Commodity Theorem and Food Demand Estimation.” *American Journal of Agricultural Economics* 87(2005): 28–37.

Strotz, R.H. "The Empirical Implications of a Utility Tree." *Econometrica* 25(1957): 269–280.
Theil, H. *The System-Wide Approach to Microeconomics*. Chicago: The University of Chicago Press, 1980.
Weiss, Y., and S. Sharir. "A Composite Good Theorem for Simple Sum Aggregates." *Econometrica* 46(1978): 1499–1501.

# Chapter 4
# Consumer Demand—Empirical Analysis I

## 4.1 Introduction

The purpose of this chapter is to discuss empirical implementation of the systems of demand functions approach presented in the last two chapters. We need to first address questions of functional form specification, data, and statistical specification. The functional form question has been a long-standing issue in the area of consumer demand analysis. There are scores of functional forms and a comprehensive review on the possibilities, strengths, and weaknesses is not possible in this book. Excellent reviews can be found elsewhere (see, e.g., Barnett and Serlitis 2008). Instead, the focus will be on the two well-known workhorses in econometric analysis: the Rotterdam Model (RM), and the almost ideal demand system (AIDS). Additional discussion will center on extensions of these two models to more general models which are currently finding popularity. In the next chapter, the RM and AIDS models will be used to estimate empirical results for an important empirical application to meat demand. This application not only serves to illustrate the relevance of the theory, but also data issues in implementing the systems of demand functions approach.

## 4.2 Brief History of Empirical Consumer Demand Models

### *4.2.1 Single-Equation Approach*

At the outset, it is important to make a distinction between single-equation commodity demand and systems of demand equations, and to discuss some of the general issues surrounding these applications. Single-equation methodology has been mostly concerned with finding appropriate demand models that best fit the data under

 
M. K. Wohlgenant, *Market Interrelationships and Applied Demand Analysis*,
Palgrave Studies in Agricultural Economics and Food Policy,
https://doi.org/10.1007/978-3-030-73144-1_4

analysis, both time-series and cross-section data, in order to obtain estimates of own-price elasticity of demand and/or income elasticity. Many of the initial applications were to agricultural and food data. These commodities are in some sense ideal for analysis because they are (a) relatively homogeneous, (b) consumer preferences are relatively stable, and (c) fluctuations in supply are large relative to changes in demand. Focusing on time-series applications, consider a typical model for the $i^{\text{th}}$ good:

$$\log q_i = a_i + b_i t + e_i \log\left(\frac{y}{P}\right) + e_{ii} \log\left(\frac{p_i}{P}\right) + \varepsilon_i \tag{4.1}$$

where $q_i$ is per capita consumption, $p_i$ is the price of the commodity, $t$ is a linear time trend, $y$ is per capita income, $P$ is a general price deflator (e.g., consumer price index), and $\varepsilon_i$ is an error term. The double-log demand model is often chosen because it produces price and income elasticities directly. It is also often supported by data plots, which show a curvilinear relationship between price and quantity. Researchers, however, have shown this functional form assumption is not compatible with any more than single-equation analysis. It is also the case that the model, as specified, does not allow for any provision for related goods—specific substitutes and/or complements to the good in question. Even with prices of related goods included, the model still fails to satisfy both adding-up and symmetry unless extreme restrictions are imposed on the elasticities, robbing it of empirical tractability. Despite these limitations, this modeling approach is still popular where the analysis is only directly concerned with single commodities[1].

### 4.2.2 *Systems of Demand Functions Derived from Directly Specified Utility Function*

The progression to analysis of systems of demand functions has proceeded through formulating models that satisfy the general restrictions of consumer behavior. The first model to satisfy these restrictions is Stone's (1954) Linear Expenditure System (LES)

$$p_i q_i = p_i \gamma_i + \beta_i \left( y - \sum_{j=1}^{n} p_j \gamma_j \right) \tag{4.2}$$

This model is the most general linear model that satisfies the general restrictions of consumer behavior. It is derivable directly from the Stone–Geary utility function,

[1]Despite these limitations of the double-log demand model, it still can be useful as part of an incomplete demand system because such a specification does not commit us to the double-log functional form for other commodities. LaFrance and Hanemann (1989) show that incomplete demand systems can be formulated whereby at least one good does not have the restrictive functional form and still be considered a valid demand system.

$u = \sum_{j=1}^{n} \beta_j \log(q_j - \gamma_j)$. The model, however, is quite restrictive because, as can be seen, utililty is strongly separable in each commodity. Moreover, the LES implies all goods must be normal, all goods are specific substitutes for one another, but gross complements to one another. At most Stone's model has applications to broad groups, but even then it can lead to unreasonable restrictions on the relationship between own-price and income elasticities[2].

### 4.2.3 Formulation of Directly Specified Demand Functions

The next development in systems of demand functions was formulation of direct demand models that satisfy the general restrictions of consumer behavior. The Rotterdam Model has its origins in this line of development. Other models include the CBS differential demand systems (Keller and van Driel 1985) and NBER models (Neves 1987). More will said about this class of models below.

### 4.2.4 Derivation of Demand Functions Using Locally Flexible Functional Forms

With the advent of duality theory, demand functions were derived from directly specified indirect utility or expenditure functions through application of Roy's identity, (2.35), or Shephard's lemma, (2.37). The idea is to specify, say, an indirect utility function through a second-order Taylor's series expansion to have enough parameters to impose general restrictions of consumer behavior. An example of such a model is the indirect transcendental logarithmic utility function—indirect translog for short (Christensen et al. 1975)—which, through application of Roy's identity, (2.34), produces the demand functions:

$$w_i = w_i(y, \boldsymbol{p}) = -\frac{\frac{\partial \varphi}{\partial \log p_i}}{\frac{\partial \varphi}{\partial \log y}} = \frac{\frac{\partial \varphi}{\partial \log\left(p_i/y\right)}}{\sum_j \frac{\partial \varphi}{\partial \log\left(p_j/y\right)}} = \frac{\beta_i + \sum_j \beta_{ji} \log\left(p_i/y\right)}{\sum_k \left(\beta_k + \sum_j \beta_{kj} \log\left(p_j/y\right)\right)} \tag{4.3}$$

where $-\frac{\partial \varphi}{\partial \log y} = \sum_j \frac{\partial \varphi}{\partial \log p_j}$ because $\varphi$ is homogeneous of degree zero in prices and income. With a normalization such as $\sum \beta_k = -1$ the model can be estimated as a system of Marshallian share demand functions. Other locally flexible

[2] If the number of groups is large, then $e_{ii} \cong \phi e_i$, known as Pigou's law (Deaton and Muellbauer 1980b, Chapt. 3)

demand systems such as generalized Leontief (Diewert 1971), where square roots of normalized prices replace logarithms of normalized prices, have also been applied extensively.

### *4.2.5 Demand Functions Derived from Globally Flexible Functional Forms*

The problem with demand systems based on second-order local flexibility is that one cannot arbitrarily choose a point in the sample, e.g., sample mean, and then assert that the elasticities estimated at that point are statistically consistent, regardless of the truth (White 1980). Gallant (1981) shows that one must choose functional forms based on the Sobolev norm in order to take into account derivatives of the indirect utility function or expenditure function when applying standard regression methods. He shows the Fourier Flexible Form satisfies the Sobolev norm. The Fourier Flexible Form is essentially the indirect translog model (4.3) with added linear functions in pairs of sine and cosine functions of normalized prices. Barnett and Jonas (1983) have proposed the Asymptotically Ideal Model, which uses as arguments fractional powers of normalized prices, and may be viewed as a generalization of the generalized Leontief model[3].

Because of the theoretical preference of the semi-nonparametric models of Gallant and Barnett and Jonas, it is somewhat surprising that they have not been used as much as other more restrictive functional forms. Reasons could be the increased complexity of the model and uncertainty about order of expansion. Whatever the reason, researchers have been satisfied to pursue empirical work with more common models such as the RM and AIDS. More will be said about why they continue to enjoy popularity as we proceed.

## 4.3 System of Demand Equations Estimation

In estimating a system of demand equations, we need to incorporate stochastic elements into the framework. It is typically assumed that the error structure is such that error terms can be added to the system of the Marshallian demand functions to obtain:

$$q_{it} = g_i\left(y_t, \boldsymbol{p}_t\right) + \varepsilon_{it} i = 1, \ldots, n; t = 1, \ldots, T \tag{4.4}$$

---

[3]There are several embellishments of Fourier Flexible Form (FFF). Chalfant (1987) embeds the Almost Ideal Demand System (AIDS) in the FFF. Piggott (2003) developed a nested PIGLOG model where both the AIDS and Translog models, as well as models incorporating pre-committed quantities, are nested within the FFF.

where $\mathrm{E}(\boldsymbol{\varepsilon}_t) = E(\varepsilon_{1t}, \varepsilon_{2t}, \ldots, \varepsilon_{nt})' = 0'$, $\mathrm{E}(\boldsymbol{\varepsilon}_t\boldsymbol{\varepsilon}_t') = E\begin{bmatrix} \varepsilon_{1t}^2 & \varepsilon_{1t}\varepsilon_{2t} & \varepsilon_{1t}\varepsilon_{nt} \\ \varepsilon_{2t}\varepsilon_{1t} & \varepsilon_{2t}^2 & \varepsilon_{2t}\varepsilon_{nt} \\ \varepsilon_{nt}\varepsilon_{1t} & \varepsilon_{nt}\varepsilon_{n2} & \varepsilon_{nt}^2 \end{bmatrix} =$ $\boldsymbol{\Omega}$, $\mathrm{E}(\boldsymbol{\varepsilon}_t\boldsymbol{\varepsilon}_s') = 0\forall s \neq t$. Berndt and Savin (1975) consider the more complicated case where $\mathrm{E}(\boldsymbol{\varepsilon}_t\boldsymbol{\varepsilon}_s') \neq 0$. Multiplying (4.4) by $p_{it}$ and summing over both sides and imposing adding-up gives: $\sum_i p_{it}q_{it} = \sum_i p_{it}g_i(y_t, \boldsymbol{p}_t) + \sum_i p_{it}\varepsilon_{it} = y$implies $\boldsymbol{\Omega}$ is singular because $\sum_i p_{it}\varepsilon_{it} = 0$. So $\boldsymbol{\Omega}^{-1}$ does not exist and has at most rank $n-1$. Barten (1969) has shown one can arbitrarily delete one equation and estimate the remaining $n-1$ equations.

Let $\boldsymbol{q}_{(n-1)t}$ be the $n-1$ vector of quantities consumed at time $t$. If $\boldsymbol{\varepsilon}_{(n-1)t}$ is multivariate normal, then $\boldsymbol{q}_{(n-1)t} \sim N\left[\boldsymbol{g}_{(n-1)t}(y_t, \boldsymbol{p}_t), \boldsymbol{\Omega}_{n-1}\right]$ and the log-likelihood function is

$$\log f(\boldsymbol{q}_{(n-1)t}) = -\frac{(n-1)}{2}\log(2\pi) - \frac{1}{2}\log|\boldsymbol{\Omega}_{n-1}| - \frac{1}{2}\left[\left(\boldsymbol{q}_{(n-1)t} - \boldsymbol{g}_{(n-1)t}(y_t, \boldsymbol{p}_t)\right)'\boldsymbol{\Omega}_{n-1}^{-1}\left(\boldsymbol{q}_{(n-1)t} - \boldsymbol{g}_{(n-1)t}(y_t, \boldsymbol{p}_t)\right)\right]$$

For all $T$ observations, the log-likelihood function is therefore:

$$\log L = \sum_{t=1}^{T} logf_t = -\frac{T(n-1)}{2}\log - \frac{T}{2}\log|\boldsymbol{\Omega}_{n-1}| - \frac{1}{2}\sum_{t=1}^{T}\left[\left(\boldsymbol{q}_{(n-1)t} - \boldsymbol{g}_{(n-1)t}(y_t, \boldsymbol{p}_t)\right)'\boldsymbol{\Omega}_{n-1}^{-1}\left(\boldsymbol{q}_{(n-1)t} - \boldsymbol{g}_{(n-1)t}(y_t, \boldsymbol{p}_t)\right)\right] \quad (4.5)$$

Maximization of (4.5) with respect to the parameters (embedded in $\boldsymbol{g}_{(n-1)t}(y_t, \boldsymbol{p}_t)$ and $\boldsymbol{\Omega}_{n-1}$, subject to constraints on the parameter estimates), yields maximum likelihood estimates. Parameter values for the $n^{th}$ equation can be obtained using the FIML estimates and general restrictions of consumer behavior.

The same framework can be used to estimate system of demand functions if there is autocorrelation in the residuals. A common assumption is that there is only serial correlation in each equation, independent of other equations. In such an instance, Berndt and Savin (1975) have shown that the autocorrelation parameter, $\rho$, should be constrained to be the same for each equation. Define the residuals in (4.4) as $u_{it} = \rho u_{it-1} + \varepsilon_{it}$. Quasi-differencing (4.4) gives the resulting equations:

$$q_{it} = \rho q_{it-1} + g_i(y_t, \boldsymbol{p}_t) - \rho g_i(y_{t-1}, \boldsymbol{p}_{t-1}) + \varepsilon_{it} i = 1, \ldots, n; t = 2, \ldots, T$$

This set of equations, after eliminating one of the equations, would then be used in formulating the log-likelihood function (4.5).

The restrictions implied by theory can be tested using the likelihood ratio test: $LR = \frac{\tilde{L}}{\hat{L}}$, where $\tilde{L}$ is the maximum likelihood value with restrictions imposed, and $\hat{L}$ is maximum likelihood value without restrictions imposed. Note though that adding-up is a maintained hypothesis because it is a construct of the data. It is well-known that

$$-2\log LR = 2\left(\log\hat{L} - \log\tilde{L}\right) \tag{4.6}$$

is distributed chi-squared with $r$ degrees of freedom (i.e., number of independent restrictions) at significance level $\alpha$, i.e.,

$$-2\log LR \sim \chi^2_\alpha(r) \tag{4.7}$$

Tests usually performed include: (i) homogeneity condition alone, (ii) homogeneity plus symmetry, and (iii) symmetry given homogeneity condition holds. The empirical record finds (i) frequently rejected, especially when the number of goods is moderate to large, and (iii) usually holding (Deaton and Muellbauer 1980b, Chapt. 3). It is still a puzzle as to why this is so, given that the "no money illusion" implication of the zero homogeneity condition seems more fundamental than the symmetry condition. Dynamic misspecification and inappropriate or mismatched data may be a cause of problem (Deaton and Muellbauer 1980b, Chapt. 3).

## 4.4 The Rotterdam Model

The RM is directly derived from the Marshallian demand function, $\boldsymbol{q} = \boldsymbol{g}(y, \boldsymbol{p})$, by first totally differentiating, converting to elasticities, and then imposing the Slutsky decomposition to obtain: $dlogq_i = e_i\left(dlogy - \sum_k w_k dlogp_k\right) + \sum_j e^*_{ij} dlogp_j$. Multiplying both sides by $w_i$ and using the result that $dlogy - \sum_k w_k dlogp_k = \sum_k w_k dlogq_k$, we get:

$$w_i dlogq_i = b_i\left(\sum_k w_k dlogq_k\right) + \sum_j c_{ij} dlogp_j \tag{4.8}$$

where $b_i = p_i\frac{\partial q_i}{\partial y}$ is the marginal expenditure of good $i$ because $\frac{\partial p_i q_i}{\partial y} = p_i\frac{\partial q_i}{\partial y}$ and $c_{ij} = w_i e^*_{ij} = p_i p_j k_{ij}/y$. Even though no assumptions have been made about constancy of coefficients, we can see that the general restrictions of consumer behavior hold exactly:

$$\sum_i w_i dlogq_i = \sum_i b_i \left( \sum_k w_k dlogq_k \right) = \sum_k w_k dlogq_k \text{implies} \sum_i b_i = 1$$

$$\text{for adding} - \text{up;} \tag{4.8.a}$$

$$\sum_j c_{ij} = 0 \text{ for homogeneity;} \tag{4.8.b}$$

$$c_{ij} = c_{ji} \text{ for symmetry;} \tag{4.8.c}$$

$$c_{ii} \leq 0 \text{ for negativity;} \tag{4.8.d}$$

$$\left[c_{ij}\right] = \left[p_i p_j k_{ij}/y\right] \text{is negative semi} - \text{definite.} \tag{4.8.e}$$

Replacing the log differentials with first differences in logarithms and making these functions constants gives us the *absolute price version* of the RM:

$$\bar{w}_{it} \Delta logq_{it} = b_i \Delta log Q_t + \sum_j c_{ij} \Delta logp_{jt} \tag{4.9}$$

where $\Delta logq_{it} = logq_{it} - logq_{it-1}$, $\Delta logp_{it} = logp_{it} - logp_{it-1}, \ldots \Delta log Q_t = \sum_k \bar{w}_{kt} \Delta logq_{kt}$ is the Divisia volume index (Theil 1980), which represents relative changes in real income; and $\bar{w}_{it} = \frac{1}{2}(w_{it} + w_{it-1})$, which are average budget shares between adjoining time periods. The restrictions are the same as above in (4.8.a), (4.8.b), (4.8.c), (4.8.d) and (4.8.e).

In addition to the absolute price version, there is also the *relative price version* of the RM. From Chapter 3, we have Eq. (3.19):

$$w_i dlogq_i = b_i \left(dlogy - \mathbf{w}' dlog\,\mathbf{p}\right) + \sum_{k=1}^{n} v_{ik} (dlogp_k - dlog\pi)$$

Replacing differentials with first differences as above we obtain the discrete time form of (3.19):

$$\bar{w}_{it} \Delta logq_{it} = b_i \left(\Delta logy_t - \bar{\mathbf{w}}'_t \Delta log\,\mathbf{p}_t\right) + \sum_{k=1}^{n} v_{ik} (\Delta logp_{kt} - \Delta log\pi_t) \quad \text{(or)}$$

$$\bar{w}_{it} \Delta logq_{it} = b_i \Delta log Q_t + \sum_{k=1}^{n} v_{ik} (\Delta logp_{kt} - \Delta log\pi_t) \tag{4.10}$$

where $v_{ik} = c_{ik} - \phi b_i b_k$. This formulation of the RM decomposes the substitution effect into specific and general effects, and allows one to estimate Frischian price elasticities of demand.

An important application of the relative price version of the RM is its application to formulating composite demand functions for first-stage income allocation equations. From (3.18), we have the discrete time version of the composite demand relative price version of the RM:

$$\bar{w}_{Gt}\Delta log Q_t^G = a_G + b_G \Delta log Q_t + \phi b_G(\Delta log \pi_{Gt} - \Delta log \pi_t) + \varepsilon_{Gt} \tag{4.11}$$

where $a_G$ is a constant measuring the time trend in demand due to exogenous preference shifts, and $\varepsilon_{Gt}$ is an error term for the composite demand equation. This composite demand equation can be combined with the absolute price version of the RM for the conditional demand functions (3.20):

$$\bar{w}_{it}\Delta log q_{it} = a_i + b_i^G\left(\bar{w}_{Gt}\Delta log Q_t^G\right) + \sum_{j\in G} c_{ik}^G \Delta log p_{kt} + \varepsilon_{it} \tag{4.12}$$

where $a_i$ and $\varepsilon_{it}$ are exogenous trend shift parameters and error terms with the properties indicated above under multivariate normality. It is important to recognize the two equations are not independent because both $\Delta log \pi_{Gt}$ and $\Delta log \pi_t$ depend on the parameters $b_i^G$ from the second stage, as indicated by the forms of these two price indices (see 3.18). However, conditional on these parameters, the system is block recursive.

A widespread critique of the RM is that it is only integrable into a community utility function if the utility function is Cobb-Douglas. However, in a significant paper, Barnett (1978) proved that the assumed constancy of parameters of the model at the *aggregate* level imposes few, if any, restrictions on the parameters at the individual or *micro* level. Barnett derives a general theoretical construct for aggregate demand systems, and then shows that the RM gives a Taylor's series local approximation to the aggregate theory throughout the RM's feasible parameter set. While the so-called "flexible functional forms" based on Taylor's series expansions of unknown indirect utility and expenditure functions also provide first-order approximations to arbitrary demand functions, the RM has the advantage of approximating a more general theoretical construct than the flexible functional forms. Based on its theoretical properties, the RM seems better fit for use with aggregate data.

## 4.5 The Almost Ideal Demand System

The Almost Ideal Demand System (AIDS) is based on the assumption that preferences are of the PIGLOG class, a class of preferences yielding exact, nonlinear aggregation over consumers (Deaton and Muellbauer 1980a). The PIGLOG class can be defined as[4]:

$$\log c(u, \boldsymbol{p}) = \log a(\boldsymbol{p}) + ub(\boldsymbol{p}) \tag{4.13}$$

Additional motivation for this form of the expenditure function is that it produces Engel curves consistent with results from empirical work. To derive demand functions from this specification we first apply Shepherd's lemma to (4.13):

$$w_i = \frac{\partial \log c(u, \boldsymbol{p})}{\partial \log p_i} = \frac{\partial \log a(\boldsymbol{p})}{\partial \log p_i} + u\frac{\partial b(\boldsymbol{p})}{\partial \log p_i}$$

Next solve (4.13) for the indirect utility function, $\psi(y, \boldsymbol{p}) = \frac{\log c(u,\boldsymbol{p}) - \log a(\boldsymbol{p})}{b(\boldsymbol{p})} = \frac{\log y - \log a(\boldsymbol{p})}{b(\boldsymbol{p})}$, and substitute above to obtain:

$$w_i = \frac{\partial \log c(u, \boldsymbol{p})}{\partial \log p_i} = \frac{\partial \log a(\boldsymbol{p})}{\partial \log p_i} + \left[\frac{\log y - \log a(\boldsymbol{p})}{b(\boldsymbol{p})}\right]\frac{\partial b(\boldsymbol{p})}{\partial \log p_i} \tag{4.14}$$

Deaton and Muellbauer (1980a) specify the two price indices as follows:

$$\log a(\boldsymbol{p}) = \alpha_0 + \sum_i \alpha_i logp_i + \frac{1}{2}\sum_j\sum_k \gamma_{jk} logp_j logp_k \tag{4.15}$$

$$b(\boldsymbol{p}) = \beta_0 \Pi p_i^{\beta_i} \tag{4.16}$$

Substituting (4.15) and (4.16) into (4.14) and noting that $\frac{\partial \log b(\boldsymbol{p})}{\partial \log p_i} b(\boldsymbol{p}) = \frac{\partial b(\boldsymbol{p})}{\partial \log p_i}$, we obtain:

$$w_i = \alpha_i^* + \sum_k \gamma_{ki} logp_k$$

$$+\beta_i\left[\log y - \sum_i \alpha_i logp_i - \frac{1}{2}\sum_j\sum_k \gamma_{jk} logp_j logp_k\right] \tag{4.17}$$

where $\alpha_i^* = \alpha_i - \beta_i\alpha_0$. The model is subject to the testable restrictions:

$$\sum_j \gamma_{ij} = 0 \text{for homogeneity;} \tag{4.17a}$$

$$\gamma_{ij} = \gamma_{ji} \text{ for symmetry;} \tag{4.17b}$$

[4]The AIDS model was initially formulated as $\log c(u, \boldsymbol{p}) = (1-u)\{\log a(\boldsymbol{p})\} + u\{\log a(\boldsymbol{p}) + b(\boldsymbol{p})\}$. Rearrangement of terms leads to (4.13).

Price elasticities can be estimated using the formula, $e_{ij} = \frac{1}{w_i}\frac{\partial \log w_i}{\partial p_j} - \delta_{ij}$, where $\delta_{ij}$ is the Kronecker delta ($\delta_{ij} = 1, i = j; \delta_{ij} = 0, i \neq j$):

$$e_{ij} = \frac{\gamma_{ij} - \beta_i\left(\alpha_j + \sum_k \gamma_{ki} logp_k\right)}{w_i} - \delta_{ij} = \frac{\gamma_{ij} + \beta_i\beta_j \log\left(\frac{y}{P}\right) - w_j\beta_i}{w_i} - \delta_{ij} \tag{4.18}$$

Income elasticities are:

$$e_i = \frac{\beta_i}{w_i} + 1 \tag{4.19}$$

Compensated elasticities can be computed using the Slutsky equation, $e_{ij}^* = e_{ij} + w_j e_i$.

A function of interest is $c_{ij} = w_i e_{ij}^*$, which for the AIDS model (4.17) is:

$$c_{ij} = w_i e_{ij}^* = \gamma_{ij} + \beta_i\beta_j \log\left(\frac{y}{P}\right) + w_i w_j - w_i\delta_{ij} \tag{4.20}$$

The matrix $\left[c_{ij}\right]$ must be negative semi-definite. In contrast to the RM, negative semi-definiteness only holds locally for the AIDS model.

The AIDS model for econometric analysis is specified from (4.17) as follows:

$$w_{it} = \alpha_i + \tau_i t + \sum_k \gamma_{ki} logp_{kt}$$

$$+\beta_i\left[\log y_t - \sum_i \alpha_i logp_{it} - \frac{1}{2}\left(\sum_j\sum_k \gamma_{jk} logp_j logp_k\right)\right] + \varepsilon_{it} \tag{4.21}$$

where $t$ is a linear time trend to reflect non-price and income changes (e.g., taste changes). The parameter $\alpha_0$ in the price index (4.15) is also set to zero so that $\alpha_i$ is identifiable (Deaton and Muellbauer 1980a). The empirical specification is now Eq. (4.21), subject to the constraints (4.17a) and (4.17b).

A problem with the AIDS model is that it does not have a global regular region. In particular, the model often violates the curvature restrictions. The generalized modified AIDS model (MAIDS) has been developed to enlarge the regular region or price-income space that satisfies curvature restrictions and monotonicity (Cooper and McLaren 1992). Other models such as the Generalized Box-Cox (Berndt and Khaled 1979) or Miniflex Laurent (Barnett 1985) also have larger regular regions but are more complex and have not been widely used. One can always check regularity conditions to see if they satisfy the model. If not, such restrictions can be imposed in estimation if needed.

## 4.6 The Linear Approximate AIDS

Because prices are often highly correlated, Deaton and Muellbauer (1980a) recommended replacing the price index from (4.15), by $\log P^* = \log a(\boldsymbol{p})$. On the assumption $P \cong \theta P^*$, Eq. (4.17) can be written as

$$w_i = \alpha_i^{**} + \sum_k \gamma_{ki} logp_k + \beta_i \log\left(\frac{y}{P^*}\right) \tag{4.22}$$

where $\alpha_i^{**} = \alpha_i - \beta_i \log\theta$, and $\log P^* = \sum_k w_k \log p_k$ is the geometric price index. In addition to mitigating the effects of multi-collinearity, this specification is linear in parameters making it easy to not only estimate with time-series data, but especially with cross-section and panel data. This model, called the Linear Approximate AIDS (LA/AIDS) model, is

$$w_{it} = \alpha_i + \tau_i t + \sum_k \gamma_{ki} logp_{kt} + \beta_i \log\left(\frac{y_t}{P_t^*}\right) + \varepsilon_{it} \tag{4.23}$$

where, as in the full AIDS model, we have set $\log\theta = 0$. This model, while appealing for empirical analysis, is not without problems. First, it is unclear what formulas to use for elasticities. If elasticities are based on the form (4.22), the formulas are complicated (Green and Alston 1990, 1991). Asche and Wessells (1997) have shown all the formulas for the different possibilities converge to (4.18) and (4.19) when elasticities are evaluated where normalized prices and income equal unity. Second, the LA/AIDS model in levels form is no longer invariant to scaling of the prices (Moschini 1995). Moschini shows replacing prices with (i) relative prices (e.g., prices in index form), (ii) shares with lagged shares, or (iii) shares with average shares will resolve the problem[5].

## 4.7 Comparison of RM with AIDS

When comparing the RM with the AIDS models, it is useful to consider the log differentials of the two forms:
$w_i dlogq_i = b_i dlogQ_t + \sum_j c_{ij} dlogp_j$ for the RM and$dw_i = \beta_i dlog\left(\frac{y}{P}\right) + \sum_j \gamma_{ij} dlogp_j$ for the AIDS model.

Aside from the two-income terms, $dlogQ$ and $dlog\left(\frac{y}{P}\right)$, the models only differ in the dependent variables. In fact, the two are related through the relationship

[5]It is interesting to note that although Deaton and Muellbauer (1980a) propose the LA/AIDS model for initial estimation, they never propose it as a replacement for the full AIDS model.

$$dw_i = w_i dlogw_i = w_i dlogq_i + w_i dlogp_i - w_i dlogy$$

Barten and Theil refer to $w_i dlogq_i$ as the quantity-change, or real change, component of the change in expenditure share. It is also the case that the normalized price coefficients in the RM, $c_{ij}$, are related to the AIDS model as shown in (4.20). Aside from the term $\log(\frac{y}{P})$ the right-hand side will be a constant. Thus, as pointed out by Deaton and Muellbauer (1980b, Chapt. 3), the AIDS model implies normalized Slutsky coefficients as almost constant.

The RM and AIDS imply different relationships between changes in income and income elasticities. With the marginal expenditure values assumed to be constant, differentiation of the income elasticity of the RM with respect to income implies $\frac{\partial e_i}{\partial y} = \frac{-b_i}{w_i^2}\frac{\partial w_i}{\partial y}$. For commodities like all food, and many individual foods, that are income inelastic, the model requires that income elasticities increase as income increases because in that case $\frac{\partial w_i}{\partial y} < 0$. On the other hand, the AIDS model, where $e_i = 1 + \frac{\beta_i}{w_i}$, implies that $\frac{\partial e_i}{\partial y} = \frac{-\beta_i}{w_i^2}\frac{\partial w_i}{\partial y}$. For income inelastic goods, $\beta_i < 0$, so that for income inelastic goods, income elasticities must decrease as income increases. While one might believe the AIDS model imposes the correct relationship, in actuality there is support for the relationship imposed by the RM. As Allen and Bowley (1935, p. 125) point out: "Demands tend to become more elastic as income rises, [because a] larger expenditure is spread over a wider range of items and the possibilities of substituting other items for a given item are thereby increased." Because income elasticities are linked to price elasticities through the Homogeneity Condition, it follows that both cross-price elasticities and income elasticities could increase as income increases. Empirical support for this proposition is provided by Wohlgenant (1984) in which US demand for food is estimated with the Fourier Flexible Form and elasticities are traced out over time. From the middle 1960s until the latter 1970s, both the own-price elasticity of demand for food and income elasticity of demand for food increase. This result contradicts the hypothesis that the income elasticity for food must decrease as income increases. This result is also consistent with the idea that the quality elasticity may be dominate in recent decades. The quality elasticity is the difference between the elasticity of expenditure with respect to income and elasticity of quantity with respect to income (see, e.g., Cramer 1973), and reflects the effect of changes in average food price for changes in income. As income rises, individuals substitute toward higher valued goods so average price of the bundle of food increases. One conclusion from this analysis might be that the RM is more suitable for time-series data while the AIDS model is more appropriate for cross-sectional data.

The RM can be reformulated to comply with the income-consumption relationship of the AIDS model by writing the model as follows:

$$\bar{w}_{it}\Delta\log\left(\frac{q_{it}}{Q_t}\right) = b_i \Delta log Q_t + \sum_j c_{ij}\Delta log p_{jt} \tag{4.24}$$

which is the so-called CBS differential demand model (Keller and van Driel 1985). In this form, it can be verified that income elasticities have exactly the same form as with the AIDS model.

Barnett and Seck (2008) have conducted extensive simulations to evaluate how the RM, AIDS, and LA/AIDS model compare empirically. They find that the RM performs as well as the AIDS model in most applications. Both the RM and full AIDS models approximate the Allen elasticities of substitution quite well if substitution is moderately high. However, the full AIDS model does a better job with a high degree of substitution[6]. The RM performs better with sub-groups of the utility function. The LA/AIDS model generally performs worse than both the RM and full AIDS model.

## 4.8 Alternative Differential Demand Systems

Because of persistence in time-series data, including problems of non-stationarity and unit roots, economists have often preferred first difference forms of demand systems. The most notable example is the RM but the AIDS model is also often specified and estimated in first differences. Two other differential demand models in the literature are the CBS model (Keller and van Driel 1985) and the NBER model (Neves 1987).

The CBS model, Eq. (4.24), has price effects equivalent to RM but income effects equivalent to the AIDS model. As discussed previously, this allows one to capture income effects widely believed to correspond to individual behavior. On the other hand, the NBER model has the same price effects as the AIDS model but income effects equivalent to the RM. The model is

$$\Delta w_{it} + \bar{w}_{it} \Delta \log Q_t = \sum_k \gamma_{ki} \Delta og p_{kt} + b_i \Delta \log Q_t + \varepsilon_{it} \tag{4.25}$$

Barten (1993) estimates a synthetic model that embeds the LA/AIDS, RM, CBS, and NBER models. Therefore, one can test each one of the four models against the synthetic model. To test each model against any alternative, non-nest testing methods would need to be employed. An advantage of the RM and CBS models over the LA/AIDS and NBER models is that they satisfy the general restrictions globally.

## 4.9 Generalization of AIDS Demand Systems

One appealing feature of the AIDS model is that it aggregates perfectly for a representative consumer, which allows for income distribution and preference shifters

[6]The Allen elasticities of substitution are related to the Hicksian elasticities as follows: $\sigma_{ij} = \frac{e^*_{ij}}{w_j}$. See Allen (1938).

(Deaton and Muellbauer 1980a). Thus, many researchers have taken the PIGLOG class of preferences (for which the AIDS is a special case) as a maintained hypothesis.

Generalizations of the AIDS demand system have occurred in two different areas: (a) through expansion of price effects and (b) expansion of income effects. The Fourier AIDS demand system (Chalfant 1987) generalizes the AIDS model by extending the price index $\log a(\boldsymbol{p})$ to be a function also of the Fourier function. The generalization delivers a model that, like the original AIDS, is a linear function of price variables, and therefore is easy to estimate. Generalizations of income response were introduced initially through GAIDS model (Bollino 1987), where pre-committed quantities are introduced into the AIDS model. That is, the expenditure function, (4.13), is modified as follows: $\log\left[c(u,\boldsymbol{p}) - \boldsymbol{p}'\boldsymbol{c}\right] = \log a(\boldsymbol{p}) + ub(\boldsymbol{p})$, where $\boldsymbol{c}$ is a vector of pre-committed quantities. Piggott (2003) includes this generalization in the Globally Flexible AIDS model of Chalfant to obtain the NEP (Nested PIGLOG) model. The model delivers share equations similar to GAIDS model with pre-committed quantities.

One limiting feature of the AIDS model is that it restricts Engel curves to be linear in log income. Empirical results from cross-sectional data show Engel curves can be quite nonlinear and do not necessarily follow the Working-Leser form. The quadratic AIDS model (QAIDS) model (Banks et al. 1997) was introduced to allow generalization of the AIDS model to include quadratic income terms. Banks et al. show that the rank 3 quadratic log share demand equations must have the following form for the indirect utility function: $u = \left\{\left[\frac{\log y - \log a(\boldsymbol{p})}{b(\boldsymbol{p})}\right]^{-1} + \lambda(\boldsymbol{p})\right\}^{-1}$, where $\lambda(\boldsymbol{p})$ is a differentiable function homogeneous of degree zero in prices. Note that the first term in brackets alone gives the indirect utility function for the AIDS model.

Lewbel and Pendakur (2009) generalize the QAIDS model to accommodate any polynomial degree of income effects. Consider the form of the log cost function

$$\log c(u, \log \boldsymbol{p}, z, \boldsymbol{\varepsilon}) = u + (\log \boldsymbol{p})'\boldsymbol{m}(u, z) + T(\log \boldsymbol{p}, z) + S(\log \boldsymbol{p}, z)u + (\log \boldsymbol{p})'\boldsymbol{\varepsilon} \tag{4.26}$$

where $z$ is a vector of demographic variables and $\boldsymbol{\varepsilon}$ is a vector of error terms. This expenditure function has Hicksian share equations: $\boldsymbol{w} = \boldsymbol{m}(u, z) + \nabla_{\log \boldsymbol{p}} T(\log \boldsymbol{p}, z) + \nabla_{\log \boldsymbol{p}} S(\log \boldsymbol{p}, z)u + \boldsymbol{\varepsilon}$. The indirect utility function can be shown to equal: $u = y^* = \frac{y - (\log \boldsymbol{p})'\boldsymbol{w} - T(\log \boldsymbol{p}, z) + (\log \boldsymbol{p})'\nabla_{\log \boldsymbol{p}} T(\log \boldsymbol{p}, z)}{1 + S(\log \boldsymbol{p}, z) - (\log \boldsymbol{p})'\nabla_{\log \boldsymbol{p}} S(\log \boldsymbol{p}, z)}$. This function is an affine transformation of the Stone Index, $\log y - (\log \boldsymbol{p})'\boldsymbol{w}$. The Marshallian implicit demand functions of this EASI (Exact Affine Stone Index) demand system are obtained by substituting for $u$ in the Hicksian share equations:

$$\boldsymbol{w} = \boldsymbol{m}\left(y^*, z\right) + \nabla_{\log \boldsymbol{p}} T(\log \boldsymbol{p}, z) + \nabla_{\log \boldsymbol{p}} S(\log \boldsymbol{p}, z)y^* + \boldsymbol{\varepsilon} \tag{4.27}$$

Lewbel and Pendakur (2009) are interested in allowing for higher-order polynomial functions of income so the function $\boldsymbol{m}(u, z) = \sum b_r u^r + \boldsymbol{C}z + \boldsymbol{D}zu$. For empirical application, the functions $T(\log \boldsymbol{p}, z)$ and $S(\log \boldsymbol{p}, z)$ are specified as quadratic functions. Following the steps leading to (4.27) we have

$$\boldsymbol{w} = \sum b_r y^{*r} + \boldsymbol{C}z + \boldsymbol{D}zy^* + \sum z_i \boldsymbol{A}_i \boldsymbol{p} + \boldsymbol{B}\boldsymbol{p}y^* + \boldsymbol{\varepsilon} \tag{4.28}$$

The EASI system would be linear in the Stone Index, $\log y - (\log \boldsymbol{p})\prime\boldsymbol{w}$, if the matrices $\boldsymbol{A}_i$ and $\boldsymbol{B}$ were zero. In this case, we have the approximate EASI demand system:

$$\boldsymbol{w} = \sum b_r \tilde{y}^r + \boldsymbol{C}z + \boldsymbol{D}z\tilde{y} + \sum z_i \boldsymbol{A}_i \boldsymbol{p} + \boldsymbol{B}\boldsymbol{p}\tilde{y} + \boldsymbol{\varepsilon} \tag{4.29}$$

where $\tilde{y} = \log y - (\log \boldsymbol{p})\prime\bar{\boldsymbol{w}}$ and $(\log \boldsymbol{p})\prime\bar{\boldsymbol{w}}$ is the Stone Index evaluated at the sample means. The approximate EASI model nests both the LA/AIDS and approximate QAIDS models.

## Problems

4.1 Show that in order for the double-log demand system to satisfy the general restrictions of consumer behavior all own-price elasticities must be $-1$, all cross-price elasticities must be zero, and all income elasticities must be 1. (Hint: Consider the expression for $\log w_i = \log q_i + \log p_i - \log y$. The Engel aggregation requires all income elasticities be constant with this functional form, implying all expenditure shares must be constant. Substitute for the double-log demand function in the above expression and differentiate with respect to prices and income.)

4.2 Show that the LES demand functions, Eq. (4.2), can be derived from the Stone-Geary Utility function, $u = \sum_{j=1}^{n} \beta_j \log(q_j - \gamma_j)$. Explain why the demand system does not admit inferior goods. Show that all uncompensated cross-price effects are complements but all compensated price effects are net substitutes.

4.2 Show that the LES demand functions, Eq. (4.2), can be derived from the Stone-Geary Utility function, $u = \sum_{j=1}^{n} \beta_j \log(q_j - \gamma_j)$. Explain why the demand system does not admit inferior goods. Show that all uncompensated cross-price effects are complements but all compensated price effects are net substitutes.

4.3 In empirical work, it is often convenient to work with share equations, particularly when one is interested in estimating substitution between closely related goods. Show that such a model, $w_i = \alpha_i + \sum_{j=1}^{n} \gamma_{ij} logp_j$, can be rationalized as a consumer demand function when preferences associated with the indirect translog function are homothetic. Also show that this model can be derived as a special case of the AIDS model.

4.4 Show that for the parametric specification of the absolute price version of the RM that Eq. (3.30) used to test for weak separability is exactly $\frac{c_{il}}{c_{jm}} = \frac{b_i b_l}{b_j b_m} \forall i, j \in G; l, m \in H, G \neq H$. Show how specification of the RM would be changed when these restrictions are imposed. Indicate how the RM would be estimated with these restrictions imposed and how the test for separability would be conducted.

4.5 Derive the Marshallian price elasticities and income elasticities from the Indirect Translog Model, Eq. (4.3). Compare with the elasticities for the RM and AIDS.

4.6 Derive the expenditure and price elasticities (both compensated and uncompensated) for the CBS and NBER models and compare with the elasticities derived from the RM and AIDS.

## References

Allen, R.G.D. *Mathematical Analysis for Economists.* London: Macmillan & Co., 1938.

Allen, R.G.D., and A.L. Bowley. *Family Expenditures: A Study of Its Variations.* London: P.S. King & Sons, 1935.

Asche, F., and C.R. Wessells. "On Price Indices in the Almost Ideal Demand System." *American Journal of Agricultural Economics* 79(1997): 1182–1185.

Barnett, W.A. "Theoretical Foundations of the Rotterdam Model." *Review of Economic Studies* 46(1978): 109–130.

Barnett, W.A. "The Miniflex Laurent Translog Flexible Functional Form." *Journal of Econometrics* 30(1985): 33–44.

Barnett, W.A., and A. Jonas. "The Muntz-Szatz Demand System: An Application of a Globally Behaved Series Expansion." *Economics Letters* 11(1983): 337–342.

Barnett, W.A., and A. Serlitis. "Consumer Preferences and Demand Systems." *Journal of Econometrics* 147(2008): 210–224.

Barnett, W.A., and O. Seck. "Rotterdam Model Versus Almost Ideal Demand System: Will the Best Specfication Please Stand Up?" *Journal of Applied Econometrics* 23(2008): 795–824.

Barten, A.P. "Maximum Likelihood Estimation of a Complete Demand Systems." *European Economic Review* 1(1969): 7–73.

Barten, A.P. "Consumer Allocation Models: Choice of Functional Forms." *Empirical Economics* 18(1993): 129–158.

Banks, J., R. Blundell, and A. Lewbel. "Quadratic Engel Curves and Consumer Demand." *The Review of Economics and Statistics* 79(1997): 527–539.

Berndt, E.R., and M.S. Khaled. "Parametric Productivity Measurement and Choice Among Flexible Functional Forms." *Journal of Political Economy* 87(1979): 1220–1245.

Berndt, E.R., and N.E. Savin. "Estimation and Hypothesis Testing in Singular Systems with Autoregressive Disturbances." *Econometrica* 43(1975): 937–957.

Bollino, C.A. "GAIDS: A Generalized Version of the Almost Ideal Demand System." *Economics Letters* 23(1987): 199–202.

Chalfant, J.A. "A Globally Flexible, Almost Ideal Demand System." *Journal of Business and Economics Statistics* 5(1987): 233–242.

Christensen, L.R., D.W. Jorgenson, and L.J. Lau. "Transcendental Logarithmic Utility Functions." *The American Economic Review* 65(1975): 367–382.

Cooper, R.J., and K.R. McLaren. "An Empirically Oriented Demand System with Improved Regularity Properties." *Canadian Journal of Economics* 25(1992): 652–657.

Cramer, J.S. "Interaction of Income and Price in Consumer Demand." *International Economic Review* 14(1973): 351–363.

Deaton, A.S., and J. Muellbauer. "An Almost Ideal Demand System." *The American Economic Review* 70(1980a): 312–326.

Deaton, A.S., and J. Muellbauer. *Economics and Consumer Behavior*. Cambridge: Cambridge University Press, 1980b.

Diewert, W.E. "An Application of the Shephard Duality Theorem: A Generalized Leontief Production Function." *Journal of Political Economy* 79(1971): 481–507.

Gallant, A.R. "On the Bias in Flexible Functional Forms and Essentially Unbiased Form: The Fourier Flexible Form." *Journal of Econometrics* 15(1981): 211–245.

Green, R., and J.M. Alston. "Elasticities in AIDS Models." *American Journal of Agricultural Economics* 72(1990): 442–445.

Green, R., and J.M. Alston. "Elasticities in AIDS Models: A Clarification and Extension." *American Journal of Agricultural Economics* 73(1991): 874–875.

Keller, W.J., and J. Van Driel. "Differential Consumer Demand Systems." *European Economic Review* 27(1985): 375–390.

LaFrance, J.T., and W. M. Hanemann. "The Dual Structure of Incomplete Demand Systems." *American Journal of Agricultural Economics* 71(1989): 262–274.

Lewbel, A., and K. Pendakur. "Tricks with Hicks: The EASI Demand System." *The American Economic Review* 99(2009): 827–863.

Moschini, G. "Units of Measurement and the Stone Index in Demand Systems Estimation." *American Journal of Agricultural Economics* 77(1995): 63–68.

Neves, P. "Analysis of Consumer Demand in Portugal, 1958–1981." Memorie de Maitrise en Sciences Economiques, Louvain-la-Neuve, France: University Catholiqque de Louvrain, 1987.

Piggott, N.E. "The Nested PIGLOG Model: An Application to U.S. Food Demand." *American Journal of Agricultural Economics* 85(2003): 1–15.

Stone, R. "Linear Expenditure Systems and Demand Analysis: An Application to the Pattern of British Demand." *The Economic Journal* 64(1954): 511–527.

Theil, H. *The System-Wide Approach to Microeconomics*. Chicago: The University of Chicago Press, 1980.

White, H. "Using Least Squares to Approximate Unknown Regression Functions." *International Economic Review* 21(1980): 149–170.

Wohlgenant, Michael K. "Conceptual and Functional Form Issues in Estimating Demand Elasticities for Food." *American Journal of Agricultural Economics* 66(1984): 211–215.

# Chapter 5
# Consumer Demand—Empirical Analysis II

## 5.1 Introduction

In this chapter, the focus is on empirical application of the system of demand functions approach using the Rotterdam Model (RM) and Almost Ideal Demand System (AIDS). Attention is given to the nature of the data sets typically available for use in time-series analysis. I discuss issues involved in implementation and interpretation using data sets created for estimation of US demand for meats. In the process, an evaluation is made of the relative performance of the RM and AIDS models. This chapter focuses mainly on time-series applications. The next chapter focuses on issues-related primarily to cross-section data and panel data.

## 5.2 Application to U.S. Meat Demand

As indicated by Brown and Heien (1972) and Christensen and Manser (1977), there are no official data on consumption of US food commodities. The US Department of Agriculture's Economic Research Service (ERS) publishes annual time series on per capita quantities of food commodities that "disappear" into the US marketing channels. These quantities are derived from production, inventory, and net trade statistics, and estimates of retail consumption are obtained by applying (fixed) coefficients to quantities available for consumption. Price indices are available for most of these food categories from the United States Department of Labor, Bureau of Labor Statistics (BLS).

 
M. K. Wohlgenant, *Market Interrelationships and Applied Demand Analysis*,
Palgrave Studies in Agricultural Economics and Food Policy,
https://doi.org/10.1007/978-3-030-73144-1_5

### 5.2.1 Development of Data Set Based on USDA Disappearance Data

For the meat group we follow Christensen and Manser (1977) and define the four commodities as: (a) beef and veal, (b) pork, (c) poultry, and (d) fish. Per capita quantities for these categories are available from ERS Food Availability (Per Capita) Demand System (https://www.ers.usda.gov/data-products/food-availability-per-capita-data-system/). Price indices for these categories were obtained from BLS Data Bases, Tables & Calculators by Subject (https://www.bls.gov/data/). The sample period for estimation is 1970–2010, a total of 41 observations. With first-differencing of the variables in estimation, this leaves a total of 40 observations for estimation.

Expenditures have to be estimated and the procedure of Brown and Heien and Christensen and Manser is used. In particular, average prices for each category for a base period are estimated and these estimates are used to construct constant dollar expenditures by multiplying each per capita quantity by its respective price. The specific prices used must match the base period of the price indices used in construction of the category prices, which is 1982–1984 = 100. The average prices of each meat product for 1971 are derived from Christian and Manser's Table 1 by dividing expenditure on each product by per capita quantity for 1971. These average prices were then converted to 1982–1984 values by dividing each price by its respective price index (divided by 100) to obtain average prices for 1982–1984 of \$2.45 for beef and veal (Beef), \$1.87 for pork (Pork), \$1.05 for poultry (Plty) and \$2.93 for fish (Fish). These average prices were then multiplied by their respective per capita quantities published by ERS to obtain constant per capita dollar expenditures as shown in Table 5.1. Table 5.2 shows the price indices for each group product. The Consumer Price Index for all goods (CPI) is also listed in Table 5.2. This index is used to deflate prices and expenditures to remove the effects of inflation. Table 5.3 lists the meat expenditures by product and the total (Sum). The last column in Table 5.3 is per capita personal consumption expenditures on all goods purchased by the consumer (PPCE). These data are personal consumption expenditures divided by July 1 civilian population for each year https://apps.bea.gov/.

### 5.2.2 Application to Absolute Price Version of Rotterdam Model

Using the data listed in Tables 5.1, 5.2 and 5.3, and after deflating all price and expenditure variables in Tables 5.2 and 5.3 by the CPI, variables for the conditional RM, Eq. (4.12), were formed and the models consisting of the equations for beef and veal, pork, and poultry were estimated by FIML using Proc Model of SAS software

**Table 5.1** Constant Dollar Expenditures Per Capita for Meats, 1970–2010

| Year | Beef ($q_1$) | Pork ($q_2$) | Plty ($q_3$) | Fish ($q_4$) |
|---|---|---|---|---|
| 1970 | 212.8533 | 103.5709 | 42.13256 | 34.40805 |
| 1971 | 211.202 | 113.2453 | 42.13531 | 33.66535 |
| 1972 | 213.7012 | 102.2233 | 43.52773 | 36.60127 |
| 1973 | 200.9779 | 91.16245 | 41.83291 | 37.33206 |
| 1974 | 214.6022 | 98.58256 | 41.68406 | 35.36212 |
| 1975 | 224.4477 | 80.22235 | 40.62014 | 35.55782 |
| 1976 | 238.6532 | 84.38155 | 44.12339 | 37.68074 |
| 1977 | 232.085 | 87.29283 | 44.85061 | 37.03758 |
| 1978 | 219.4119 | 87.03972 | 46.9826 | 39.17461 |
| 1979 | 195.089 | 99.41243 | 50.05888 | 38.04163 |
| 1980 | 190.939 | 106.1778 | 49.72651 | 36.37314 |
| 1981 | 193.0133 | 101.3303 | 51.14029 | 36.85975 |
| 1982 | 192.3937 | 90.9134 | 51.39309 | 36.31773 |
| 1983 | 196.426 | 95.94968 | 51.4773 | 38.97796 |
| 1984 | 196.1494 | 95.42695 | 53.43925 | 41.33151 |
| 1985 | 198.2032 | 96.23431 | 55.09667 | 43.9747 |
| 1986 | 197.3932 | 90.81774 | 55.79853 | 45.18257 |
| 1987 | 184.3342 | 91.22438 | 59.43923 | 47.17126 |
| 1988 | 180.9571 | 97.38716 | 59.49167 | 44.36477 |
| 1989 | 171.626 | 96.3463 | 60.67408 | 45.57135 |
| 1990 | 168.1072 | 92.31408 | 63.665 | 43.78624 |
| 1991 | 165.1204 | 93.08609 | 66.07861 | 43.27504 |
| 1992 | 163.9265 | 97.81873 | 69.78457 | 42.79337 |
| 1993 | 160.0182 | 96.48857 | 72.40061 | 43.31025 |
| 1994 | 164.2815 | 97.48828 | 73.17608 | 43.83277 |
| 1995 | 165.1152 | 96.26408 | 72.33 | 43.22062 |
| 1996 | 166.9624 | 90.01058 | 73.21115 | 42.42881 |
| 1997 | 163.0306 | 89.04668 | 74.94878 | 41.75254 |
| 1998 | 164.8895 | 95.89695 | 75.54605 | 42.46731 |
| 1999 | 166.6278 | 98.19681 | 80.25763 | 43.50493 |
| 2000 | 167.0758 | 95.07715 | 81.24185 | 44.52017 |
| 2001 | 163.2199 | 93.44921 | 80.89369 | 43.09745 |
| 2002 | 166.7592 | 95.8985 | 85.05774 | 45.74694 |
| 2003 | 160.0766 | 96.38443 | 86.13108 | 47.80177 |
| 2004 | 162.5259 | 95.22623 | 88.72872 | 48.39004 |
| 2005 | 161.3826 | 92.7579 | 90.73313 | 47.3561 |

(continued)

**Table 5.1** (continued)

| Year | Beef ($q_1$) | Pork ($q_2$) | Plty ($q_3$) | Fish ($q_4$) |
|---|---|---|---|---|
| 2006 | 162.096 | 91.60337 | 91.28 | 48.427 |
| 2007 | 160.3666 | 94.17162 | 89.68359 | 47.70133 |
| 2008 | 153.2622 | 91.46027 | 88.01343 | 46.72846 |
| 2009 | 149.9316 | 92.6767 | 84.01271 | 46.20306 |
| 2010 | 146.4055 | 88.278 | 86.92515 | 46.23745 |

version 9.4[1]. Recall one equation has to be dropped prior to estimation because of the adding-up property, so the fish equation was dropped. Unrestricted, homogeneity restricted, and homogeneity plus symmetry versions of the models were estimated. The p-values for the homogeneity restriction applied equation by equation were all above 0.46, indicating failure to reject the null hypothesis that the zero homogeneity condition holds. The chi-squared likelihood ratio test for symmetry, given homogeneity, was 2.71 with a p-value of 0.44. Thus, symmetry, given homogeneity, holds as well. Finally, the chi-squared value for homogeneity and symmetry holding jointly was 10.76 with a p-value of 0.10. The adjusted R-squared values were 0.83 for beef and veal, 0.87 for pork, and 0.31 for poultry. The Durbin-Watson statistics were 1.85 for beef and veal, 1.95 for pork, and 1.80 for poultry. Finally, the matrix $\left[c_{ij}\right]$ is negative semi-definite.

Parameter values of the conditional RM are shown in Table 5.4. All three commodities have significant own-price effects as indicated by $c_{11}$, $c_{22}$, and$c_{33}$. Pork is a strong substitute for beef and veal, poultry is a substitute for beef and veal, and fish is a substitute for pork. Other relationships are unclear given insignificance of coefficients. The marginal expenditure values are all positive indicating normal goods within the meat group. Finally, the trend variables for beef and veal and pork are insignificant, but significant for poultry.

Compensated elasticities for the conditional RM are presented in Table 5.5. Price elasticities are computed by dividing each estimated $c_{ij}$ by $w_i$. The sample mean expenditure shares are 0.0171118 for beef and veal, 0.0086883 for pork, 0.0058103 for poultry, 0.0038688 for fish, and 0.0354792 for all meats. The elasticities for fish are obtained by imposing the general restrictions as indicated previously. The compensated elasticities give indication of the degree of substitutability among individual commodities within the meat group[2]. Own-price elasticities indicate all goods are price inelastic. Pork is the most elastic and fish is very inelastic. Beef and veal and

[1]The data analysis of this book was generated using SAS software version 9.4. Copyright © 2013 SAS Institute inc. SAS and all other SAS Institute inc. product or service names are registered trademarks of SAS Institute inc., Cary, NC, USA.

[2]As shown in footnote 18, the Allen elasticities of substitution can be computed by dividing these elasticities by budget shares. Blackorby and Russell (1989) contend Morishma elasticities give a better indication of substitutability than Allen elasticities. These elasticities can be computed directly from the information provided in Table 5 with the estimates of the budget shares used to calculate the compensated elasticities.

**Table 5.2** Price Indices for Meats (1982–1984 = 100), 1970–2010

| Year | Beef ($p_1$) | Pork ($p_2$) | Plty ($p_3$) | Fish ($p_4$) | CPI |
|---|---|---|---|---|---|
| 1970 | 43.5 | 45.4 | 53.2 | 31.3 | 38.84167 |
| 1971 | 45.5 | 41.1 | 53.5 | 34.5 | 40.48333 |
| 1972 | 49.7 | 47.6 | 54.2 | 37.6 | 41.80833 |
| 1973 | 59.6 | 63.3 | 76 | 43.1 | 44.425 |
| 1974 | 61.3 | 63 | 72.1 | 49.7 | 49.31667 |
| 1975 | 61.9 | 77.1 | 79.7 | 53.9 | 53.825 |
| 1976 | 59.9 | 78.1 | 76.4 | 60.2 | 56.93333 |
| 1977 | 59.5 | 73.9 | 76.9 | 66.7 | 60.61667 |
| 1978 | 73.1 | 83.4 | 84.9 | 73 | 65.24167 |
| 1979 | 93.1 | 84.7 | 89.1 | 80.1 | 72.58333 |
| 1980 | 98.4 | 81.9 | 93.7 | 87.5 | 82.38333 |
| 1981 | 99.2 | 89.5 | 97.5 | 94.8 | 90.93333 |
| 1982 | 100.6 | 101 | 95.8 | 98.2 | 96.53333 |
| 1983 | 99.1 | 100.1 | 97 | 99.3 | 99.58333 |
| 1984 | 100.3 | 98.8 | 107.3 | 102.5 | 103.9333 |
| 1985 | 98.2 | 99.1 | 106.2 | 107.5 | 107.6 |
| 1986 | 98.8 | 107.2 | 114.2 | 117.4 | 109.6917 |
| 1987 | 106.3 | 116 | 112.6 | 129.9 | 113.6167 |
| 1988 | 112.1 | 112.5 | 120.7 | 137.4 | 118.275 |
| 1989 | 119.3 | 113.2 | 132.7 | 143.6 | 123.9417 |
| 1990 | 128.8 | 129.8 | 132.5 | 146.7 | 130.6583 |
| 1991 | 132.4 | 134.1 | 131.5 | 148.3 | 136.1667 |
| 1992 | 132.3 | 127.8 | 131.4 | 151.7 | 140.3083 |
| 1993 | 137.1 | 131.7 | 136.9 | 156.6 | 144.475 |
| 1994 | 136 | 133.9 | 141.5 | 163.7 | 148.225 |
| 1995 | 134.9 | 134.8 | 143.5 | 171.6 | 152.3833 |
| 1996 | 134.5 | 148.2 | 152.4 | 173.1 | 156.8583 |
| 1997 | 136.8 | 155.9 | 156.6 | 177.1 | 160.525 |
| 1998 | 136.5 | 148.5 | 157.1 | 181.7 | 163.0083 |
| 1999 | 139.2 | 145.9 | 157.9 | 185.3 | 166.5833 |
| 2000 | 148.1 | 156.5 | 159.8 | 190.4 | 172.1917 |
| 2001 | 160.5 | 162.4 | 164.9 | 191.1 | 177.0417 |
| 2002 | 160.6 | 161.8 | 167 | 188.1 | 179.8667 |
| 2003 | 175.1 | 164.9 | 169.1 | 190 | 183.9667 |
| 2004 | 195.3 | 174.2 | 181.7 | 194.3 | 188.9 |
| 2005 | 200.425 | 177.7333 | 185.2667 | 200.0833 | 195.2667 |

(continued)

**Table 5.2** (continued)

| Year | Beef ($p_1$) | Pork ($p_2$) | Plty ($p_3$) | Fish ($p_4$) | CPI |
|---|---|---|---|---|---|
| 2006 | 202.05 | 177.2667 | 182.0083 | 209.5083 | 201.55 |
| 2007 | 211.0597 | 180.8953 | 191.3638 | 219.0865 | 207.3354 |
| 2008 | 220.586 | 185.034 | 200.901 | 232.122 | 215.303 |
| 2009 | 218.273 | 181.366 | 204.22 | 240.556 | 214.537 |
| 2010 | 224.511 | 189.957 | 203.978 | 243.229 | 218.056 |

pork are expenditure elastic, but poultry and fish are expenditure inelastic. It should be recalled that these elasticities only account for substitutability within the meat group and expenditure elasticities are calculated holding expenditure on meats constant. I will present unconditional demand elasticities below after including estimates of the first-stage income allocation equations. I do not present uncompensated conditional price elasticities because income effects are not reflective of total income effects because they are computed using meat expenditures rather than total expenditures to compensate price changes.

### 5.2.3 *Application to LA/AIDS and AIDS Models*

Both the LA/AIDS and AIDS models, Eqs. (4.23) and (4.21), are used to estimate conditional demand functions for meats. The LA/AIDS model, as in Deaton and Muellbauer (1980), is used to test for the restrictions of consumer behavior and then the full AIDS model is used to estimate the final parameter estimates with elasticities. As indicated in Chapter 4, empirical implementation of the LA/AIDS model requires we normalize all prices and meat expenditures. This was done by first deflating each price index and total meat expenditures by the CPI (Table 5.2) and then dividing each deflated price index and deflated meat expenditures by its sample mean value. The resulting data were then used with the expenditure shares (relative to meat consumption) computed from Table 5.2. In initial estimations, first-order autocorrelation in the residuals was found present in all three meats. Thus, all equations were corrected for first-order autocorrelation in estimation with the common autocorrelation parameter, $\rho$. Estimation proceeded by estimating each conditional demand Eq. (4.23) separately and testing for the homogeneity condition equation by Eq. (4.17a). The null hypothesis of the homogeneity condition was not rejected for any of the three meats: beef and veal, pork, and poultry. The model was then estimated by FIML to test for symmetry (4.17b), given that the homogeneity condition holds. The p-value for the likelihood ratio test is 0.32; therefore, we fail to reject symmetry, given homogeneity. I then test homogeneity and symmetry jointly and estimate a p-value of 0.03; this time, however, we reject homogeneity and symmetry holding jointly.

**Table 5.3** Expenditures Per Capita for Meats ($ per person), 1970–2010

| Year | Beef ($x_1$) | Pork ($x_2$) | Plty ($x_3$) | Fish ($x_4$) | Sum ($x_m$) | PPCE |
|---|---|---|---|---|---|---|
| 1970 | 92.59121 | 47.0212 | 22.41452 | 10.76972 | 172.7966 | 3153.951 |
| 1971 | 96.09691 | 46.5438 | 22.54239 | 11.61455 | 176.7976 | 3370.575 |
| 1972 | 106.2095 | 48.65829 | 23.59203 | 13.76208 | 192.2219 | 3659.684 |
| 1973 | 119.7828 | 57.70583 | 31.79301 | 16.09012 | 225.3718 | 4009.15 |
| 1974 | 131.5512 | 62.10701 | 30.05421 | 17.57497 | 241.2874 | 4349.514 |
| 1975 | 138.9331 | 61.85143 | 32.37425 | 19.16567 | 252.3245 | 4771.647 |
| 1976 | 142.9533 | 65.90199 | 33.71027 | 22.68381 | 265.2493 | 5263.678 |
| 1977 | 138.0906 | 64.5094 | 34.49012 | 24.70407 | 261.7941 | 5784.511 |
| 1978 | 160.3901 | 72.59112 | 39.88823 | 28.59746 | 301.4669 | 6389.703 |
| 1979 | 181.6279 | 84.20233 | 44.60246 | 30.47135 | 340.904 | 7044.589 |
| 1980 | 187.884 | 86.95963 | 46.59374 | 31.8265 | 353.2638 | 7687.603 |
| 1981 | 191.4691 | 90.6906 | 49.86178 | 34.94305 | 366.9646 | 8409.726 |
| 1982 | 193.5481 | 91.82254 | 49.23458 | 35.66401 | 370.2692 | 8920.599 |
| 1983 | 194.6582 | 96.04563 | 49.93298 | 38.70512 | 379.3419 | 9737.673 |
| 1984 | 196.7379 | 94.28183 | 57.34031 | 42.3648 | 390.7248 | 10545.21 |
| 1985 | 194.6356 | 95.3682 | 58.51266 | 47.2728 | 395.7892 | 11376.17 |
| 1986 | 195.0244 | 97.35661 | 63.72192 | 53.04433 | 409.1473 | 11993.63 |
| 1987 | 195.9473 | 105.8203 | 66.92857 | 61.27546 | 429.9716 | 12669.8 |
| 1988 | 202.8529 | 109.5606 | 71.80645 | 60.95719 | 445.1771 | 13590.72 |
| 1989 | 204.7498 | 109.064 | 80.5145 | 65.44047 | 459.7688 | 14460.78 |
| 1990 | 216.522 | 119.8237 | 84.35613 | 64.23442 | 484.9363 | 15227.94 |
| 1991 | 218.6194 | 124.8285 | 86.89337 | 64.17689 | 494.5181 | 15556.44 |
| 1992 | 216.8747 | 125.0123 | 91.69693 | 64.91754 | 498.5015 | 16339.65 |
| 1993 | 219.385 | 127.0754 | 99.11644 | 67.82386 | 513.4007 | 17106.24 |
| 1994 | 223.4228 | 130.5368 | 103.5441 | 71.75425 | 529.258 | 17920.73 |
| 1995 | 222.7404 | 129.764 | 103.7936 | 74.16659 | 530.4646 | 18617.37 |
| 1996 | 224.5644 | 133.3957 | 111.5738 | 73.44427 | 542.9781 | 19448.42 |
| 1997 | 223.0258 | 138.8238 | 117.3698 | 73.94375 | 553.1632 | 20287.82 |
| 1998 | 225.0742 | 142.407 | 118.6828 | 77.16309 | 563.3271 | 21285.51 |
| 1999 | 231.9459 | 143.2691 | 126.7268 | 80.61464 | 582.5565 | 22481.88 |
| 2000 | 247.4393 | 148.7957 | 129.8245 | 84.76641 | 610.8259 | 23946.54 |
| 2001 | 261.9679 | 151.7615 | 133.3937 | 82.35922 | 629.4823 | 24768.49 |
| 2002 | 267.8153 | 155.1638 | 142.0464 | 86.04999 | 651.0755 | 25492.96 |
| 2003 | 280.2941 | 158.9379 | 145.6477 | 90.82337 | 675.7031 | 26566.92 |
| 2004 | 317.4132 | 165.8841 | 161.2201 | 94.02185 | 738.5392 | 27999.94 |
| 2005 | 323.451 | 164.8617 | 168.0983 | 94.75165 | 751.1626 | 29551.67 |

(continued)

**Table 5.3** (continued)

| Year | Beef ($x_1$) | Pork ($x_2$) | Plty ($x_3$) | Fish ($x_4$) | Sum ($x_m$) | PPCE |
|---|---|---|---|---|---|---|
| 2006 | 327.515 | 162.3822 | 166.1372 | 101.4586 | 757.493 | 30995.31 |
| 2007 | 338.4692 | 170.352 | 171.6219 | 104.5072 | 784.9502 | 32170.97 |
| 2008 | 338.075 | 169.2326 | 176.8199 | 108.467 | 792.5945 | 32776.46 |
| 2009 | 327.2602 | 168.084 | 171.5708 | 111.1442 | 778.0592 | 32058.63 |
| 2010 | 328.6964 | 167.6902 | 177.3082 | 112.4629 | 786.1578 | 32928.68 |

**Table 5.4** Parameter Estimates of Conditional RM for Meats

| Parameter | Estimate | Approx Std Err | t Value | Approx Pr > \|t\| |
|---|---|---|---|---|
| $c_{11}$ | −0.00776 | 0.000924 | −8.40 | <.0001 |
| $c_{12}$ | 0.006717 | 0.000692 | 9.71 | <.0001 |
| $c_{13}$ | 0.001262 | 0.000701 | 1.80 | 0.0802 |
| $c_{14}$ | −0.00021 | 0.000585 | −0.37 | 0.7155 |
| $c_{21}$ | 0.006717 | 0.000692 | 9.71 | <.0001 |
| $c_{22}$ | −0.00801 | 0.000985 | −8.13 | <.0001 |
| $c_{23}$ | 0.000465 | 0.000487 | 0.95 | 0.3467 |
| $c_{24}$ | 0.000824 | 0.000386 | 2.14 | 0.0395 |
| $c_{31}$ | 0.001262 | 0.000701 | 1.80 | 0.0802 |
| $c_{32}$ | 0.000465 | 0.000487 | 0.95 | 0.3467 |
| $c_{33}$ | −0.00149 | 0.000666 | −2.24 | 0.0316 |
| $c_{34}$ | −0.00024 | 0.000347 | −0.69 | 0.4977 |
| $a_1$ | −0.00006 | 0.000078 | −0.79 | 0.4328 |
| $b_1$ | 0.623717 | 0.0720 | 8.66 | <.0001 |
| $a_2$ | −0.00007 | 0.000067 | −1.11 | 0.2756 |
| $b_2$ | 0.283756 | 0.0984 | 2.88 | 0.0066 |
| $a_3$ | 0.0001 | 0.000031 | 3.24 | 0.0025 |
| $b_3$ | 0.059164 | 0.0220 | 2.68 | 0.0109 |

The fully restricted LA/AIDS model parameter estimates are shown in Table 5.6. Compensated elasticities for the fully restricted LA/AIDS model are shown in Table 5.7. Note that fish has the wrong sign for its compensated own-price elasticity. The other elasticities are similar to the RM, except that the own-price elasticities are notably smaller in absolute value for beef and veal and pork.

Parameter estimates and elasticities for the conditional full AIDS model are shown in Tables 5.8 and 5.9. As in the case of the LA/AIDS model, we reject the joint hypothesis of homogeneity and symmetry, this time at the 0.01 level. Moreover, one of the eigenvalues of the estimated matrix $\left[c_{ij}\right]$ is positive, indicating violation of negative semi-definiteness condition. This should be clear by the incorrect sign

**Table 5.5** Compensated Price and Expenditure Elasticities for Conditional RM Model of Meats

| Elasticity | Estimate | Approx Std Err | t Value | Approx Pr > \|t\| |
|---|---|---|---|---|
| $e_{11}$* | −0.45375 | 0.0540 | −8.40 | <.0001 |
| $e_{12}$* | 0.392531 | 0.0404 | 9.71 | <.0001 |
| $e_{13}$* | 0.073774 | 0.0410 | 1.80 | 0.0802 |
| $e_{14}$* | −0.01255 | 0.0342 | −0.37 | 0.7155 |
| $e_1$ | 1.2932 | 0.1493 | 8.66 | <.0001 |
| $e_{21}$* | 0.773099 | 0.0796 | 9.71 | <.0001 |
| $e_{22}$* | −0.92144 | 0.1134 | −8.13 | <.0001 |
| $e_{23}$* | 0.05347 | 0.0561 | 0.95 | 0.3467 |
| $e_{24}$* | 0.09487 | 0.0444 | 2.14 | 0.0395 |
| $e_2$ | 1.158735 | 0.4018 | 2.88 | 0.0066 |
| $e_{31}$* | 0.21727 | 0.1207 | 1.80 | 0.0802 |
| $e_{32}$* | 0.079955 | 0.0839 | 0.95 | 0.3467 |
| $e_{33}$* | −0.25626 | 0.1146 | −2.24 | 0.0316 |
| $e_{34}$* | −0.04096 | 0.0598 | −0.69 | 0.4977 |
| $e_3$ | 0.361268 | 0.1346 | 2.68 | 0.0109 |
| $e_{41}$* | −0.05552 | 0.1512 | −0.37 | 0.7155 |
| $e_{42}$* | 0.213052 | 0.0997 | 2.14 | 0.0395 |
| $e_{43}$* | −0.06152 | 0.0898 | −0.69 | 0.4977 |
| $e_{44}$* | −0.09601 | 0.1479 | −0.65 | 0.5205 |
| $e_4$ | 0.30596 | 0.3865 | 0.79 | 0.4338 |

Note: The sample mean expenditure shares are 0.0171118 for beef and veal, 0.0086883 for pork, 0.0058103 for poultry, 0.0038688 for fish, and 0.0354792 for all meats

on compensated own-price elasticity of fish. In addition to the incorrect sign on fish demand and violation of negative semi-definiteness, a significant negative trend is shown in beef demand and positive trend in poultry demand. In the RM, only poultry shows a significant positive shift in preferences. Elasticities are similar to the LA/AIDS model.

### 5.2.4 *Unconditional Demand Elasticities from Rotterdam Model*

Based on the overall quality of results, I use the RM to estimate unconditional demand elasticities. I assume there are three separable groups: meats (M), non-meat foods

**Table 5.6** Parameter Estimates of Conditional Demand Functions for LA/AIDS Model

| Parameter | Estimate | Approx Std Err | t Value | Approx Pr > \|t\| |
|---|---|---|---|---|
| $\gamma_{11}$ | 0.088586 | 0.0404 | 2.19 | 0.0352 |
| $\gamma_{12}$ | 0.007578 | 0.0156 | 0.49 | 0.6301 |
| $\gamma_{13}$ | −0.0474 | 0.0289 | −1.64 | 0.1103 |
| $\gamma_{14}$ | −0.11653 | 0.0668 | −1.74 | 0.0902 |
| $\gamma_{22}$ | 0.013599 | 0.0222 | 0.61 | 0.5440 |
| $\gamma_{23}$ | −0.02218 | 0.0136 | −1.63 | 0.1124 |
| $\gamma_{24}$ | 0.022429 | 0.0453 | 0.50 | 0.6234 |
| $\gamma_{33}$ | 0.089099 | 0.0276 | 3.23 | 0.0028 |
| $\gamma_{34}$ | −0.03104 | 0.0368 | −0.84 | 0.4052 |
| $\beta_1$ | 0.094585 | 0.0703 | 1.35 | 0.1875 |
| $\beta_2$ | −0.0033 | 0.0607 | −0.05 | 0.9570 |
| $\beta_3$ | −0.05841 | 0.0395 | −1.48 | 0.1481 |
| $\alpha_1$ | 0.560267 | 0.0274 | 20.45 | <.0001 |
| $\alpha_2$ | 0.254405 | 0.0157 | 16.22 | <.0001 |
| $\alpha_3$ | 0.095768 | 0.0142 | 6.73 | <.0001 |
| $\rho$ | 0.829308 | 0.0821 | 10.10 | <.0001 |
| $\tau_1$ | −0.00394 | 0.000807 | −4.89 | <.0001 |
| $\tau_2$ | −0.00082 | 0.000551 | −1.49 | 0.1464 |
| $\tau_3$ | 0.003614 | 0.000468 | 7.73 | <.0001 |

(NM), and non-food (NF)[3]. For three groups, the composite demand Eqs. (4.11) consist of two estimating equations:

$$\begin{aligned}\bar{w}_{Mt}\Delta\log Q_t^M =& a_M + b_M\Delta log Q_t\\ &+\phi b_M(1-b_M)(\Delta log\pi_{Mt}-\Delta log\pi_{NFt})\\ &-\phi b_M(1-b_{NM})(\Delta log\pi_{NMt}-\Delta log\pi_{NFt})+\varepsilon_{Mt}\end{aligned} \tag{5.1}$$

$$\begin{aligned}\bar{w}_{NMt}\Delta\log Q_t^{NM} =& a_{NM} + b_{NM}\Delta log Q_t\\ &-\phi b_M(1-b_{NM})(\Delta log\pi_{Mt}-\Delta log\pi_{NFt})\\ &+\phi b_{NM}(1-b_{NM})(\Delta log\pi_{NMt}-\Delta log\pi_{NFt})+\varepsilon_{NMt}\end{aligned} \tag{5.2}$$

where the parameters of the third equation, non-food, can be estimated from the parameter estimates from the meats and non-meats expenditure allocation equations.

[3]Past researchers (George and King 1971; Bieri and de Janvry 1972; Brown and Heien 1972; Huang 1993; Okrent and Alston 2011) have assumed between four and fifteen separable food groups. Pollack (1970) points out the researcher has flexibility in the case of strong separability. By adding groups together, we can think of resulting groups as "super groups".

**Table 5.7** Compensated Price and Expenditure Elasticities for Conditional LA/AIDS Model of Meats

| Elasticity | Estimate | Approx Std Err | t Value | Approx Pr > \|t\| |
|---|---|---|---|---|
| $e_{11}$* | −0.34165 | 0.0860 | −3.97 | 0.0004 |
| $e_{12}$* | 0.259789 | 0.0332 | 7.83 | <.0001 |
| $e_{13}$* | 0.070716 | 0.0615 | 1.15 | 0.2587 |
| $e_{14}$* | −0.1331 | 0.1422 | −0.94 | 0.3562 |
| $e_1$ | 1.201341 | 0.1497 | 8.03 | <.0001 |
| $e_{21}$* | 0.500876 | 0.0640 | 7.83 | <.0001 |
| $e_{22}$* | −0.70053 | 0.0911 | −7.69 | <.0001 |
| $e_{23}$* | 0.080566 | 0.0559 | 1.44 | 0.1587 |
| $e_{24}$* | 0.206999 | 0.1858 | 1.11 | 0.2732 |
| $e_2$ | 0.98647 | 0.2493 | 3.96 | 0.0004 |
| $e_{31}$* | 0.193578 | 0.1684 | 1.15 | 0.2587 |
| $e_{32}$* | 0.190948 | 0.0793 | 2.41 | 0.0218 |
| $e_{33}$* | −0.30921 | 0.1609 | −1.92 | 0.0633 |
| $e_{34}$* | −0.06592 | 0.2146 | −0.31 | 0.7606 |
| $e_3$ | 0.659669 | 0.2300 | 2.87 | 0.0071 |
| $e_{41}$* | −0.54396 | 0.5813 | −0.94 | 0.3562 |
| $e_{42}$* | 0.558892 | 0.3938 | 1.42 | 0.1652 |
| $e_{43}$* | −0.09841 | 0.3203 | −0.31 | 0.7606 |
| $e_{44}$* | 0.20359 | 0.2548 | 0.80 | 0.4299 |
| $e_4$ | 0.713939 | 0.4174 | 1.71 | 0.0966 |

Note: The sample mean expenditure shares are 0.0171118 for beef and veal, 0.0086883 for pork, 0.0058103 for poultry, 0.0038688 for fish, and 0.0354792 for all meats

Note that with this specification of three groups, in addition to the intercepts, there are three parameters ($\phi$, $b_M$, $b_{NM}$) with six reduced-form parameters. This highlights the importance of restricting compensated price elasticities to the form indicated in (3.28) and (3.29). Because the money flexibility parameter, $\phi$, is over-identified, a unique estimate of $\phi$ can be obtained only through imposing the restrictions on the reduced form.

Additional data are required for estimation of the first-stage expenditure allocation equations. We need expenditures on other, non-meat food and non-food commodities. In addition, we do not have price indices for non-meat commodities, so I use published BLS price indices to approximate the marginal price indices. Following Clements and Johnson (1983), we approximate the non-meat food price index as follows:

**Table 5.8** Parameter Estimates of Conditional Demand Functions for Full AIDS Model

| Parameter | Estimate | Approx Std Err | t Value | Approx Pr > \|t\| |
|---|---|---|---|---|
| $\gamma_{11}$ | 0.094126 | 0.0401 | 2.35 | 0.0248 |
| $\gamma_{12}$ | 0.005621 | 0.0159 | 0.35 | 0.7259 |
| $\gamma_{13}$ | −0.05239 | 0.0281 | −1.86 | 0.0709 |
| $\gamma_{14}$ | −0.13482 | 0.0668 | −2.02 | 0.0515 |
| $\gamma_{22}$ | 0.012583 | 0.0238 | 0.53 | 0.5999 |
| $\gamma_{23}$ | −0.02229 | 0.0143 | −1.56 | 0.1275 |
| $\gamma_{24}$ | 0.026229 | 0.0447 | 0.59 | 0.5614 |
| $\gamma_{33}$ | 0.094867 | 0.0284 | 3.34 | 0.0021 |
| $\gamma_{34}$ | −0.02075 | 0.0409 | −0.51 | 0.6149 |
| $\beta_1$ | 0.084502 | 0.0784 | 1.08 | 0.2887 |
| $\beta_2$ | −0.01175 | 0.0702 | −0.17 | 0.8679 |
| $\beta_3$ | −0.05523 | 0.0399 | −1.39 | 0.1748 |
| $\alpha_1$ | 0.559982 | 0.0282 | 19.83 | <.0001 |
| $\alpha_2$ | 0.255173 | 0.0151 | 16.95 | <.0001 |
| $\alpha_3$ | 0.095793 | 0.0147 | 6.50 | <.0001 |
| $\rho$ | 0.82467 | 0.0873 | 9.45 | <.0001 |
| $\tau_1$ | −0.00391 | 0.000826 | −4.74 | <.0001 |
| $\tau_2$ | −0.00086 | 0.000545 | −1.57 | 0.1259 |
| $\tau_3$ | 0.003602 | 0.000469 | 7.68 | <.0001 |

$$\Delta log \pi_{NMt} \cong \frac{1}{[(1-(\bar{w}_{Mt}/\bar{w}_{FOODt}))]}\left[\Delta log P_{FOODt} - \sum_{j \in M}\left(\frac{\bar{w}_{jt}}{\bar{w}_{FOODt}}\right)\Delta log p_{jt}\right] \tag{5.3}$$

where $P_{FOODt}$ is the price index of food,$\bar{w}_{FOODt}$ is the average expenditure share of food, and the $p_{jt}$'s are price indices of individual meat commodities. Relative changes in group quantities are estimated as follows:

$$\Delta log Q_t^{NM} = \Delta log y_{NMt} - \Delta log P_{NMt};\ \Delta log Q_t^{NF} = \Delta log y_{NFt} - \Delta log P_{NFt} \tag{5.4}$$

Per capita (total) personal consumption expenditures (ppce, Table 5.3), and food expenditures are the sum of food and nonalcoholic beverages purchased for off-premise consumption and meals and nonalcoholic beverages purchased on premise (https://apps.bea.gov/). Price indices come from BLS (https://www.bls.gov/data/). Data on per capita food expenditures (xfood), non-meat food expenditures (xnmeats), non-food expenditures (xnfood), and price indices are presented in Table 5.10.

**Table 5.9** Compensated Price and Expenditure Elasticities for Conditional Full AIDS Model of Meats

| Elasticity | Estimate | Approx Std Err | t Value | Approx Pr > \|t\| |
|---|---|---|---|---|
| $e_{11}$* | −0.32986 | 0.0853 | −3.87 | 0.0005 |
| $e_{12}$* | 0.255624 | 0.0338 | 7.55 | <.0001 |
| $e_{13}$* | 0.060102 | 0.0598 | 1.00 | 0.3223 |
| $e_{14}$* | −0.17203 | 0.1422 | −1.21 | 0.2350 |
| $e_1$ | 1.179877 | 0.1669 | 7.07 | <.0001 |
| $e_{21}$* | 0.492845 | 0.0653 | 7.55 | <.0001 |
| $e_{22}$* | −0.7047 | 0.0975 | −7.23 | <.0001 |
| $e_{23}$* | 0.080133 | 0.0586 | 1.37 | 0.1805 |
| $e_{24}$* | 0.222595 | 0.1835 | 1.21 | 0.2338 |
| $e_2$ | 0.951766 | 0.2879 | 3.31 | 0.0023 |
| $e_{31}$* | 0.164521 | 0.1637 | 1.00 | 0.3223 |
| $e_{32}$* | 0.190333 | 0.0832 | 2.29 | 0.0286 |
| $e_{33}$* | −0.2756 | 0.1657 | −1.66 | 0.1057 |
| $e_{34}$* | −0.00598 | 0.2382 | −0.03 | 0.9801 |
| $e_3$ | 0.678176 | 0.2322 | 2.92 | 0.0063 |
| $e_{41}$* | −0.70305 | 0.5811 | −1.21 | 0.2350 |
| $e_{42}$* | 0.591949 | 0.3890 | 1.52 | 0.1376 |
| $e_{43}$* | −0.00892 | 0.3556 | −0.03 | 0.9801 |
| $e_{44}$* | 0.240131 | 0.2560 | 0.94 | 0.3551 |
| $e_4$ | 0.84759 | 0.4341 | 1.95 | 0.0594 |

Note: The sample mean expenditure shares are 0.0171118 for beef and veal, 0.0086883 for pork, 0.0058103 for poultry, 0.0038688 for fish, and 0.0354792 for all meats

There are two ways to estimate the unconditional elasticities. One way is to use the estimates of the marginal expenditure values from Table 5.4 to calculate the weights in the marginal price index, $\Delta log\pi_{Mt}$, and then estimate Eqs. (5.1) and (5.2) jointly treating this price index as data like the other price indices. This approach will produce consistent parameter estimates and is most advantageous when we have a relatively large number of groups. A more efficient approach is to substitute the formula for the marginal price index into the expression for the marginal price index and then estimate all the parameters, including the marginal expenditure values for the meats group, jointly with the first-stage and second-stage demand functions.

In this case, Eqs. (5.1) and (5.2) would have the form:

$$\bar{w}_{Mt}\Delta\log Q_t^M = a_M + b_M \Delta log\, Q_t$$

**Table 5.10** Expenditure Per Capita and Price Indices for Food, Nmeats, Nfood, 1970–2010

| Year | xfood | xnmeats | xnfood | foodp | nfoodp |
|---|---|---|---|---|---|
| 1970 | 587.7192 | 414.9226 | 2566.232 | 39.2 | 39.01667 |
| 1971 | 600.4642 | 423.6666 | 2770.111 | 40.35 | 40.79167 |
| 1972 | 640.1932 | 447.9713 | 3019.491 | 42.09167 | 42.025 |
| 1973 | 707.2375 | 481.8658 | 3301.913 | 48.175 | 43.64167 |
| 1974 | 789.0991 | 547.8117 | 3560.415 | 55.11667 | 47.975 |
| 1975 | 866.3583 | 614.0338 | 3905.289 | 59.79167 | 52.48333 |
| 1976 | 932.7998 | 667.5504 | 4330.878 | 61.63333 | 55.95 |
| 1977 | 1000.44 | 738.6463 | 4784.071 | 65.51667 | 59.60833 |
| 1978 | 1093.933 | 792.4658 | 5295.77 | 72.05833 | 63.88333 |
| 1979 | 1211.699 | 870.7954 | 5832.89 | 79.91667 | 71.15 |
| 1980 | 1309.706 | 956.4417 | 6377.897 | 86.775 | 81.50833 |
| 1981 | 1394.241 | 1027.276 | 7015.485 | 93.55833 | 90.38333 |
| 1982 | 1452.874 | 1082.605 | 7467.724 | 97.35 | 96.325 |
| 1983 | 1512.827 | 1133.485 | 8224.846 | 99.40833 | 99.66667 |
| 1984 | 1592.195 | 1201.47 | 8953.018 | 103.2333 | 104 |
| 1985 | 1647.036 | 1251.246 | 9729.135 | 105.5667 | 108.0167 |
| 1986 | 1722.652 | 1313.505 | 10270.97 | 108.9417 | 109.7583 |
| 1987 | 1798.743 | 1368.771 | 10871.06 | 113.4833 | 113.6417 |
| 1988 | 1920.215 | 1475.038 | 11670.51 | 118.175 | 118.2583 |
| 1989 | 2036.387 | 1576.618 | 12424.39 | 125.075 | 123.7083 |
| 1990 | 2160.107 | 1675.171 | 13067.83 | 132.3667 | 130.2833 |
| 1991 | 2198.455 | 1703.937 | 13357.99 | 136.25 | 136.1417 |
| 1992 | 2210.854 | 1712.352 | 14128.8 | 137.8917 | 140.75 |
| 1993 | 2258.124 | 1744.723 | 14848.11 | 140.8583 | 145.1333 |
| 1994 | 2322.594 | 1793.336 | 15598.13 | 144.275 | 148.95 |
| 1995 | 2356.393 | 1825.928 | 16260.98 | 148.4167 | 153.1 |
| 1996 | 2409.127 | 1866.149 | 17039.29 | 153.2833 | 157.4917 |
| 1997 | 2458.357 | 1905.193 | 17829.47 | 157.275 | 161.1 |
| 1998 | 2510.675 | 1947.348 | 18774.83 | 160.6833 | 163.425 |
| 1999 | 2608.658 | 2026.101 | 19873.23 | 164.1 | 167.025 |
| 2000 | 2711.73 | 2100.905 | 21234.81 | 167.8167 | 172.9833 |
| 2001 | 2787.848 | 2158.366 | 21980.65 | 173.0833 | 177.7833 |
| 2002 | 2828.433 | 2177.358 | 22664.53 | 176.2167 | 180.5167 |
| 2003 | 2943.881 | 2268.178 | 23623.04 | 179.975 | 184.65 |
| 2004 | 3096.867 | 2358.328 | 24903.07 | 186.175 | 189.3583 |
| 2005 | 3249.603 | 2498.44 | 26302.07 | 190.725 | 196.0417 |

(continued)

**Table 5.10** (continued)

| Year | xfood | xnmeats | xnfood | foodp | nfoodp |
|---|---|---|---|---|---|
| 2006 | 3382.011 | 2624.518 | 27613.3 | 195.175 | 202.6833 |
| 2007 | 3522.067 | 2737.117 | 28648.9 | 202.9159 | 208.0979 |
| 2008 | 3632.823 | 2840.229 | 29143.64 | 214.1064 | 215.5284 |
| 2009 | 3600.584 | 2822.525 | 28458.04 | 217.9551 | 214.0078 |
| 2010 | 3651.78 | 2865.623 | 29276.9 | 219.6251 | 217.8285 |

$$+\phi b_M(1-b_M)\left[\left(\sum_{j\in M} b_j^M \Delta log p_{jt}\right) - \Delta log \pi_{NFt}\right]$$
$$-\phi b_M b_{NM}(\Delta log \pi_{NMt} - \Delta log \pi_{NFt}) + \varepsilon_{Mt} \quad (5.5)$$

$$\bar{w}_{NMt}\Delta \log Q_t^{NM} = a_{NM} + b_{NM}\Delta log Q_t$$
$$-\phi b_M b_{NM}\left[\left(\sum_{j\in M} b_j^M \Delta log p_{jt}\right) - \Delta log \pi_{NFt}\right]$$
$$+\phi b_{NM}(1-b_{NM})(\Delta log \pi_{NMt} - \Delta log \pi_{NFt}) + \varepsilon_{NMt} \quad (5.6)$$

Equations (5.5) and (5.6) with the three conditional meat demand equations from (4.9),

$$\bar{w}_{it}\Delta log q_{it} = a_i + b_i^M(\bar{w}_{Mt}\Delta log Q_t^M) + \sum_{j\in G} c_{ik}^M \Delta log p_{kt} + \varepsilon_{it} (i = 1, 2, 3) \quad (5.7)$$

comprise the set of five equations estimated jointly by FIML.

Parameter estimates of Eqs. (5.5) through (5.7), a system of five equations, are presented in Table 5.11. Compensated unconditional elasticities are presented in Table 5.12. Own-price elasticities, except pork, are smaller than one in absolute value. All four meats are net substitutes. The strongest substitutes are beef and pork. Pork and fish also appear to be strong substitutes. Expenditure elasticities are close for beef, pork, and poultry, but quite smaller for fish. Because the parameter estimates of the conditional demand functions have changed from Table 5.8, the new conditional demand elasticities are presented in Table 5.13.

The largest difference is between the unconditional and conditional demand elasticities, as can be seen by comparing the results in Table 5.12 with those in Table 5.13. The difference is especially striking for beef and veal. The compensated own-price elasticity of demand for beef and veal is −0.49 for the conditional demand model (Table 5.13) and −0.74 for the unconditional demand model (Table 5.12). The expenditure elasticity for beef and veal from the conditional demand model is 1.07 but 0.62 from the unconditional demand model. Similar differences exist for poultry, but the

**Table 5.11** Parameter Estimates of First-Stage Allocation Equations for Relative Price Version of RM, Eqs. (5.5) and (5.6), and Second-Stage Conditional Demand Eqs. (5.7)

| Parameter | Estimate | Approx Std Err | t Value | Approx Pr > \|t\| |
|---|---|---|---|---|
| $\phi$ | −0.78683 | 0.2568 | −3.06 | 0.0041 |
| $b_1$ | 0.514999 | 0.1311 | 3.93 | 0.0004 |
| $b_2$ | 0.292225 | 0.0759 | 3.85 | 0.0005 |
| $b_3$ | 0.133901 | 0.0623 | 2.15 | 0.0385 |
| $b_4$ | 0.058876 | 0.0704 | 0.84 | 0.4082 |
| $c_{11}$ | −0.00832 | 0.00106 | −7.85 | <.0001 |
| $c_{12}$ | 0.006228 | 0.000963 | 6.47 | <.0001 |
| $c_{13}$ | 0.001866 | 0.000899 | 2.07 | 0.0450 |
| $c_{14}$ | 0.00023 | 0.000866 | 0.27 | 0.7923 |
| $c_{22}$ | −0.00795 | 0.000811 | −9.80 | <.0001 |
| $c_{23}$ | 0.000679 | 0.000457 | 1.49 | 0.1455 |
| $c_{24}$ | 0.001042 | 0.000480 | 2.17 | 0.0365 |
| $c_{33}$ | −0.00171 | 0.000891 | −1.92 | 0.0628 |
| $c_{34}$ | −0.00084 | 0.000507 | −1.65 | 0.1077 |
| $a_m$ | −0.0004 | 0.000222 | −1.78 | 0.0829 |
| $b_m$ | 0.02068 | 0.00748 | 2.76 | 0.0090 |
| $b_{nm}$ | 0.071465 | 0.0197 | 3.63 | 0.0009 |
| $a_{nm}$ | −0.0005 | 0.000484 | −1.04 | 0.3038 |
| $a_1$ | −0.00007 | 0.000087 | −0.80 | 0.4313 |
| $a_2$ | −0.00007 | 0.000071 | −1.04 | 0.3068 |
| $a_3$ | 0.000109 | 0.000035 | 3.13 | 0.0034 |

differences between pork and fish between conditional and unconditional elasticities are not as dramatic.

For completeness, I report the uncompensated unconditional elasticities associated with the compensated elasticities in Table 5.14. These elasticities are obtained applying the generalized Slutsky equation, $e_{ij} = e^*_{ij} - w_j e_i$ to the elasticities reported in Table 5.12. These elasticities, as can be seen in comparison with Table 5.12, are very similar in magnitude. This is because the income effects are small. A comparison with other estimates in the literature indicates more elastic demand elasticities for beef and veal and for pork in this study. For example, Huang (1993) estimates own-price uncompensated elasticities for beef and veal of −0.62 and pork of −0.73; and expenditure elasticities of 0.39 and 0.66, respectively.

For meats as a composite good, the uncompensated own-price elasticity is −0.45 with a t-value of −5.70. The expenditure elasticity is 0.58 with a t-value of 2.76. Huang (1993) estimated the own-price elasticity of meats as −0.36 and expenditure elasticity as 0.52. The money flexibility estimate $\phi$ from Table 5.11 is −0.79 with a

**Table 5.12** Compensated Unconditional Price and Expenditure Elasticities for Meats when Eqs. (5.5), (5.6), and (5.7) are Jointly Estimated

| Elasticity | Estimate | Approx Std Err | t Value | Approx Pr > \|t\| |
|---|---|---|---|---|
| $e_{11}$* | −0.73615 | 0.1295 | −5.69 | <.0001 |
| $e_{12}$* | 0.22466 | 0.0607 | 3.70 | 0.0007 |
| $e_{13}$* | 0.044976 | 0.0423 | 1.06 | 0.2949 |
| $e_{14}$* | 0.006101 | 0.0427 | 0.14 | 0.8871 |
| $e_{22}$* | −1.07564 | 0.1090 | −9.87 | <.0001 |
| $e_{21}$* | 0.442491 | 0.1197 | 3.70 | 0.0007 |
| $e_{23}$* | 0.006381 | 0.0623 | 0.10 | 0.9190 |
| $e_{24}$* | 0.088767 | 0.0434 | 2.04 | 0.0483 |
| $e_{33}$* | −0.34389 | 0.1779 | −1.93 | 0.0611 |
| $e_{31}$* | 0.132209 | 0.1244 | 1.06 | 0.2949 |
| $e_{32}$* | 0.067774 | 0.0818 | 0.83 | 0.4130 |
| $e_{34}$* | −0.16576 | 0.1123 | −1.48 | 0.1485 |
| $e_{44}$* | −0.12671 | 0.2548 | −0.50 | 0.6221 |
| $e_{41}$* | −0.06534 | 0.1461 | −0.45 | 0.6574 |
| $e_{42}$* | 0.19801 | 0.0969 | 2.04 | 0.0483 |
| $e_{43}$* | −0.24776 | 0.1678 | −1.48 | 0.1485 |
| $e_1$ | 0.624729 | 0.3003 | 2.08 | 0.0447 |
| $e_2$ | 0.698202 | 0.2788 | 2.50 | 0.0169 |
| $e_3$ | 0.477475 | 0.2568 | 1.86 | 0.0712 |
| $e_4$ | 0.313789 | 0.3940 | 0.80 | 0.4310 |

t-value of −3.06. This estimate is in the range to be expected for developed countries like the US (Frisch, 1959), and is in the range of values reported by a large number of studies over a long period of time (Clements 2008).

A comparison between the RM and the LA/AIDS and AIDS models indicates a preference for the RM for this data set. Much of the difference in performance seems to center on fish demand. Because the fish data appear to be weak, perhaps not too much should be made of the differences. The RM may very well be a preferred model for aggregate data such as these. It is certainly easier to apply because of its linear structure for the absolute price version and almost linear structure for the relative price version.

**Table 5.13** Compensated Conditional Price and Expenditure Elasticities for Meats when Eqs. (5.5), (5.6), and (5.7) are Jointly Estimated

| Elasticity | Estimate | Approx Std Err | t Value | Approx Pr > \|t\| |
|---|---|---|---|---|
| $e_{11}$* | −0.48824 | 0.0622 | −7.85 | <.0001 |
| $e_{12}$* | 0.365334 | 0.0565 | 6.47 | <.0001 |
| $e_{13}$* | 0.109435 | 0.0528 | 2.07 | 0.0452 |
| $e_{14}$* | 0.01347 | 0.0508 | 0.27 | 0.7924 |
| $e_{21}$* | 0.719564 | 0.1113 | 6.47 | <.0001 |
| $e_{22}$* | −0.91843 | 0.0937 | −9.80 | <.0001 |
| $e_{23}$* | 0.07842 | 0.0527 | 1.49 | 0.1458 |
| $e_{24}$* | 0.120442 | 0.0555 | 2.17 | 0.0367 |
| $e_{31}$* | 0.321688 | 0.1551 | 2.07 | 0.0452 |
| $e_{32}$* | 0.117039 | 0.0787 | 1.49 | 0.1458 |
| $e_{33}$* | −0.29463 | 0.1536 | −1.92 | 0.0630 |
| $e_{34}$* | −0.1441 | 0.0874 | −1.65 | 0.1079 |
| $e_{41}$* | 0.059181 | 0.2232 | 0.27 | 0.7924 |
| $e_{42}$* | 0.268668 | 0.1238 | 2.17 | 0.0367 |
| $e_{43}$* | −0.21538 | 0.1306 | −1.65 | 0.1079 |
| $e_{44}$* | −0.11247 | 0.2268 | −0.50 | 0.6229 |
| $e_1$* | 1.068882 | 0.2721 | 3.93 | 0.0004 |
| $e_2$* | 1.194591 | 0.3102 | 3.85 | 0.0005 |
| $e_3$* | 0.816937 | 0.3802 | 2.15 | 0.0385 |
| $e_4$* | 0.536878 | 0.6415 | 0.84 | 0.4082 |

Note: The sample mean expenditure shares are 0.0171118 for beef and veal, 0.0086883 for pork, 0.0058103 for poultry, 0.0038688 for fish, and 0.0354792 for all meats

## 5.3 Imposing Negative Semi-Definiteness

As indicated previously, the violation of negative semi-definiteness (nsd) can be resolved empirically by specifying and imposing nsd on the model. Barten and Geyskens (1975) develop a method for imposing nsd on the RM model. For this model, we can impose nsd by equating the $(n-1)x(n-1)$ matrix of price coefficients $\boldsymbol{\Theta} = \left[c_{ij}\right]$ with the matrix $-\boldsymbol{T}'\boldsymbol{T}$ where $\boldsymbol{T}$ is an upper triangular matrix (Diewert and Wales, 1988). Estimation with respect to the coefficients in $\boldsymbol{T}$ will lead to imposition of nsd on the matrix of price coefficients.

If one were using the AIDS model, nsd could be imposed locally using the method proposed by Moschini (1998). This method starts with imposing nsd at the point where prices and income are normalized to one. At that point, the transformed price coefficients of the AIDS model, Eq. (4.10), can be written as

**Table 5.14** Uncompensated Unconditional Price and Expenditure Elasticities for Meats when Eqs. (5.5), (5.6), and (5.7) are Jointly Estimated

| Elasticity | Estimate | Approx Std Err | t Value | Approx Pr > \|t\| |
|---|---|---|---|---|
| $e_{11}$ | −0.74681 | 0.1337 | −5.59 | <.0001 |
| $e_{12}$ | 0.219253 | 0.0606 | 3.62 | 0.0009 |
| $e_{13}$ | 0.041353 | 0.0422 | 0.98 | 0.3341 |
| $e_{14}$ | 0.003677 | 0.0425 | 0.09 | 0.9315 |
| $e_{22}$ | −1.08169 | 0.1097 | −9.86 | <.0001 |
| $e_{21}$ | 0.430588 | 0.1214 | 3.55 | 0.0011 |
| $e_{23}$ | 0.002331 | 0.0629 | 0.04 | 0.9707 |
| $e_{24}$ | 0.086058 | 0.0433 | 1.99 | 0.0544 |
| $e_{33}$ | −0.34666 | 0.1785 | −1.94 | 0.0600 |
| $e_{31}$ | 0.124069 | 0.1230 | 1.01 | 0.3200 |
| $e_{32}$ | 0.063641 | 0.0828 | 0.77 | 0.4473 |
| $e_{34}$ | −0.16762 | 0.1130 | −1.48 | 0.1468 |
| $e_{44}$ | −0.12792 | 0.2561 | −0.50 | 0.6205 |
| $e_{41}$ | −0.07069 | 0.1444 | −0.49 | 0.6274 |
| $e_{42}$ | 0.195294 | 0.0972 | 2.01 | 0.0521 |
| $e_{43}$ | −0.24958 | 0.1696 | −1.47 | 0.1498 |
| $e_1$ | 0.624729 | 0.3003 | 2.08 | 0.0447 |
| $e_2$ | 0.698202 | 0.2788 | 2.50 | 0.0169 |
| $e_3$ | 0.477475 | 0.2568 | 1.86 | 0.0712 |
| $e_4$ | 0.313789 | 0.3940 | 0.80 | 0.4310 |

Note: The sample mean expenditure shares are 0.0171118 for beef and veal, 0.0086883 for pork, 0.0058103 for poultry, 0.0038688 for fish, 0.0354792 for all meats, 0.1058140 for non-meat foods, and 0.8588030 for non-food

$$\theta_{ij} = c_{ij} = w_i e^*_{ij} = \gamma_{ij} + \alpha_i \alpha_j - \alpha_i \delta_{ij} \tag{5.8}$$

Setting $\boldsymbol{\Theta} = -\boldsymbol{T}'\boldsymbol{T}$ as in the RM, and rewriting the AIDS model in terms of these coefficients yields

$$w_{it} = \alpha_i + \alpha_i \log\left(\frac{p_{it}}{P^\alpha_t}\right) + \sum_{j=1}^{n-1} \theta_{ij} \log\left(\frac{p_{jt}}{p_{nt}}\right) + \beta_i \log\left(\frac{y_t}{P_t}\right) \tag{5.9}$$

where $\log P^\alpha_t = \sum_{i=1}^{n} \alpha_i \log p_{it}$ and the homogeneity condition has been imposed. The translog price index with homogeneity and symmetry imposed is

$$\log P_t = \log P_t^{\alpha} - \frac{1}{2}\left(\log P_t^{\alpha}\right)^2 + \frac{1}{2}\sum_i \alpha_i (logp_{it})^2$$

$$+\frac{1}{2}\sum_{j=1}^{n-1}\sum_{j=1}^{n-1}\theta_{jk}log\left(\frac{p_{jt}}{p_{nt}}\right)log\left(\frac{p_{kt}}{p_{nt}}\right) \tag{5.10}$$

As in the case of the RM, estimation can then proceed by estimating with respect to the parameters in $\boldsymbol{T}$ which are related to the parameters of (5.9) and (5.10) through the relationship $\boldsymbol{\Theta} = -\boldsymbol{T}'\boldsymbol{T}$. If unconstrained estimation reveals one or more eigenvalues of $\boldsymbol{\Theta}$ positive, then the rank can be reduced by sequentially reducing the number of linearly independent vectors in $\boldsymbol{T}$ (Moschini 1998). In a recent application, Srivastava et al (2014), in estimation of a system of demand functions for alcoholic beverages, find four out of eleven of the eigenvalues were positive. Therefore, negative semi-definiteness was imposed by deleting four of the vectors in $\boldsymbol{T}$.

## 5.4 Other Data Sets

Two other data sets used for time-series applications of consumer demand are the US Department of Commerce, Bureau of Economic Analysis (BEA), and the US Department of Labor, Bureau of Labor Statistics (BLS) data sets. The BEA publishes Personal Consumption Expenditures and Price Indices by major product types on a monthly, quarterly, and annual basis. The data are the most comprehensive data published by the federal government. The price indices are Fisher Ideal price indices. The source for these data is https://apps.bea.gov/. Food and beverage data are available for individual products at the same level as ERS. The one problem with these data is that they are only available on a commodity basis for consumption off premises. Purchased meals and beverage data are only available for the aggregate. Thus, for issues like taxation policy, these data would be insufficient because of a lack of information on commodities purchased to produce meals and beverages for on-premise consumption. For broader aggregates (e.g., food, durables, etc.), data from this source are readily available for econometric analysis.

The BLS data are from cross sections of households and can be aggregated across households to weekly, monthly, quarterly, or annual basis. These data have the same limitations as the BEA data in that they only provide detailed commodity data for at home consumption. A complete description of both the BEA and BLS data can be found in Okrent and Alston (2011).

However, it is possible to use these data in a meaningful way by supplementing the consumer demand models with relationships between commodity prices and expenditures on purchased meals and beverages, which can be estimated with appropriate economic relationships. Commodities consumed away from home are not identifiable generally because final purchases are meals. However, commodities in this instance may be estimated as the amounts purchased by restaurants, institutions, and fast food stores. In this case, think of there being a production function for food purchased and/or consumed on premise, or away from home, that depends on all the quantities of individual food commodities. Associated with this production function we have a cost function of the form:

$$C = c\left(P^1, \ldots, P^N, \boldsymbol{w}\right) \cdot Q_{op} \tag{5.10}$$

where $P^G\left(p_1, \ldots, p_{n_G}\right)$ is a price index corresponding to the $N$-good partition of the utility function, $\boldsymbol{w}$ is a vector of input prices of non-food prices used in producing food consumed away from home, and $Q_{op}$ is the quantity of food produced for restaurants, institutions, and fast food stores. By Shephard's lemma, Eq. (2.37), demand for the $i$th good purchased associated with the $G^{\text{th}}$ branch is:

$$q_{iop} = \frac{\partial C}{\partial p_i} = \left[\frac{\partial c\left(P^1, \ldots, P^N, \boldsymbol{w}\right) \cdot Q_{op}}{\partial P^G}\right]\left(\frac{\partial P^G}{\partial p_i}\right) \tag{5.11}$$

where it is assumed the composite on-premise good represents the $N^{\text{th}}$ good.

In market equilibrium, $Q_{op} = D_{op}\left(\pi_{op}, \pi, y\right)$, i.e., demand for the composite good of food sold to restaurants, institutions, and fast food stores. The variables $\pi_{op}$ and $\pi$ are marginal price indices for the composite good and marginal price index for all goods, respectively. The specification for demand will be valid when strong separability holds for the aggregate food commodities purchased at home and for the aggregate good away from home good.

Empirical implementation would include estimating the $N-1$ first-stage equations corresponding to the food at home and non-food groups, and the one away from home group, on the assumption these $N$ goods are distinct, strongly separable groups. The away from home conditional demand functions and cost function, equations, (5.10) and (5.11), would also be estimated. The estimated demand function, $D_{op}\left(\pi_{op}, \pi, y\right)$, would then be substituted into (5.11) and the resulting function differentiated to obtain elasticities for the commodities consumed away from home. Thus, we are able to link price changes to change in demand for goods consumed off and on premise.

It is important to recognize that the choice of data for demand estimation can have consequences for the way in which the model is formulated and how the elasticities are estimated. Use of ERS data is more straightforward, but as discussed previously, it involves assumptions about the dataset developed for use in estimation, one of which is that goods consumed away from home are valued at the same price as goods consumed at home. Another assumption is that the price indices, which only cover goods purchased for at home consumption, are adequate proxies for goods consumed away from home. The final assumptions are that the simple sum aggregates of per capita consumption are adequate proxies for food consumption, and the average prices are adequate for representation of commodity prices[4]. More will be said on this issue in the next chapter.

## Problems

5.1 Given the elasticities and sample mean shares for the compensated conditional demand elasticities in Table 5.5, calculate the matrix of uncompensated conditional demand elasticities. Why are the uncompensated conditional elasticities so different from the compensated conditional elasticities, yet the uncompensated unconditional elasticities are very similar to the compensated unconditional elasticities?

5.2 Verify that the eigenvalues of the matrix $\left[c_{ij}\right]$ from Table 5.5 are all nonpositive.

5.3 Derive the compensated cross-price elasticities for the four meat goods with respect to non-meat food and non-food goods using the parameter estimates from Table 5.12. Sample mean estimates of the relevant budget shares are shown in Table 5.14. The relevant formulas can be found in Chapter 3.

5.4 Explain why the money flexibility coefficient $\phi$ must be estimated jointly with the other parameters of the first-stage equations.

5.5 Use the data in Tables 5.1, 5.2 and 5.3 to estimate the Indirect Translog demand system. Compare the compensated price and expenditure elasticities with those obtained from the RM and AIDS in this chapter.

## References

Barten, A.P., and E. Geyskens. "The Negativity Condition in Consumer Demand." *European Economic Review* 6(1975): 227–260.

Bieri, J., and Alain de Janvry. *Empirical Analysis of Demand under Consumer Budgeting*. University of California, Giannini Foundation Monograph No. 30, Calif. Agric. Exp. Sta., Berkeley, CA, 1972.

Blackorby, C., and R.R. Russell. "Will the Real Elasticity of Substitution Please Stand Up? *The American Economic Review* 79(1989): 882–888.

Brown, M., and D. Heien. "The S-Branch Utility: A Generalization of the Linear Expenditure System." *Econometrica* 40(1972): 737–747.

Christensen, L.R., and M.F. Manser. "Estimating U.S. Consumer Preferences for Meats with a Flexible Utility Function." *Journal of Econometrics* 5(1977): 37-53.

Clements, K.W. "Price Elasticities of Demand are Minus One-Half." *Economics Letters* 99(2008): 490–493.

[4]As discussed in the next chapter, both of these assumptions can produce quality effects in the demand analysis. Such a practice of using simple sum aggregates and average prices is commonplace in empirical work.

Clements, K.W., and L.W. Johnson. “The Demand for Beer, Wine, and Spirits: A Systemwide Analysis.” *Journal of Business* 56(1983): 273–304.

Deaton, A.S., and J. Muellbauer. “An Almost Ideal Demand System.” *The American Economic Review* 70(1980): 312–326.

Diewert, W.E., and T.J. Wales. “A Normalized Quadratic Semiflexible Functional Form.” *Journal of Econometrics* 37(1988): 327–342.

Frisch, R.A. “A Complete Scheme for Computing All Direct and Cross Demand Elasticities.” *Econometrica* 27(1959): 177–196.

George, P.S., and G.A. King. *Consumer Demand for Food Commodities in the United State with Projections for 1980.* Giannini Foundation Monograph No. 26, California Agricultural Experiment Station, Berkeley, CA, 1971.

Huang, K.S. *A Complete System of U.S. Demand for Food.* USDA Technical Bulletin No. 1821, Washington, 1993.

Moschini, G. The Semiflexible Almost Ideal Demand System.” *European Economic Review* 42(1998): 349–364.

Okrent, A. and J.M. Alston. *Demand for Food in the United States: A Review of Literature, Evaluation of Previous Estimates, and Presentation of New Estimates.* University of California, Giannini Foundation Monograph No. 48, California Agricultural Experiment Station, Berkeley, CA, 2011.

Pollack, R.A. “Conditional Demand Functions and the Implications of Separable Utility.” *Southern Economic Journal* 37(1970): 423–433.

Srivastava, P., K.R. McLaren, M. Wohlgenant, and X. Zhao. “Disaggregated Econometric Analysis of Consumer Demand Response by Alcoholic Beverage Types.” *The Australian Journal of Agricultural and Resource Economics* 59(2014): 412–432.

# Chapter 6
# Quality, Heterogeneous Goods, and Cross-Section Demand

## 6.1 Introduction

The data set used in the last chapter is a time series data set. In recent years, attention has focused more on cross section and panel data sets that have become available to researchers for applied demand analysis. Such data sets present unique challenges to analysts as discussed in this chapter. This chapter addresses the issue of specification of commodity demand when estimated with cross-sectional and/or panel data where the role of quality through price changes becomes an issue. The chapter also discusses how to model systems of heterogeneous demand functions and panel data models for food demand systems. Finally, issues of zero values and censoring are also addressed with a focus on empirical implementation with systems of demand functions.

## 6.2 Unit Values, Prices, and Quality

### *6.2.1 Problem of Average Prices Varying Across Households*

Historically, economists have been interested in estimating Engel curves and cross-sectional data have been well suited for that purpose. Two early studies by Allen and Bowley (1935) and Prais and Houthakker (1955), and a more recent study by George and King (1971), are comprehensive works on estimating income elasticities from cross-section data. The assumption typically made with cross-sectional data is that all consumers face the same price. Prais and Houthakker (1955) showed this assumption is questionable, particularly when the focus is on commodities as opposed to goods. Goods are aggregated into commodities, which tend to be heterogeneous in nature. Therefore, average commodity prices may vary across households as households choose different combinations of goods within the commodity aggregates. This not



M. K. Wohlgenant, *Market Interrelationships and Applied Demand Analysis*,
Palgrave Studies in Agricultural Economics and Food Policy,
https://doi.org/10.1007/978-3-030-73144-1_6

only raises questions about the effect of such price variation on income-consumption relationships but also how price effects should be modeled with cross-sectional data (Cox and Wohlgenant 1986; Deaton 1988).

With exogenous preference shift variables such as product or goods characteristics, demand for the $i^{\text{th}}$ good from Eq. (2.3) is

$$q_i = g_i\left(y, p_i, \boldsymbol{p}_s, \boldsymbol{s}\right) \tag{6.1}$$

where $\boldsymbol{p}_s$ is the vector of all other prices. Using the comparative static result (2.24), we can show that changes in demand for the good in question are

$$dq_i = \sum_j k_{ij}\left(dp_j - \lambda^{-1}\sum_{k=1}^{r}\frac{\partial^2 v}{\partial q_i \partial s_k}ds_k\right) + \frac{\partial g_i}{\partial y}\left(dy - \sum_j q_j dp_j\right) \tag{6.2}$$

This means we can account for exogenous utility function shift variables by adjusting prices for changes in the monetized marginal value of these characteristics. This can be done directly through hedonic regressions based on the first-order conditions for utility maximization, Eq. (2.1). This also means that the income–consumption relationship—the Engel curve—can be estimated directly because prices will have been purged of their dependence on product characteristics, including income, which often is used to proxy for these characteristics.

On the interpretation that the demand functions (6.1) are for commodities, as opposed to goods, average prices are often used in applied demand analysis with cross-sectional and panel data sets. While the (elementary) goods are homogeneous, the composite goods as sums of the elementary goods are not. Average prices are unit values, $V_i = \frac{\sum_{i\in G} p_i x_i}{\sum_{i\in G} x_i}$, which are no longer exogenous but are a function of choices of elementary goods made by the consumer. As discussed by Nelson (1991), the consumer problem then becomes one of choosing quality as well as quantity, where both variables appear in the utility function. This is the approach taken by Houthakker (1952–1953) and Theil (1952–1953).

### 6.2.2 *Income and Price Elasticities of Quality*

Nelson (1991) suggests controlling for quality variation through use of separability and commodity aggregation theory. In particular, if one views the composite good or commodity as a separable group of the elementary goods, say $Q_G = Q_G\left(x_1, \ldots, x_{n_G}\right)$, then the quality problem is solved. Consumers choose composite goods in a first-stage optimization problem and then choose elementary goods in a second-stage problem. With the Paasche or Laspeyres price indices for the composite good, the problem is solved. To see why this is so, consider the set of relationships:

$$V_G = P_G \upsilon_G \tag{6.3}$$

$$Q_G = q_G \upsilon_G \tag{6.4}$$

where, as before, $V_G$, is the unit value, $P_G = \frac{\sum_{i\in G} p_i x_i}{\sum_{i\in G} p_i^* x_i}$, is a quality-invariant price index,$q_G = \sum_{i\in G} x_i$ and $\upsilon_G = \frac{\sum_{i\in G} p_i^* x_i}{\sum_{i\in G} x_i}$ is the quality index. Taking logs of (6.3) and (6.4) and differentiating with respect to log income and log prices yields:

$$\eta_{Vy} = \frac{\partial \log V_G}{\partial \log y} = \eta_{\upsilon y};\ \eta_{VP} = \frac{\partial \log V_G}{\partial \log P_G} = 1 + \eta_{\upsilon P} \tag{6.5}$$

$$\eta_{Qy} = \frac{\partial \log Q_G}{\partial \log y} = \eta_{qy} + \eta_{\upsilon y};\ \eta_{QP} = \frac{\partial \log Q_G}{\partial \log P_G} = \eta_{qP} + \eta_{\upsilon P} \tag{6.6}$$

where an account has been taken of the facts that $\frac{\partial \log P_G}{\partial \log y} = 0$ and $\frac{\partial \log P_G}{\partial \log P_G} = 1$. The elasticity $\eta_{\upsilon y} = \frac{\partial \log \upsilon_G}{\partial \log y}$ is the so-called "elasticity of quality" or income elasticity of quality (see, e.g., Prais and Houthakker 1955; George and King 1971; Cramer 1973), and $\eta_{\upsilon P} = \frac{\partial \log \upsilon_G}{\partial \log P_G}$ is the price elasticity of quality.

The goal then is to estimate $\eta_{Qy}$ and $\eta_{QP}$, elasticities of demand with respect to income and price. These elasticities are the true, quality invariant, elasticities corresponding to consumer theory. As can be seen from (6.5) and (6.6), these elasticities are not equal to the elasticities estimated using either simple sum quantities or elasticities estimated using unit values. Some studies (e.g., Deaton 1987, 1988, 1990) are interested primarily in the quantity elasticities $\eta_{qy}$ and $\eta_{qP}$, apparently because of food policy. However, these elasticities can be derived from the relationships in (6.5) and (6.6). The problem from an empirical standpoint is how to consistently estimate demand elasticities when only unit values, not the appropriate quality-invariant price indices, are available. There are two approaches that have been proposed to address this problem: the Cox and Wohlgenant (1986) approach and the Deaton (1988) approach. Each approach rests on different assumptions and may or may not be appropriate for any given data set.

## 6.3 Cox and Wohlgenant Approach to Modeling Unit Values

In the original Cox and Wohlgenant (1986) paper, the goal was to show that, after adjusting unit values for quality change using hedonic-type regressions, there was sufficient price variation to estimate price elasticities of demand with cross-section data. Moreover, by purging the unit values of quality effects, consistent estimates of income elasticities and household characterisitcs could be obtained.

The model of quality adjustment by Cox and Wohlgenant (1986) is an extension of the approach of Cowling and Raynor (1970). Their method first estimates hedonic values for the specified commodity characteristics, and then uses the residuals as estimates of the quality-adjusted prices in the model. Cowling and Raynor (1970) use specific product characteristics (e.g., horsepower for tractor price), while Cox and Wohlgenant (1986) use income and household characteristics in the hedonic regressions.

The demand functions with quality-invariant prices are modeled in two steps. In the first step, we estimate the unit value functions as a function of income and household characteristics (after removing region/quarterly fixed effects) to obtain

$$V_{ijc} = \bar{V}_{ic} + \hat{b}_{iy} y_{jc} + \hat{c}\prime_i \boldsymbol{hc}_{jc} + \hat{u}_{ijc} \tag{6.7}$$

where the subscript $i$ refers to the good, $j$ to the individual, and $c$ to cluster, which could be region/quarter or other specific category of people. Following Houthakker (1952–1953), the unit values equal the sum of quality prices, $\hat{b}_{iy} y_{jc} + \hat{c}\prime_i \boldsymbol{hc}_{jc}$, and quantity prices, $\bar{V}_{ic} + \hat{u}_{ijc}$. Next, quality-adjusted prices are formed:

$$V_{ijc} - \hat{b}_{iy} y_{jc} - \hat{c}\prime_i \boldsymbol{hc}_{jc} = \bar{V}_{ic} + \hat{u}_{ijc} \tag{6.8}$$

In the second step, the quality-adjusted prices are substituted for the unobserved prices (i.e., quantity prices) in the demand specification and the model is estimated by OLS. For example, in the single-commodity case:

$$q_{ijc} = g_i\left(y_j, \bar{V}_{ic} + \hat{u}_{ijc}, \boldsymbol{b}_{ij}\right) + \varepsilon_{ijc} \tag{6.9}$$

where $\boldsymbol{b}_{ij}$ represent other demand shift variables. With other prices in the demand equation, a similar procedure would be followed to replace these prices with quality-adjusted unit values. Murphy and Topel (1985) show that this type of two-step procedure is statistically consistent.

The Cross-sectional data used by Cox and Wohlgenant (1986) to estimate demand for fresh vegetables, canned vegetables, and frozen vegetables are truncated data. The parameters were estimated using Tobit. For non-consuming households, prices are unobservable so the average region/quarter mean values were used for those households[1].

The Cox and Wohlgenant (1986) model can be extended to decompose both income and price elasticities into quantity and quality effects. We can do this through

[1]Dong et al. (1998) show that this approach can produce inconsistent parameter estimates. The same criticism can be made of the papers by Deaton and other applications where researchers assign missing prices values based on averages or even regression imputations. While the methodology used by Cox and Wohlgenant can be challenged, one should not make too much of the empirical application of Dong et al., which is not credible because it excludes substitutes for beef. More realistic applications, with multiple commodities, lead to complications with Dong et al's methodology. More will be said about how to model systems of equations with missing prices in Sect. 6.8.

using an additional piece of information, derived by Deaton (1988, Eq. 10), showing that

$$\eta_{Vp} = 1 + \eta_{Vy}\frac{\eta_{qP}}{\eta_{qy}}, \text{ or } \eta_{vp} = \eta_{vy}\frac{\eta_{qP}}{\eta_{qy}} \tag{6.10}$$

in light of (6.5) and (6.6). To understand where this important relationship comes from, recall the assumption that individual goods within a group are weakly separable from goods in other groups implies there exist conditional demand functions of the form: $x_i = g_i^G(y_G, \boldsymbol{p}_G) \forall i \in G$. Assume that prices within the group move proportionately with one another so that $\boldsymbol{p}_G = P_G \boldsymbol{p}_G^*$, where $\boldsymbol{p}_G^*$ is a vector of fixed prices for goods within the group and $P_G$ is the scalar commodity price index. Thus, we can write a demand for good $i$ as: $x_i = g_i^G(y_G, \boldsymbol{p}_G) = g_i^G(y_G, P_G \boldsymbol{p}_G^*) = g_i^G(y_G/P_G, \boldsymbol{p}_G^*)$, the last step imposing the zero homogeneity property of Marshallian demand functions. Noting that the quality function, $v_G = \frac{\sum_{i \in G} p_i^* x_i}{\sum_{i \in G} x_i}$, depends only on the $x_i$'s and each demand function only depends on $y_G/P_G$ for fixed prices $\boldsymbol{p}_G^*$, there is a unique relationship between $\log v_G$ and $\log(y_G/P_G)$, say $\log v_G = f[\log(y_G/P_G)]$. Differentiating with respect to log price gives: $\frac{\partial \log v_G}{\partial \log P_G} = \frac{\partial \log v_G}{\partial \log y_G}\left(\frac{\partial \log y_G}{\partial \log P_G} - 1\right)$. But we also know that $\frac{\partial \log y_G}{\partial \log P_G} = \left(1 + \frac{\partial \log v_G}{\partial \log P_G} + \frac{\partial \log q_G}{\partial \log P_G}\right)$ and through differentiating $f[\log(y_G/P_G)]$ with respect to $y$ : $\frac{\partial \log v_G}{\partial \log y} = \frac{\partial \log v_G}{\partial \log y_G} \cdot \frac{\partial \log y_G}{\partial \log y}$. Upon substituting into the above expression and rearranging terms we get (6.10). Also, one can show, using (6.5) and (6.6) and rearranging terms, that

$$\eta_{vp} = \eta_{vy}\frac{\eta_{QP}}{\eta_{Qy}} \text{ or } \eta_{Vp} = 1 + \eta_{Vy}\frac{\eta_{QP}}{\eta_{Qy}} \tag{6.11}$$

Either the ratio of own-price elasticity to income elasticity of demand or the ratio of own-price elasticity of quantity demand to income elasticity of quantity demand can be used to estimate the ratio of price elasticity of quality to income elasticity of quality, $\eta_{vP}/\eta_{vy}$.

We can use the relationships in (6.10) to decompose changes into quantity and quality effects for the results obtained by Cox and Wohlgenant (1986). From Cox (1984), additional data are obtained to estimate the elasticity values at the sample means. From Cox (1984, Table 18, Model 3) we find the value of the quantity to equal 7.34. The ratio of total elasticity to total slope from Model 3 in the same table, multiplied by the mean quantity value, gives \$8.3200223 thousand dollars for mean income. The sample mean quality-adjusted price for fresh vegetables from Cox (1984, Table 10) is \$0.203. With this information, the quality elasticity from Cox and Wohlgenant (1986, Table 3) is 0.0526. The price elasticity of quality using Eq. (6.10) is therefore $\eta_{vp} = (0.0526)(-0.2036)/0.0713) = -0.15$. Using (6.5) and (6.6) we can then estimate the own-price and income elasticities of the quality-invariant demand functions: $\eta_{QP} = -0.15 - 0.2036 = -0.35$, and $\eta_{Qy} = 0.0526 + 0.0713 = 0.12$. Both demand elasticities are over twice their (absolute) values for the quantity demand relationships. These results may be useful for food policy analysis, suggesting almost half of the price response for fresh vegetable consumption is due to a change in the mix of fresh vegetables consumed. As overall vegetable prices increase (decrease) by one percent, the average quality of fresh vegetables decreases (increases) by 0.15 percent.

Estimation of quantity demand functions, i.e., estimation of demand functions with quantity measured as the sum of individual items within the group, will produce measured demand elasticities that are the true demand elasticities net of the respective quality elasticities, i.e., $\frac{\partial \log q_G}{\partial \log P_G} = \frac{\partial \log Q_G}{\partial \log P_G} - \frac{\partial \log v_G}{\partial \log P_G}$ and $\frac{\partial \log q_G}{\partial \log y} = \frac{\partial \log Q_G}{\partial \log y} - \frac{\partial \log v_G}{\partial \log y}$. The use of expenditure shares rather than simple sum quantities gives directly estimates of price and income elasticities of demand when quality-adjusted prices are used. To see this, note that price and income elasticities of demand are both derived through differentiation of the budget share, i.e., $\frac{\partial w_i}{\partial \log P_j} \cdot \frac{1}{w_i} = \frac{\partial \log Q_i}{\partial \log P_j} + \delta_{ij}$ and $\frac{\partial w_i}{\partial \log y} \cdot \frac{1}{w_i} = \frac{\partial \log Q_i}{\partial \log y} - 1$ when prices are quality-adjusted prices. These results follow from (6.5)–(6.6) and the fact that $w_i = \frac{P_i Q_i}{y} = \frac{P_i q_i v_i}{y} = \frac{V_i q_i}{y}$.

## 6.4 Deaton Approach to Unit Values in Estimating Demand Functions

Deaton in a series of papers (1987, 1988, and 1990) has developed an alternative approach to estimate demand elasticities from cross-sectional data where unit values are used for prices. The assumptions of his methodology are that prices only vary between clusters, and prices are constant within clusters of respondents within villages, where surveys of consumers are undertaken. The key assumption he makes is that there is no variation in market prices so that within cluster estimators can identify income and quality effects. For simplicity, consider the single-good case consisting of the following two equations (Deaton 1988):

$$w_{ic} = \alpha_1 + \beta_1 \log y_{ic} + \boldsymbol{\gamma}'_1 \mathbf{z}_{ic} + \theta_1 \log p_c + f_c + u_{1ic} \tag{6.12}$$

$$\log V_{ic} = \alpha_2 + \beta_2 \log y_{ic} + \boldsymbol{\gamma}'_2 \mathbf{z}_{ic} + \theta_2 \log p_c + u_{2ic} \tag{6.13}$$

where $w_{ic}$ is budget share of good, $y_{ic}$ is total expenditures, $\mathbf{z}_{ic}$ is a vector of household characteristics, $p_c$ is the unobserved market price, $V_{ic}$ is the calculated unit value, and $f_c$ is a cluster fixed effect.

The model is estimated in three stages. In the first stage, the within cluster means are removed so that

$$\tilde{y}_{1ic} = w_{ic} - \tilde{\beta}_1 \log y_{ic} - \tilde{\boldsymbol{\gamma}}'_1 \mathbf{z}_{ic} \tag{6.14}$$

$$\tilde{y}_{2ic} = \log V_{ic} - \tilde{\beta}_2 \log y_{ic} - \tilde{\boldsymbol{\gamma}}'_2 \mathbf{z}_{ic} \tag{6.15}$$

The population analogs to these two equations are

$$y_{1c} = \alpha_1 + \theta_1 \log p_c + f_c + u_{1c} \tag{6.16}$$

$$y_{2c} = \alpha_2 + +\theta_2 \log p_c + u_{2c} \tag{6.17}$$

Over $C$ clusters with cluster $c$ having $n_c$ households, $n_c^+$ of which consume positive amounts, the covariances and variances of (6.16) and (6.17) are

$$cov(y_{1c}, y_{2c}) = \theta_1\theta_2 m_p + {}^{\sigma_{12}}\!/_{n_c} \tag{6.18}$$

$$var(y_{2c}) = \theta_2^2 m_p + {}^{\sigma_{22}}\!/_{n_c^+} \tag{6.19}$$

where $m_p$ is the between cluster variance of log $p_c$. Letting $\tau = C/\left(\sum n_c^{-1}\right)$ and $\tau^+ = C/\left(\sum n_c^{+-1}\right)$, and solving for $m_p$, we obtain the population OLS estimator

$$\tilde{\phi} = \frac{cov(\tilde{y}_{1c}, \tilde{y}_{2c}) - {}^{\tilde{\sigma}_{12}}\!/_{\tau}}{var(\tilde{y}_{2c}) - {}^{\tilde{\sigma}_{22}}\!/_{\tau^+}} \tag{6.20}$$

which consistently estimates the ratio $\theta_1/\theta_2$. The estimated variances and covariances are from the correlation of errors and cross-errors in the first-stage estimation. Deaton (1988) shows that the separability restriction that individual goods of each commodity are weakly separable from individual goods of other groups, Eq. (6.10), implies the result $\theta_2 = 1+\beta_2\varepsilon_p/\varepsilon_x$, where $\varepsilon_p$ is the quantity price elasticity and $\varepsilon_x$ is the quantity income elasticity (see Eq. 6.10). Through manipulation with derivatives of the budget share and quality equations, (6.12) and (6.13), an estimator for $\theta_1$ is obtained:

$$\theta_1 = \frac{\phi[\beta_1 + w(1+\beta_2)]}{(\beta_1 + w - \beta_2\phi)} \tag{6.21}$$

The one significant feature of Deaton's model is accounting for errors in variables in the estimator in (6.20). The formulas would be the methods of moment estimator for OLS if the covariance and variance terms, ${}^{\tilde{\sigma}_{12}}\!/_{\tau}$ and ${}^{\tilde{\sigma}_{22}}\!/_{\tau^+}$, were absent. Their presence is based on assumption that both expenditures and quantities in calculating unit values are error-ridden. The modeling approach of Cox and Wohlgenant (1986) does not directly account for measurement error but modeling approaches are available to deal with that problem. They would seem to be relatively easy to deal with when panel or pseudo-panel data are used. With repeated observations on the same cross-section units, available instruments might include lagged unit values if the panel collecting data changed over time, which is often the case. Another possibility would be to use unit values from an adjacent region, similar to the approach of Hausman et al. (1994). Such unit values, although possibly error-ridden, would be viable so long as the errors in the unit values from the different regions are uncorrelated.

Another difference in the Cox and Wohlgenant and Deaton modeling approaches is that all individuals within a cluster are assumed to face the same prices in Deaton's approach. The Cox and Wohlgenant model can be reconciled with the Deaton model by assuming the quantity price in (6.8) equals $\overline{\bar{V}_{ic} + \hat{u}_{ijc}}$ (Hoang 2009). As can be seen, the cluster prices are now independent of individual consumers within the cluster.

The Deaton model has been generalized to more than one good and multivariate statistical models have been developed to estimate the parameters (Deaton 1987, 1990). In empirical work with individual survey data, no effort is made in these studies to model missing values and zero observations due to censoring. While Deaton argues that this is not a problem if one is interested in the average response to price and income changes across the whole population, in general, the degree of censoring can cause statistical problems as indicated below in Sect. 6.8.

## 6.5 Theil-Clement Approach to Quality Measurement

Theil (1975/76) introduced the idea that if affluence grows faster than necessities, then the market basket will grow in a more desirable direction. Using income elasticities of component goods alone, Theil's quality index can be defined as (Clements and Gao 2012):

$$y_{eq} = \sum_i w_i(e_i - 1)\left(\tilde{Q}_i - \tilde{Q}\right) \tag{6.22}$$

where $\tilde{Q}_i$ is the relative change in quantity of $i^{\text{th}}$ good and $\tilde{Q}$ is the relative change in quantity of all goods ($\tilde{Q} = \sum_i w_i \Delta \log Q_i$). Whether income elasticities are larger or smaller than one does not in itself determine whether quality is increasing or decreasing. A quality component $(e_i - 1)\left(\tilde{Q}_i - \tilde{Q}\right)$ is increasing either if the income elasticity is larger (smaller) than one and quantity is increasing (decreasing) relative to the whole. On average, however, we can say quality is increasing if consumption of luxuries is increasing more on average than necessities are growing.

We can likewise define the index of price of quality and index of spending as follows (Clements and Gao 2012):

$$y_{ep} = \sum_i w_i(e_i - 1)(\tilde{p}_i - \tilde{p}) \tag{6.23}$$

$$y_{ew} = \sum_i w_i(e_i - 1)\tilde{w}_i \tag{6.24}$$

where $\tilde{p}_i$ is the relative change in price of $i^{\text{th}}$ good, $\tilde{w}_i$ is the relative change in expenditure share of $i^{\text{th}}$ good, and $\tilde{p} = \sum_i w_i \tilde{p}_i$ is the Divisia price index. For the price increase, luxuries become relatively more expensive and necessities relatively cheaper. The sum of these two indices, (6.22), and (6.23) equals (6.24):

$$y_{ew} = y_{eq} + y_{ep} \tag{6.25}$$

Another way of stating (6.25) is that deflated spending $y_{ew} - y_{ep}$ equals the quality index $y_{eq}$.

Clements and Gao (2012) and Clements and Si (2017) use this framework to measure diversity and quality of diets across countries. Diets are more diverse for wealthier countries and the quality of diets increases with income, although the elasticity is small (Clements and Si 2017).

## 6.6 Modeling Systems of Demand Functions for Heterogeneous Goods

Modeling demand for heterogeneous goods with the goal of estimating disaggregated elasticities presents challenges beyond the approaches discussed so far. The three major approaches in the literature to this problem are discussed below. The first is an extension of the two-stage budgeting process to multiple stages in order to isolate goods by successfully more homogeneous sub-groups. The second approach is the goods characteristics, linear utility approach whereby goods are modeled directly in terms of their characteristics. The third approach is the Hedonic Metric approach where elasticities are estimated through qualitative factor dependencies.

### *6.6.1 Multi-Stage Budgeting Approaches to Quality*

Theil (1980) proposed extending the two-stage budgeting procedure to estimating demand for heterogeneous and branded goods. A nice example of this approach is Hausman et al. (1994), who estimate brand-level demand for beer using a three-level budgeting procedure. In the first stage, the consumer chooses between beer and all other goods. In the second stage, given expenditures on beer, the consumer chooses between different market segments (premium beer, light beer, popular-priced beer). In the third stage, given expenditures on each market segment, the consumer chooses among different brands within the market segment.

The Hausman et al. model has three sets of equations:

Upper level:

$$\log q_t = \beta_0 + \beta_1 \log y_t + \beta_2 \log p_t + \mathbf{Z_t}\boldsymbol{\delta} + \varepsilon_t \tag{6.26}$$

Middle level:

$$\log q_{mnt} = \beta_m \log y_{mnt} + \sum\nolimits_1^M \theta_k \log p_{knt} + \varepsilon_{mnt} \tag{6.27}$$

Brand level:

$$w_{int} = \alpha_{in} + \beta_i \log\left(\frac{y_{nt}}{p_{nt}}\right) + \sum\nolimits_1^J \gamma_{ij} \log p_{jnt} + \varepsilon_{int} \tag{6.28}$$

where $q_t$ is beer per capita consumption; $y_t$ is per capita income; $p_t$ is the price index of beer; $\mathbf{Z}_t$ is the vector of exogeneous demand shifters for beer demand; $q_{mnt}$ is per capita quantity of beer consumed of segment *m*, city *n*, at time *t*;$y_{mnt}$ is per capita beer expenditures of segment *m*, city *n*, at time *t*; $p_{knt}$ is an index of beer prices for the corresponding middle-level segment;$w_{int}$ is the market share of brand *i* associated with city *n*, at time *t*; $\frac{y_{nt}}{P_{nt}}$ is real income of city *n*, at time *t*; $P_{nt}$ the Stone's price index; and $p_{jnt}$ is the price of brand *j* in city *n*, at time *t*.

Aggregate monthly time series data are used to estimate overall demand for beer, Eq. (6.26). Panel data of cities over time are used to estimate the middle level (6.27) and brand-level demands (6.28). Fixed effects for cities are included in brand-level demand functions and these effects are eliminated through the within-group estimator by demeaning all variables prior to estimation. The instrumental variables estimator was used because of endogenous prices resulting from market power by beer retailers. Prices of adjacent cities were used as instruments.

The formulas for estimating three-stage budgeting need to be modified in this application. The formulas based on weak separability for within-group estimation, Eqs. (3.25) and (3.27) for the approach taken by Hausman et al., are as follows:

$$e_{ij}^* = \frac{b_i^M b_j^M \varphi_{MM}^* + c_{ij}^M}{w_i} \forall i, j \in M \tag{6.29}$$

$$e_i = \frac{b_i^M b_M}{w_i} \tag{6.30}$$

$$e_{MM}^* = \frac{b_i^G b_j^G \varphi_{GG}^* + c_{ij}^G}{w_i} \forall i, j \in G \tag{6.31}$$

$$e_i = \frac{b_i^G b_G}{w_i} \tag{6.32}$$

where M denotes middle-level segments. Equations (6.29) and (6.30) are compensated conditional elasticities at brand level for each market segment. Equations (6.31) and (6.32) are compensated conditional elasticities at middle-level segments for producing the aggregate good beer. Recall that if there are more than two groups within each utility or sub-utility group, then strong separability or homogeneous separability must be used to ensure consistent two-stage budgeting. In this case, because we have three middle-level market segments, the brand-level demand functions need to be restricted. The most plausible assumption in this case would be homogeneous separability. Even then the assumption would imply unitary income elasticities, which in light of our previous discussion on quality change would rule out quality differences among brands (see, e.g., equation 6.22). Another limitation of the Hausman et al. (1994) approach is the assumption that the middle-level demand functions have the double-log demand form, Eq. (6.27). This system of demand functions fails to satisfy globally adding-up and symmetry. Other functional forms like the LA/AIDS would be more appropriate.

### 6.6.2 Nested Logit Framework Approach to Modeling Heterogeneous Goods

The linear random utility goods characteristics modeling approach has enjoyed popularity among econometricians in the past two decades. The modeling assumptions of this approach allow one to develop a demand model that is linear in the log of market share so that linear econometric methods can be applied. Often the demand model is formulated and estimated jointly with a pricing model based on imperfect competition. The pricing model will not be discussed here, except to indicate the importance of it with regard to endogeneity of price in the demand model and how that is modeled empirically. Extensive discussion of the random utility goods characteristics model can be found elsewhere, especially Berry (1994). Only the rudimentary aspects of the model are presented here. In order to make the modeling approach more transparent, I discuss its features and implementation with respect to demand for rural accommodation from a published article by Tchetchick et al (2008).

Utility of tourist $i$, $i \in \{1, 2, \ldots, N\}$, from staying at accommodation $j \in \{1, 2, \ldots, L\}$ is

$$u_{ij} = \boldsymbol{X}_j\beta - \alpha p_j + \zeta_j + \xi_{ir} + (1-\sigma)\varepsilon_{ij} \tag{6.33}$$

where $\boldsymbol{X}_j$ is a vector of accommodation characteristics, $p_j$ is price per night stay, $\zeta_j + \xi_{ir} + (1-\sigma)\varepsilon_{ij}$ are unobserved characteristics of the utility function, for region $r = \{1, 2, \ldots, R\}$. The consumer chooses $j$ if $u^*_{ij} \geq u_{ik} \forall k \neq j$.

Average utility to the $j^{th}$ firm is

$$\delta_j = \boldsymbol{X}_j\beta - \alpha p_j + \zeta_j \tag{6.34}$$

so that

$$v_{ij} = \xi_{ir} + (1-\sigma)\varepsilon_{ij} \tag{6.35}$$

with choice set $A = \{v_{ij}|\delta_j + v_{ij} \geq \delta_k + v_{ik}, \forall k \neq j\}$. With $F(v)$ the cumulative distribution function, the percentage of tourists choosing accommodation $j$ is

$$\delta_j = \int_A dF(v) \tag{6.36}$$

Let $\delta_o = 0$ be an outside good with exogenous price, and assume the joint pdf of $v_{ij}$ is the extreme-value function. With this empirical specification for the error distribution, we can derive closed-form solutions for the market share and outside good and after manipulation of these two functions we obtain the following expression:

$$\log(s_j/s_o) = \delta_j + \sigma \log s_{j/r} \tag{6.37}$$

where $\log s_{j/r}$ is the within region share of the $j^{th}$ firm. Substituting for $\delta_j$ from (6.34) yields:

$$\log(s_j/s_o) = \boldsymbol{X}_j\beta - \alpha p_j + \sigma \log s_{j/r} + \zeta_j \tag{6.38}$$

Equation (6.38) is the estimating equation but OLS will be inconsistent as price and regional market share can be expected to be correlated with the error term, $\zeta_j$. Tchetchik et al (2008) estimate the model using generalized method of moments (GMM) with instruments selected from exogenous variables independent of $\zeta_j$ but correlated with price and regional market share. Instruments for price include cost shifters that do not appear in the demand equation but are correlated with price. Instruments for regional market share include characteristics of competing accommodation units. The results of estimation produce a significant price elasticity of –1.76 and elasticity of substitution of 0.35, the latter indicating greater substitution within the region than between regions.

The linear utility approach outlined here is a convenient way to estimate the market share of heterogeneous goods. Market demand must be determined from another line of research. Another advantage is that the model deals with the problem of zero purchases by consumers, although it assumes consumers purchase only one unit of the good. Extension to multiple purchases is possible (Chan 2006), but more complicated requiring use of the simulated method of moments. Another limitation of the model is the assumption of constant marginal utility of income. This is a clear violation of one of the most basic tenets of consumer choice, and means that, at best, the price elasticities from this model are Frischian elasticities.

### 6.6.3 *Hedonic Metric Approach to Estimating Differentiated Demand Functions*

A more recent and potentially more powerful method to estimate price elasticities of demand for heterogeneous products is the Hedonic Metric Approach of Gulseven and Wohlgenant (2015), which is an extension of the Distance Metric approach of Penske et al (2002). In this approach, a multi-dimensional hedonic space, based on qualitative information available to consumers, is created. Second, the differentiated products are allocated into this space and demand elasticities for these goods are estimated using qualitative factor distances.

To make the ideas of this approach concrete, consider the absolute price version of the RM augmented to account for product differentiation through hedonic measures of commodity attributes:

$$w_i dlogq_i = b_i dlogy + \beta_0 dlogp_i + \left(\beta_1 \chi_i^s + \beta_2 \chi_i^c\right) dlogp_i + \sum_{j \neq i} \left(\lambda_h d_{ij}^h + \lambda_{nn} d_{ij}^{nn}\right) dlogp_j \quad (6.39)$$

where $\chi_i^s$ is the market share of good $i$, $\chi_i^c$ is the closeness index, $d_{ij}^h$ is the hedonic distance metric, and $d_{ij}^{nn}$ is a dummy variable matrix created according to the nearest neighbor concept. The distance measures are reciprocals of the Euclidean norm in attribute space between products. Hedonic distance components are differences between values of hedonic attributes for two goods. The values of these hedonic attributes are estimated through hedonic regressions.

Gulseven and Wohlgenant (2015) applied the Hedonic Metric methodology to five milk products from Nielsen Homescan data on a weekly basis over the period 2002–2006. The results were consistent with the theory and produced quite plausible results. For the 17 major UPC's for soy milk, the own-price elasticities ranged from about −2 to −10. All cross-price elasticities were positive, indicating net substitutes as one would expect.

## 6.7 Specifying and Estimating Systems of Demand Functions with Panel Data

Access to Consumer Expenditure data, Nielsen Homescan data, and Information Resources, Inc. (IRI) data has popularized panel data models. In this section, the basic features of these models and challenges are reviewed.

### *6.7.1 Structure of Panel Data Models*

Consider the form of the LA/AIDS model, which is often used for demand estimation with panel data:

$$w_{ij} = a_i + \delta_j + \tau{\prime}_i s_{jt} + \sum\nolimits_k \gamma_{ik} logp_{kjt} + \beta_i \log\left(\frac{y_{jt}}{p^*_{jt}}\right) + \varepsilon_{ijt} \tag{6.40}$$

where the subscripts refer to commodity ($i$), individual ($j$), and time period ($t$). The vector $\boldsymbol{s}_{jt}$ represents household and product characteristics. Individual heterogeneity $\delta_j$ maybe modeled as either a fixed or random effect. As a fixed effect, the parameter $\delta_j$ is typically eliminated through demeaning all the variables. Alternatively, it could be eliminated through first-differencing. For random effects, the effect is included in the error term and it is modeled as part of the error structure. However, individual heterogeneity is often correlated with other variables in the model so the random effects model would produce inconsistent parameter estimates. The inconsistency can be tested using the Hausman and Taylor (1981) test for endogeneity.

When there are missing values on the dependent variable (to be discussed below), individual heterogeneity is often modeled as correlated random effects. In this case, a simple approach is to model $\delta_j$ as a linear function of the time-means of all the exogeneous variables (Wooldridge 2010, Chapt. 10). This has the effect of making the error term uncorrelated with all the exogenous variables. A less structured, but more challenging approach, is to project $\delta_j$ on all the exogenous variables of the model for all time periods (Meyerhoefer et al. 2005; Choi et al. 2013).

### 6.7.2 Demographic Variables

Demographic variables used in empirical analysis include household size, education, age, race, ethnicity, presence of children, and region. Typically, these variables are modeled in an unrestricted reduced-form manner. One could restrict these effects using one of the various forms of structural models. The four main types of models include (Pollack and Wales 1992): (i) demographic translating, (ii) demographic scaling, (iii) the Gorman specification, and (iv) the Modified Prais-Houthakker procedure. As an example, the Gorman specification on the Marshallian demand functions would have the form:

$$q_i = d_i + g_i\left(y - \sum p_k d_k, p_1 m_1, p_2 m_2, \ldots, p_n m_n\right) \tag{6.41}$$

where the $d$'s and $m$'s depend on the various demographic variables. These demand functions can be shown to be derived from the direct utility function of the form:

$$u = v\left[\frac{(q_1 - d_1)}{m}, \frac{(q_2 - d_2)}{m}, \ldots, \frac{(q_n - d_n)}{m}\right] \tag{6.42}$$

The purpose of such demographic models is for welfare analysis between individuals or households with different demographic characteristics. The problem, as highlighted by Pollack and Wales (1992, Chapt. 3) is that that such specifications may involve interpersonal comparisons of utility, which economists usually reject.

### 6.7.3 *Modeling Higher Order Engel Curves*

The LA/AIDS model (6.40) is not the only functional form used in empirical analysis. If the estimates are used for welfare analysis, the full AIDS model may be used, although its nonlinearity can preclude estimation with large data sets. The EASI demand system, in particular the approximate EASI demand system, Eq. (4.29), could be used for welfare analysis (Lewbel and Pendakur, 2009). It also allows one to estimate more general Engel curves. Lewbel and Pendakur (2009), using Canadian Expenditure survey data, and Zhen et al. (2014), using Nielsen Homescan data, find polynomials in income to the 5th order.

## 6.8 Systems of Demand Functions with Missing Observations

### 6.8.1 *Missing Values on Exogenous Variables*

While accounting for quality and product differentiation present challenges in estimating systems of demand functions, missing observations, particularly with cross-section data, also present challenges. The first significant question facing the researcher is what the cause of missing values is. First, if the missing values occur in the right-hand side, independent variables (e.g., income), then estimating demand parameters with these missing values produces consistent estimates using OLS and other linear estimators like SUR. Replacing exogenous missing values like this with predicted values from multiple regressions on other exogenous variables also produces consistent estimates. Dagenais (1973) and Gourieroux and Monfort (1981) derive efficient estimators for regression imputation methods of this type.

### 6.8.2 *Missing Values on Dependent Variable*

Missing values on the dependent variable, such as quantity or expenditure share, result from the consumer unit not purchasing any of the commodity during the period in which the consumer survey was conducted. Non-purchasing could mean infrequent purchase by the consumer or through abstinence—consumers unwilling to purchase commodity under any circumstances. A commodity may not be purchased in a given time period because of durability. If the commodity is a durable good, we would expect a pattern of purchase in one period and no purchases over several time periods as service flows from that durable good are consumed. The commodity purchased, while non-durable, could be purchased and placed in inventory. Incentives for inventory holding include economizing on transaction costs, holding precautionary balances, and speculative motive. For food items, the less perishable the item, the longer the consumer could be expected to hold the good in inventory, everything else equal. If the reason for zero consumption is infrequent purchases, then under certain conditions standard regression methods can be employed, so long as all the data are included in estimation (Blundell and Meghir, 1987). Of course, consumers may not consume a product at any price due to abstinence. For example, if the person does not drink alcohol, then the person is unlikely to consume at any price.

The more problematic cause of missing values in the dependent variable is censoring due to corner solutions. Recall from Chapter 2 that if $q_i = 0$ then $\frac{\partial v(\boldsymbol{q})}{\partial q_i} - \lambda p_i \leq 0$. We then have what is called an endogenous selection problem in that the consumer chooses to purchase (or not purchase) the good depending upon whether its marginal utility is equal (or less than equal) to its price. For purposes of discussion, consider the LA/AIDS model often used in the empirical analysis:

$$w_{ijt}^* = \alpha_i + \delta_j + \boldsymbol{\tau'}_i \boldsymbol{s}_{jt} + \sum_k \gamma_{ik} logp_{kjt} + \beta_i \log\left(\frac{y_{jt}}{P_{jt}^*}\right) + \varepsilon_{ijt} \quad (6.43)$$

$$w_{ijt}^* = max\left(0, w_{ijt}\right) \quad (6.44)$$

where the subscripts refer to commodity ($i$), individual ($j$), and time period ($t$). The variables are as defined in Eq. (6.40).

### 6.8.3 *Tobit Model*

With censoring, (6.43) and (6.44) constitute a Tobit model. While maximum likelihood estimation is feasible, it is computationally demanding for more than two commodities. In lieu of that approach, researchers often use the Heckman method (Heckit) whereby the model is estimated in two steps. In the first step, a probit model is estimated for the portion of the sample containing positive values of expenditure shares. A separate model is estimated for each commodity and the inverse mills' ratio is formed from each model. The set of Eqs. (6.43) is then augmented to include the estimated inverse mills' ratio, $\hat{\lambda}_{it}$, as an additional explanatory variable in the model. The set of equations to be estimated then takes the form:

$$w_{ijt} = \alpha_i + \delta_j + \boldsymbol{\tau'}_i \boldsymbol{s}_{jt} + \sum_k \gamma_{ik} logp_{kjt} + \beta_i \log\left(\frac{y_{jt}}{P_{jt}^*}\right) + \mu_i \hat{\lambda}_{it} + \varepsilon_{ijt} \quad (6.45)$$

Including the estimated inverse mills' ratios in the model corrects for the problem of non-zero means caused by truncation of the probability distribution at zero. Full details on estimation, including correcting for heteroskesticity, can be found elsewhere, e.g., Amemyia (1985) or Wooldridge (2010). See Heien and Wessells (1990) for a notable empirical application.

### 6.8.4 An Alternative Two-Stage Approach

Shonkwiler and Yen (1999) point out that estimation of a system of demand equations requires the use of the whole sample because each dependent variable may have a different pattern of censoring. Let $\boldsymbol{x\prime}_{ijt}\hat{\boldsymbol{\beta}}_i$ be the vector of predictions from Tobit model. In this case, the appropriate model to estimate should be:

$$w_{ijt} = \Phi\left(\boldsymbol{x\prime}_{ijt}\hat{\boldsymbol{\beta}}_i\right)\left(\alpha_i + \delta_j + \boldsymbol{\tau\prime}_i \boldsymbol{s}_{jt} + \sum_k \gamma_{ik} logp_{kjt} + \beta_i \log\left(\frac{y_{jt}}{P^*_{jt}}\right)\right)$$
$$+\mu_i \phi\left(\boldsymbol{x\prime}_{ijt}\hat{\boldsymbol{\beta}}_i\right) + \varepsilon_{ijt} \tag{6.46}$$

where $\Phi\left(\boldsymbol{x\prime}_{ijt}\hat{\boldsymbol{\beta}}_i\right)$ is the cumulative distribution function (cdf) and $\phi\left(\boldsymbol{x\prime}_{ijt}\hat{\boldsymbol{\beta}}_i\right)$ is the probability density function (pdf) for the normal distribution. Shonkwiler and Yen (1999) show that the model can be estimated in two steps: (i) Obtain parameter estimates $\hat{\boldsymbol{\beta}}_i$ for each equation using the Probit model; (ii) calculate the cdf and pdf for each good and estimate the system (6.46) using SUR or FIML including both zero and non-limit observations. Yen and Lin (2006) extend the method to the estimation of a complete system with FIML in one step. Owing to the number of integrals involving censored variables, this method is limited to only two or three commodities.

### 6.8.5 Problem of Missing Prices and Amemyia Principle

An important issue that has not been given enough attention is how to deal with missing prices. When quantity demanded, or expenditure share, is zero, prices will not be observed for those not purchasing. If the problem is corner solutions with products not being purchased because of relative prices, then we have what is called by Amemyia (1985) a Type 3 Tobit model.

To understand the problem of missing prices with censoring, consider the case with one censored good:

$$w_{ij}^{*} = a_1 + \delta_j + \tau\prime_1 s_{jt} + \gamma_{11}\log p_{1jt} + \sum\nolimits_{k\neq 1}\gamma_{1k}logp_{kjt} + \beta_1\log\left(\frac{y_{jt}}{p_{jt}^{*}}\right) + \varepsilon_{1jt} \tag{6.46}$$

In this model, $\log p_{1jt}$ is observable only when $w_{1jt}^{*} = w_{1jt} > 0$. The solution to this problem is discussed by Wooldrige (2010, Sect. 19.7.3). Let $\log p_{1jt} = z\prime_{1jt}\hat{\boldsymbol{\theta}}_{1j}$ be the function estimated by Tobit, where the $z$'s represent the set of variables explaining the price variable. Substituting for the price variable in (6.46) then gives an equation with predicted values for $\log p_{1jt}$ for both observed and unobserved values of $\log p_{1jt}$. Such a method could be employed for other missing prices as well, but the estimator has been shown to be relatively inefficient compared to the Amemyia GLS estimator (Lee 1981).

The Amemyia principle (Amemyia 1985, sec. 10.8.4) can be explained as follows. Define

$$\boldsymbol{y} = \boldsymbol{Y\gamma} + \boldsymbol{X}_1\boldsymbol{\beta} + \boldsymbol{u} \tag{6.47}$$

$$\left[\boldsymbol{y}, \boldsymbol{Y}\right] = \boldsymbol{X}[\boldsymbol{\pi\Pi}] + \boldsymbol{V} \tag{6.48}$$

where (6.47) is a structural equation for a single commodity ($\boldsymbol{y}$) and (6.47) gives the reduced-form equations for the single commodity and the set of jointly dependent variables ($\boldsymbol{Y}$) included in (6.47). The matrix $\boldsymbol{X}$ consists of all the exogenous variables in the structural equation (i.e., 6.46) and $\boldsymbol{X}_1$ is a subset of $\boldsymbol{X}$. From Eqs. (6.47) and (6.48), the structural and reduced-form parameters can be shown to be related as follows:

$$\pi = \boldsymbol{\Pi\gamma} + \boldsymbol{J\beta} \tag{6.49}$$

where $\boldsymbol{J}$ is a matrix of 0's and 1's such that $\boldsymbol{X}_1 = \boldsymbol{XJ}$. Lee (1981) shows that GLS applied to $\hat{\boldsymbol{\pi}} = \hat{\boldsymbol{\Pi}}\boldsymbol{\gamma} + \boldsymbol{J\beta} +$ error is relatively more efficient than the two-step estimator discussed above. Wilde (2004) has generalized the Amemyia Principle to the multivariate case. The approach essentially involves estimating the reduced-form parameters and then forming relationships of the form (6.49) and estimating all the structural parameters jointly using the minimum distance estimator[2].

While the two-step estimators discussed above are theoretically sound, as a practical manner they do not always perform that well empirically. In fact, OLS applied to the subsample with censoring may do as well as the two-step estimators (Puhani 2000). Cases where the two-step procedures are supposed to be used are when the error terms between the selection equation and outcome equation are highest and where the degree of censoring is high. However, it is in those cases that the two-step procedure is found to be most inefficient. Moreover, OLS applied to the subsample

[2]Davis and Wohlgenant (1993), in the context of the random utility framework, apply Amemyia's principle to demand for natural and artificial Christmas trees.

of censored values will perform best. As a practical matter, two step, OLS, and FIML (where feasible) should be used to determine the most efficient results (Puhani, 2000).

### *6.8.6 Stone–Lewbel Prices*

It is often the case that no specific prices are observed for individuals or individual households. For example, the CEX household survey collects expenditures on households but prices are only available as regional price indexes. Lewbel (1989) shows that most methods of incorporating demographic variation into separable models can be represented as Barten equivalence scales, except that the scales depend on the exact mix of goods for each group, as well as on demographic variables. In particular, he shows that the demand functions can be represented as $Q^G = g^G\left(y, P^1M^1, \ldots, P^GM^G, \ldots, P^NM^N\right)$, where $M^G = v_G\left(\boldsymbol{q}_G, \boldsymbol{a}_G^*\right)/v_G\left(\boldsymbol{q}_G, \boldsymbol{a}_G\right)$. With homogeneous separability, Lewbel (1989) shows that $M^G = V_G\left(\boldsymbol{p}_G, \boldsymbol{a}_G\right)/V_G\left(\boldsymbol{p}_G, \boldsymbol{a}_G^*\right)$. Moreover, budget shares for individual goods within the separable group can be written as $w_i^G = \frac{\partial \log V_G}{\partial \log p_i}$. Because variation in demographic variables are linked to variation in prices through the relationship $V_G = M^GP^G$, one can use within group prices to represent demographic variation between households. Lewbel (1989) shows in particular if group preferences are Cobb-Douglas, the equivalence scales can be represented as

$$M^GP^G = M^G = \frac{1}{k_i}\prod\nolimits_{i=1}^{n_G}\left(w_i^G\right)^{-w_i^G} \tag{6.50}$$

where $P^G = 1$, and $k_i = \prod_{i=1}^{n_G}\left(w_i^{G*}\right)^{-w_i^{G*}}$ denotes the value for the reference level household. This means that the demand equations may simply be augmented with Stone–Lewbel prices, (6.50). For two notable applications, see Hoderlein and Mihaleva (2008) and Koksal and Wohlgenant (2016).

## 6.9 An Alternative Approach Based on Pseudo-Panel Data

An alternative approach to individual cross-sectional and panel data is pseudo-panel data. Deaton (1985) suggested using this approach as an alternative way for estimating individual behavior models. This approach enables one to follow cohorts of individuals over repeated cross-sectional surveys. Because cohorts are followed over time, they are constructed based on characteristics that are time invariant, such as the birth year of the reference person. Cohorts can be constructed from a single characteristic or multiple characteristics. For example, Koksal and Wohlgenant (2016) formed pseudo-panels based on the geographic region and the household head's year of birth from US Household Expenditure Survey data (CEX). Cohorts are defined by the interaction of three generations (born before 1950, born between 1950–1964, born in 1965 or later) and four geographic regions (northeast, midwest, south, west). For example, all household heads born between 1950–1964 that reside in the south would form one cohort and all households born between 1950–1964 that reside in the west would form another cohort. The resulting pseudo-panel consists of a total of 336 observations over 12 cohorts and 28 quarters. This allocation results in an average cohort size of around 100 households. Verbeek and Nijman (1992) show that if the sample size in each cohort is sufficiently large, the intercept can be treated as the unobserved cohort fixed effect. When cohorts contain at least 100 individuals and time variation in the cohort means is sufficiently large, the bias in the standard fixed effects estimator will be small and can be ignored. While information on individuals is lost, this comes at a benefit of not having to deal with missing data while still capturing demographic effects common to certain important groups.

## Problems

6.1 Using (6.10) and the formulas in (6.5) and (6.6), derive the quality relationships in (6.11). Discuss the economic significance of these relationships.

6.2 What is the theoretical basis for Eq. (6.38)? What underlying assumptions of the model restrict its applications? Why will OLS produce inconsistent parameter estimates and what types of instruments would produce consistent estimate?

6.3 Show how individual heterogeneity in (6.40) through the term $\delta_j$ can be eliminated through either first-demeaning all the variables (i.e., subtracting the mean form of Eq. [6.40] from Eq. [6.40]) or through first-differencing by commodity and by household. Why would neither one of these methods be expected to work if the model is a censored demand equation like Eq. (6.43)?

6.4 Derive the relationship between reduced form and structural parameters, (6.49), used to estimate the structural parameters via the Amemyia principle. How does the Amemyia principle differ from the two-step procedure discussed by Wooldridge (2010)?

## References

Allen, R.G.D., and A.L. Bowley. *Family Expenditures: A Study of Its Variations*. London: P.S. King & Sons, 1935.

Amemyia, T. *Advanced Econometrics*. Cambridge, MA: Harvard University Press, 1985.

Berry, S.L. “Estimating Discrete Choice Models of Product Differentiation.” *The Rand Journal of Economics* 25(1994): 242–262.

Blundell, R., and C. Meghir. "Bivariate Alternatives to the Tobit Model." *Journal of Econometrics* 34(1987): 179–200.
Chan, T.Y. "Estimating a Continuous Hedonic-Choice Model with an Application to Demand for Soft Drinks." *Rand Journal of Economics* 37(2006): 466–482.
Choi, Hee-Jung, Michael K. Wohlgenant, and Xiaoyong Zheng. "Household Level Welfare Effects of Organic Milk Introduction." *American Journal of Agricultural Economics* 45(2013): 1009–1028.
Clements, K.W., and G. Gao. "Quality, Quantity, Spending, and Prices." *European Economic Review* 56(2012): 1376–1391.
Clements, K.W., and J. Si. "Diet Diversity, Engel's Law, and the Quality of Food Consumption." *American Journal of Agricultural Economics* 100(2017): 1–22.
Cox, T. "An Analysis of Price Effects in Cross-Section Demand." Ph.D. Thesis, Texas A&M University, 1984.
Cox, T., and M.K. Wohlgenant. "Prices and Quality Effects in Cross-Sectional Demand Analysis." *American Journal of Agricultural Economics* 68(1986): 908–919.
Cowling, K., and A.J. Raynor. "Price, Quality, and Market Share." *Journal of Political Economy* 78(1970): 1292–1309.
Cramer, J.S. "Interaction of Income and Price in Consumer Demand." *International Economic Review* 14(1973): 351–363.
Dageneis, M.G. "The Use of Incomplete Observations in Multiple Regression Analysis." *Journal of Econometrics* 1(1973): 317–328.
Davis, G. C., and M. K. Wohlgenant. "Demand Elasticities from a Discrete Choice Model: The Natural Christmas Tree Market." *American Journal of Agricultural Economics* 75(1993): 730–738.
Deaton, A. "Panel Data from Time Series of Cross Sections." *Journal of Econometrics* 30(1985): 109–126.
Deaton, A. "Estimation of Own- and Cross-Price Elasticities from Household Survey Data." *Journal of Econometrics* 36(1987): 7–30.
Deaton, A. "Quality, Quantity, and Spatial Variation of Price." *The American Economic Review* 78(1988): 418–430.
Deaton, A. "Price Elasticities from Survey Data: Extensions and Indonesian Results." *Journal of Econometrics* 44(1990): 281–309.
Dong, D., J.S. Shonkwiler, and O.A. Capps, Jr. "Estimation of Demand Functions using Household Data: The Problem Revisited." *American Journal of Agricultural Economics* 80(1998): 466–473.
George, P.S., and G.A. King. *Consumer Demand for Food Commodities in the United State with Projections for 1980*. Giannini Foundation Monograph No. 26, California Agricultural Experiment Station, Berkeley, CA, 1971.
Gourieroux, C., and A. Monfort. "On the Problem of Missing Data in Linear Models." *Review of Economic Studies* 48(1981): 579–586.
Gulseven, O., and M. Wohlgenant. "A Quality Based Approach to Estimating Quantitative Elasticities for Differentiated Products: An application to Retail Milk Demand." *Quality & Quantity* 49(2015): 2077–2096.
Hausman, J.A., and W.E. Taylor. "Panel Data and Unobservable Individual Effects." *Econometrica* 49(1981): 1377–1398.
Hausman, J.A., G.K. Leonard, and J.D. Zona. "Competitive Analysis with Differenciated Products." *Annales d'Économie et de Statistique* (1994): 160–180.
Heien, D.M., and C.R. Wessells. "Demand Systems Estimation with Microdata: A Censored Regression Approach." *Journal of Business & Economic Statistics* 8(1990): 365–381.
Hoang, L.V. "Estimation of Food Demand with Survey Data from Vietnam," DEPOCEN Working Paper Series No. 2009/12, Center for Agricultural Policy, Institute of Policy and Strategy for Agriculture and Rural Development, Vietnam, 2009.
Hoderlein, S., and S. Mihaleva. "Increasing the Price Variation in a Cross Section." *Journal of Econometrics* 147(2008): 316–325.

Houthakker, H.S. "Compensated Changes in Quantities and Qualities Consumed." *Review of Economic Studies* 19(1952–53): 155–164.

Koksal, A., and Michael Wohlgenant. "How Do Smoking Bans in Restaurants Affect Restaurant and at Home Alcohol Consumption? *Empirical Economics* 50(2016): 1193–1213.

Lee, L.F. "Simultaneous Equations Models with Discrete and Censored Variables." In C.F. Manski and D. McFadden (eds.) *Structural Analysis of Discrete Data with Econometric Applications*, pp. 346-364. Cambridge, MA: MIT Press, 1981.

Lewbel, A. "Identification and Estimation of Equivalence Scales under Weak Separability." *The Review of Economic Studies* 56(1989): 311–316.

Lewbel, A., and K. Pendakur. "Tricks with Hicks: The EASI Demand System." *The American Economic Review* 99(2009): 827–863.

Meyerhoefer, C.D., C.K. Ranney, and D.E. Sahn. "Consistent Estimation of Censored Demand Systems Using Panel Data." *American Journal of Agricultural Economics* 87(2005): 660–672.

Murphy, K.M., and R.H. Topel. "Estimation and Inference in Two-Step Econometric Models." *Journal of Business & Economics Statistics* 3(1985): 370–379.

Nelson, J.A. "Quality Variation and Quantity Aggregation in Consumer Demand for Food." *American Journal of Agricultural Economics* 73(1991): 1204–1212.

Pinske, S., M. Slade, and C. Brett. "Spatial Price Competition: A Semiparametric Approach." *Econometrica* 70(2002): 1111–1155.

Pollack, R.A., and T.J. Wales. *Demand System Specification and Estimation*. New York: Oxford University Press, 1992.

Prais, S.J., and H.S. Houtkakker. *The Analysis of Family Budgets*. Cambridge: Cambridge University Press, 1955.

Puhani, P.A. "The Heckman Correction for Sample Selection and Its Critique." *Journal of Economic Surveys* 14(2000): 53–67.

Shonkwiler, J.S., and S.T. Yen. "Two-Step Estimation of a Censored Demand System." *American Journal of Agricultural Economics* 81(1999): 972–982.

Tchetchik, A., A. Fleischer, and I. Finkelshtain. "Differentiation and Synergies in Rural Tourism: Estimation and Simulation of the Israeli Market." *American Journal of Agricultural Economics* 90(2008): 553–570.

Theil, H. "Qualities, Prices, and Budget Enquiries." *Review of Economic Studies* 19(1952–53): 129–147.

Theil, H. *Theory and Measurement of Consumer Demand*, Vol. I. Chicago: University of Chicago Press, 1975/1976.

Theil, H. *The System-Wide Approach to Microeconomics*. Chicago: The University of Chicago Press, 1980.

Verbeek, M., and T. Nijman. "Can Cohort Data be Treated as Genuine Panel Data?" *Empirical Economics* 17(1992): 9–23.

Wilde, J. "Estimating Multiple Equation Hybrid Models with Endogenous Dummy Regressors." *Statistica Neerlandica* 58(2004): 296–312.

Wooldridge, J.M. *Econometric Analysis of Cross Section and Panel Data*. Cambridge, MA: The MIT Press, 2010.

Yen, S.T., and B-W Lin. "A Sample-Selection Approach to Systems of Demand Functions." *American Journal of Agricultural Economics* 88(2006): 742–749.

Zhen, Chen, Eric A. Finkelstein, James M. Nonnemaker, Shawn A. Karns and Jessica E. Todd. "Predicting the Effects of Sugar-Sweetened Beverage Taxes on Food and Beverage Demand in a Large Demand System." *American Journal of Agricultural Economics* 96(2014): 1–25.

# Chapter 7
# Derived Demand, Marketing Margins, and Relationship Between Output and Raw Material Prices

## 7.1 Introduction

Conceptually, most demand applications are derived demand applications, not consumer demand. This is because we often do not observe final demand directly, but rather only purchases made by consumers that are inputs into final goods consumed. For policy analysis, it is often the case that we are primarily interested in quantities and prices of producers, not those of consumers. In the case of agricultural and food policy, the object of interest is often derived demand for the agricultural raw materials used in processing and distributing finished goods to consumers.

The theory of derived demand is based on the premise that final consumer demand is a joint demand for all the inputs used in making and producing the final product (Marshall 1920). An insightful way to view derived demand is through the theory of household production. In this approach, the consumer is viewed as maximizing the utility of the final (possibly unobserved) consumer goods (Stigler and Becker 1977):

$$\max_{\{z_i\}} u = v(z_1, z_2, \ldots, z_n) \tag{7.1}$$

subject to

$$z_i = f_i(q_{1i}, q_{2i}, \ldots, q_{mi}; l_i; k_i) \tag{7.2}$$

$$q_j = \sum\nolimits_{i=1}^{n} q_{ji}; l_j = \sum\nolimits_{i=1}^{n} l_{ji}; k_j = \sum\nolimits_{i=1}^{n} k_{ji} \tag{7.3}$$

$$y = \sum\nolimits_{i=1}^{m} p_i q_i + \sum\nolimits_{i=1}^{n} w l_i = wT + \mu \tag{7.4}$$

where (7.2) is a production function relating (unobserved) final goods $z_i$ to quantities of raw materials purchased, $q_{ji}$, other variable factors, $l_{ji}$, and fixed inputs, $k_{ji}$.

 
M. K. Wohlgenant, *Market Interrelationships and Applied Demand Analysis*, Palgrave Studies in Agricultural Economics and Food Policy,
https://doi.org/10.1007/978-3-030-73144-1_7

The relationships in (7.3) are identities on the allocation of inputs across different categories; and Eq. (7.4) is the budget constraint, where $w$ is a wage rate, T is total time available, and $\mu$ is non-labor income. The solutions to this maximization problem include the derived demands for the purchased raw materials:

$$q_i = f_i(y, p_1, p_2, \ldots p_m, w) \tag{7.5}$$

Equation (7.5) shows that derived demand depends on income and factor prices of all inputs used in producing the final products. While (7.5) has a similar form with consumer demand functions, it is different with the inclusion of $w$, which represents the time cost of producing the final goods. Moreover, application to commodities like purchased raw materials for food indicates that we have demand functions for raw materials that depend on prices of raw materials instead of consumer goods. Indeed, at any level of the marketing channel, we can view derived demand as a function of prices of all inputs used in producing the final downstream goods. At the wholesale level, systems of wholesale demand functions with wholesale prices are appropriate. At the primary production level, say the farm level, systems of farm demand functions with farm prices are appropriate.

The household production problem is somewhat unique where the individual is both a producer and consumer. Most markets are specialized with consumption and production being separate activities. For manufactured goods, which constitute most commodities including food commodities in the US, final consumer demand is a joint demand for raw materials produced by primary producers and services, such as processing and marketing, provided by market intermediaries. Thus, in general, derived demand relationships will depend upon consumer demand relationships and market intermediary relationships depicting production and marketing of final products, as well as the acquisition of raw materials used in the production of final products.

The following section discusses the historical approach to modeling derived demand for raw materials, with a focus primarily on derived demand for agricultural inputs. This discussion is followed by the presentation of a more general model of derived demand that allows one to link the system of consumer demand functions to the corresponding system of derived demand functions for agricultural inputs. The focus is on developing a framework that is theoretically consistent with consumer demand behavior and market intermediary behavior. The focus is on price-taking behavior. This chapter is mainly concerned with the theoretical foundations of derived demand. Extensions to a more general model as well as imperfect competition and short-run food price determination are discussed in the next chapter. The material covered in this chapter draws from Brandow (1958), Waugh (1964), George and King (1971), Gardner (1975), Wohlgenant (1989, 2001) and Wohlgenant and Haidacher (1989).

## 7.2 Historical Approaches to Modeling Derived Demand for Raw Materials

To begin with, consider an industry where a single, homogenous good is produced with the industry production function.

$$q = f[m, va(l_1, l_2, \ldots, l_m)] = f[m, va(\boldsymbol{l})] \tag{7.6}$$

where $q$ is quantity produced (say at the retail level), $m$ is the quantity of the raw material (say at the farm level), and $va$ is a function depicting value-adding services, which depends upon a vector $\boldsymbol{l}$ of variable factors like labor, packaging, and energy. Both $f$ and $va$ depend upon a capital input, which is suppressed for notational convenience.

### 7.2.1 *Price Spread Relationships with Quantity/Price*

In the simplest case, the production function would exhibit fixed proportions so that,

$$q = \min\left[\frac{m}{a}, \frac{va(\boldsymbol{l})}{b}\right] \tag{7.7}$$

Let $p$ be output price, $r$ the price of the raw material, and $\boldsymbol{w}$ the price vector of intermediate inputs, $\boldsymbol{l}$. With the cost of value-adding services equal to $c = c(q, w) = \min_{\boldsymbol{l}}\{\boldsymbol{w}'\boldsymbol{l} | q = (1/b) \cdot va(\boldsymbol{l})\}$, where $w$ is the price index of value-adding inputs $va(\boldsymbol{l})$, the market intermediary solves the problem:

$$\max_q \pi = (p - ar)q - c(q, w) \tag{7.8}$$

The first-order condition for profit maximization is

$$\frac{\partial \pi}{\partial q} = (p - ar) - \frac{\partial c(q, w)}{\partial q} = 0 \tag{7.9}$$

The second-order condition is that $-\frac{\partial^2 c(q,w)}{\partial q^2} < 0$ or $\frac{\partial^2 c(q,w)}{\partial q^2} > 0$. This means that the price spread is

$$s = p - ar = c_q(q, w) \tag{7.10}$$

which increases as $q$ increases because of rising marginal cost. The price spread could also remain constant if marginal cost is constant and be compatible with the theory provided the solution is not a corner solution. Although a negative relationship between output and the price spread is incompatible with price-taking behavior at the firm level, such a relationship could exist if marginal costs of individual firms shift downward as industry output increases. This would occur if there were technical externalities to the industry. The price spread could have a negative relationship with output if there were pecuniary economies. That is, if supply curves of factors other than the raw material were negatively sloped, then these factor prices would decrease and marginal costs of individual firms would shift downward as industry output increases. Thus, in general, we can expect the price spread and output to take on all three different relationships.[1]

The price spread relationship with price-taking behavior is often viewed in terms of changes in output price instead of output quantity. When output demand is stationary, change in the price spread will either increase, decrease, or remain constant as output price changes. For this simple theory, derived demand for the raw product for any given quantity is the difference between output price and the raw material price. Output price is the maximum price consumers are willing to pay for that quantity and the marginal costs of processing and marketing services depict minimum costs of producing that output. The difference, therefore, represents the maximum price the market is willing to pay for the raw material per unit of output. The derived demand schedule is obtained by finding the locus of points between output price and marginal cost at each output level.

### 7.2.2 Derived Demand Elasticities as Products Between Elasticities of Price Transmission and Retail Demand Elasticities

In light of the above discussion, we can obtain a formula for the derived demand elasticity through differentiating $m_i = a_i q_i = a_i D_i(p_1, p_2, \ldots, p_n)$, $p_i = f_i(r_i)$, with respect to $r_j$ (Waugh 1964):

$$\frac{\partial m_i}{\partial r_j} = a_i \frac{\partial D_i}{\partial p_j} \frac{\partial f_j}{\partial r_j}$$

or

$$E_{ij} = e_{ij} \eta_j \quad \forall i, j \tag{7.11}$$

where $E_{ij} = \frac{\partial m_i}{\partial r_j} \frac{r_j}{m_i}$, $e_{ij} = \frac{\partial D_i}{\partial p_j} \frac{p_j}{q_i}$, $\eta_j = \frac{\partial p_j}{\partial r_j} \frac{r_j}{p_j}$. The derived demand elasticity for quantity of the $i^{\text{th}}$ raw material with respect to price of the $j^{\text{th}}$ raw material is equal to the product of the consumer demand elasticity of good $i$ with respect to the price of good $j$, and the elasticity of price transmission from price of the $j^{\text{th}}$ raw material to price of the $j^{\text{th}}$ final product.

---

[1] See Tomek and Robinson (1981, Chapter 6) for a graphical analysis of these relationships.

### 7.2.3 Derived Demand Elasticities Constrained to Be Less Than Retail Demand Elasticities

George and King (1971) define the raw-to-final product price relationship for empirical work as

$$s_j = p_j - a_j r_j = \alpha_j + \beta_j p_j \tag{7.12}$$

The price spread model includes two special cases: (i) $\beta_j = 0$, constant absolute spread; and (ii) $\alpha_j = 0$, constant percentage spread. In the first case, it can be shown that the elasticity of price transmission equals the raw product share of the final product (farmers' share of the retail dollar in agricultural economics literature) i.e., $\eta_j = \frac{r_j m_j}{p_j q_j} = \frac{r_j a_j}{p_j}$. In the second case of a constant percentage spread, $\eta_j = 1$. Thus, so long as the raw material price is less than the output price, the elasticity of price transmission is bounded by zero and one. This means according to (7.11), that the absolute value of the price elasticity of derived demand must be less than or equal to the absolute value of the corresponding consumer demand elasticity. That is

$$|E_{ij}| \leq |e_{ij}| \forall i, j \tag{7.13}$$

We show in the next section that this relationship is quite restrictive. This should cause the researcher to carefully consider using the Leontief production function in applied work, especially when the results can be sensitive to the assumption of fixed proportions.

## 7.3 Gardner Model of Retail and Farm Price Relationships

### 7.3.1 Long-Run Competitive Model with Variable Proportions Production Function

It is useful to view the price spread in a more general way by considering it as the outcome of supply-demand relationships for the output price, raw material price, and other factor prices. Gardner (1975), using a single-product, two-factor model of the food industry, evaluates the relationship between output (retail) and raw material (farm) prices. The model is a long-run, perfectly competitive model of the food industry, whose production function at the industry level is (7.6) with two inputs, $m$ and $l = va$. With free entry into and exit from the industry, the production function exhibits constant returns to scale. In addition to the production function, the model consists of consumer demand for the output and two equations depicting the first-order conditions for profit maximization: value marginal product equals factor price for $m$ and $l$. The model is closed with supply equations for the two inputs. One could proceed directly with these six equations to find comparative statics of long-run equilibrium. An equivalent and somewhat easier approach is to work with the dual relationships: industry total cost, the profit-maximizing condition price equals marginal cost, and conditional factor demands to characterize market intermediary behavior. Following Wohlgenant (2011), in this approach, the set of relationships depicting long-run competitive equilibrium in the food industry are:

$$q = D(p, z) \quad \text{(retail demand)} \tag{7.14}$$

$$p = uc(r, w) \quad \text{(inverse retail supply)} \tag{7.15}$$

$$m = \frac{\partial uc(r, w)}{\partial r} q \quad \text{(conditional farm demand)} \tag{7.16}$$

$$l = \frac{\partial uc(r, w)}{\partial w} q \quad \text{(conditional marketing input demand)} \tag{7.17}$$

$$r = h(m, t_m) \quad \text{(supply of farm input)} \tag{7.18}$$

$$w = i(l, t_l) \quad \text{(supply of marketing input)} \tag{7.19}$$

The first equation, (7.14), is consumer demand with $z$ representing exogenous demand shifters, including income, population, prices of other consumer goods, and exogenous preference shift parameters. Equation (7.15) is the condition that price equals marginal cost. With constant returns to scale, marginal cost equals unit costs, $uc(r, w)$. This equation also can be thought of as the inverse of the industry supply of the output, holding factor prices constant. Equations (7.16) and (7.17) are conditional factor demands obtained by applying Shepard's lemma to the industry cost function, $C = uc(r, w)q$. The final two equations, (7.18) and (7.19) are inverse supply functions for the two factors; the variables, $t_m$ and $t_l$, denote exogenous supply shifters, like technical change or taxes.

### 7.3.2 Comparative Statics of Retail-to-Farm Price Ratio

We proceed as usual by totally differentiating Eqs. (7.14)–(7.19). We do this while at the same time converting the differentials to log differentials, defined as $Eq = \frac{dq}{q}$, $Ep = \frac{dp}{p}$, $Em = \frac{dm}{m}$, $Er = \frac{dr}{r}$, $Ew = \frac{dw}{w}$, $Ez = \frac{dz}{z}$, $Et_m = \frac{dt_m}{t_m}$, and $Et_l = \frac{dt_l}{t_l}$. These equations can be written as follows:

$$Eq = eEp + e_z Ez \tag{7.20}$$

$$Ep = s_m Er + s_l Ew \tag{7.21}$$

$$Em = -s_l \sigma Er + s_l \sigma Ew + Eq \tag{7.22}$$

$$El = s_m \sigma Er - s_m \sigma Ew + Eq \tag{7.23}$$

$$Er = \left({}^1\!/\varepsilon_m\right) Em + \varepsilon_{rt_m} Et_m \tag{7.24}$$

$$Ew = (1/\varepsilon_l) El + \varepsilon_{wt_l} Et_l \tag{7.25}$$

In Eq. (7.20), I have used the same notation for retail demand elasticities as in Chapter 2. For Eq. (7.21) note that elasticities of unit cost function with respect to $r$ and $w$ equal their respective cost shares, $s_m$ and $s_l$. Because of constant returns to scale, the cost shares are value shares, i.e., $s_m = rm/pq$ and $s_l = wl/pq$. The conditional price elasticities of the input demand elasticities are, by definition, Allen elasticities of substitution multiplied by cost-shares (Allen 1938). The coefficient multiplying $Er$ in (7.22) is $\sigma_{mm} s_m$. Likewise, the coefficient for $Ew$ in (7.23) is $\sigma_{ll} s_l$. Conditional demand functions are homogeneous of degree zero in prices, implying $\sigma_{mm} s_m + \sigma_{ml} s_l = 0$. Let $\sigma_{ml} = \sigma$ and we obtain $\sigma_{mm} s_m = -\sigma_{ml} s_l = -s_l \sigma$ for the elasticity of $m$ with respect to $r$ in Eq. (7.24).[2] Similar reasoning leads to the elasticity of $m$ with respect to $w$ and elasticities of $l$ with respect to $r$ and $w$ in (7.23). Finally, $\varepsilon_m$, and $\varepsilon_l$ in (7.24) and (7.25) are price elasticity of supplies for inputs $m$ and $l$. Note that the elasticities $\varepsilon_{rt_m}$ and $\varepsilon_{wt_l}$ are for vertical shifts in these supply curves.

To proceed further, we can reduce the set of six equations to two by (a) substituting (7.21) into (7.20) and that result for $Eq$ into (7.22) and (7.23); and (b) substituting the results from (a) into (7.24) and (7.25). This gives the two-equation system:

$$\begin{bmatrix} \varepsilon_m + s_l \sigma - s_m e & -s_l(\sigma + e) \\ -s_m(\sigma + e) & \varepsilon_l + s_m \sigma - s_l e \end{bmatrix} \begin{bmatrix} Er \\ Ew \end{bmatrix} = \begin{bmatrix} e_z Ez + \varepsilon_m \varepsilon_{rt_m} Et_m \\ e_z Ez + \varepsilon_l \varepsilon_{wt_l} Et_l \end{bmatrix} \tag{7.27}$$

Solutions to this system, $\boldsymbol{Ax} = \boldsymbol{b}$ for the total effects of exogenous shifts in demand and supply on-farm and marketing input prices can be obtained readily through the application of Cramer's rule (e.g., Hadley 1961):

$$E_{r,z} = \frac{e_z(\varepsilon_l + \sigma)}{Det\,\boldsymbol{A}}; \; E_{w,z} = \frac{e_z(\varepsilon_m + \sigma)}{Det\,\boldsymbol{A}} \tag{7.28}$$

$$E_{r,t_m} = \frac{\varepsilon_m \varepsilon_{rt_m}(\varepsilon_l + s_m \sigma - s_l e)}{Det\,\boldsymbol{A}}; \; E_{w,t_m} = \frac{s_m \varepsilon_m \varepsilon_{rt_m}(\sigma + e)}{Det\,\boldsymbol{A}} \tag{7.29}$$

[2] See, e.g., Varian (1992) for properties of conditional input demand functions.

$$E_{r,t_l} = \frac{s_l \varepsilon_l \varepsilon_{wt_l}(\sigma + e)}{Det\mathbf{A}}; \ E_{w,t_l} = \frac{\varepsilon_l \varepsilon_{wt_l}(\varepsilon_m + s_l\sigma - s_m e)}{Det\mathbf{A}} \tag{7.30}$$

where $Det\mathbf{A} = (\varepsilon_m + s_l\sigma - s_m e)(\varepsilon_l + s_m\sigma - s_l e) - s_m s_l(\sigma + e)^2 > 0$ in all normal cases.[3] These comparative statics are total elasticities: $E_{r,z}$ is the total elasticity of $r$ with respect to a one percent change in $z$, holding $t_m$ and $t_l$ constant; $E_{w,z}$ is the total elasticity of $w$ with respect to $z$; $E_{r,t_m}$ is the total elasticity of $r$ with respect to $t_m$; $E_{w,t_m}$ is the total elasticity of $w$ with respect to $t_m$; $E_{r,t_l}$ is the total elasticity of with respect to $r$ with respect to $t_l$; and $E_{w,t_l}$ is the elasticity of $w$ with respect to $t_l$.

Gardner (1975) defines the price spread as the retail-to-farm price ratio, $p/r$. In elasticity form, $E(p/r) = Ep - Er$. Subtracting $Er$ from both sides of (7.21) and rearranging terms we get $E(p/r) = s_l(Ew - Er)$. Given the above comparative static results we can derive expressions for total elasticity of the price ratio:

$$E_{p/r,z} = \frac{-e_z(\varepsilon_l - \varepsilon_m)}{Det\mathbf{A}} \tag{7.31}$$

$$E_{p/r,t_m} = -\frac{s_l \varepsilon_m \varepsilon_{mt_m}(\varepsilon_l - e)}{Det\mathbf{A}} \tag{7.32}$$

$$E_{p/r,t_l} = \frac{s_l \varepsilon_l \varepsilon_{lt_l}(\varepsilon_m - e)}{Det\mathbf{A}} \tag{7.33}$$

With $Det\mathbf{A} > 0$, the signs of Eqs. (7.31)–(7.33) are determined by the numerators. If the supply elasticity of the marketing input is larger than the elasticity of the farm input, which we would expect to be the normal case, then (7.31) is negative. An increase in retail demand is expected to decrease the retail-to-farm price ratio. Recall that the partial elasticities $\varepsilon_{mt_m}$ and $\varepsilon_{lt_l}$ refer to vertical shifts in the supply curves. Therefore, an upward shift in farm supply leads to a decrease in the retail-to-farm price ratio. On the other hand, an upward shift in the supply curve of marketing inputs increases the retail-to-farm price ratio.

### *7.3.3 Comparative Statics of Farm Value Share*

With the above elasticities and Eqs. (7.21)–(7.22), we can find the effects of the exogenous demand and supply variables on the farmer's share of the retail dollar, i.e., $s_m = \frac{rm}{pq}$. Note that $Es_m = -E(p/r) + E(m/q)$. Solving for $E(m/q)$ from (7.22), substituting into (7.21), and rearranging variables we obtain $Es_m = -(1-\sigma)E(p/r)$. Therefore, we find that the total elasticities $Es_{m,z}$, $Es_{m,t_m}$, and $Es_{m,t_l}$ are all proportional to (7.31)–(7.33) and depend upon the relative magnitude of $\sigma$. If $\sigma < 1$, then the farmers' share will increase: (a) when consumer demand increases, (b) when the farm supply curve shifts upward, and (c) when the marketing input supply curve shifts

[3] Normal means downward sloping demand for output and upward-sloping supply curves for inputs.

downward. The opposite holds true in each case when $\sigma > 1$. The parameter $\sigma < 1$ is most consistent with food commodities unless we are dealing with very disaggregate goods. The farmer's share has consistently declined over time for all food and most major food commodities. With consumer demand consistently increasing over time, increases in consumer demand (e.g., through increases in population) cannot explain the decline in the farmers' share. However, the supply of farm inputs has consistently increased over time as have the costs of marketing (through upward shifts in marketing input supply). So increases in supply of farm inputs and marketing costs have apparently outweighed increases in demand for food to cause the farmers' share of the retail dollar to decline.[4]

### 7.3.4 Biased Estimates of Markup Price Equation

For empirical analysis, George and King (1971) estimated (7.12) in the form:

$$r_i = \gamma_i + \delta_i p_i \tag{7.34}$$

where $\gamma_i = -\frac{\alpha_i}{a_i}$ and $\delta_i = \frac{(1-\beta_i)}{a_i}$. We can evaluate the validity of this model by considering the form of the elasticity of price transmission for increases in retail demand and increases in farm supply. In the first case, the elasticity of price transmission is obtained by resolving Eqs. (7.27) when $e_n En$ is replaced with $Ep$. This gives the expression:

$$E_{r,p} = \frac{(\varepsilon_l + \sigma)}{(s_m \varepsilon_l + s_l \varepsilon_m + \sigma)} \tag{7.35}$$

Likewise, the elasticity of price transmission for increases in farm supply will have the form:

$$E_{r,p} = \frac{\varepsilon_l + s_m \sigma - s_l e}{s_m (\varepsilon_l + \sigma)} \tag{7.36}$$

As can be seen from these formulas, increases in consumer demand have a different effect on the elasticity of price transmission than increases in farm supply. Thus, Eq. (7.34) cannot yield estimates of $\gamma_i$ and $\delta_i$ consistent with supply changes that are applicable to conditions from retail demand changes. It should be noted that Eq. (7.34) will be valid only if the supply elasticity of the marketing input becomes infinite.

Equation (7.34) can be modified to yield consistent results with shifts in supply and demand. Wohlgenant and Mullen (1987) propose augmenting (7.12) to include

[4]The analysis ignores technical change. If technical change is farm-input saving then the farmer's share of the retail dollar would decrease. See Miedema (1976) or Wohlgenant (2011).

the quantity of the farm input, as well as account for the effect of marketing input prices:

$$\frac{s_j}{w} = \alpha_j + \beta_j \frac{p_j}{w} + \theta_j m_j \tag{7.37}$$

Wohlgenant (2014) provides a rigorous justification for this specification by deriving the equation as the inverse input demand function from a short-run profit function, conditional on $m$ being predetermined. In particular, Wohlgenant (2014) shows that $\beta_j$ will be positive if there are diminishing marginal returns to $m_j$. In the case of fixed input proportions, the price spread becomes independent of both $\frac{p_j}{w}$ and $m_j$. In that case, the price spread becomes a constant absolute margin. With $\beta_j \geq 0$, the elasticity of price transmission can take on any value between the farm value share and one.

## *7.3.5 Derived Demand Elasticities not Proportional to Retail Demand Elasticities*

The elasticity of demand for the farm input can also be derived from Eqs. (7.27) when $r$ is taken as exogenous:

$$E_{m,r} = \frac{l(s_m e - s_l \sigma) + \sigma e}{\varepsilon_l + s_m \sigma - s_l e} \tag{7.38}$$

This is Hicks (1957) definition of elasticity of derived demand. It is derived allowing for adjustments in final product demand and the market for the competing input. Allen's (1938) expression is obtained by taking the limit as $\varepsilon_l \rightarrow \infty$:

$$E_{m,r} = s_m e - s_l \sigma \tag{7.39}$$

Comparing (7.39) with (7.11), we immediately see that ignoring substitutability between the farm and marketing inputs results in an understatement of the derived demand elasticity for the farm input. In fact, it is possible for the elasticity of derived demand to be larger in absolute value than the elasticity of retail demand as can be seen by observing (7.39). This would occur if substitution in production (through $\sigma$) is larger than substitution in consumption (through $e$). This equation also is consistent with the margin specification (7.37) as opposed to (7.12).

## 7.4 Empirical Analysis: The Wohlgenant Model of Retail-to-Farm Price Linkages

### 7.4.1 *Importance of Input Substitutability in Food Industry*

In light of the above analysis, it is conceptually appealing to view farm output as an input into the food marketing process. The food marketing sector produces a large number and variety of food products (for both at-home and away-from-home consumption) from any given agricultural raw material. This means there are many opportunities for substitution with value-adding inputs and other raw materials in production of the final products. By varying the proportion of the raw material in each final good produced, different conversion amounts are obtained as weights of the final product per unit volume changes. Moreover, there is inherent randomness in processing, handling, and transporting these goods because of differences in variety, size, etc., in addition to differences in workers' skills on the assembly line and in the distribution channel. In contrast to a manufacturing process like microchip production, conversion factors can exhibit considerable randomness, which in itself is a source of input substitution (Walters 1960). Output uncertainty can produce variation in input proportions (Liviatan 1971). In addition, allocation of the raw material from lower-valued goods to higher-valued goods increases the ratio of composite demand to quantity of the raw material (Buccola 2000). Finally, input substitution can occur at the industry level even though it is not present in individual firms. This occurs when firms are different so that changes in industry output lead to changes in the allocation of industry output across firms in the industry (Diewert 1981).[5]

### 7.4.2 *No Direct Estimates of Food Consumption by Commodity*

In the empirical application to follow, the commodities evaluated are meats: beef and veal, pork, and poultry. Quantities of the raw materials are obtained prior to processing but other resources (primarily labor services) are generally freely available. In the appendix to this chapter, following Liviahan (1971), I show how kinked isoquants resulting from the linear programming model of the firm, in combination with output uncertainty, result in smoothed isoquants that relate labor to expected output and the predetermined quantity of raw materials. The key finding is that the marginal rate of substitution (MRS) between labor and raw material is a continuous weighted average of the individual fixed MRS's of adjoining fixed input-output

[5]Wohlgenant (1989) found significant input substitution for six out of seven disaggregate food commodities for earlier time period. Goodwin and Brester (1995) estimate an input demand system for all food and find significant input substitution between agricultural raw materials and each other input.

points. The weights are continuous and differentiable functions of the quantity of the raw material. The gradual change in these weights produces continuous variation in the MRS with $m$, for expected output constant, as $m$ is substituted for the freely variable input.

For most disaggregated food commodities, data are unavailable for food quantities consumed. Estimated per capita food consumption quantities are obtained by multiplying wholesale quantities, calculated as quantities disappearing in the food channel, by a fixed conversion factor that is representative of the technologies in that industry. As indicated above, these are not necessarily the actual quantities consumed because the conversion factors can change as input quantities change for a variety of reason as indicated above. Thus, it is best to regard final goods produced through a variable proportions production function of the form indicated by Eq. (7.6).

### *7.4.3 Reduced-Form Model of Retail and Farm Prices*

Because retail consumption is generally unobservable, the model of retail-to-farm linkage developed is based on reduced-form relationships for retail price and farm price for the commodity. With price-taking behavior, the following set of equations represent short-run market equilibrium:

$$q_d = D(p, z) \tag{7.40}$$

$$q_s = S(p, r, w) \tag{7.41}$$

$$m_d = D_m(p, r, w) \tag{7.42}$$

$$q_s = q_d = q \tag{7.43}$$

$$m_s = m_d = m \tag{7.44}$$

where (7.40) is consumer or retail demand as defined previously, (7.41) is the retail supply function, (7.42) is farm-level demand, and (7.43)–(7.44) represent market-clearing conditions for the retail and farm-level markets. Farm-level supplies of most commodities are predetermined with respect to price because of biological lags in production. Thus, supplies are taken as fixed in the short run.[6] We also assume that prices of value-adding inputs are exogenous to the industry in question so a demand function for the composite input of value-adding inputs is not included in the above

[6]If supply is jointly determined with price, then the analysis is still valid, conditional on the quantity of the raw material supply being fixed. In empirical estimation, the quantity $m$ can be taken as endogenous with appropriate instruments used in estimation.

set of equations. The Eqs. (7.41) and (7.42) are summations of supplies and demands across individual firms and therefore allow for the fact that firms may differ in size. Uniqueness in talent and ability (entrepreneurial capacity) are major reasons firms differ in size (Friedman 1976), and are a source of upward-sloping supply curves in the long run (Panzar and Willig 1978), even when factor prices are constant. Allowing for diversity among firms is important empirically as we often observe a wide range of sizes of firms in food processing and marketing.

Because $q$ is unobservable, we eliminate this variable from consideration by using Eq. (7.43), and substituting (7.41) into (7.40) to obtain the two-equation model:

$$S(p, r, w) = D(p, z) \tag{7.45}$$

$$m = D_m(p, r, w) \tag{7.46}$$

This two-equation system for given exogenous variables yields reduced-form solutions for retail and farm prices which, in log differential form, may be written as:

$$Ep = \pi_{pz}Ez + \pi_{pw}Ew + \pi_{pm}Em \tag{7.47}$$

$$Er = \pi_{rz}Ez + \pi_{rw}Ew + \pi_{rm}Em \tag{7.48}$$

Equation (7.47) is the reduced-form equation for retail price and Eq. (7.48) is the reduced-form equation for the farm price. Equation (7.48) may also be viewed as the industry inverse-demand function for the farm input because it shows the maximum price the marketing sector is willing to pay for this input, holding the retail demand curve constant and the price of the value-adding composite input constant (Friedman 1976; Heiner 1982). The law of demand holds for derived demand, and the demand curve can be shown to be bounded between the aggregate input demand curve holding output constant, and the aggregate demand curve holding output price constant. It also has symmetrical price relationships with all other inputs (Heiner 1982), and a symmetrical relationship with the output price reduced-form equation as shown below.

### 7.4.4 Comparative Statics of Reduced Form

The comparative statics of the reduced-form Eqs. (7.47) and (7.48) can be determined through total differentiation of (7.45) and (7.46), and converting to elasticities:

$$\begin{bmatrix} \varepsilon - e & \varepsilon_{sr} \\ -\varepsilon_{mp} & -\varepsilon_{mr} \end{bmatrix} \begin{bmatrix} Ep \\ Er \end{bmatrix} = \begin{bmatrix} e_z Ez - \varepsilon_{sw} Ew \\ \varepsilon_{mw} Ew - Em \end{bmatrix} \tag{7.49}$$

where $E$ denotes relative change as before (e.g., $Ep = dp/p$), $\varepsilon$ is the retail price elasticity of supply, $e$ is the own-price elasticity of retail demand,$\varepsilon_{sr}$ is the elasticity of retail supply with respect to the farm price, $e_z$ is the elasticity of retail demand with respect to $z$, $\varepsilon_{sw}$ is the elasticity of retail supply with respect to $w$, $\varepsilon_{mp}$ is the elasticity of farm input demand with respect to price $p$, $\varepsilon_{mr}$ is the elasticity of farm input demand with respect to $r$, and $\varepsilon_{mw}$ is the elasticity of farm input demand with respect to $w$. We also set $e_z = 1$, because by definition $Ez$ is the proportionate horizontal change in retail demand. As before, solutions to the system of equations, $\boldsymbol{Bx} = \boldsymbol{c}$, for the total effects of changes in the exogenous variables on retail and farm prices, can be obtained through application of Cramer's rule:

$$E_{p,z} = \pi_{pz} = \frac{-\varepsilon_{mr}}{Det\boldsymbol{B}} \tag{7.50}$$

$$E_{p,w} = \pi_{pw} = \frac{\varepsilon_{sw}\varepsilon_{mr} - \varepsilon_{mw}\varepsilon_{sr}}{Det\boldsymbol{B}} \tag{7.51}$$

$$E_{p,m} = \pi_{pm} = \frac{\varepsilon_{sr}}{Det\boldsymbol{B}} \tag{7.52}$$

$$E_{r,z} = \pi_{rz} = \frac{\varepsilon_{mp}}{Det\boldsymbol{B}} \tag{7.53}$$

$$E_{r,w} = \pi_{rw} = \frac{(\varepsilon - e)\varepsilon_{mw} - \varepsilon_{mp}\varepsilon_{sw}}{Det\boldsymbol{B}} \tag{7.54}$$

$$E_{r,m} = \pi_{rm} = \frac{-(\varepsilon - e)}{Det\boldsymbol{B}} \tag{7.55}$$

where $Det\boldsymbol{B} = -(\varepsilon - e)\varepsilon_{mr} + \varepsilon_{sr}\varepsilon_{mp}$. We know from Heiner (1982) that $E_{r,m} < 0$; therefore, $Det\boldsymbol{B}$ >0 because the numerator of (7.55) is negative. Because the farm input is a normal input, $\varepsilon_{sr} < 0$ and $\varepsilon_{mp} > 0$. Thus, $E_{p,z} > 0$, $E_{p,m} < 0$, $E_{r,z} > 0$. The signs of $E_{p,w}$ and $E_{r,w}$ are generally indeterminate.

As indicated above, Eq. (7.48), with appropriate parameterization, may be regarded as a structural equation of inverse industry derived demand for the agricultural raw material input. It can be estimated using linear least-squares methods like OLS. In a multivariate context, with many inputs, Eq. (7.48) would become a system of inverse industry derived demand functions with the property, collectively of negative semi-definiteness (Heiner 1982). Braulke (1984, 1987) extended the results of Heiner to multiple products and long-run entry/exit decisions. His results are essentially the same as Heiner's, with the additional requirement of negative semi-definiteness imposed on the output demand functions. More will be said about this requirement later.

### 7.4.5 Relationship of Reduced Form to Structure

If one were interested in the relationship between the reduced form and a particular structure, e.g., equations (7.40)–(7.44) then, assuming local identifiability so that the total elasticities and partial elasticities exist, the structure and reduced form are related as follows:

$$\begin{bmatrix} \varepsilon - e & \varepsilon_{sr} \\ -\varepsilon_{mp} & -\varepsilon_{mr} \end{bmatrix} \begin{bmatrix} \pi_{pz} & \pi_{pw} & \pi_{pm} \\ \pi_{rz} & \pi_{rw} & \pi_{rm} \end{bmatrix} = \begin{bmatrix} 1 & -\varepsilon_{sw} & 0 \\ 0 & \varepsilon_{mw} & -1 \end{bmatrix} \tag{7.56}$$

With knowledge of the retail price elasticity of demand, $e$, the structural (partial) elasticities of the output supply and farm input demand functions are just identified: There are six reduced-form parameters and six structural parameters in six equations.

In solving for the structure in terms of the reduced form, it is useful to follow Amemyia (1985, Chapter 10) and first rewrite the two equations in (7.49) where the first equation is normalized on price of the output and the second is normalized on the price of the raw material:

$$Ep = \varepsilon_{pr} Er + \varepsilon_{pw} Ew + \varepsilon_{pz} Ez \tag{7.57}$$

$$Er = \varepsilon_{rp} Ep + \varepsilon_{rw} Ew + \varepsilon_{rm} Em \tag{7.58}$$

where $\varepsilon_{pr} = -\frac{\varepsilon_{sr}}{\varepsilon - e}$, $\varepsilon_{pw} = -\frac{\varepsilon_{sw}}{\varepsilon - e}$, $\varepsilon_{pz} = \frac{1}{\varepsilon - e}$, $\varepsilon_{rp} = -\frac{\varepsilon_{mp}}{\varepsilon_{mr}}$, $\varepsilon_{rw} = -\frac{\varepsilon_{mw}}{\varepsilon_{mr}}$, and $\varepsilon_{rm} = \frac{1}{\varepsilon_{mr}}$. Next write the model in standard notation for simultaneous equations:

$$\boldsymbol{y} = \boldsymbol{Y\gamma} + \boldsymbol{X}_1\boldsymbol{\beta} + \boldsymbol{u}$$

$$\left[\boldsymbol{y}\ \boldsymbol{Y}\right] = \boldsymbol{X}\left[\boldsymbol{\pi}\ \boldsymbol{\Pi}\right] + \boldsymbol{V}$$

where $\boldsymbol{y}$ is the vector of observations on the normalized endogenous variable (i.e., either $E\boldsymbol{p}$ or $E\boldsymbol{r}$); $\boldsymbol{Y}$ is the matrix of included endogenous variables on the right-hand side of equation (in this case a vector of either $E\boldsymbol{r}$ or $E\boldsymbol{p}$); $\boldsymbol{X}_1$ is the subset of all exogenous variables $\boldsymbol{X}$; $\boldsymbol{\gamma}$ and $\boldsymbol{\beta}$ are the structural parameters associated with the endogenous and exogenous variables in the equation of interest; $\boldsymbol{\pi}$ and $\boldsymbol{\Pi}$ are the matrices of reduced-form parameters; and $\boldsymbol{u}$ and $\boldsymbol{V}$ are vector and matrix of error terms, respectively. The set of reduced-form equations for $\boldsymbol{Y}$ can be substituted into the structural equation $\boldsymbol{y}$ with $\boldsymbol{X}_1$ defined as $\boldsymbol{JX}$, where $\boldsymbol{J}$ is a given matrix consisting of only ones and zeros, to obtain the relationship between reduced form and structural parameters, shown in (6.49) but repeated here:

$$\boldsymbol{\pi} = \boldsymbol{\Pi\gamma} + \boldsymbol{J\beta} \tag{7.59}$$

In terms of the reduced form and structural parameters of (7.47) and (7.57) we have:

$$\begin{bmatrix} \pi_{pm} \\ \pi_{pz} \\ \pi_{pw} \end{bmatrix} = \begin{bmatrix} \pi_{rm} \\ \pi_{rz} \\ \pi_{rw} \end{bmatrix} \varepsilon_{pr} + \begin{bmatrix} 0\,0\,0 \\ 0\,1\,0 \\ 0\,0\,1 \end{bmatrix} \begin{bmatrix} \varepsilon_{pm} \\ \varepsilon_{pz} \\ \varepsilon_{pw} \end{bmatrix}$$

Multiplying out the matrix and solving for the structural parameters:

$$\varepsilon_{pr} = \pi_{rm}^{-1} \pi_{pm} \tag{7.60}$$

$$\varepsilon_{pz} = \pi_{pz} - \pi_{rz}\varepsilon_{pr} = \pi_{pz} - \pi_{rz}\pi_{rm}^{-1}\pi_{pm} \tag{7.61}$$

$$\varepsilon_{pw} = \pi_{pw} - \pi_{rw}\varepsilon_{pr} = \pi_{pw} - \pi_{rw}\pi_{rm}^{-1}\pi_{pm} \tag{7.62}$$

Following the same method, we can come up with solutions for the structural parameters in (7.58):

$$\varepsilon_{rp} = \pi_{pz}^{-1} \pi_{rz} \tag{7.63}$$

$$\varepsilon_{rm} = \pi_{rm} - \pi_{pm}\varepsilon_{rp} = \pi_{rm} - \pi_{pm}\pi_{pz}^{-1}\pi_{rz} \tag{7.64}$$

$$\varepsilon_{rw} = \pi_{rw} - \pi_{pw}\varepsilon_{rp} = \pi_{rw} - \pi_{pw}\pi_{pz}^{-1}\pi_{rz} \tag{7.65}$$

### 7.4.6 Empirical Specification

Without any restrictions on the parameters, we see that unique solutions for the structural parameters may be obtained from the reduced-form model. There are, however, restrictions from the theory of the firm and aggregated output supply and demand functions. The first two are homogenous restrictions. That is, the aggregate supply and input demand functions should be homogeneous of degree zero in all prices, implying $\varepsilon_{sr} + \varepsilon_{sw} + \varepsilon = 0$ and $\varepsilon_{mr} + \varepsilon_{mw} + \varepsilon_{mp} = 0$. These restrictions are as follows[7]:

$$\varepsilon_{pr} + \varepsilon_{pw} = 1 + \varepsilon_{pz} e^0$$

[7]From the first equation, $\varepsilon_{pr} + \varepsilon_{pw} = \varepsilon \cdot \varepsilon_{pz}$. Because $\varepsilon = \frac{1}{\varepsilon_{pz}} + e$, it follows that $\varepsilon \cdot \varepsilon_{pz} = \left(\frac{1}{\varepsilon_{pz}} + e\right)\varepsilon_{pz} = 1 + e \cdot \varepsilon_{pz}$.

$$\varepsilon_{rp} + \varepsilon_{rw} = 1$$

where $e^0$ denotes a given and fixed value of the retail demand elasticity. Substituting from (7.60)–(7.65) gives:

$$\left(1 - \pi_{rw} + \pi_{rz}e^0\right) + \pi_{pw} = 1 + \pi_{pz}e^0 \tag{7.66}$$

$$\pi_{rw} + \left(1 - \pi_{pw}\right)\pi_{pz}^{-1}\pi_{rz} = 1 \tag{7.67}$$

In addition to the homogeneity restrictions, there is a reciprocal relationship between output supply and farm input demand: $\frac{\partial S}{\partial r} = -\frac{\partial D_m}{\partial p}$, or in elasticity form $\varepsilon_{sr} = -s_m \varepsilon_{mp}$ (Mosak 1938). In terms of reduced-form parameters, this symmetry relationship is:

$$\pi_{pm} = -s_m \pi_{rz} \tag{7.68}$$

It is also useful to test for constant returns to scale, given homogeneity and symmetry hold. The reason for this test is that it is the case of long-run competitive equilibrium with identical firms. This test result can be shown to result when the two restrictions hold[8]:

$$\pi_{pz} = -\pi_{pm} \tag{7.69}$$

$$\pi_{rz} = -\pi_{rm} \tag{7.70}$$

To sum up, a rigorous theoretical framework has been developed to estimate retail-to-farm price linkages. With a specification for exogenous changes in retail demand and selection of an appropriate functional form, we are ready to specify an empirical model to estimate and to test the model with time series data. For the exogenous demand shift variable, consider the definition of a horizontal relative change in demand for the $i^{\text{th}}$ commodity:

$$Ez_i = \sum_{j \neq i} e_{ij} Ep_j + e_i Ey + Epop$$

where $Epop$ is the relative change in population. For empirical application, elasticities estimated from a system of demand function must be selected in order to provide a consistent basis for linking retail demand to farm-level demand. It is useful to use the Slutsky decomposition in the above definition to segment relative price changes

[8]These two restrictions result from the fact that proportionate changes in both $m$ and $va$ will lead to a proportional change in industry output. This must occur with input prices and output price constant. As can be seen from (7.47) and (7.48), $r$ and $p$ will remain constant for proportional changes in m and z only if the conditions in (7.69) and (7.70) hold.

from changes in real income. In particular, as shown in Chapter 2, this decomposition allows us to write $Ez_i$ as[9]:

$$Ez_i = \sum_{j \neq i} e_{ij}^*(Ep_j - Ew) + e_i\Big(Ey - \sum\nolimits_{k=1}^{n} w_k Ep_k\Big) + Epop \tag{7.71}$$

This specification allows us to deflate all prices by a numeraire price and express income as real income. In the empirical application, we shall use the relative change in overall consumer price index (cpi) to approximate the geometric index, $\sum_{k=1}^{n} w_k Ep_k$, and divide all prices by the price index of value-adding inputs, $w$. The reason we can use $w$ is the retail supply and raw material input demand functions are both homogeneous of degree zero in prices. The demand indices, Eq. (7.71), are constructed using elasticities from the system of demand functions for meats in Chapter 5.

## 7.5 Empirical Application to US Retail-to-Farm Price Linkages of Meats

### *7.5.1 Data Set Consistent with Data Set for Consumer Demand for Meats*

The empirical application is to retail-to-farm price linkages for beef and veal, pork, and poultry. The data set used to estimate retail demand elasticities in Chapter 5 is combined with data on prices and quantities of these commodities at the farm level. Quantity data come from the same source as retail quantities, beef (Beefm), pork (Porkm), and (Poultm) in carcass weight (https://www.ers.usda.gov/data-products/food-availability-per-capita-data-system/).[10] Prices are Producer Price Indices (PPI) for slaughter steers and heifers (Beefr), slaughter barrows and gilts (Porkr), and for slaughter poultry (Poultr) (https://www.bls.gov/data/). The price index of value-adding inputs, $w$, is proxied by the average hourly earnings of production and non-supervisory workers in non-durable goods industries, also from the BLS source.[11] These data, including US civilian population (pop) for 1970–2010, are shown in Table 7.1. The data correspond to the same time period for meat retail demand estimation in Chapter 5.

[9] Note that this implies that the own-price elasticity is the compensated elasticity as well.

[10] To be consistent with retail demand, beef and veal quantities are added together for "beef" quantity designation.

[11] Initially, an index of wage rates and index of fuels and related products and power was constructed and used but was found to be inferior to simply the wage rate index. Therefore, the index of wage rate was used in estimation.

**Table 7.1** Farm Quantities (Mil. Lb.), Prices & Wage (1982-100), and Population (000)

| year | beefm | porkm | poultm | beefr | porkr | poultr | wage | pop |
|---|---|---|---|---|---|---|---|---|
| 1970 | 24063.24 | 14956.83 | 9886.258 | 44.34167 | 45.375 | 51.825 | 38.02222 | 205.052 |
| 1971 | 24122.28 | 16417.3 | 10071.33 | 49.50833 | 37.275 | 52.175 | 40.52222 | 207.661 |
| 1972 | 24680.94 | 14959.63 | 10601.04 | 55.54167 | 53.05 | 54.21667 | 43.3 | 209.896 |
| 1973 | 23443.95 | 13451.46 | 10203.81 | 70.175 | 80.49167 | 93.525 | 46.26667 | 211.909 |
| 1974 | 25251.59 | 14660.57 | 10327.56 | 65.175 | 71.11667 | 82.05 | 50.46667 | 213.854 |
| 1975 | 26627.43 | 12032.36 | 10168.67 | 67.00833 | 96.125 | 98.925 | 55.15556 | 215.973 |
| 1976 | 28596 | 12761.01 | 11072.64 | 60.5 | 87.35 | 86.95833 | 59.63333 | 218.035 |
| 1977 | 28090.41 | 13317.23 | 11331.61 | 61.95833 | 81.66667 | 91.41667 | 65.01111 | 220.239 |
| 1978 | 26858.33 | 13402.7 | 11913.39 | 80.75 | 93.83333 | 104.1 | 70.7 | 222.585 |
| 1979 | 24161.75 | 15457.77 | 12944.65 | 104.8083 | 80.025 | 101.2333 | 77.02222 | 225.055 |
| 1980 | 23932.35 | 16684.11 | 13358.21 | 103.9667 | 74.53333 | 105.3083 | 84.25556 | 227.726 |
| 1981 | 24427.56 | 16058.3 | 14016.74 | 99.075 | 83.78333 | 104.85 | 92.67778 | 229.966 |
| 1982 | 24583.01 | 14527.97 | 14406.67 | 100 | 99.99167 | 99.99167 | 100.0111 | 232.188 |
| 1983 | 25328.92 | 15452.81 | 14905.13 | 96.73333 | 85.80833 | 107.6333 | 104.5444 | 234.307 |
| 1984 | 25509.11 | 15482.6 | 15483.5 | 100.9583 | 87.825 | 125.3833 | 108.5222 | 236.348 |
| 1985 | 26004.97 | 15733.31 | 16189.27 | 90.75833 | 80.99167 | 117.875 | 112.9333 | 238.466 |
| 1986 | 26484.98 | 15003.04 | 17082.09 | 89.225 | 98.025 | 129.6833 | 116.0667 | 240.651 |
| 1987 | 25652.78 | 15224.59 | 18614.34 | 99.99167 | 97.675 | 101.2417 | 119.1 | 242.804 |
| 1988 | 25597.53 | 16422.85 | 19472.92 | 107.4083 | 82.86667 | 121.5 | 122.5667 | 245.021 |
| 1989 | 24513.6 | 16421.93 | 20641.5 | 111.4667 | 81.025 | 128.7667 | 126.6 | 247.342 |
| 1990 | 24286.8 | 15912.34 | 21997.07 | 119 | 93.675 | 118.825 | 131.5444 | 250.132 |
| 1991 | 24350.64 | 16261.21 | 23103.51 | 113.1083 | 82.6 | 111.2417 | 135.7 | 253.493 |
| 1992 | 24497.15 | 17316.71 | 24218.4 | 113.575 | 70.79167 | 112.575 | 139.3889 | 256.894 |
| 1993 | 24230.54 | 17313.52 | 24937.38 | 114.7167 | 76.09167 | 121.9417 | 142.6667 | 260.255 |
| 1994 | 25360.98 | 17703.26 | 25620.61 | 104.075 | 66.075 | 124.4167 | 146.1556 | 263.436 |
| 1995 | 25786.17 | 17684.82 | 25820.77 | 99.41667 | 70.375 | 125.6333 | 150.7 | 266.557 |
| 1996 | 26182.28 | 16726.82 | 26571.1 | 97.55833 | 88.58333 | 140.525 | 155.6778 | 269.667 |
| 1997 | 25882.26 | 16745.44 | 27385.15 | 98.74167 | 86.725 | 130.975 | 160.5111 | 272.912 |
| 1998 | 26498.62 | 18278.27 | 27996.03 | 92.71667 | 52.63333 | 141.3667 | 166.0333 | 276.115 |
| 1999 | 27092.67 | 18874.99 | 29743.77 | 98.43333 | 54.425 | 129.9333 | 171.3667 | 279.295 |
| 2000 | 27471.55 | 18498.83 | 30326.22 | 104.4083 | 72.875 | 124.6583 | 177.4889 | 282.385 |
| 2001 | 27121.88 | 18397.43 | 30588.69 | 108.2083 | 73.24167 | 130.675 | 183.4222 | 285.267 |
| 2002 | 27986.19 | 19043.5 | 32285.04 | 101.2417 | 55.51667 | 119.9333 | 188.6778 | 288.028 |
| 2003 | 27131.26 | 19341.51 | 32884.76 | 126.95 | 66.16667 | 138.025 | 195.0333 | 290.704 |
| 2004 | 27819.92 | 19296.53 | 33918.08 | 125.425 | 87.4 | 172.5667 | 200.6778 | 293.31 |
| 2005 | 27822.81 | 18899.44 | 34723.24 | 130.775 | 82.05833 | 168.5583 | 203.5222 | 295.994 |

(continued)

**Table 7.1** (continued)

| year | beefm | porkm | poultm | beefr | porkr | poultr | wage | pop |
|---|---|---|---|---|---|---|---|---|
| 2006 | 28209.46 | 18864.98 | 35295.13 | 127.175 | 76.99167 | 150.8333 | 204.3556 | 298.766 |
| 2007 | 28186.89 | 19559.33 | 35329.11 | 138.7833 | 75.83333 | 187.9583 | 208.9111 | 301.714 |
| 2008 | 27203.96 | 19211.06 | 35095.36 | 138.35 | 78.15 | 199 | 215.4 | 304.3748 |
| 2009 | 26838 | 19633.48 | 33825.4 | 124.6417 | 67.99167 | 188.925 | 220.7556 | 307.0066 |
| 2010 | 26387.52 | 18845.46 | 34921.46 | 141.925 | 91.10833 | 208.7583 | 224.0333 | 309.3302 |

**Table 7.2** Cross-Price and Income Elasticity Estimates, and Farm Value Shares

| Beef (b) | | | Pork (pk) | | | Poultry (py) | | |
|---|---|---|---|---|---|---|---|---|
| Elasticity | Estimate | Std Error | Elasticity | Estimate | Std Error | Elasticity | Estimate | Std Error |
| ebbc | -0.73615 | 0.1295 | epkpkc | -1.07564 | 0.109 | epypy | -0.34389 | 0.1779 |
| ebpkc | 0.22466 | 0.0607 | epkbc | 0.442491 | 0.1197 | epybc | 0.132209 | 0.1244 |
| ebpyc | 0.044976 | 0.0423 | epkpyc | 0.006381 | 0.0623 | epypkc | 0.067774 | 0.0818 |
| ebfc | 0.006101 | 0.0427 | epkfc | 0.088767 | 0.0434 | epyfc | -0.16576 | 0.1123 |
| ebnmc | 0.035129 | 0.0123 | epknmc | 0.03926 | 0.013 | epynmc | 0.026849 | 0.0163 |
| ebnfc | 0.446262 | 0.1108 | epknfc | 0.498746 | 0.1485 | epynfc | 0.341074 | 0.186 |
| sbeefm | 0.599075 | | sporkm | 0.454894 | | spoultm | 0.427301 | |
| (1990 value) | | | | | | | | |
| ebeef | 0.624729 | 0.3003 | | | | | | |
| epork | | | | 0.698202 | 0.2788 | | | |
| poult | | | | | | | 0.477475 | 0.2568 |

## 7.5.2 *Weights in Retail Demand Index*

The coefficients for the demand index, (7.71), are the cross-price elasticities and income elasticities of each meat. Table 7.2 presents the sample mean estimates of these compensated price and expenditure elasticities. Own-price elasticities for each of the meats are also presented. In addition, median farm value shares, as shares of retail value, for beef and veal, pork, and poultry are shown.[12]

We need a functional form for empirical analysis. While many functional forms are available, I select a model that is first-differences in natural logs. The empirical model for the $i^{\text{th}}$ commodity consists of the two discrete counterparts to (7.47) and (7.48):

$$\Delta \log(p_{it}/w_t) = \pi_{pio} + \pi_{piz}\Delta \log z_{it} + \pi_{pim}\Delta \log m_{it} + u_{pit} \tag{7.72}$$

[12] Complete time series data for poultry are unavailable, so median shares are used rather than mean shares in estimation. Comparison of median with mean values for beef and veal and pork indicates only small differences between the two measures of central tendency.

$$\Delta \log(r_{it}/w_t) = \pi_{rio} + \pi_{riz}\Delta \log z_t + \pi_{rim}\Delta \log m_{it} + u_{rit} \tag{7.73}$$

where $u_{pt}$ and $u_{rt}$ are error terms, assumed to be i.i.d. with zero means; and $\pi_{po}$ are $\pi_{ro}$ are constants to account for trend effects. All the coefficients are assumed to be constant. Note that terms associated with the wage rate, $w_t$, have been deleted because it is used as deflator for all other prices. The demand index variable is:

$$\Delta \log z_{it} = \sum_{j \neq i} \widehat{e_{ij}^*}\Delta \log\big(p_{jt}/w_t\big) + \widehat{e_i}\Delta \log(y_t/cpi_t) + \Delta \log pop_t \tag{7.74}$$

where hats denote estimates from Table 7.2, and $cpi_t$ denotes the consumer price index for all goods.

### 7.5.3 Testing Zero Homogeneity Condition

A test for the zero homogeneity condition is to augment both retail and farm price equations with the nominal variable, $\Delta \log w_t$. A test of the null hypothesis that only relative prices matter is then a joint test of the hypothesis that the coefficients on this variable in both equations equal zero. The results of this test indicate failure to reject the null hypothesis at p-values larger than 0.5 when tested equation by equation. In light of this result, I have imposed the hypothesis of zero homogeneity in prices and income. In other words, I have assumed only real prices and income have an effect on consumers and producers. With the Slutsky decomposition, I have deflated per capita total expenditures by the cpi as discussed previously. All commodity prices and the wage rate are relative prices and I have chosen the wage rate as the numeraire. This means the parameter space for estimation has been reduced to four reduced-form parameters: $\pi_{pim}, \pi_{piz}, \pi_{rim}, \pi_{riz}$; and four structural parameters: $\varepsilon_{pir}, \varepsilon_{piz}, \varepsilon_{rim}, \varepsilon_{rip}$. The reduced-form parameters $\pi_{piw}$ and $\pi_{riw}$ are recovered through the relationships $1 + \pi_{piz}\widehat{e}_{ii}$ and $1 + \pi_{riz}\widehat{e}_{ii}$, respectively. The structural parameters $\varepsilon_{piw}$ and $\varepsilon_{riw}$ are estimated through (7.62) and (7.65), respectively.

### 7.5.4 Model Estimation with Symmetry Restriction

With the zero homogeneity condition imposed, there is only one testable constraint per set of retail and farm prices:

$$\pi_{pim} = -\widehat{s_{im}}\pi_{riz} \tag{7.75}$$

which arises from the symmetry restriction between retail supply and farm input demand. Because of the logarithmic functional form, which leads to constant elasticities, this restriction can only be imposed at one data point and we choose the median shares as reported in Table 7.2.

If symmetry holds, we can then test for constant returns to scale (CRTS) from (7.69) and (7.70):

$$\pi_{piz} = -\pi_{pim} \tag{7.76}$$

$$\pi_{riz} = -\pi_{rim} \tag{7.77}$$

The overall approach to estimation and testing is constrained indirect least squares (Wegge 1978). The Eqs. (7.72) and (7.73) are the reduced form, which with a given value of $\hat{e}_{ii}$ lead to just identification of the economic structure given by (7.57) and (7.58). The existence of other constraints on the reduced-form parameter causes these structural parameters to be overidentified, and therefore allows us to test the theory. As shown by Wegge (1978), this is a powerful way to test the theory. In principle, the reduced form could correspond with many different theories and the data should be confronted with different theories to see if they are compatible with the hypothesized theory. In this application, we impose and test the symmetry constraint, (7.75), to test the theory of price-taking behavior of market intermediaries in the beef, pork, and poultry industries. If symmetry holds, we then proceed to test if the CRTS restrictions hold.

The specific estimator used is SUR.[13] The model was estimated using Proc Model of SAS software version 9.4. The likelihood ratio tests statistics for all three meats had p-values above 0.14 (p-values of 0.14, 0.35, and 0.36 for beef, pork, and poultry, respectively), indicating failure to reject the basic theory of price-taking behavior in meat processing and marketing. Results for the reduced form and structure are shown in Tables 7.3, 7.4 and 7.5.[14] Individual R-squared values are all quite respectable (all larger than 0.44), realizing that the models are in first-differences. Furthermore, there is little evidence of serial correlation indicated by the Durbin–Watson statistics. Most of the reduced-form parameters are highly significant and have the anticipated signs. The exogenous demand shift variable, $\Delta \log z_{it}$, is strongly positively related to both

[13]The general form of the SUR estimator is nonlinear SUR, for which the likelihood ratio test is $L = S(\tilde{\theta}, \hat{\Omega}) - S(\hat{\theta}, \hat{\Omega})$, distributed chi-squared with $r$ (number of restrictions), where $S(\theta, \hat{\Omega}) = \sum_{t=1}^{T} [y_t - f(x_t, \theta)]' \hat{\Omega}^{-1} [y_t - f(x_t, \theta)]$. Note that both $S(\cdot)$ functions are minimized with respect to the vector of parameters, $\theta$. Because of the estimation method, each uses the same variance-covariance matrix, $\hat{\Omega}$, estimated using residuals from OLS estimation in the first stage. For estimation of reduced-form parameters, the function $f(x_t, \theta)$ is linear in both variables and parameters. For estimation of structural parameters, the estimator is linear in variables but nonlinear in parameters. See Gallant (1987, Chapter 5) for more details.

[14]Because cross-price and income elasticities are taken as deterministic, the reported asymptotic standard errors underestimate the true standard errors. These standard errors are not reported here. Murphy and Topel (2001) provide formulas for this case.

**Table 7.3** Parameter Estimates of Constrained Reduced Form and Structural Retail-to-Farm Price Linkage Equations, Beef and Veal, 1970–2020

SUR Parameter Estimates

| **Parameter** | **Estimate** | **Approx Std Err** | **t Value** | **Approx Pr > \|t\|** |
|---|---|---|---|---|
| $\pi_{pm}$ | −1.02456 | 0.1386 | −7.39 | <.0001 |
| $\pi_{rz}$ | 1.707608 | 0.2310 | 7.39 | <.0001 |
| $\pi_{pz}$ | 1.03358 | 0.2158 | 4.79 | <.0001 |
| $\pi_{rm}$ | −1.75202 | 0.2724 | −6.43 | <.0001 |
| $\pi_{po}$ | −0.01775 | 0.00667 | −2.66 | 0.0115 |
| $\pi_{ro}$ | −0.03897 | 0.0104 | −3.76 | 0.0006 |
| **Term** | **Estimate** | **Approx Std Err** | **t Value** | **Approx Pr > \|t\|** |
| $\pi_{pw}$ | 0.23851 | 0.1590 | 1.50 | 0.1421 |
| $\pi_{rw}$ | −0.25808 | 0.1702 | −1.52 | 0.1379 |
| $e_{pr}$ | 0.584792 | 0.0949 | 6.17 | <.0001 |
| $e_{pz}$ | 0.034985 | 0.3088 | 0.11 | 0.9104 |
| $e_{rp}$ | 1.652128 | 0.3660 | 4.51 | <.0001 |
| $e_{rm}$ | −0.0593 | 0.5190 | −0.11 | 0.9097 |
| $e_{pw}$ | 0.389433 | 0.1748 | 2.23 | 0.0321 |
| $e_{rw}$ | −0.65213 | 0.3660 | −1.78 | 0.0830 |

*Note* Values for $\pi_{pw}$ and $\pi_{rw}$ and structural elasticities computed from formulas in text

retail and farm prices, with its effect being greater on farm prices than retail prices. Changes in raw material supply, $\Delta \log m_t$, also strongly negatively affect both retail and farm prices, with again the effect being greater on farm prices than retail prices in all instances. Changes in the wage rate generally have a positive effect on retail prices but a negative effect on farm prices. A major reason effects on farm price are greater than on retail price is because farm prices are smaller than retail prices so retail price changes in levels require smaller percentage changes to equal levels changes in farm prices.

The elasticities of retail supply and farm-level demand are also shown in Tables 7.3–7.5 for the structure normalized on output price and raw material price (Eqs. 7.57 and 7.58). Most of the signs of the parameters are as expected. Output price is positively related to farm price, the wage rate, and the exogenous retail demand shift variable. The farm price is negatively related to its own quantity, positively related to output price, and negatively related to the wage rate. The only exceptions are the effect of exogenous retail demand shift variable on retail price of pork and farm quantity on farm price of pork, but in both instances parameters are very insignificant. In fact, the results overall indicate very elastic retail supplies and output price constant raw material input demands, consistent with an underlying constant-returns-to scale production function. Poultry is the only exception where we find

**Table 7.4** Parameter Estimates of Constrained Reduced Form and Structural Retail-to-Farm Price Linkage Equations, Pork, 1970–2020

SUR Parameter Estimates

| Parameter | Estimate | Approx Std Err | t Value | Approx Pr > \|t\| |
|---|---|---|---|---|
| $\pi_{pm}$ | −0.95883 | 0.0787 | −12.18 | <.0001 |
| $\pi_{rz}$ | 2.130726 | 0.1749 | 12.18 | <.0001 |
| $\pi_{pz}$ | 0.806692 | 0.1533 | 5.26 | <.0001 |
| $\pi_{rm}$ | −2.50535 | 0.2660 | −9.42 | <.0001 |
| $\pi_{po}$ | −0.01809 | 0.00589 | −3.07 | 0.0040 |
| $\pi_{ro}$ | −0.05224 | 0.0168 | −3.12 | 0.0035 |
| **Term** | **Estimate** | **Approx Std Err** | **t Value** | **Approx Pr > \|t\|** |
| $\pi_{pw}$ | 0.132636 | 0.1649 | 0.80 | 0.4262 |
| $\pi_{rw}$ | −1.29098 | 0.1881 | −6.86 | <.0001 |
| $e_{pr}$ | 0.382712 | 0.0488 | 7.84 | <.0001 |
| $e_{pz}$ | −0.00876 | 0.2030 | −0.04 | 0.9658 |
| $e_{rp}$ | 2.641313 | 0.5191 | 5.09 | <.0001 |
| $e_{rm}$ | 0.027212 | 0.6328 | 0.04 | 0.9659 |
| $e_{pw}$ | 0.626709 | 0.1910 | 3.28 | 0.0023 |
| $e_{rw}$ | −1.64131 | 0.5191 | −3.16 | 0.0031 |

*Note* Values for $\pi_{pw}$ and $\pi_{rw}$ and structural elasticities computed from formulas in text

significant effects of exogenous retail demand on retail price and farm quantity on farm price. The implied retail supply elasticity of poultry is 1.0 and output price constant input demand elasticity is –0.9.[15]

### 7.5.5 *Model Estimation with CRTS Restriction*

Of interest is whether there exist underlying aggregate production functions that exhibit constant returns to scale. If so, then marginal and inframarginal firms can be characterized as having similar cost structures and the industry can be described with one cost function, or equivalently as one representative firm. To test for constant returns to scale we impose the restrictions (7.76) and (7.77). In each case, we fail to reject this market structure with p-values for the likelihood ratio test of 0.99, 0.24, and 0.06 for beef, pork, and poultry, respectively. The implication is that, although firm diversity within the meat industries exists, all three industries behave as though each is efficiently organized by single firm. In each industry, over time, there has been a small group of firms accounting for a large proportion of output. These firms have all

[15]The supply elasticity is computed as $\frac{1}{\varepsilon_{pz}} + e$ and the input demand elasticity is computed as $\frac{-1}{\varepsilon_{rm}}$, using the appropriate parameters from Table 7.2 and Table 7.5.

**Table 7.5** Parameter Estimates of Constrained Reduced Form and Structural Retail-to-Farm Price Linkage Equations, Poultry, 1970–2020

SUR Parameter Estimates

| Parameter | Estimate | Approx Std Err | t Value | Approx Pr > \|t\| |
|---|---|---|---|---|
| $\pi_{pm}$ | −1.38254 | 0.2530 | −5.46 | <.0001 |
| $\pi_{rz}$ | 3.21522 | 0.5885 | 5.46 | <.0001 |
| $\pi_{pz}$ | 2.18295 | 0.4182 | 5.22 | <.0001 |
| $\pi_{rm}$ | −3.13604 | 0.5810 | −5.40 | <.0001 |
| $\pi_{po}$ | 0.001252 | 0.00987 | 0.13 | 0.8998 |
| $\pi_{ro}$ | 0.042853 | 0.0208 | 2.06 | 0.0469 |
| **Term** | **Estimate** | **Approx Std Err** | **t Value** | **Approx Pr > \|t\|** |
| $\pi_{pw}$ | 0.248126 | 0.1440 | 1.72 | 0.0933 |
| $\pi_{rw}$ | −0.10742 | 0.2027 | −0.53 | 0.5993 |
| $e_{pr}$ | 0.440857 | 0.0625 | 7.05 | <.0001 |
| $e_{pz}$ | 0.7655 | 0.3613 | 2.12 | 0.0409 |
| $e_{rp}$ | 1.472878 | 0.2478 | 5.94 | <.0001 |
| $e_{rm}$ | −1.09972 | 0.4794 | −2.29 | 0.0276 |
| $e_{pw}$ | 0.295482 | 0.1146 | 2.58 | 0.0141 |
| $e_{rw}$ | −0.47288 | 0.2478 | −1.91 | 0.0642 |
| $e_{pw}$ | 0.961906 | 0.6165 | 1.56 | 0.1272 |
| $e_{rw}$ | −0.90932 | 0.3964 | −2.29 | 0.0276 |

*Note* Values for $\pi_{pw}$ and $\pi_{rw}$ and structural elasticities computed from formulas in text

been similar in structure. Studies in agricultural economics have consistently shown economies of scale exist in the livestock and other agricultural processing industries. These studies also show the existence of "L-shaped" long-run average cost curves, indicating economies of scale can be achieved with a range of firm sizes, albeit rather large sizes. Apparently, the smaller firms in each industry supply mostly to niche and specialty markets and have little influence on the overall structure of these commercial industries.

The comparative statics of the reduced-form price relationships with CRTS can be inferred quite readily from Eqs. (7.28)–(7.30) and the relationship between retail and input prices, $Ep = s_m Er + s_l Ew$. With farm input supply fixed and the wage rate exogenous to the industry, we know from (7.24) and (7.25) that $\varepsilon_m \varepsilon_{rt_m} Et_m = -Em$ and $\varepsilon_{wt_l} Et_l = Ew$. Therefore,

$$\pi_{piz} = \frac{s_{mi}}{s_{il}\sigma_i - s_{mi}e_{ii}}, \quad \pi_{riz} = \frac{1}{s_{il}\sigma_i - s_{mi}e_{ii}} \tag{7.78}$$

$$\pi_{pim} = \frac{-s_{mi}}{s_{il}\sigma_i - s_{mi}e_{ii}}, \quad \pi_{rim} = \frac{-1}{s_{il}\sigma_i - s_{mi}e_{ii}} \tag{7.79}$$

$$\pi_{piw} = \frac{s_{li}\sigma}{s_{il}\sigma_i - s_{mi}e_{ii}}, \quad \pi_{riw} = \frac{s_{li}(\sigma + e_{ii})}{s_{il}\sigma_i - s_{mi}e_{ii}} \tag{7.80}$$

As can be seen, for a given value of the retail demand elasticity, there is a single structural parameter, $\sigma_i$, the elasticity of substitution between the farm input and value-adding input.

Results of the reduced-form and structural parameters of the model with CRTS are presented in Tables 7.6, 7.7 and 7.8. The effects of retail demand and farm supply on both retail and farm prices have correct signs and even more significant due to imposition of CRTS constraints. The effects of wage rate on retail prices are positive and significant for beef and poultry, but negative and highly insignificant for pork. All effects of wage on farm prices are negative and are insignificant except for pork. The difference in the results between beef and poultry on the one hand and pork on the other hand stems from fact that the results point to fixed input proportions for pork. As can be seen, the elasticity of substitution between the farm and value-adding inputs, σ, is positive and significant for beef and poultry but not different from zero for pork. As shown by Eq. (7.80), this explains why the effect of the wage rate on retail price of pork is also zero. In fact, a joint test for fixed proportions is that $H_0$: $\pi_{piw} = 0, \pi_{rim} = \frac{1}{\hat{s}_{mi}\hat{e}_{ii}}$. This hypothesis is equivalent to the hypothesis: $H_0$: $\sigma = 0$, which we fail to reject for pork, given estimates of the farm value share and retail demand elasticity.

Input substitution for beef and veal and poultry is clearly important and, given the relative magnitudes of the parameters, is consistent with the explanation offered

**Table 7.6** Parameter Estimates of Constrained Reduced Form and Structural Retail-to-Farm Price Linkage Equations with CRTS, Beef and Veal, 1970–2010

| Parameter | **Estimate** | **Approx Std Err** | **t Value** | **Approx Pr > \|t\|** |
|---|---|---|---|---|
| $\pi_{pm}$ | 1.036772 | 0.1163 | 8.91 | <.0001 |
| $\pi_{rz}$ | −1.03677 | 0.1163 | −8.91 | <.0001 |
| $\pi_{pz}$ | 1.727954 | 0.1939 | 8.91 | <.0001 |
| $\pi_{rm}$ | −1.72795 | 0.1939 | −8.91 | <.0001 |
| $\pi_{po}$ | −0.01777 | 0.00578 | −3.07 | 0.0039 |
| $\pi_{ro}$ | −0.03936 | 0.0101 | −3.88 | 0.0004 |
| **Term** | **Estimate** | **Approx Std Err** | **t Value** | **Approx Pr > \|t\|** |
| $\pi_{pw}$ | 0.236158 | 0.0857 | 2.76 | 0.0089 |
| $\pi_{rw}$ | −0.27307 | 0.1428 | −1.91 | 0.0634 |
| σ | 0.341673 | 0.1623 | 2.11 | 0.0420 |

*Note* Values for $\pi_{pw}$ and $\pi_{rw}$ and structural elasticities computed from formulas in text

**Table 7.7** Parameter Estimates of Constrained Reduced Form and Structural Retail-to-Farm Price Linkage Equations with CRTS, Pork, 1970–2010

SUR Parameter Estimates

| Parameter | Estimate | Approx Std Err | t Value | Approx Pr > \|t\| |
|---|---|---|---|---|
| $\pi_{pm}$ | 0.97922 | 0.0659 | 14.87 | <.0001 |
| $\pi_{rz}$ | −0.97922 | 0.0659 | −14.87 | <.0001 |
| $\pi_{pz}$ | 2.176044 | 0.1464 | 14.87 | <.0001 |
| $\pi_{rm}$ | −2.17604 | 0.1464 | −14.87 | <.0001 |
| $\pi_{po}$ | −0.02119 | 0.00517 | −4.10 | 0.0002 |
| $\pi_{ro}$ | −0.05498 | 0.0167 | −3.29 | 0.0021 |
| **Term** | **Estimate** | **Approx Std Err** | **t Value** | **Approx Pr > \|t\|** |
| $\pi$pw | −0.05287 | 0.0708 | −0.75 | 0.4599 |
| $\pi$rw | −1.3397 | 0.1574 | −8.51 | <.0001 |
| $\sigma$ | −0.04417 | 0.0562 | −0.79 | 0.4367 |

*Note* Values for $\pi_{pw}$ and $\pi_{rw}$ and structural elasticities computed from formulas in text

**Table 7.8** Parameter Estimates of Constrained Reduced Form and Structural Retail-to-Farm Price Linkage Equations with CRTS, Poultry, 1970–2010

SUR Parameter Estimates

| Parameter | Estimate | Approx Std Err | t Value | Approx Pr > \|t\| |
|---|---|---|---|---|
| $\pi_{pm}$ | 1.405379 | 0.2341 | 6.00 | <.0001 |
| $\pi_{rz}$ | −1.40538 | 0.2341 | −6.00 | <.0001 |
| $\pi_{pz}$ | 3.268324 | 0.5445 | 6.00 | <.0001 |
| $\pi_{rm}$ | −3.26832 | 0.5445 | −6.00 | <.0001 |
| $\pi_{po}$ | 0.013237 | 0.00870 | 1.52 | 0.1365 |
| $\pi_{ro}$ | 0.046257 | 0.0182 | 2.55 | 0.0150 |
| **Term** | **Estimate** | **Approx Std Err** | **t Value** | **Approx Pr > \|t\|** |
| $\pi_{pw}$ | 0.515945 | 0.0806 | 6.40 | <.0001 |
| $\pi_{rw}$ | −0.12571 | 0.1875 | −0.67 | 0.5067 |
| $\sigma$ | 0.276951 | 0.0894 | 3.10 | 0.0037 |

*Note* Values for $\pi_{pw}$ and $\pi_{rw}$ and structural elasticities computed from formulas in text

in the Appendix. With demand uncertainty and with the quantity of the farm input quasi-fixed due to biological lags and contracting, input substitution occurs between value-adding inputs (i.e., labor) and the farm input. As the farm input is increased, holding expected retail demand constant, labor used in slaughtering and cutting meat is adjusted as one moves from one production technique to another determined in part by the probability distribution defining retail demand. In other words, with freely available labor, varying amounts of it are applied to the fixed carcass to achieve a given level of expected retail demand.

The overall implication of input substitution is that the industry price elasticity of demand for the farm input in general is not equal to the product of the elasticity of price transmission and elasticity of retail demand. In other words, for beef and veal and poultry, the elasticity of derived demand for the farm input is calculated through the formula given by Eq. (7.39). Values for beef and veal and poultry are obtained directly as the reciprocals of $\pi_{rim}$ from Tables (7.6) and (7.8). These elasticities are: $E_{bb} = -0.58$ with t-value $= -8.9$ and $E_{py,py} = -0.31$ with t-value $= -6.00$. The corresponding output-constant (compensated) derived demand elasticities are $E^*_{bb} = -0.16$ with a t-value of $-2.11$ and $E^*_{py,py} = -0.16$ with a t-value of $-3.10$.[16] Note that the industry demand elasticities are bounded by the output-constant elasticities and the output price constant elasticities, which approach infinity in this case. Finally, the derived demand elasticities with fixed proportions are calculated according to Eq. (7.11) as elasticities of price transmissions times retail demand elasticities. In this case, because of CRTS restriction, all elasticities of price transmission are equal to farm value shares. The estimated derived demand elasticities with fixed proportions are $E_{bb} = -0.44$, $E_{pk,pk} = -0.48$, $E_{py,py} = -0.15$. Because $\sigma = 0$ for pork, the value of $-0.48$ with fixed proportions is its estimated derived demand elasticity. For beef and veal and poultry, the differences are $-0.58$ versus $-0.44$ for beef and veal, and $-0.31$ versus $-0.15$ for poultry. While the differences may not seem all that large for these commodities, even small elasticities of substitution can have important policy implications for vertical integration (Vernon and Graham 1971) and producer-funded checkoff programs (Alston and Scobie 1983; Wohlgenant 1993), among other applications.

### 7.5.6 Sensitivity of Results to Specification of Retail Demand Index

Some attention should be given to the retail demand shift variables, $\Delta \log z_{it}$, used in estimation because these are constructed data and are measured with error due to the use of elasticities estimated from a system of consumer demand functions. Moreover, each demand shift variable depends on retail prices of other goods, some of which are endogenous and may make $\Delta \log z_{it}$ endogenous. We take each $\Delta \log m_{it}$ as predetermined because of biological lags in production and also contracting which predetermines quantities for future delivery. I have looked at the efficacy of these demand indices two ways. First, because the cross-price and income elasticities are estimated from data derived from disappearance data, I consider what problems this creates by re-estimating the system of demand functions with different data as estimates for consumption. In particular, I use consumer expenditure data provided

[16]The compensated industry derived demand elasticities hold output constant and are measured by setting the term $\hat{s}_{mi}\hat{e}_{ii} = 0$.

by BLS on expenditures per consumer unit by region, aggregated over all regions with weights equal to a relative number of consumer units per region (https://www.bls.gov/data/). The data are available only starting in 1984 so I have linked the expenditure data I derived in Chapter 5 with these data from 1970–1983. The new expenditure series were then used to construct the dependent variables of the RM as

$$\overline{w}_{it} \Delta log q_{it} = \overline{w}_{it} \Delta log w_{it} - \overline{w}_{it} (\Delta \log p_{it} - \Delta \log y_t) \tag{7.81}$$

Expenditure data for fish are not reported so only beef and veal, pork, and poultry expenditure are used. The results turned out very similar to the results derived from the disappearance data. In fact, the compensated price elasticities and income elasticities were in most instances within two decimal places of one another. No elasticity was found to be over one standard deviation from the previously estimated ones. The reason for this close correspondence is likely the form of the transformation taken to convert to RM. As can be seen by Eq. (7.81), the dependent variable indirectly only depends on the disappearance data. To the extent that the average budget shares and change in logs of budget shares differ from one another, we would expect to have error in the dependent variables of the RM.

Another way to look at the problem is to note from Chapter 6 that the difference between the true demand quantity and simple sum quantity used is the quality index. From Eq. (6.4), $\log q_i^* = \log q_i + \log v_i$, where $q_i^*$ is the unobserved constant dollar expenditure. The quality index is a weighted average of quantity shares of components of the composite commodity, with weights equal to fixed prices for some base time period. Over time, the index changes as the quantity shares change. For a number of reasons, we would not expect large changes in these shares, even though substitution among goods within the composite commodity occurs, as discussed earlier in this chapter. Relative price movements within the composite commodity would not be large because of arbitrage. In turn, this would limit changes in relative quantity shares. The bottom line is that, with time-series data, we should not expect large deviations between changes in constant dollar expenditures and changes in the simple sum aggregates.

A rigorous way to evaluate the validity of the $\Delta \log z_{it}$ variables is through use of the Hausman (1978) specification test. To the extent that the weights used in the index are biased the Hausman test can be used to test for misspecification. Moreover, the Hausman test can be used to test for exogeneity by using instruments for the perceived endogenous components of the index. The Hausman test is that the null hypothesis is the correct specification of the index $\Delta \log z_{it}$, both with respect to correct specification of weights on elasticities and exogeneity of retail prices of beef and veal, pork, and poultry. The Hausman test is constructed as follows:

$$H = T\hat{q}'\hat{V}^{-1}(\hat{q})\hat{q}$$

where $\widehat{q} = \left(\widehat{\boldsymbol{\beta}}_1 - \widehat{\boldsymbol{\beta}}_0\right)$ and $\widehat{V} = \widehat{V}\left(\widehat{\boldsymbol{\beta}}_1\right) - \widehat{V}\left(\widehat{\boldsymbol{\beta}}_0\right)$. The vector $\widehat{\boldsymbol{\beta}}_0$ is the vector of parameter estimates under the null hypothesis and $\widehat{\boldsymbol{\beta}}_1$ is the vector under the alternative hypothesis. The matrices $\widehat{V}\left(\widehat{\boldsymbol{\beta}}_0\right)$ and $\widehat{V}\left(\widehat{\boldsymbol{\beta}}_1\right)$ are the variance-covariance estimates under the null and alternative hypotheses. The statistic $H$ is a Wald-type statistic and is distributed chi-squared with the number of explanatory variables equal to the degrees of freedom. In the present case, I estimate the unrestricted versions of (7.72) and (7.73). Under the null hypothesis, OLS is the consistent and efficient estimator while under the alternative hypothesis 2SLS is the consistent estimator as required for the Hausman test. I use change in logs of farm quantities for beef and veal, pork, and poultry; changes in logarithms of ppce, retail fish price, retail price of non-meats, retail price of nonfood, and population as instrumental variables. The chi-squared values for the three models have p-values of 0.27, 0.48, and 0.99 for beef and veal, pork, and poultry, respectively. Thus, we fail to reject that the constructed $\Delta \log z_{it}$ variables are the correct estimates for retail demand shifters.[17]

### 7.5.7 *Results for Retail-to-Farm Price Linkage Equations*

The final issue I address in this chapter is the effect of retail demand, farm supply, and value-adding costs on the retail-to-farm price ratio, the measure of price spreads introduced by Gardner (1975). The elasticities are obtained by subtracting Eq. (7.73) from Eq. (7.72). These results are presented in Table 7.9. These results show that all variables, including intercepts reflecting time trends, are highly significant determinants of the retail-to-farm price ratio. As predicted by Gardner (1975), decreases in retail demand, increases in farm supply, and increases in marketing costs all increase the price spread. Business cycles exist in livestock operations (especially beef—see, e.g., Mundlak and Huang 1996). This means both demand decreases and supply increases often occur concurrently. As can be seen from Table 7.9, a one percent simultaneous decrease in demand and increase in supply results in well over a one percent increase in the price spread (i.e., approximately 1.4% for beef, 2.4% for pork, and over 3.7% for poultry). It is not surprising, then, why primary produces often complain about price gauging, market power, etc., during such times. The effect of the wage rate as a proxy for marketing costs is also large and significant for all meats, consistent with what we would expect. The price spreads for beef and pork have positive, unexplained trends over time, while poultry shows a negative trend.

---

[17] A third approach to testing the validity of the retail consumption data is to model demand for meats as derived demand functions directly (Brester and Wohlgenant 1993). This results in a model with an index of marketing inputs as an additional variable in the model. Under constant returns to scale, the elasticity of derived demand with respect to this variable and elasticity of demand with respect to retail price can be used to identify the true retail demand elasticity. The wage rate variable was included in the conditional demand functions for beef and veal, pork, and poultry, and found statistically insignificant in all three cases, suggesting no significant bias with use of disappearance data in this application.

**Table 7.9** Estimates of Retail-to-Farm Price Ratios for Beef and Veal, Pork, and Poultry, 1970–2010

| Term | Estimate | Approx Std Err | t Value | Approx Pr > \|t\| |
|---|---|---|---|---|
| Beef and Veal | | | | |
| $\pi_{pr0}$ | 0.021585 | 0.00821 | 2.63 | 0.0123 |
| $\pi_{prz}$ | −0.69118 | 0.0775 | −8.91 | <.0001 |
| $\pi_{prm}$ | 0.691182 | 0.0775 | 8.91 | <.0001 |
| $\pi_{prw}$ | 0.509228 | 0.0571 | 8.91 | <.0001 |
| Pork | | | | |
| $\pi_{pr0}$ | 0.033794 | 0.0169 | 2.00 | 0.0528 |
| $\pi_{prz}$ | −1.19682 | 0.0805 | −14.87 | <.0001 |
| $\pi_{prm}$ | 1.196824 | 0.0805 | 14.87 | <.0001 |
| $\pi_{prw}$ | 1.286837 | 0.0866 | 14.87 | <.0001 |
| Poultry | | | | |
| **πpr0** | −0.03302 | 0.0127 | −2.61 | 0.0130 |
| **πprz** | −1.86294 | 0.3104 | −6.00 | <.0001 |
| **πprm** | 1.862945 | 0.3104 | 6.00 | <.0001 |
| **πprw** | 0.641654 | 0.1069 | 6.00 | <.0001 |

Again, primary producers often point to this as evidence of increasing market power, but other factors omitted from the models (e.g., technical change) could explain these trends.

In summary, the model developed here while simple in structure, overall seems to do an adequate job of explaining changes in retail and farm prices over time in the three meat industries. These sets of equations can be combined with the retail demand equations estimated in Chapter 5 to derive the total impact of exogenous retail demand variables (e.g., income), farm supplies, and marketing costs on the retail and farm prices of the three meat commodities. Next chapter will illustrate through the empirical applications in Chapters 5 and 7 how to compute these impacts. The next chapter will also discuss how to test and modify the model for imperfect competition. Finally, models of short-run food price determination will be presented with a focus on the determinants of lags between retail and farm prices.

Terms estimated as $\pi_{pro} = \pi_{po} - \pi_{ro}$, $\pi_{prz} = \pi_{pz} - \pi_{rz}$, $\pi_{prm} = \pi_{pm} - \pi_{rm}$, and $\pi_{prw} = \pi_{pw} - \pi_{rw}$ using parameter estimates from Tables 7.6–7.8.

## Appendix: Input Substitution and Output Demand Uncertainty

The purpose of this Appendix is to show how continuous, convex-shaped isoquants can result from a linear programming problem of choosing a variable factor, $v$, in combination with a quasi-fixed factor, $m$, via two production techniques to minimize input use subject to given expected output, $q$, and a fixed available level of the factor, $b$. It is assumed that both factors, $v$ and $m$ are divisible and that $v$ is freely available in supply. This corresponds closely to livestock slaughter and processing where predetermined quantities of the livestock are scheduled for processing ahead of time, and where the plant adjusts its variable factors to meet expected demand. The Appendix parallels Liviathan (1971) for the simplest case of two production techniques.

The processor minimizes $v_1 + v_2$ (equivalently, minimizing costs, $w(v_1 + v_2)$, where$w$is fixed) subject to the production function, $q \le a_{q1}v_1 + a_{q2}v_2$, and the restriction on the availability of the raw material, $b \ge a_{m1}v_1 + a_{m2}v_2$, with $v_i \ge 0, \forall i$. The deterministic solution can be seen graphically from the figure below.

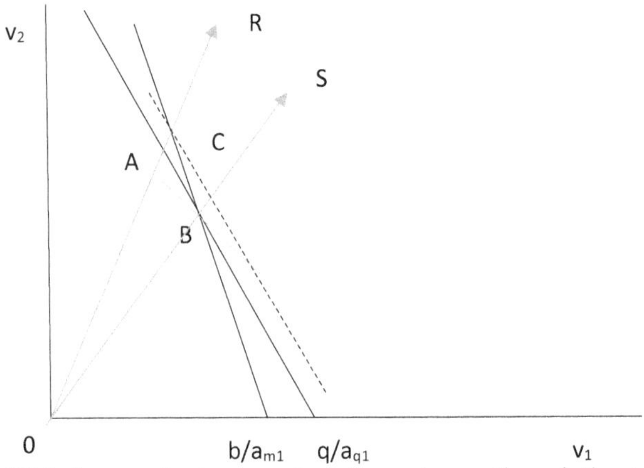


With the way the two constraints are shown, the solution to the problem is at point B where the curve intersecting point B gives the lowest possible sum of $v_1$ and $v_2$. For a given level of output, represented by the ordinate q/$a_{q1}$, there is a tradeoff between $v$ and $m$ between points A and B. At point B both constraints are satisfied, but at point A only the production constraint is met. Suppose point C is the ex ante choice of inputs with expected output given by the dotted line. This point predetermines the quasi-fixed input $m$. Suppose ex post output is given by the line segment AB. With the quasi-fixed factor fixed by point C, the input combination $v_1$ and $v_2$ will be directly below point C on the line segment AB. With the variable factor freely available, it will adjust downward to meet output $q$. In general, for the output $q$, combinations of $v_1$ and $v_2$ would be distributed between A and B. For points to the left of the ray OC, whose slope is $\frac{a_{q1}}{a_{m1}}$, the optimum relationship between $v$and$b$ for given $q$ is $v = \gamma^1 q - \beta^1 b$ where $\beta^1 = 0$. For points to the right of $\frac{a_{q1}}{a_{m1}}$, the optimum relationship between $v$and$m$ for given $q$ is $v = \gamma^2 q - \beta^2 b$.

Define $\alpha(b) = \frac{a_{q1}}{a_{m1}}$ and let $f(q, m) = \gamma q - \beta b$ and let the probability density function for demand be $h(q)$ such that $\int_L^U h(q)dq = 1$. The relationship between the

expected value of $v$ and output is $E(v) = \int_{L}^{\alpha(b)} f(q,b)h(q)dq + \int_{\alpha(b)}^{U} f(q,b)h(q)dq$.
Partially differentiating with respect to $b$ we obtain

$$\frac{\partial E(v)}{\partial b} = \int_{L}^{\alpha(b)} \frac{\partial f(q,b)}{\partial b}h(q)dq - \int_{\alpha(b)}^{U} \frac{\partial f(q,b)}{\partial b}h(q)dq$$

$$= \int_{L}^{\alpha(b)} \beta^1 h(q)dq - \int_{\alpha(b)}^{U} -\beta^2 h(q)dq \quad \text{or}$$

$$\frac{\partial E(v)}{\partial b} = \beta^2 \int_{\alpha(b)}^{U} h(q)dq$$

because $\beta^1 = 0$. The marginal rate of substitution between $b$ and $v$ is MRS $= -\frac{\partial E(v)}{\partial b}$. Differentiating with respect to $b$:

$$\frac{\partial MRS}{\partial b} = -\beta^2 h(\alpha(b))\alpha(b) < 0$$

Therefore, the MRS is continuously differentiable and convex to the origin as postulated.

**Problems**

7.1 It is frequently observed that income and the farm value share are negatively correlated. Using the Gardner long-run competitive model of the food industry, explain two ways in how this could occur. Do these conditions seem reasonable?

7.2 For pork where we find the elasticity of substitution is not significantly different from zero, calculate the new reduced-form parameters using Eqs. (7.78)–(7.80) using data from Table 7.2.

7.3 Define incidence of marketing charges on farmers as $I_{r,w} = \frac{\left|\frac{dlogr}{dlogw}\right|}{\left(\left|\frac{dlogr}{dlogw}\right| + \left|\frac{dlogp}{dlogw}\right|\right)}$. Calculate values of $I_{r,w}$ for beef and veal, pork, and poultry from the empirical results in Tables 7.6 and 7.8 for beef and veal and poultry, and from problem 7.2 for pork. Explain why there are differences in the incidence of marketing charges across commodities.

7.4 The Wohlgenant (1989) model takes farm quantities as predetermined in the short run. Suppose over a period of time, producers are able to adjust supplies in response to the change in farm price. In particular, suppose that the supply elasticities for beef and veal, pork, and poultry are 0.5, 1.0, and 3.0. Using the results from Tables 7.6–7.8 estimate the effects of exogenous shifts in demand, processing costs, and farm supplies on retail and farm prices for each commodity. Assume that for each commodity, supply changes can be written as $Er_i = (1/\varepsilon_i)Em_i + Es_i$, where $\varepsilon_i$ is the supply elasticity of commodity and $Es_i$

is the (vertical) relative change in supply. Discuss the new results incorporating the supply functions, and compare with the results in Tables 7.6–7.8.

7.5 The COVID-19 pandemic caused disruptions in red meat and poultry processing. In some instances, there was more than a 40 percent reduction in the workforce. Using the comparative static results from Gardner's model with the parameter estimates from this study, calculate the effect of a 10 percent reduction in employment on retail-to-farm price ratios for the three meat commodities. For determinate solutions, assume that the short-run supply elasticity for each farm input is 0.1. Discuss the results and explain why meat processors would not necessarily profit from the increase in the price spread, in this instance.

## References


Allen, R.G.D. *Mathematical Analysis for Economists.* London: Macmillan & Co., 1938.

Alston, J.A., and G.M. Scobie. "Distribution of Research Gains in Multistage Production Systems: Comment." *American Journal of Agricultural Economics* 65(1983): 353–356.

Amemyia, T. *Advanced Econometrics.* Cambridge, MA: Harvard University Press, 1985.

Braulke, M. "The Firm in Short-Run Equilibrium: Comment." *The American Economic Review* 74(1984): 750–753.

Braulke, M. "On the Comparative Statics of a Competitive Industry." *The American Economic Review* 77(1987): 479–485.

Brester, Gary W., and Michael K. Wohlgenant. "Correcting for Measurement Error in Food Demand Estimation." *The Review of Economics and Statistics* 75(1993): 352–356.

Buccola, S.T. "Material and Value-Adding Inputs in Manufacturing Enterprises." *Journal of Productivity Analysis* 13(2000): 231–247.

Diewert, W.E. "The Comparative Statics of Long-Run Equilibrium." *Canadian Journal of Economics* 14(1981): 78–92.

Friedman, M. *Price Theory.* Chicago: Aldine Publishing Co., 1976.

Gallant, A.R. *Nonlinear Statistical Models.* New York: Wiley, 1987.

Gardner, B. "The Farm-Retail Price Spread in a Competitive Food Industry." *American Journal of Agricultural Economics* 57(1975): 399–409.

George, P.S., and G.A. King. *Consumer Demand for Food Commodities in the United State with Projections for 1980.* Giannini Foundation Monograph No. 26, *California Agricultural Experiment Station,* Berkeley, CA, 1971.

Goodwin, B.K., and G.W. Brester. "Structural Change in Factor Demand Relationships in the U.S. Food and Kindred Products Industry." *American Journal of Agricultural Economics* 77(1995): 69–79.

Hadley, G. *Linear Algebra.* Reading, MA: Addison-Wesley Publishing Company, Inc., 1961.

Hausman, J.A. "Specification Tests in Econometrics." *Econometrica* 46(1978): 1251–1271.

Heiner, R.A. "Theory of the Firm in 'Short-Run' Industry Equilibrium." *The American Economic Review* 82(1982): 555–562.

Hicks, J.R. *The Theory of Wages.* New York: St. Martin's Press, 1957.

Liviatan, N. "The Marginalist Principle in a Discrete Production Model under Uncertain Demand." *Quarterly Journal of Economics* 85(1971): 684–709.

Marshall, A. *Principles of Economics.* New York: MacMillan Co. Ltd., Inc., 1920.

Miedema, A.K. "The Retail-Farm Price Ratio, the Farmer's Share and Technical Change." *American Journal of Agricultural Economics* 58(1976): 750–756.

Mosak, J.L. "Interrelations of Production, Price, and Derived Demand." *Journal of Political Economy* 46(1938): 761–787.

Mundlak, Y., and H. Huang. "International Comparisons of Cattle Cycles." *American Journal of Agricultural Economics* 78(1996): 855–868.

Panzar, J.C., and R.D. Willig. "On the Comparative Statics of a Competitive Industry with Inframarginal Firms." *The American Economic Review* 68(1978): 474–478.

Stigler, G.J., and G.S. Becker. "De Gustibus Non Est Disputandum." *The American Economic Review* 67(1977): 76–90.

Vernon, J.M., and D.A. Graham. "Profitability of Monopolization by Vertical Integration." *Journal of Political Economy* 79(1971): 924–925.

Walters, A.A. "Marginal Productivity and Probability Distributions of Factor Services." *The Economic Journal* 70(1960): 325–330.

Wegge, L.L. "Constrained Indirect Least Squares Estimators." *Econometrica* 46(1978): 435–449.

Wohlgenant, M.K. "Demand for Farm Output in a Complete System of Demand Functions." *American Journal of Agricultural Economics* 71 (1989): 241–252.

Wohlgenant, M.K. "Marketing Margins: Empirical Analysis." In B.L. Gardner and G.C. Rausser (eds.) *Handbook of Agricultural Economics*, Vol. 1B, pp. 934–970. Amsterdam: Elsevier Science B.V., 2001, Chapter 16.

Wohlgenant, M.K., and J.D. Mullen. "Modeling the Farm-Retail Price Spread for Beef." *Western Journal of Agricultural Economics* 12(1987): 119–125.

Wohlgenant, M.K., and R.C. Haidacher. *Retail to Farm Demand Linkages of a Complete System of Demand Functions*, USDA Technical Bulletion No. 1775, Washington, 1989.

Wohlgenant, Michael K. "Consumer Demand and Welfare in Equilibrium Displacement Models." In Lusk, J., J. Roosen, and J. Shogren (eds.) *Handbook on the Economics of Food Consumption and Policy*. London: Oxford University Press, 2011, Chapter 11.

Wohlgenant, Michael K. "Distribution of Gains from Research and Promotion in Multi-Stage Production Systems: The Case of the U.S. Beef and Pork Industries." *American Journal of Agricultural Economics* 75(1993): 642–651. (Errata: 75(1993): 1072.).

Wohlgenant, Michael K. "Market Middlemen and Determinants of the Price Spread Under Competition." *Theoretical Economics Letters* 4(2014): 834–838.

# Chapter 8
# Retail-to-Farm Demand Linkages, Imperfect Competition, and Short-Run Price Determination

## 8.1 Introduction

In this chapter, we build on Chapter 7 in three important ways. First, we consider both vertical and horizontal effects on derived demand for raw materials. In the last chapter, we showed how retail-to-farm price linkages could be formulated and estimated consistently. While the approach allows us to go one step further and derive total impacts of retail demand, farm supply, and marketing costs on derived demand, we need to derive the properties of these generalized derived demands first. Second, we need to evaluate the approach in light of role imperfect competition may play on the price relationships. Finally, how does short-run price determination differ via lags between retail and farm prices and the role played by inventories?

## 8.2 Generalized Derived Demand Relationships

Consider the most general case where we have a set of outputs and inputs combined via a general multi-output, multi-input production function, $f(\boldsymbol{q}, \boldsymbol{m}, \boldsymbol{va}) = 0$ where $\boldsymbol{q}$ is a vector of outputs, $\boldsymbol{m}$ is a corresponding vector of raw material inputs, and $\boldsymbol{va}$ is a vector of value-adding inputs associated with the $n$ products. Under quite general conditions, we know there exists a profit function, $\pi(\boldsymbol{p}, \boldsymbol{r}, \boldsymbol{w}) = \max_{\boldsymbol{q},\boldsymbol{m}}\left[\boldsymbol{p}'\boldsymbol{q} - \boldsymbol{r}'\boldsymbol{m} - c(\boldsymbol{q}, \boldsymbol{m}, \boldsymbol{w})\right]$ where $c(\boldsymbol{q}, \boldsymbol{m}, \boldsymbol{w}) = \min_{l}\left[\boldsymbol{w}'\boldsymbol{l} : f(\boldsymbol{q}, \boldsymbol{m}, \boldsymbol{va}(\boldsymbol{l})) = 0\right]$. The profit function is homogeneous of degree one and convex in prices. Application of Hotelling's theorem yields:

$$\frac{\partial \pi(\boldsymbol{p}, \boldsymbol{r}, \boldsymbol{w})}{\partial \boldsymbol{p}} = \boldsymbol{S}(\boldsymbol{p}, \boldsymbol{r}, \boldsymbol{w})$$

 
M. K. Wohlgenant, *Market Interrelationships and Applied Demand Analysis*, Palgrave Studies in Agricultural Economics and Food Policy,
https://doi.org/10.1007/978-3-030-73144-1_8

$$\frac{\partial \pi(\boldsymbol{p}, \boldsymbol{r}, \boldsymbol{w})}{\partial \boldsymbol{r}} = -\boldsymbol{m}(\boldsymbol{p}, \boldsymbol{r}, \boldsymbol{w})$$

These multi-product, multi-input supply, and input demand functions may be combined with the corresponding system of consumer demand functions, $\boldsymbol{q} = \boldsymbol{D}(\boldsymbol{p}, z)$ where **z** is a vector of exogenous demand shift variables. In total differential form, market equilibrium, taking $\boldsymbol{r}$ and $\boldsymbol{w}$ exogenous, is:

$$d\boldsymbol{q} = \boldsymbol{D}_{\boldsymbol{p}}(\boldsymbol{p}, z)d\boldsymbol{p} + \boldsymbol{D}_z(\boldsymbol{p}, z)dz \tag{8.1}$$

$$d\boldsymbol{q} = \boldsymbol{S}_{\boldsymbol{p}}(\boldsymbol{p}, \boldsymbol{r}, \boldsymbol{w})d\boldsymbol{p} + \boldsymbol{S}_{\boldsymbol{r}}(\boldsymbol{p}, \boldsymbol{r}, \boldsymbol{w})d\boldsymbol{r} + \boldsymbol{S}_{\boldsymbol{w}}(\boldsymbol{p}, \boldsymbol{r}, \boldsymbol{w})d\boldsymbol{w} \tag{8.2}$$

$$d\boldsymbol{m} = \boldsymbol{m}_{\boldsymbol{p}}(\boldsymbol{p}, \boldsymbol{r}, \boldsymbol{w})d\boldsymbol{p} + \boldsymbol{m}_{\boldsymbol{r}}(\boldsymbol{p}, \boldsymbol{r}, \boldsymbol{w})d\boldsymbol{r} + \boldsymbol{m}_{\boldsymbol{w}}(\boldsymbol{p}, \boldsymbol{r}, \boldsymbol{w})d\boldsymbol{w}$$

Using the Slutsky decomposition, $\boldsymbol{D}_{\boldsymbol{p}}(\boldsymbol{p}, z) = \boldsymbol{D}^c_{\boldsymbol{p}}(\boldsymbol{p}, z) - \boldsymbol{q}_y\boldsymbol{q}'$ from (2.15) in (8.1) and equating the result with (8.2) yields the two-equation system:

$$\boldsymbol{S}_{\boldsymbol{p}}d\boldsymbol{p} + \boldsymbol{S}_{\boldsymbol{r}}d\boldsymbol{r} + \boldsymbol{S}_{\boldsymbol{w}}d\boldsymbol{w} = \boldsymbol{D}^c_{\boldsymbol{p}}d\boldsymbol{p} + \boldsymbol{q}_y\left(dy - \boldsymbol{q}'d\boldsymbol{p}\right) + \boldsymbol{D}_z dz$$

$$d\boldsymbol{m} = \boldsymbol{m}_{\boldsymbol{p}}d\boldsymbol{p} + \boldsymbol{m}_{\boldsymbol{r}}d\boldsymbol{r} + \boldsymbol{m}_{\boldsymbol{w}}d\boldsymbol{w}$$

or

$$\left(\boldsymbol{S}_{\boldsymbol{p}} - \boldsymbol{D}^c_{\boldsymbol{p}}\right)d\boldsymbol{p} + \boldsymbol{S}_{\boldsymbol{r}}d\boldsymbol{r} + \boldsymbol{S}_{\boldsymbol{w}}d\boldsymbol{w} = \boldsymbol{D}_{\boldsymbol{I}}d\boldsymbol{I} \tag{8.3}$$

$$d\boldsymbol{m} = \boldsymbol{m}_{\boldsymbol{p}}d\boldsymbol{p} + \boldsymbol{m}_{\boldsymbol{r}}d\boldsymbol{r} + \boldsymbol{m}_{\boldsymbol{w}}d\boldsymbol{w} \tag{8.4}$$

where $\boldsymbol{D}_{\boldsymbol{I}}d\boldsymbol{I} = \boldsymbol{q}_y\left(dy - \boldsymbol{q}'d\boldsymbol{p}\right) + \boldsymbol{D}_z dz$. This model is obviously a generalization of (7.49) because it allows for multiple products and multiple raw materials. For food processing and marketing, this is especially important because raw materials are often used in different products. Conceptually, the demand functions, which account for the endogeneity of retail prices and quantities are industry derived demand functions and of interest directly for applied demand and policy analysis. These generalized derived demand functions can be characterized as the solutions to (8.3) and (8.4):

$$\begin{aligned} d\boldsymbol{m}^*(\boldsymbol{r}, \boldsymbol{w}, \boldsymbol{I}) &= \boldsymbol{m}_{\boldsymbol{p}}\left(\boldsymbol{S}_{\boldsymbol{p}} - \boldsymbol{D}^c_{\boldsymbol{p}}\right)^{-1}\boldsymbol{D}_{\boldsymbol{I}}d\boldsymbol{I} \\ &+\left[-\boldsymbol{m}_{\boldsymbol{p}}\left(\boldsymbol{S}_{\boldsymbol{p}} - \boldsymbol{D}^c_{\boldsymbol{p}}\right)^{-1}\boldsymbol{S}_{\boldsymbol{r}} + \boldsymbol{m}_{\boldsymbol{r}}\right]d\boldsymbol{r} \\ &+\left[-\boldsymbol{m}_{\boldsymbol{p}}\left(\boldsymbol{S}_{\boldsymbol{p}} - \boldsymbol{D}^c_{\boldsymbol{p}}\right)^{-1}\boldsymbol{S}_{\boldsymbol{w}} + \boldsymbol{m}_{\boldsymbol{w}}\right]d\boldsymbol{w} \end{aligned} \tag{8.5}$$

where the *nxn* matrix of partial derivatives of the derived demand functions are:

$$m_r^*(r, w, I) = -m_p\left(S_p - D_p^c\right)^{-1} S_r + m_r \tag{8.6}$$

### 8.2.1 Properties of System of Derived Demand Functions

Heiner (1982, 1984), Braulke (1984, 1987), and Chavas and Cox (1997) develop the theoretical properties of the generalized derived demand functions, including implications for welfare measurement (Chavas and Cox 1997).[1] The properties of these demand functions are stated in Theorem 3.

***Theorem 3*** The generalized derived demand response matrix, $m_r^*(r, w, I)$ is bounded between two negative semi-definite matrices, one being the matrix of output-constant demand responses, $m_r^c(r, w, q)$ and the other the matrix of output-price constant demand responses, $m_r(r, w, p)$. Thus, the difference between the two matrices, $m_r^*(r, w, I)$ is negative semi-definite.

Proof:

From (8.3), define $P_r = -\left(S_p - D_p^c\right)^{-1} S_r$ and rewrite (8.6) as: $m_r^* = m_p P_r + m_r$. From the properties of the profit function, we know that $m_r$ is a negative semi-definite matrix. Also, $-m_p P_r = S_r' P_r = -S_r'\left(S_p - D_p^c\right)^{-1} S_r$ is negative semi-definite. This is because of the reciprocity condition, $m_p = -S_r'$ and the fact that $\left(S_p - D_p^c\right)^{-1}$ is positive semi-definite. Therefore, $m_r - m_r^* = -m_p P_r$ is negative semi-definite.

We can characterize the output-constant demand response functions by solving (8.3) for $dp$ when $D_p^c = 0$ and substituting into (8.4) to obtain: $m_r^c = m_r + m_p P_r^c = m_r^* - m_p P_r + m_p P_r^c \leq 0$, $P_r^c = -S_p^{-1} S_r$. We thus have, $m_r^* - m_r^c = m_p\left(P_r - P_r^c\right) = S_r'\left[\left(S_p - D_p^c\right)^{-1} - S_p^{-1}\right] S_r$, which is a negative semi-definite matrix.[2] Hence, $m_r^*(r, w, I)$, is bounded by two negative semi-definite matrices and therefore is a negative semi-definite matrix. QED

[1] The theorem here is different and new in that it is for derived demand functions that depend on real income through the Slutsky decomposition. The past studies cited assumed "normal" conditions on Marshallian demand elasticities such that own-price elasticities exceed cross-price elasticities. Such a requirement is not implied by Theory. Use of Hicksian demand functions insures negative semi-definiteness and is actually more relevant for policy analysis (Friedman 1976, Chapter 2).

[2] This is because $\left(S_p - D_p^c\right) - S_p \geq 0$. Multiplying both sides by $\left(S_p - D_p^c\right)^{-1}$ gives $I - \left(S_p - D_p^c\right)^{-1} S_p \geq 0$. Finally post-multiplying by $S_p^{-1}$ gives $S_p^{-1} - \left(S_p - D_p^c\right)^{-1} \geq 0$. Thus, $S_r'\left[\left(S_p - D_p^c\right)^{-1} - S_p^{-1}\right] S_r = -S_r'\left[S_p^{-1} - \left(S_p - D_p^c\right)^{-1}\right] S_r \leq 0.$,

In addition to the property of negative semi-definiteness, the generalized demand functions, $\boldsymbol{m}^*(\boldsymbol{r}, \boldsymbol{w}, \boldsymbol{I})$ are homogeneous of degree zero in prices.[3] The significance of Theorem 3 is that the matrix of total effects of farm quantities on farm prices derived from the three sets of equations from (7.72) and (7.73) will be negative semi-definite because it will be precisely the inverse of the generalized derived demand functions. We shall now derive these total effects from changes in farm supplies as well as effects of other exogenous variables on farm prices and retail prices. We shall also derive the generalized derived demand elasticities for beef and veal, pork, and poultry.

Define $\boldsymbol{\pi}_{pz} = [\pi_{piz}], \boldsymbol{\pi}_{rz} = [\pi_{riz}], \boldsymbol{\pi}_{pw} = [\pi_{piw}], \boldsymbol{\pi}_{rw} = [\pi_{riw}], \boldsymbol{\pi}_{pm} = [\pi_{pim}]$, and $\boldsymbol{\pi}_{rm} = [\pi_{rim}]$. With exception of $\boldsymbol{\pi}_{pm}$ and $\boldsymbol{\pi}_{rm}$, these are square, diagonal matrices; $\boldsymbol{\pi}_{pm}$ and $\boldsymbol{\pi}_{rm}$ are $3 \times 1$ vectors. The parameter estimates for three matrices and vectors are obtained from Tables 7.6–7.8. Also define $\boldsymbol{e}^-$ as the square matrix of cross-price elasticities for beef, pork, and poultry, whose diagonal elements are zero. Parameters for this matrix come from Table 7.2. Define $\boldsymbol{e}^o$ as the $3 \times 5$ matrix of exogenous demand shift parameters corresponding to retail fish price (fishp), retail nonmeat prices (nmeatsp), retail nonfood prices (nfoodp), real per capita pce (ppce), and population (pop). The parameter values are obtained from Table 7.2. Given these definitions, the six retail and farm price equations, (7.72) and (7.73) can be written in matrix notation as follows:

$$E\boldsymbol{p} = \boldsymbol{\pi}_{pm} E\boldsymbol{m} + \boldsymbol{\pi}_{pw} E w + \boldsymbol{\pi}_{pz} \boldsymbol{e}^- E\boldsymbol{p} + \boldsymbol{\pi}_{pz} \boldsymbol{e}^o E\boldsymbol{I} \tag{8.7}$$

$$E\boldsymbol{r} = \boldsymbol{\pi}_{rm} E\boldsymbol{m} + \boldsymbol{\pi}_{rw} E w + \boldsymbol{\pi}_{rz} \boldsymbol{e}^- E\boldsymbol{p} + \boldsymbol{\pi}_{rz} \boldsymbol{e}^o E\boldsymbol{I} \tag{8.8}$$

where $E\boldsymbol{I}$ is the $4 \times 1$ vector of proportional changes in the exogenous retail demand shift variables. The formulas for solutions to retail and farm prices are as follows:

$$E\boldsymbol{p} = \left(\boldsymbol{I} - \boldsymbol{\pi}_{pz}\boldsymbol{e}^-\right)^{-1}\left(\boldsymbol{\pi}_{pm} E\boldsymbol{m} + \boldsymbol{\pi}_{pw} E w + \boldsymbol{\pi}_{pz} \boldsymbol{e}^o E\boldsymbol{I}\right) \tag{8.9}$$

$$\begin{aligned} E\boldsymbol{r} &= \left[\boldsymbol{\pi}_{rm} + \boldsymbol{\pi}_{rz}\boldsymbol{e}^-\left(\boldsymbol{I} - \boldsymbol{\pi}_{pz}\boldsymbol{e}^-\right)^{-1}\boldsymbol{\pi}_{pm}\right] E\boldsymbol{m} \\ &+ \left[\boldsymbol{\pi}_{rw} + \boldsymbol{\pi}_{rz}\boldsymbol{e}^-\left(\boldsymbol{I} - \boldsymbol{\pi}_{pz}\boldsymbol{e}^-\right)^{-1}\boldsymbol{\pi}_{pw}\right] E w \\ &+ \left[\boldsymbol{\pi}_{rz} + \boldsymbol{\pi}_{rz}\boldsymbol{e}^-\left(\boldsymbol{I} - \boldsymbol{\pi}_{pz}\boldsymbol{e}^-\right)^{-1}\boldsymbol{\pi}_{pm}\right] \boldsymbol{e}^0 E\boldsymbol{I} \end{aligned} \tag{8.10}$$

Finally, the solutions to relative change in the generalized derived demand functions are:

[3] As in Chapter 7, with the Slutsky decomposition, consumer demand relationships are expressed in terms of relative prices and real income. With multi-product supply and multi-input demand functions homogeneous of degree zero in prices, it follows that the industry derived demand functions must also be homogenous of degree zero in prices.

$$
\begin{aligned}
Em = \\
&\left[\pi_{rm} + \pi_{rz}e^{-}\left(I - \pi_{pz}e^{-}\right)^{-1}\pi_{pm}\right]^{-1} Er \\
-&\left[\pi_{rm} + \pi_{rz}e^{-}\left(I - \pi_{pz}e^{-}\right)^{-1}\pi_{pm}\right]^{-1}\left[\pi_{rw} + \pi_{rz}e^{-}\left(I - \pi_{pz}e^{-}\right)^{-1}\pi_{pw}\right]Ew \\
-&\left[\pi_{rm} + \pi_{rz}e^{-}\left(I - \pi_{pz}e^{-}\right)^{-1}\pi_{pm}\right]^{-1}\left[\pi_{rz} + \pi_{rz}e^{-}\left(I - \pi_{pz}e^{-}\right)^{-1}\pi_{pm}\right]e^{0}E
\end{aligned}
\tag{8.11}
$$

### 8.2.2 *Total Demand Elasticities for Retail-to-Farm Demand Linkages for Meats*

Equations (8.9)–(8.11) are used to compute total effects of farm supplies, the wage rate, and exogenous retail demand shifters on farm prices, retail prices, and industry derived demands as shown in Table 8.1.[4] The results are completely consistent with both the theory of consumer demand relationships estimated in Chapter 5 and the retail-to-farm price linkage equations, depicting market intermediary behavior, from Chapter 7. They show how prices and quantities would expect to be affected from changes in the relevant exogenous variable. The impact of farm supplies on both farm and retail prices is quite large as one might expect. The cross-quantity effects are all negative as well, indicating these inputs are net substitutes for one another. Somewhat surprisingly, the wage rate representing marketing costs only has small effects on farm and retail prices when farm supplies are regarded as predetermined. Also, real nonfood prices, real personal consumption expenditures, and population have relatively large effects on farm and retail prices. Note that other food nonmeat prices have relatively small effects on prices. Because of strong separability we could disaggregate this price variable into subgroups such as dairy, fats and oils, bakery products, and fruits and vegetables, etc. We would need to know the relative weights on these indices which, in theory, would be marginal price indices. However, as discussed in Chapter 3, one might approximate these weights by relative expenditure shares. At any rate, the effects would be expected to be small because of the small relative impacts of nonmeat prices as a composite good.

The last two sets of elasticities in Table 8.1 are parameters of the system of derived demand functions and retail price equations as functions of raw material prices and the wage rate. We know from Theorem 3 that the matrix of compensated price effects should be negative semi-definite. The derived demand own-price elasticities are negative as expected. Cross-price elasticities are all positive indicating net substitutes for one another. Because the underlying industry structure exhibits constant-returns-to-scale (CRTS), the cross-price effects result from retail demand

[4]Standard errors are not reported. Asymptotic standard errors could be computed using, for example, the formulas provided by Theil (1971, pp. 537–538).

**Table 8.1** Total Impacts of Farm Supplies, Wage Rate, and Exogenous Retail Demand Shift Variables on Farm Prices, Retail Prices, and Derived Demands for Beef and Veal, Pork, and Poultry

| | | | | | | **Elasticity** | | | | |
|---|---|---|---|---|---|---|---|---|---|---|
| Farm price | | **beefm** | **porkm** | **poultm** | **wage** | **fishp** | **nmeatp** | **nfoodp** | **ppce** | **pop** |
| beef | | -1.92774 | -0.4107 | -0.12553 | -0.16621 | 0.02741 | 0.087214 | 1.107927 | 1.551122 | 2.463971 |
| pork | | -1.06122 | -2.29404 | -0.08765 | -0.6306 | 0.195581 | 0.129697 | 1.647621 | 2.306594 | 3.44291 |
| poultry | | -0.60557 | -0.33515 | -3.30961 | 0.032181 | -0.51516 | 0.12329 | 1.566215 | 2.192606 | 4.250319 |
| | | | | | | **Elasticity** | | | | |
| **Retail price** | | **beefm** | **porkm** | **poultm** | **wage** | **fishp** | **nmeatp** | **nfoodp** | **ppce** | **pop** |
| beef | | -1.15664 | -0.24642 | -0.07532 | -0.00227 | 0.016446 | 0.052328 | 0.664757 | 0.930673 | 1.478382 |
| pork | | -0.47755 | -1.03232 | -0.03944 | -0.28377 | 0.088011 | 0.058364 | 0.741429 | 1.037967 | 1.54931 |
| poultry | | -0.26039 | -0.14411 | -1.42313 | 0.307926 | -0.22152 | 0.053015 | 0.673472 | 0.942821 | 1.827637 |
| | | | | | | **Elasticity** | | | | |
| **Farm Quanity** | | **beefr** | **porkr** | **poultr** | **wage** | **fishp** | **nmeatp** | **nfoodp** | **ppce** | **pop** |
| beef | | -0.58047 | 0.101097 | 0.01934 | -0.03335 | 0.006101 | 0.035129 | 0.446262 | 0.62479 | 1 |
| pork | | 0.265495 | -0.48384 | 0.002744 | -0.26107 | 0.088767 | 0.03926 | 0.498746 | 0.698202 | 1 |
| poultry | | 0.079325 | 0.030498 | -0.30597 | 0.042263 | -0.16576 | 0.026849 | 0.341074 | 0.477475 | 1 |
| | | | **Elasticity** | | | | | | | |
| **Retail price** | | **beefr** | **porkr** | **poultr** | **wage** | | | | | |
| beef | | 0.6 | | | 0.4 | | | | | |
| pork | | | 0.45 | | 0.55 | | | | | |
| poultry | | | | 0.43 | 0.57 | | | | | |

interdependencies. For example, an increase in the price of swine increases the retail price of pork, which in turn increases retail beef demand and farm-level demand for beef. Relative to own-price effects, the cross-price elasticities are small. As in the case of consumer demand, the closest substitutes are between beef and veal and pork. Exogenous retail demand shift variables are all equal to the horizontal increases in retail demand because of CRTS. Likewise, the elasticities of the retail prices with respect to farm prices and wage rates are the value shares of those inputs due to CRTS.

## 8.3 Imperfect Competition and Market Intermediaries

Mainly because of high concentration ratios, market intermediaries in the food industry have been accused of exercising market power in both output and input markets. Nowhere have these accusations been more common than in the meat industries. As a result, numerous studies have been conducted to both test for and estimate the degree of market power. In what follows, I will review the basic approaches taken to model imperfect competition and discuss their implications for the food industry, especially the meat industries.

### *8.3.1 Review of Different Models*

The New Empirical Industrial Organization (NEIO) literature (Breshnahan 1989) has been the source of the majority of models developed to test for and estimate the degree of market power. Breshnahan (1989) starts with the basic relationship for a given firm:

$$p = -\theta q \frac{\partial p}{\partial q} + MC$$

Where $\theta$ is an index of market power, ranging from zero to one. If $\theta = 0$, we have price-taking behavior with price equaling marginal cost; if, at the other extreme, $\theta = 1$, we have monopoly. On the input side, we have the condition (Murray 1995; Muth and Wohlgenant 1999b):

$$r = -\phi m \frac{\partial r}{\partial m} + MVP$$

where $\phi$ is an index of market power in the market for the raw material, ranging from zero to one as in market power in the output market. Here $\frac{\partial r}{\partial m}$ is the slope of the market inverse supply function as $\frac{\partial p}{\partial q}$ above is the slope of the market inverse demand function. $MVP$ refers to marginal value product, which could either be $p \cdot mp$ or

$mr \cdot mp$, depending upon competitive conditions in the output market. Noting that the price elasticity of demand is $e = \frac{1}{\frac{\partial p}{\partial q} \cdot \frac{q}{p}}$ and the price elasticity of supply is $e = \frac{1}{\frac{\partial p}{\partial q} \cdot \frac{q}{p}}$, the above two expressions for the output and raw material markets can be written as follows:

$$p\left(1 + \frac{\theta}{e}\right) = c_q(q, w) \tag{8.12}$$

$$r\left(1 + \frac{\phi}{\varepsilon_m}\right) = \pi_m(m, p, w) \tag{8.13}$$

where I have used as a fact that the partial derivative of the restricted profit function with respect to quantity of the raw material quantity is the marginal factor cost (Diewert 1974). The restricted profit function is defined as $\pi(m, p, w) = \max_{q,l}\left\{pq - \mathbf{w}'\mathbf{l} \middle| q = f[(m, va(\mathbf{l}))]\right\}$, where, as before, $w$ is the price index of value-adding inputs. The reason for this last formulation, (8.13), is because we often do not have quantities of inputs other than the farm input (Muth and Wohlgenant 1999b).

Breshnahan (1982) and Lau (1982) have shown that the market power parameter in (8.12) is not identifiable unless the demand function is non-separable in at least one of the exogenous demand shifters. By extension, market power in the farm input market would not be identifiable unless the supply function is non-separable in at least one of the exogenous supply shifters. One of the earliest, and most notable applications, is Appelbaum (1982), who used a constant elasticity demand function with a separable cost function (marginal cost independent of output) applied to four industries: rubber, textiles, electrical machinery, and tobacco industries. Muth and Wohlgenant (1999b) make beef supply a non-linear function of corn price and inventory of cattle. Just and Chern (1980) make the supply of tomatoes a function of non-linear technical change from introducing the tomato harvester.

As indicated by Lau (1982), the above results do not consider restrictions on the cost function which can help us identify the market power parameter. One common assumption in agricultural economics studies is fixed input proportions, in which case the cost function can be written as follows: $c = raq + c^p(q, w)$, where $m = aq$, according to (7.7), and $c^p(q, w)$ is the processing component of costs. This is the approach of Schroeter (1988) applied to the beef industry. He shows that this specification implies the indices of market power for the output and farm input markets are the same. The resulting equation for estimation is:

$$p\left(1 + \frac{\theta}{e}\right) = ar\left(1 + \frac{\theta}{\varepsilon_m}\right) + \frac{\partial c^p(q, w)}{\partial q} \tag{8.14}$$

Another approach to specifying and testing for market power was originally proposed by Diewert (1974, 1978). In this approach, we can replace retail price by its marginal price, and by extension, the farm price by its marginal price in the profit function. Define $p^0 = p(q^0) - \theta q^0 \frac{\partial p^0}{\partial q} = p\left(1 + \frac{\theta}{e^0}\right)$

and $r^0 = r(m^0) - \phi m^0 \frac{\partial r^0}{\partial m} = r\left(1 + \frac{\phi}{\varepsilon_m^0}\right)$. Then the profit function, $\pi = \max_{q,m,l}\left[p^0 q - r^0 m - \boldsymbol{w}'\boldsymbol{l} \middle| q = f(m, va(\boldsymbol{l}))\right] = \pi(p^0, r^0, w) = p^0 q^0 - r^0 m^0 - \boldsymbol{w}'\boldsymbol{l}^0$. That is, maximum profit with marginal prices substituted for average prices has the same value as the firm's true profit function. This is because this modified profit function is a supporting hyperplane to the profit maximization problem when marginal prices replace average prices (Diewert 1978). Following Diewert, Appelbaum (1979), Roberts (1984), and Muth and Wohlgenant (1999a) used this framework to develop a test and/or estimate the degree of imperfect competition. The profit function can be differentiated with respect to the marginal prices to obtain:

$$q^0 = S(p^0, r^0, w) = \frac{\partial \pi(p^0, r^0, w)}{\partial p^0} \tag{8.15}$$

$$m^0 = m(p^0, r^0, w) = -\frac{\partial \pi(p^0, r^0, w)}{\partial r^0} \tag{8.16}$$

The comparative statics of (8.15) and (8.16) can be characterized in terms of the marginal prices. We find with the profit function convex in prices that the supply relation, $S(p^0, r^0, w)$, is positively related to $p^0$ and negatively related to both factor prices.[5] The farm input demand relation is negatively related to $r^0$, positively related to $p^0$, and either negatively or positively related to $w$. In addition to these comparative statics, we have reciprocity relationships of the form:

$$\frac{\partial m}{\partial w} = \frac{\partial va}{\partial r^0} \tag{8.17}$$

$$\frac{\partial S}{\partial r^0} = -\frac{\partial m}{\partial p^0} \tag{8.18}$$

where $va = va(p^0, r^0, w)$ is the value-adding input demand relation, obtained as $-\frac{\partial \pi(p^0, r^0, w)}{\partial w}$.

We usually do not have data on input quantities of value-adding inputs so a test statistic will be based on (8.18). We can rewrite this relationship in terms of elasticities:

$$\varepsilon_{Sr^0} = -\frac{r^0 m}{p^0 q}\varepsilon_{mp^0} = -\frac{\left(1 + \frac{\phi}{\varepsilon_m}\right)}{\left(1 + \frac{\theta}{e}\right)} s_m \varepsilon_{mp^0} \tag{8.19}$$

---

[5]Following Breshnahan (1989), the term "relation" is used instead of relationship or function to describe both (8.15) and (8.16). The reason for this distinction is that neither a supply function nor input demand function exists in the case of imperfect competition, but rather only points in the price-quantity space. On the other hand, derivatives with respect to marginal prices can be used to properly characterize displacement from equilibrium for small changes from the initial equilibrium.

Under the null hypothesis of price-taking behavior, this relationship reduces to $\varepsilon_{Sr} = -s_m \varepsilon_{mp}$, which is the condition for competitive price-taking behavior we derived in Chapter 7. We can apply and test this condition using Eq. (7.68), $\pi_{pm} = -s_m \pi_{rz}$. I already conducted this test to see if the reduced-form models were consistent with the theory of price-taking behavior and failed to reject the restriction for all three meats. Holloway (1991) also derived a test for market power in the retail market based on the assumption of monopolistic competition. His test is equivalent to the test for CRTS, Eqs. (7.69) and (7.70), plus the restriction, $\pi_{pz} + \pi_{pm} - \pi_{rz} - \pi_{rm} = 0$, which is a restriction on the retail-farm price ratio equation. I also test for this restriction, jointly with (7.69) and (7.70), and find that I fail to reject at p-values of 0.98, 0.2, and 0.07 for beef and veal, pork, and poultry, respectively.[6]

### 8.3.2 Implications for Reduced-Form Retail and Farm Price Models

The full market interrelationships can be summarized by the set of equations depicting market equilibrium for the retail product and farm input:

$$S(p^0, r^0, w) = D((1 - L)^{-1} p^0, z) \tag{8.20}$$

$$m = D_m(p^0, r^0, w) \tag{8.21}$$

where $L = \frac{-\theta}{e}$ is the Lerner's index of market power. Let $N = \frac{\phi}{\varepsilon_m}$ be the market power index for the raw material input. Then the solutions to (8.20) and (8.21) are:

$$p = Lp + p^0(z, w, m) \tag{8.22}$$

$$r = -Nr + r^0(z, w, m) \tag{8.23}$$

because $p^0 = p - Lp$ and $r^0 = r + Nr$. Aside from the percentage markup, $L$, and percentage markdown, $N$, Eqs. (8.22) and (8.23) have the same form as the reduced form for competitive behavior as discussed in Chapter 7. In terms of structural coefficients in $p^0(z, w, m)$ and $r^0(z, w, m)$ the only difference is with respect to the own-price elasticity of demand for retail product, which now is $(1 - L)^{-1}e$, as

[6] Holloway (1991) contends that one should not use deflated data for this test. However, this is incorrect because the price elasticity of demand will be zero homogeneous in prices and income if the demand function is. This follows from the fact that first-order derivatives of a demand function will be homogeneous of degree $-1$ so when multiplied by ratio of price/quantity to obtain the elasticity, the resulting function must be homogeneous of degree zero. So long as the index of market power is independent of proportional price changes, the zero homogeneity condition will be preserved.

indicated by (8.20).[7] In general, $L$ could depend upon retail price and exogenous retail demand shifters. Likewise, $N$ could depend upon farm price and exogenous supply shifters, say $c$. Both $L$ and $N$ could also depend upon some exogenous components, $L_0$and$N_0$, respectively, which could represent things like concentration ratios. Thus, the general form of reduced-form price equations under imperfect competition would be

$$p - p(z, w, m, L_0) \tag{8.24}$$

$$r = r(z, w, m, c, N_0) \tag{8.25}$$

Note that now farm supply, $m$, would be endogenous, so that the two equations must be estimated by a simultaneous equation estimator, such as 3SLS.

It is interesting to examine in more detail Eqs. (8.22) and (8.23) when both $L$ and $M$ are approximately constant, which might occur when both the output demand and input supply functions are of the constant elasticity form. Then, after imposing the zero homogeneity restriction by deflating prices by the wage rate, we have the augmented form of model (7.72) and (7.73):

$$\Delta \log(p_{it}/w_t) = (1 - L)\big(\pi_{pio} + \pi_{piz}\Delta \log z_{it} + \pi_{pim}\Delta \log m_{it}\big) + u_{pit} \tag{8.26}$$

$$\Delta \log(r_{it}/w_t) = (1 + N)(\pi_{rio} + \pi_{riz}\Delta \log z_t + \pi_{rim}\Delta \log m_{it}) + u_{rit} \tag{8.27}$$

where now the parameters, $\pi_{ij}$, are evaluated at the marginal prices and exogenous variables. It should be clear from these two relationships that the symmetry condition, $\pi_{pm} = -s_m\pi_{rz}$, as discussed above, is altered to

$$\pi_{pm} = -\frac{(1 + N)}{(1 - L)} s_m\pi_{rz} \tag{8.28}$$

Consider the following relationship between retail and farm prices:

$$(1 - L)\pi_{pz} - (1 + N)\pi_{rz} = -(1 - L)\pi_{pm} + (1 + N)\pi_{rm} \tag{8.29}$$

Recall that when CRTS holds, $\pi_{pz} + \pi_{pm} = 0$ and $\pi_{rz} + \pi_{rm} = 0$. Thus, the relationship (8.29) will hold. Therefore, a more complete test for price-taking behavior, given the alternative hypothesis of imperfect competition, would be the two CRTS restrictions jointly with Eq. (8.29). These are precisely the conditions of Holloway (1991) in his proposition. Although his analysis only focused on the alternative of monopolistic competition, the test results here are for more general

[7]Note that $L$ must be less than one so long as marginal cost is positive. It still can be zero, which would define price-taking behavior. On the other hand, there is really no upper bound on $N$ but a value of zero would define price-taking behavior.

types of imperfect competition. So, in summary, we have as a null hypothesis: $\pi_{pm} = -s_m \pi_{rz}, \pi_{pz} + \pi_{pm} = 0, \pi_{rz} + \pi_{rm} = 0,$ and $\pi_{pz} + \pi_{pm} - \pi_{rz} - \pi_{rm} = 0.$ The joint test of these four restrictions on the three meats leads to failure to reject the null hypothesis with p-values of 0.51, 0.24, and 0.12 for beef and veal, pork, and poultry, respectively.

A relatively large number of studies conducted over the past four decades indicate little or no evidence of market power in food markets, especially livestock and meat industries, despite several calls for congressional investigations into anti-competitive behavior. A summary of these studies can be found in Wohlgenant (2001, 2013). It is a bit of a puzzle why this is so, given the relatively high concentration ratios found in many of these industries, especially the meat industries. Some possible explanations are: (a) economies of scale in processing, (b) relatively homogeneous products, and (c) competitive pricing. Morrison-Paul (2000) has shown economies of scale exist in the U.S. Beef Industry and are captured at large volumes. The goods produced by each processor in the respective meat industry are very similar to each other, although some differentiation exists through product labeling, etc. Finally, but very importantly, is the fact that number of firms does not necessarily correlate with market power. Fama and Laffler (1972) show that, under fairly general conditions, price-taking behavior can exist with only two firms. There is a growing literature on contestable markets (Baumol 1982). The idea is that existing competitors, as well as potential competitors, can replicate existing firms' costs, undercut their prices slightly, and still earn a profit. This will continue until zero economic profits are earned by existing firms.

## 8.4 Short-Run Lags in Price Determination

The discussion so far has focused on prices and price spreads in equilibrium. In the short run, it has often been observed that retail food prices lag farm price changes (Tomek and Robinson 1981). In addition, it is sometimes claimed that retail prices rise faster than they fall (Ward 1982; Kinnucan and Forker 1987; Pelzman 2000). A major concern of producers is that when production increases and farm prices fall, market middlemen fail to decrease retail prices enough.

### *8.4.1 Causes of Lags Between Retail and Farm Prices*

The main causes of lagged prices hypothesized include: (a) costs of changing prices (Parish 1967; Heien 1980; Azzam 1999); costs of holding inventories (Heien 1980; Wohlgenant 1985); and imperfect competition (Parish 1967; Ward 1982; Azzam 1999). Government intervention (e.g., price floors) can be a cause of price asymmetry (e.g., Kinnucan and Forker 1987).

One of the most comprehensive empirical studies of farm-to-retail price spreads was by Heien (1980), in which he analyzed price spreads for 22 food commodities. He found uni-directional lags from farm to retail for the large majority of the commodities. The equations were simple unrestricted distributed lags of up to four months. Other variables included a unit labor cost variable and the aggregate unemployment rate. One could also add other embellishments such as lagged prices of substitutes and income (Lamm and Westcott 1981; Freebairn 1984), or marketing margins of competing products (Griffith 1974). He also tested for asymmetry in price response with rejection of symmetry in a small number of cases. While his model was motivated by disequilibrium theory of price determination and inventory holding, the empirical models were entirely reduced-form specifications and not directly linked to the theoretical models.

### *8.4.2 Model of Short-Run Price Determination with Inventory Behavior*

A major criticism of all the approaches above is their lack of theoretical justification. Wohlgenant (1985) developed a short-run theory of food price determination by linking inventory holding to short-run price expectations and margin behavior. Inventories are held as a buffer against unanticipated demand and cost shocks, where the firm must balance the costs of holding inventories with costs of depleting inventories. Firms attempt to smooth costs by using inventories to purchase and process when raw materials are less costly. If raw material costs are expected to rise (fall) next period over this period, firms will increase (decrease) inventories to reduce costs, the sum of costs now and expected costs next period. This production cost smoothing model is consistent with the widely observed phenomena of production being more variable than sales, and consistent with the linear-quadratic inventory model with an inventory target level, and with cost changes (Eichenbaum 1989; Peeters 1997).

I assume a short time interval so that the Leontief production function, Eq. (7.7), may be used. This means production and procurement costs for time $t$ equal

$$c_{pt} = (ar_t + bw_t)q_t \tag{8.30}$$

Expected inventory costs consist of holding and depletion costs

$$\overline{c}_I = c_h \int_0^{\overline{h}+\overline{x}} \left(\overline{h} + \overline{x} - x\right) f(x)dx + c_d \int_{\overline{h}+\overline{x}}^{\infty} \left(x - \overline{h} - \overline{x}\right) f(x)dx$$

where overbars denote expected values, $h$ is inventories, $x$ is sales, $c_h$ is unit costs of holding inventories, $c_d$ is unit costs of depleting inventories, and $f(x)$ is the probability distribution of sales. In the Appendix, I show the marginal cost of expected inventories equals

$$mc_I = \frac{\partial \overline{c}_I}{\partial \overline{h}} = c_h - (c_h + c_d)\left[1 - F\left(\overline{h} + \overline{x}\right)\right] \tag{8.31}$$

where $F\left(\overline{h} + \overline{x}\right)$ is the probability of end-of-the period inventories being positive so that $\left[1 - F\left(\overline{h} + \overline{x}\right)\right]$ is the probability of inventory depletion. The formula shows that the larger $c_h$ the larger marginal costs, while the larger $c_d$ the smaller marginal costs. Notice also that marginal costs can be negative so that positive inventories can exist to provide a convenience yield (Brennan 1958).

Following Holt et al. (1960), I assume that inventory costs can be approximated by the quadratic function

$$c_{It} = \frac{c_I}{2}[h_t - g_0 - gx_t]^2 \tag{8.32}$$

As shown in the Appendix, the marginal cost function from (8.32), $c_I[h_t - g_0 - gx_t]$, has cost coefficients that match exactly the first-order derivatives of (8.31) with respect to expected inventories and expected sales. Of particular interest is the fact that the parameter $g_0$ is equal to the negative of initial marginal cost divided by $c_I$. Therefore, marginal cost could be written as

$$mc_I^0 + c_I[h_t - gx_t]$$

where $mc_I^0$ is the initial marginal cost. Therefore, (8.32) reflects total inventory costs. Also, the parameter $g$ is the inventory-sales ratio, $h^0/x^0$, which is the average length of time the product is held in inventories.

The final component of inventories is the inventory identity:

$$h_t = h_{t-1} + q_t - x_t \tag{8.33}$$

where $h_t$ is the end-of-period inventory level, $h_{t-1}$ is the beginning-of-period inventory, $q_t$ is production during that period of time, and $x_t$ is sales during time $t$.

Let $E_t$ denote expected value, conditional on information available to the firm at time $t$, and let $\beta$ be the one-period discount rate such that, $0 < \beta < 1$. The problem facing the firm is to maximize the expected present discounted value of current and future net revenues:

$$E_t \sum_{j=t}^{\infty} \beta^{j-t}\left[p_j x_j - c_{Ij} - c_{pj}\right]$$

subject to (8.33). After substituting from (8.30) and (8.32), the Lagrangian function to maximize is

$$L = E_t \sum_{j=t}^{\infty} \beta^{j-t} \left[ \begin{array}{l} p_j x_j - \frac{c_I}{2}\left[h_j - g_0 - g x_j\right]^2 - \left(a r_j + b w_j\right) q_j \\ \qquad -\lambda_j \left(h_j - h_{j-1} - q_j + x_j\right) \end{array} \right]$$

The first-order conditions at time $t$ are as follows:

$$\frac{\partial L}{\partial x_t} = E_t p_t + E_t g c_I [h_t - g_0 - g x_t] - E_t \lambda_t = 0 \tag{8.34}$$

$$\frac{\partial L}{\partial q_t} = -E_t(a r_t + b w_t) + E_t \lambda_t = 0 \tag{8.35}$$

$$\frac{\partial L}{\partial h_t} = -E_t c_I [h_t - g_0 - g x_t] - E_t \lambda_t + E_t \beta \lambda_{t+1} = 0 \tag{8.36}$$

$$\frac{\partial L}{\partial \lambda_t} = -E_t h_t + h_{t-1} + q_t - E_t x_t = 0 \tag{8.37}$$

where all variables take on positive values.[8]

We can eliminate inventories, sales, and the Lagrange multipliers by substituting (8.35) into (8.34) and (8.36), and substituting that result into (8.34) to obtain the single price equation:

$$E_t p_t = (1 + g)(a r_t + b w_t) - g\beta(a E_t r_{t+1} + b E_t w_{t+1})$$

where I assume the raw material and value-adding input prices are known at time $t$. Noting that $E_t p_t = p_t - u_{pt}$, where $u_{pt}$ is a random error term, and rearranging terms we obtain:

$$p_t = [1 + g(1 - \beta)](a r_t + b w_t) - g\beta a(E_t r_{t+1} - r_t) - g\beta b(E_t w_{t+1} - w_t) + u_{pt} \tag{8.38}$$

The above equation can be simplified. First, with high frequency data such as weekly and monthly data, the discount rate will be very close to one. Thus, for all practical purposes we can set $\beta = 1$. Moreover, we can assume $E_t w_{t+1} = w_t$ with little loss. Firms often contract for labor and do not regularly forecast wages (or benefits). Changes occur less regularly and are not important from the standpoint of forecasting input costs like raw material unit costs. With these two simplifications, Eq. (8.38) becomes

$$p_t = (a r_t + b w_t) - g a(E_t r_{t+1} - r_t) + u_{pt} \tag{8.39}$$

[8] In principle, inventories could take on negative values. Following Holt et al. (1960), I assume any excess demand is treated as unfilled orders and is filled at the beginning of the next time period. However, firms can essentially avoid this by setting depletion costs high enough.

In this form, Eq. (8.39) points out that short-run equilibrium occurs when product price equals unit raw material and processing costs minus any capital gains (loss) from purchasing more (less) raw materials to reduce inventory costs. The latter expression only plays a role in determination of prices when raw material prices are changing significantly from one period to the next. In the steady state, we would have the standard markup pricing equation where price equals unit cost plus a possible markup over costs.[9]

One could also write (8.39) in terms of the so-called farm-to-retail price spread, $s_t = p_t - ar_t$, as follows:

$$s_t = bw_t - ga(E_t r_{t+1} - r_t) + u_{pt} \tag{8.40}$$

Equation (8.40) provides a simple explanation for why the price spread could vary negatively with the farm price. If middlemen expect the price to fall compared to its previous level, the price spread will be positively correlated with the negative price change. Conversely, if the farm price is expected to rise over last period's price, the price spread will be negatively correlated with the positive price change. The reason for these relationships is inventory holding. The implicit cost of inventories rises when middlemen expect price next period to fall; when next period's price is expected to rise, middlemen will be better off holding inventories and their implicit cost of inventories will fall. Although these costs are implicit, they are nevertheless real and can actually be quite significant because of the amount of time the product is held in inventory. In the case of meat, the product after slaughtering is held in cold storage and can be held in package form for several days, even weeks. In the case of beef, for example, the carcasses are chilled right after slaughtering for two weeks or longer for aging. The carcass is then cut into primal cuts and shipped to final destinations (i.e., supermarkets) for additional storage and cutting into individual meat cuts. The whole process from carcass to consumer can take up to six weeks, and longer for highly processed goods. The estimated parameter, $g$, shows the average length of time the product is in storage. The longer the time in storage, the larger the effect expected future price changes will have on implicit inventory costs, and therefore the price spread.

### 8.4.3 Empirical Application to the US Beef Short-Run Farm-to-Retail Price Spreads

To test the short-run theory of price determination discussed in the previous section, I apply the model to US beef farm-to-retail price spreads with monthly data over

[9] If the firm is imperfectly competitive and faces a constant elasticity demand curve, then we could generalize the first part of (8.39) to $p_t = \mu(ar_t + bw_t)$, where $\mu > 1$. See, e.g., Sumner (1981) in the context of the cigarette industry. Of course, markup pricing could result from other concerns such as uncertainty (e.g., Mills 1959).

the time period, January 2009–December 2018, a total of 120 observations. The price spreads are retail price of fresh beef minus net farm value of cattle prices for choice beef (cents/lb). Net farm values are farm prices less byproduct allowances on a retail equivalent basis (cents/lb). These data were obtained from USDA, ERS (https://www.ers.usda.gov/data-products/meat-price-spreads.aspx). The wage data are average hourly earnings of all employees, animal slaughtering and processing from Employment, Hours, and Earnings from the Current Employment Statistics national survey (https://beta.bls.gov/dataQuery/find?fq=survey:[ce]&s=id:A&q=CES3231160003). These data together with the monthly cpi for all goods are shown in Table 8.2.[10]

Consistent with other applications in econometrics, I assume firms form rational expectations so that $E_t r_{t+1} = r_{t+1} - u_{rt+1}$, where $u_{rt+1}$ is an error term with zero conditional expectation and constant variance. The error term is also orthogonal to $E_t r_{t+1}$. Substituting for this price expectation in Eq. (8.40), and noting that $a = 1$ in this case, we have

$$s_t = a_0 + \sum_{i=1}^{11} a_i d_i + a_t t + bw_t - g(r_{t+1} - r_t) + v_t \tag{8.41}$$

where $v_t = (u_{pt} - gu_{rt+1})$. I have also included an intercept, denoting the December value of the price spread, all else constant. Monthly dummies, $d_1 - d_{11}$, represent deviations from December for January through February. The term $t$ is a linear time trend. The error term is correlated with $r_{t+1}$ because of the specification $E_t r_{t+1} = r_{t+1} - u_{rt+1}$. This is the classical errors-in-variables model. This means OLS will be biased and inconsistent. If we could find instruments that are uncorrelated with the error term but correlated with $r_{t+1} - r_t$, consistent parameter estimates of (8.41) could be obtained. Another complication is that there are reasons to believe the error term, $v_t$, is serially correlated, i.e., $v_t = \rho v_{t-1} + \varepsilon_t$. Applying the quasi-difference operator, $1 - \rho L$ to Eq. (8.41) we obtain

$$\begin{aligned} s_t =& a_0 + \sum_{i=1}^{11} a_i d_i + a_t t + bw_t \\ & -g(r_{t+1} - r_t) + \rho s_{t-1} \\ & -\rho L\left( a_0 + \sum_{i=1}^{11} a_i d_i + a_t t + bw_t - g(r_{t+1} - r_t) \right) + \varepsilon_t \end{aligned} \tag{8.42}$$

where $L$ is the lag operator such that $Lz_t = z_{t-1}$.

Consider as instruments for $(r_{t+1} - r_t)$, $r_t$, $r_{t-1}$, and $r_{t-2}$. These instruments would be expected to be correlated with $(r_{t+1} - r_t)$ and uncorrelated with the error term $\varepsilon_t$, provided there is no more than *1*st order serial correlation. In addition, we want

[10] All price and spread data are divided by CPI. The values are expressed as real prices for December 2018 by multiplying each real variable by 252.723.

**Table 8.2** Farm-to-Retail Price Spread and Wage Rates for US Beef, January 2009–December 2018

| Date | Spread | Farm Value | Wage | CPI |
|---|---|---|---|---|
| 200901 | 248.7859 | 183.2260904 | 14.2 | 211.933 |
| 200902 | 256.6868 | 179.1107177 | 14.1 | 212.705 |
| 200903 | 247.804 | 181.798194 | 14.14 | 212.495 |
| 200904 | 234.8927 | 191.9846359 | 13.96 | 212.709 |
| 200905 | 246.2216 | 186.1426009 | 14.14 | 213.022 |
| 200906 | 249.7681 | 177.4788626 | 14.17 | 214.79 |
| 200907 | 237.294 | 179.5689911 | 14.17 | 214.726 |
| 200908 | 245.7154 | 176.27205 | 14.18 | 215.445 |
| 200909 | 234.138 | 179.8400892 | 14.27 | 215.861 |
| 200910 | 232.3736 | 182.1671273 | 14.34 | 216.509 |
| 200911 | 250.2739 | 180.143078 | 14.31 | 217.234 |
| 200912 | 254.0822 | 174.0103569 | 14.34 | 217.347 |
| 201001 | 236.0861 | 181.179716 | 14.42 | 217.488 |
| 201002 | 227.4842 | 191.0679262 | 14.6 | 217.281 |
| 201003 | 227.7438 | 202.6296962 | 14.47 | 217.353 |
| 201004 | 232.3202 | 211.2835305 | 14.55 | 217.403 |
| 201005 | 234.4803 | 211.1739064 | 14.57 | 217.29 |
| 201006 | 239.1048 | 208.0625521 | 14.59 | 217.199 |
| 201007 | 243.9214 | 197.5715982 | 14.66 | 217.605 |
| 201008 | 230.3304 | 204.93042 | 14.74 | 217.923 |
| 201009 | 235.2222 | 206.5388788 | 14.67 | 218.275 |
| 201010 | 240.3794 | 207.3772535 | 14.81 | 219.035 |
| 201011 | 239.6198 | 209.2214933 | 14.83 | 219.59 |
| 201012 | 226.4903 | 216.558033 | 14.98 | 220.472 |
| 201101 | 230.194 | 221.9341208 | 15.01 | 221.187 |
| 201102 | 231.3541 | 226.94014 | 15.03 | 221.898 |
| 201103 | 229.8809 | 242.5801461 | 15.03 | 223.046 |
| 201104 | 228.0104 | 251.4299284 | 15.1 | 224.093 |
| 201105 | 253.791 | 229.9165758 | 15.08 | 224.806 |
| 201106 | 255.3317 | 222.685117 | 15.13 | 224.806 |
| 201107 | 245.8063 | 230.8548648 | 15.08 | 225.395 |
| 201108 | 249.1713 | 237.6196806 | 15.03 | 226.106 |
| 201109 | 244.9387 | 245.8300758 | 15.22 | 226.597 |
| 201110 | 233.603 | 259.1835479 | 15 | 226.75 |
| 201111 | 235.398 | 263.4108376 | 14.99 | 227.169 |

(continued)

**Table 8.2** (continued)

| Date | Spread | Farm Value | Wage | CPI |
|---|---|---|---|---|
| 201112 | 241.2166 | 257.6343044 | 14.95 | 227.223 |
| 201201 | 244.1525 | 261.3442367 | 14.99 | 227.842 |
| 201202 | 234.6421 | 266.1690962 | 15.09 | 228.329 |
| 201203 | 234.2477 | 267.1436887 | 15.1 | 228.807 |
| 201204 | 239.7511 | 254.4785972 | 15.07 | 229.187 |
| 201205 | 237.1552 | 255.0050414 | 15.33 | 228.713 |
| 201206 | 235.8233 | 253.5632852 | 15.11 | 228.524 |
| 201207 | 254.3473 | 243.4332226 | 15.2 | 228.59 |
| 201208 | 238.1627 | 253.2782554 | 15.04 | 229.918 |
| 201209 | 227.4243 | 263.8685725 | 15.12 | 231.015 |
| 201210 | 233.3415 | 267.0133703 | 15.24 | 231.638 |
| 201211 | 241.9515 | 268.9555921 | 15.08 | 231.249 |
| 201212 | 240.7237 | 267.0478633 | 14.96 | 231.221 |
| 201301 | 256.7316 | 263.8438504 | 15.1 | 231.679 |
| 201302 | 255.1216 | 262.7854883 | 15.06 | 232.937 |
| 201303 | 259.8773 | 266.468828 | 15.12 | 232.282 |
| 201304 | 254.8784 | 267.5117764 | 15.17 | 231.797 |
| 201305 | 252.1422 | 270.4696906 | 15.14 | 231.893 |
| 201306 | 262.6921 | 264.7495312 | 15.12 | 232.445 |
| 201307 | 285.0677 | 248.0249872 | 15.21 | 232.9 |
| 201308 | 282.4743 | 252.5963288 | 15.31 | 233.456 |
| 201309 | 265.2321 | 264.1918729 | 15.42 | 233.544 |
| 201310 | 261.0383 | 274.4256813 | 15.31 | 233.669 |
| 201311 | 263.3917 | 277.4657325 | 15.43 | 234.1 |
| 201312 | 257.8009 | 278.2408684 | 15.52 | 234.719 |
| 201401 | 237.4418 | 297.12922 | 15.55 | 235.288 |
| 201402 | 247.1342 | 310.4043374 | 15.63 | 235.547 |
| 201403 | 251.8581 | 320.1575556 | 15.56 | 236.028 |
| 201404 | 275.485 | 311.6430859 | 15.61 | 236.468 |
| 201405 | 286.4616 | 304.8547816 | 15.63 | 236.918 |
| 201406 | 272.6973 | 318.9960629 | 15.63 | 237.231 |
| 201407 | 256.2505 | 338.8859647 | 15.59 | 237.498 |
| 201408 | 287.4697 | 336.492868 | 15.56 | 237.46 |
| 201409 | 280.5562 | 345.0609859 | 15.52 | 237.477 |
| 201410 | 271.0636 | 352.9990567 | 15.58 | 237.43 |

(continued)

**Table 8.2** (continued)

| Date | Spread | Farm Value | Wage | CPI |
|---|---|---|---|---|
| 201411 | 263.2843 | 367.0223803 | 15.68 | 236.983 |
| 201412 | 280.7152 | 350.2603256 | 15.73 | 236.252 |
| 201501 | 277.6221 | 355.6802176 | 15.72 | 234.718 |
| 201502 | 281.1727 | 345.8123546 | 15.78 | 235.236 |
| 201503 | 278.5593 | 352.3166661 | 15.93 | 236.005 |
| 201504 | 287.3653 | 352.7917843 | 15.93 | 236.156 |
| 201505 | 289.2397 | 351.9453912 | 15.83 | 236.974 |
| 201506 | 309.5807 | 331.055973 | 16.15 | 237.684 |
| 201507 | 309.652 | 326.8383592 | 16.21 | 238.053 |
| 201508 | 304.959 | 327.8556417 | 16.28 | 238.028 |
| 201509 | 325.8663 | 297.1513074 | 16.46 | 237.506 |
| 201510 | 330.8761 | 292.2028557 | 16.49 | 237.781 |
| 201511 | 339.1955 | 281.7260081 | 16.56 | 238.016 |
| 201512 | 324.1216 | 273.0433749 | 16.56 | 237.817 |
| 201601 | 299.596 | 297.9434756 | 16.59 | 237.833 |
| 201602 | 300.964 | 297.5904684 | 16.47 | 237.469 |
| 201603 | 322.5027 | 299.7677825 | 16.51 | 238.038 |
| 201604 | 325.0698 | 285.3817724 | 16.61 | 238.827 |
| 201605 | 323.3177 | 284.8120295 | 16.72 | 239.464 |
| 201606 | 351.0879 | 268.8774011 | 16.86 | 240.167 |
| 201607 | 354.034 | 254.9507975 | 16.87 | 240.15 |
| 201608 | 338.6108 | 252.9028516 | 16.97 | 240.602 |
| 201609 | 359.435 | 227.3661035 | 16.89 | 241.051 |
| 201610 | 355.188 | 218.4796464 | 16.97 | 241.691 |
| 201611 | 341.7007 | 234.669465 | 17 | 242.029 |
| 201612 | 317.1659 | 244.9850048 | 17.01 | 242.772 |
| 201701 | 307.4503 | 258.7435398 | 17.03 | 243.78 |
| 201702 | 322.8106 | 261.2278096 | 17.14 | 243.961 |
| 201703 | 314.9265 | 275.4676603 | 17.16 | 243.749 |
| 201704 | 308.9653 | 284.3250373 | 16.99 | 244.051 |
| 201705 | 310.6967 | 303.318239 | 17.14 | 243.962 |
| 201706 | 330.5838 | 290.0943595 | 17.06 | 244.182 |
| 201707 | 351.5557 | 258.4787879 | 17.18 | 244.39 |
| 201708 | 355.865 | 241.1441094 | 17.09 | 245.297 |
| 201709 | 345.3841 | 232.8183509 | 17.28 | 246.418 |

(continued)

**Table 8.2** (continued)

| Date | Spread | Farm Value | Wage | CPI |
|---|---|---|---|---|
| 201710 | 328.4704 | 246.9800709 | 17.32 | 246.587 |
| 201711 | 313.2062 | 267.4974921 | 17.38 | 247.332 |
| 201712 | 318.5937 | 261.6767193 | 17.42 | 247.901 |
| 201801 | 307.1643 | 268.5874822 | 17.51 | 248.884 |
| 201802 | 301.7401 | 281.0345938 | 17.52 | 249.369 |
| 201803 | 311.4205 | 275.6322639 | 17.63 | 249.498 |
| 201804 | 339.8633 | 266.1665529 | 17.74 | 249.956 |
| 201805 | 328.8833 | 267.5614213 | 17.75 | 250.646 |
| 201806 | 354.8251 | 243.0028746 | 17.75 | 251.134 |
| 201807 | 354.3729 | 247.619792 | 17.7 | 251.597 |
| 201808 | 363.0363 | 245.2041972 | 17.81 | 251.879 |
| 201809 | 349.5761 | 243.8882635 | 17.74 | 252.01 |
| 201810 | 334 | 250 | 17.87 | 252.794 |
| 201811 | 332 | 259.1 | 17.78 | 252.76 |
| 201812 | 317.9 | 265.4 | 17.81 | 252.723 |

to include as instruments all the right-hand side exogenous variables for the current period and the previous period, as well as $s_{t-1}$, because of nature of the relationship, (8.42) (Davidson and MacKinnon 1993, p. 370). The selection of the lag length $r_t, r_{t-1,}$and$r_{t-2}$ as instruments for $(r_{t+1} - r_t)$ is based on a time-series analysis of the regression model of $r_t$ on lagged prices, monthly dummies, and a time trend. Results with two lags were found to be adequate. On the assumption middlemen use only these variables in predicting future price, $E_t r_{t+1}$ will be the optimal predictor when the main source of change in market price is in farm supply, aside from trend and seasonal factors (Wohlgenant 1985). Expectations like these, which are formed based on past prices, are called quasi-rational expectations, and perform quite well in describing producers' price expectations (Nerlove and Bessler 2001).

The price spread model is estimated in two steps. I first estimate $(r_{t+1} - r_t)$ as a function of $r_t, r_{t-1,}$and $r_{t-2}, w_t, w_{t-1}, s_{t-1}, t$, intercept, and $d_i - d_{11}$. The actual values for $(r_{t+1} - r_t)$ and $(r_t - r_{t-1})$ are then replaced by their predicted values in correcting for serial correlation according to (8.42). The resulting estimates are consistent. I use the Prais-Winston estimator in order to use all the observations in estimation. SAS software version 9.4 with both Proc Syslin and Proc Autoreg were used in estimation: Proc Syslin for first-stage estimates predicted values and Proc Autoreg for correction of serial correlation.

The results of estimation of the price spread equation are shown in Table 8.3. The wage rate and expected change in price are both highly significant and have the correctly anticipated signs. The value of $g$, the parameter premultiplying $(r_{t+1} - r_t)$, indicates beef is held on average about five weeks, in agreement with industry practice. Results are also in agreement with Wohlgenant (1985) for wholesale-retail

**Table 8.3** Econometric Estimates of the Farm-to-Retail Price Spread Model for Beef, January 2009–December 2018

| Parameter Estimates | | | | |
|---|---|---|---|---|
| Variable | Estimate | Standard Error | *t* Value | Approx Pr > \|t\| |
| Intercept | −253.7766 | 134.0863 | −1.89 | 0.0613 |
| $\mathbf{E_t r_{t+1} - r_t}$ | −1.2495 | 0.3184 | −3.92 | 0.0002 |
| $\mathbf{w_t}$ | 31.1765 | 8.1122 | 3.84 | 0.0002 |
| **t** | 0.3770 | 0.1378 | 2.74 | 0.0073 |
| $\mathbf{d_1}$ | 12.2070 | 5.5519 | 2.20 | 0.0302 |
| $\mathbf{d_2}$ | −3.3558 | 5.5836 | −0.60 | 0.5492 |
| $\mathbf{d_3}$ | 0.2802 | 6.5308 | 0.04 | 0.9659 |
| $\mathbf{d_4}$ | −6.1877 | 6.1294 | −1.01 | 0.3151 |
| $\mathbf{d_5}$ | −2.7397 | 6.2758 | −0.44 | 0.6634 |
| $\mathbf{d_6}$ | −10.4359 | 6.7882 | −1.54 | 0.1273 |
| $\mathbf{d_7}$ | 4.1070 | 6.3575 | 0.65 | 0.5197 |
| $\mathbf{d_8}$ | 13.4516 | 6.0640 | 2.22 | 0.0288 |
| $\mathbf{d_9}$ | 10.6010 | 5.6480 | 1.88 | 0.0634 |
| $\mathbf{d_{10}}$ | 14.1632 | 5.4241 | 2.61 | 0.0104 |
| $\mathbf{d_{11}}$ | 10.2308 | 4.6421 | 2.20 | 0.0298 |

*Note* Estimated by IV with correction for first-order serial correlation $\widehat{\rho} = 0.700768$ with *t*-value = 9.87

price spread for beef for an earlier time period. The economic significance of this result cannot be overstated. Middlemen use inventories to smooth production costs. Achievement of a stable flow of meat at lowest cost is an important goal of meat-packers. The fact that the price spread is negatively correlated with anticipated changes in the farm price of beef means competitive forces, driven by inventory behavior, can explain this relationship. In the earlier part of the data period, price spreads were falling as farm prices were increasing. In recent years, the opposite has been true: the price spread has been widening as the farm price has been declining. These results support the hypothesis that inventory costs decline when farm prices are rising because of the decline in opportunity costs of holding inventories. On the other hand, the opportunity costs of holding inventories rise when farm prices are falling so the price spread must rise to offset these losses. The fact that beef is held in inventory for a considerable amount of time means that the price spread is quite sensitive to expected changes in farm price. If, for example, prices are expected to fall \$0.10 per lb., the price spread would be expected to rise almost \$0.125 per lb., ceteris paribus.

It is useful to obtain the empirical model in which the price spread is related to current and lagged farm prices. This can be obtained by incorporating an expectations model into the framework. As indicated above, a second-order AR process yields the best forecast of future price, given the forecast is based on the past history of its own price. This method of developing an expectations model is called quasi-rational expectations (Nerlove and Bessler 2001) because the subjective forecasts are assumed equal to the "best" market forecasts based on lagged prices alone. Using Box–Jenkins (1970) techniques, the model identified and estimated was of the form: $\Delta r_t = b_0 + b_1 \Delta r_{t-1} +$ seasonal dummies + trend + error. Using the Dickey–Fuller (1979) test (both simple and augmented), the null hypothesis of a unit root in the deflated farm price of beef and veal was not rejected.[11] Therefore, the model was estimated in first differences and one lag was found to be sufficient. The parameter estimate of the slope of $\Delta r_{t-1}$ is $\widehat{b}_1 = 0.2036$ with standard error equal to 0.0963. The optimal forecast of the change in next period's price is $E_t r_{t+1} - r_t = \widehat{b}_1 \Delta r_t = 0.2042 \Delta r_t$, plus effect of seasonal dummies and trend. Multiplying this forecast times the estimate of $g = 1.2495$ from Table 8.3 gives the marginal effect of $\Delta r_t$ on the price spread of $\frac{\partial s_t}{\partial \Delta r_t} = -0.2551$ Thus, on average, the price spread was negatively correlated with the current change in farm price of beef over the time period January 2009 to December 2018. Therefore, the model is able to account for the empirical regularity of a negative relationship between the farm-to-retail price spread for beef and veal and the farm price.

### 8.4.4 Asymmetry in Price Changes

Another issue that exists but has only really been addressed empirically, but not theoretically, is asymmetry in changes in price. That is, price changes increase faster (slower) than they decrease (increase). Pelzman (2000) has conducted an extensive study on goods where individual linkages among commodities between retail and wholesale can be identified. He found evidence of wholesale-to-retail price change and differential response for the vast majority of commodities. He attempted to test (informally but not rigorously) for causes of prices rising faster than they fall but was unsuccessful in explaining why that is the case. The two leading explanations for this irreversibility are costly changes in prices and costs of changing inventories. Despite being presented some sixty years ago, Holt et al. (1960) provide a solid theoretical foundation for asymmetric changes. They show that when inventory depletion costs are larger than holding costs, it is still economically rational to hold inventories in the face of negative marginal returns from holding inventories. In other words, if the expected price difference is negative, positive inventory holding may still exist because of the higher expected costs of stocking-out versus holding inventories. With respect to the present application, where the price spread, $E_t r_{t+1} - r_t < 0$, we showed that this encourages the firm to reduce inventories because it expects to buy the input

[11] The Dickey–Fuller test is a test of the coefficient on the lagged dependent variable in the regression: $\Delta y_t = \alpha + \beta y_{t-1} + \varepsilon_t$. The null hypothesis is unit root and, because it is a non-normal distribution, calculated probability levels of the distribution are tabled values in Dickey and Fuller (1979). The augmented Dickey–Fuller test includes lags in first differences of $\Delta y_t$.

at a lower price next period and thereby reduce inventory costs. This means current price will adjust downward more rapidly than in the absence of this incentive. On the other hand, if $E_t r_{t+1} - r_t > 0$, the incentive will be to increase inventories so that price increases next period will take longer to occur. This simple idea is, in fact, part of the construction of the inventory cost function, (8.32), where the target inventory, $h_t^* = g_0 + gx_t$, is linearly related to sales during time period $t$. The parameter, $g_0$, is negative so that the target level will occur with positive inventory at a level where marginal returns can be negative.

Empirically, researchers use a modified framework developed by Houck (1977) and Ward (1982). Following Heien (1980), I separate the effect of $\Delta r_{t+1} = r_{t+1} - r_t$ on the price spread into two parts: $\Delta r_{t+1,inc}$ when $\Delta r_{t+1} > 0$; $\Delta r_{t+1,dec}$ when $\Delta r_{t+1} < 0$. I then test for the equality of the two effects. The results of the modeling effort applied to the farm-to-retail price spread produce an F-statistic of 2.12, which has a p-value equal to 0.15. Therefore, we fail to reject the null hypothesis of no asymmetric price response for the beef price spread. This lends further support to the inventory theory presented in this chapter. While asymmetry may not be present in this application, it is something that should be tested for in future applications for specification bias. For other industry applications, the source of price stickiness and, therefore, possible price asymmetry may be different (e.g., asymmetry in supply response).

## Appendix: Derivation of Inventory Cost Function

The purpose of this Appendix is to derive the inventory cost function according to the method used by Holt et al. (1960, Chapter 11). The more realistic case of $n$ products is analyzed by Holt et al. (1960), but I analyze the simpler case of a single product, which produces essentially the same result. The inventory balance condition is

$$h_t = h_{t-1} + q_t - x_t$$

where $h_t$ is the end-of-period inventory level, $h_{t-1}$ is the beginning-of-period inventory, $q_t$ is production during that period of time, and $x_t$ is sales during time $t$. Letting overbars denote expected values, we know that with production known at time $t$,

$$h_t = \overline{h}_t + \overline{x}_t - x_t$$

For simplicity, the firm only incurs inventory holding costs (e.g., storage rental, handling, insurance, interest, etc.) and inventory depletion costs. Let $c_h$ denote per unit holding costs and $c_d$ denote per unit depletion costs from unmet demand. Then, omitting time subscripts for notational convenience, expected inventory holding and depletion costs equals:

$$\overline{c}_I = c_h \int_0^{\overline{h}+\overline{x}} \left(\overline{h} + \overline{x} - x\right) f(x) dx + c_d \int_{\overline{h}+\overline{x}}^{\infty} \left(x - \overline{h} - \overline{x}\right) f(x) dx$$

where $\overline{c}_i$ is expected inventory costs and $f(x)$ is the probability density function (pdf) of sales. Noting that expected end-of-period inventory equals

$$\overline{h} = \int_0^{\overline{h}+\overline{x}} \left(\overline{h} + \overline{x} - x\right) f(x) dx + \int_{\overline{h}+\overline{x}}^{\infty} \left(\overline{h} + \overline{x} - x\right) f(x) dx$$

expected inventory costs can be written as:

$$\overline{c}_I = c_h \overline{h} - (c_h + c_d) \int_{h+\overline{x}}^{\infty} \left(x - \overline{h} - \overline{x}\right) f(x) dx$$

Differentiating with respect to expected inventory gives the marginal cost of inventory holding:

$$mc_I = \frac{\partial \overline{c}_I}{\partial \overline{h}} = c_h - (c_h + c_d)\left[1 - F\left(\overline{h} + \overline{x}\right)\right]$$

where $F\left(\overline{h} + \overline{x}\right) = \int_0^{\overline{h}+\overline{x}} f(x) dx$ is the probability distribution function.

To proceed further, we need to specify a specific pdf for $f(x)$. Following Holt et al. (1960), I assume a normal distribution so that

$$\left[1 - F\left(\overline{h} + x\right)\right] = \left[1 - N\left(\overline{h}/\sigma\right)\right] = N\left(-\overline{h}/\sigma\right)$$

where $N(t) = \int_{-\infty}^{t} \frac{1}{\sqrt{2\pi}} e^{-z^2/2} dz$. Totally differentiating the above marginal cost function yields:

$$dmc_I = \left[N'\left(-\overline{h}/\sigma\right)(c_h + c_d)/\sigma\right]\left[d\overline{h} - \left(\overline{h}/\sigma\right) d\sigma\right]$$

If we also assume as in Holt et al. (1960) that the standard deviation of demand is proportional to expected demand or sales, i.e., $\sigma = \nu \overline{x}$, then the total differential of marginal costs equals:

$$dmc_I = \left[N'\left(\frac{\overline{h}}{\nu \overline{x}}\right) \frac{(c_h + c_d)}{\nu \overline{x}}\right]\left[d\overline{h} - \left(\overline{h}/\overline{x}\right) d\overline{x}\right]$$

The linear approximation at $\overline{h}^0$, $\overline{x}^0$, and $mc_i^0$ is:

$$mc_I = mc_I^0 + \left[N'\left(\frac{\overline{h}}{\nu\overline{x}}\right)\frac{(c_h + c_d)}{\nu\overline{x}}\right]\left[\left(\overline{h} - \overline{h}^0\right) - \left(\frac{\overline{h}}{\overline{x}}\right)\left(\overline{x} - \overline{x}^0\right)\right] \tag{A.1}$$

Consider now the quadratic approximation for inventory costs presented in Eq. (8.32):

$$c^* = \frac{1}{2}c_I[h - g_0 - gx]^2 \tag{A.2}$$

The parameters of (A.1) can then be matched with those of the derivative of (A.2):

$$\frac{\partial c^*}{\partial h} = c_I[h - g_0 - gx]$$

This will be the same formula for marginal costs in (A.1) if:

$$c_I = \left[N'\left(\frac{\overline{h}}{\nu\overline{x}}\right)\frac{(c_h + c_d)}{\nu\overline{x}}\right]$$

$$g_0 = \frac{-mc_I^0}{c_I}$$

$$g = \frac{\overline{h}}{\overline{x}}$$

These results therefore give us the desired cost coefficients.

**Problems**

8.1 Show that the submatrix of price effects, $\boldsymbol{m}_r^*(\boldsymbol{r}, \boldsymbol{w}, \boldsymbol{I})$, from Table 8.1 is negative semi-definite at the sample means. Use data from Table 5.2 and Table 7.1 in your calculations.

8.2 Re-calculate the incidence of market charges using the formula shown in problem 7.2 using the results from Table 8.1. Compare the results with those obtained in problem 7.2. If there are differences, explain why you think they are different.

8.3 The food stamp program, SNAP (Supplemental Nutrition Assistance Program), is said to have significant effects on commodity prices. The maximum amount spent by consumers through SNAP was $76 billion in 2011. PCE was $ 10,641.1 billion in 2011. SNAP benefits can only be used for food consumed at home. Proportions of meats consumed at home are estimated to be approximately 0.47 for beef and veal, 0.79 for pork, and 0.78 for poultry (Reed et al. 2002). Estimate the effects of SNAP on retail and farm prices of beef and veal, pork, and poultry using the elasticities reported in Table 8.1.

8.4 Suppose that market intermediaries form quasi-rational expectations on raw material prices such that $E_t r_{t+1} = b_0 + b_1 r_t + b_2 r_{t-1}$ Substitute into (8.40) to show the price spread can be expressed as a distributed lag in current and past raw material prices. Under what conditions would this specification result in a negative relationship between the price spread and the current period raw material price? Is this purely coincidental or does it have a theoretical basis? (Hint: see Wohlgenant [1985]).

## References


Appelbaum, E. "Testing Price Taking Behavior." *Journal of Econometrics* 9(1979): 283–294.

Appelbaum, E. "The Estimation of the Degree of Oligopoly Power." *Journal of Econometrics* 19(1982): 287–299.

Azzam, Azzeddine M. "Asymmetry and Rigidity in Farm-Retail Price Transmission." *American Journal of Agricultural Economics* 81(3)(1999): 525–533.

Baumol, W.J. "Contestable Markets: An Uprising in the Theory of Industry Structure." *The American Economic Review* 72(1982): 1–15.

Box, G.E.P., and G.M. Jenkins. *Time Series Analysis: Forecasting and Control.* San Francisco: Holden-Day, Inc., 1970.

Braulke, M. "On the Comparative Statics of a Competitive Industry." *The American Economic Review* 77(1987): 479–485.

Braulke, M. "The Firm in Short-Run Equilibrium: Comment." *The American Economic Review* 74(1984): 750–753.

Brennan, M.J. "The Supply of Storage." *The American Economic Review* 48(1958): 50–72.

Breshnahan, T.F. "Empirical Studies of Industries with Market Power." In R. Schmalansee and R. Willig (eds.) *Handbook of Industrial Organization*, Vol. II, pp. 1011–1057. Amsterdam: Elsevier Science Publishers B.V., 1989.

Breshnahan, T.F. "The Oligopoly Solution is Identified." *Economics Letters* 10(1982): 87–92.

Chavas, J-P., and T.L. Cox. "On Market Equilibrium Analysis." *American Journal of Agricultural Economics* 79(1997): 500–513.

Davidson, R., and J.G. MacKinnon. *Estimation and Inference in Econometrics.* New York: Oxford University Press, 1993.

Dickey, D.A., and W.A. Fuller. "Distributions of the Estimators for Autoregressive Time Series with Unit Roots." *Journal of the American Statistical Association* 74(1979): 427–431.

Diewert, W.E. "Applications of Duality Theory." In M.D. Intriligator and D.A. Kendrick (eds.) *Frontiers of Quantitative Economics.* Amsterdam: North-Holland Publishing Co., 1974.

Diewert, W.E. "Duality Approaches to Microeconomic Theory." The Economic Series, Technical Report No. 281, Institute for Mathematical Studies in the Social Sciences, Stanford University, 1978.

Eichenbaum, M. "Some Empirical Evidence on the Production Level and Production Cost Models of Inventory Investment." *The American Economic Review* 79(1989): 853–864.

Fama, E.F. and A.B. Laffer. "The Number of Firms and Competition." *The American Economic Review* 62(1972): 670–674.

Freebairn, J.W. "Farm and Retail Food Prices." *Review of Marketing and Agricultural Economics* 52(1984): 71–90.

Friedman, M. *Price Theory.* Chicago: Aldine Publishing Co., 1976.

Griffith, G.R. "Sydney Meat Marketing Margins: An Econometric Analysis." *Review of Marketing and Agricultural Economics* 43(1974): 223–239.

Heien, D.M. "Markup Pricing in a Dynamic Model of the Food Industry." *American Journal of Agricultural Economics* 62(1980): 10–18.

Heiner, R.A. "Theory of the Firm in 'Short-Run' Industry Equilibrium." *The American Economic Review* 82(1982): 555–562.

Heiner, R.A. "Theory of the Firm in Short-Run Industry Equilibrium: Further Comment." *American Economic Review* 74(1984): 754.

Holloway, G.J. "The Farm-Retail Price Spread in an Imperfectly Competitive Food Industry." *American Journal of Agricultural Economics* 73(1991): 979–989.

Holt, C., F. Modigliani, J. Muth, and H. Simon. *Planning Production, Inventories, and Work Force.* Englewood Cliffs, N.J.: Prentice Hall, 1960.

Houck, J.P. "An Approach to Specifying and Estimating Nonreversible Functions." *American Journal of Agricultural Economics* 15(1977): 570–572.

Just, R.E., and W.S. Chern. "Tomatoes, Technology, and Oligopsony." *Bell Journal of Economics* 11(1980): 584–602.

Kinnucan, H.W., and O.D. Forker. "Asymmetry in Farm-Retail Price Transmission for Major Dairy Products." *American Journal of Agricultural Economics* 69(1987): 285–292.

Lamm, R.M., and P.C. Westcott. "The Effect of Changing Input Costs on Food Prices." *American Journal of Agricultural Economics* 63(1981): 187–196.

Lau, L.J. "On Identifying the Degree of Competitiveness from Industry Price and Output Data." *Economics Letters* 10(1982): 93–99.

Mills, E.S. "Uncertainty and Price Theory." *Quarterly Journal of Economics* 73(1959): 116–130.

Murray, B.C. "Measuring Oligopsony Power with Shadow Prices: U.S. Markets for Pulpwood and Sawlogs." *The Review of Economics and Statistics* 77(1995): 486-498.

Muth, M.K., and M.K. Wohlgenant. "A Test for Market Power Using Marginal Input and Output Prices with Application to the U.S. Beef Processing Industries." *American Journal of Agricultural Economics* 81(1999a): 638–643.

Muth, M.K., and M.K. Wohlgenant. "Measuring the Degree of Oligopsony Power in the Beef Packing Industry in the Absence of Marketing Input Quantity Data." *Journal of Agricultural and Resource Economics* 24(1999b): 299–312.

Nerlove, M., and D.A. Bessler. "Expectations, Information and Dynamics." In B.L. Gardner and G.C. Rausser (eds.) *Handbook of Agricultural Economics*, Vol. 1A, pp. 155–206. Amsterdam: Elsevier Science B.V., 2001, Chapter 17.

Parish, R.M. "Price Leveling and Averaging." *Farm Economist* 11(1967): 187–198.

Peeters, H.M.M. "The (Mis-)Specification of Production Costs in Production Smoothing Models." *Economics Letters* 57(1997): 69–77.

Pelzman, S. "Prices Rise Faster Than They Fall." *Journal of Political Economy* 108(2000): 466–502.

Roberts, J.M. "Testing Oligopolistic Behavior." *International Journal of Industrial Organization* 2(1984): 367–383.

Schroeter, J.R. "Estimating the Degree of Market Power in the Beef Industry." *The Review of Economics and Statistics* 70(1988): 158–162.

Sumner, D.A. "Measurement of Monopoly: An Application to the Cigarette Industry." *Journal of Political Economy* 89(1981): 1010–1019.

Theil, H. *Principles of Econometrics.* New York: Wiley, 1971.

Tomek, W.G., and K.L. Robinson. *Agricultural Product Prices.* Ithaca: Cornell University Press, 1981.

Ward, R.W. "Asymmetry in Retail, Wholesale, and Shipping Point Pricing for Fresh Vegetables." *American Journal of Agricultural Economics* 64(1982): 205–212.

Wohlgenant, M.K. "Marketing Margins: Empirical Analysis." In B.L. Gardner and G.C. Rausser (eds.) *Handbook of Agricultural Economics*, Vol. 1B, pp. 934–970. Amsterdam: Elsevier Science B.V., 2001, Chapter 16.

Wohlgenant, Michael K. "Competition in the U.S. Meat Industry." *Annual Review of Resource Economics* 5(2013): 1–12.

Wohlgenant, Michael K. "Competitive Storage, Rational Expectations, and Short-Run Food Price Determination." *American Journal of Agricultural Economics* 67(1985): 739–748.

# Chapter 9
# Dynamic Consumer Demand

## 9.1 Introduction

Thus far, we have focused on static models of economic behavior. Dynamic models are relevant when the consumer responds with a lag to a change in price or income, with the implication that the adjustment to equilibrium is spread over several time periods. The two origins of lags are (a) durability of the good, and (b) habit formation. For a durable good (e.g., automobile), the individual consumes a flow of services (e.g., mileage, transportation) from a given level of stock. As income increases, demand for the stock will increase. This will lead to an increase in the stock level, but only after enough time has elapsed so the consumer is sure the income change is permanent. For habit formation, after a price increase for which the consumer has developed habits, the consumer may appear to buy quantities, which are larger than equilibrium values indicated by static demand function. At first sight, the consumer is out of equilibrium. One may then imagine a slow adaptive process by which he/she gradually reduces consumption to the "correct" level.

In this chapter, I present alternative dynamic models of consumer behavior. I first review historical models, which are mainly empirical in nature. Next, models based on the theory of the consumer are presented. These modeling approaches are both myopic models (i.e., models that ignore consumer's choices on future marginal utility), and fully intertemporal models. The intertemporal models discussed include both single-equation models and multivariate models. To show how to empirically implement the system of dynamic consumer demand functions approach, I present a data set for alcoholic beverages and estimate demand parameters from a model developed by Wohlgenant (2012). Much of the following review of myopic models owes to Phlips (1983) excellent book on dynamic models.



M. K. Wohlgenant, *Market Interrelationships and Applied Demand Analysis*,
Palgrave Studies in Agricultural Economics and Food Policy,
https://doi.org/10.1007/978-3-030-73144-1_9

## 9.2 History of Empirical Models of Dynamic Consumer Demand

Like the static theory of consumer demand, initial work in this area was motivated by empirical applications. The general problem addressed can be described by Eq. (9.1):

$$\begin{aligned} q_t &= a + b_0 p_t + b_1 p_{t-1} + \ldots + c_0 y_t \\ &+ c_1 y_{t-1} + \ldots + \varepsilon_t \\ &= a + \sum_{i=0}^{\infty} b_i p_{t-i} + \sum_{i=0}^{\infty} c_i y_{t-i} + \varepsilon_t \end{aligned} \tag{9.1}$$

where, for sake of convenience, I have ignored the effects of all other prices on demand for the good in question.

### 9.2.1 *Geometric Distribution*

As can be seen, such a model, in principle, involves a large, possibly infinite, number of lags. Thus, unless the lag distribution only involves a few time periods, some restriction must be imposed on the coefficients of the lag distribution prior to estimation. One of the most popular models historically is the geometric distribution. Ignoring for the moment the lag distribution of income, rewrite Eq. (9.1) as

$$q_t = a + b \sum_{i=0}^{\infty} \theta_i p_{t-i} + c y_t + \varepsilon_t$$

where $\sum_{i=0}^{\infty} \theta_i = 1$. Assume that $\theta_i = \delta(1-\delta)^i$, then

$$q_t = a + b\delta \sum_{i=0}^{\infty} (1-\delta)^i p_{t-i} + c y_t + \varepsilon_t$$

Because $\sum_{i=0}^{\infty} (1-\delta)^i p_{t-i} = \frac{p_t}{[1-(1-\delta)L]}$, where $L$ is the lagged operator and provided $\delta < 1$, the equation can be written as

$$q_t = a\delta + (1-\delta) q_{t-1} + b\delta p_t + c y_t - c(1-\delta) y_{t-1} + \varepsilon_t^* \tag{9.2}$$

where $\varepsilon_t^* = \varepsilon_t - (1-\delta)\varepsilon_{t-1}$.

### 9.2.2 Partial Adjustment Model

Of course, the geometric distribution is not the only form that lag distributions can take. Other forms that have proved popular are the Almon distributed lag model (1965) and the rational distributed lag model (Jorgenson 1966). One of the most popular models has been the partial adjustment model (Nerlove 1958):

$$q_t^* = a + bp_t + cy_t + \varepsilon_t \tag{9.3}$$

$$q_t - q_{t-1} = \delta\left(q_t^* - q_{t-1}\right) \tag{9.4}$$

The first equation is long-run desired demand. The consumer is envisioned as partially adjusting to that level each time period according to Eq. (9.4). Substituting (9.3) into (9.4) gives the estimating equation:

$$q_t = (1 - \delta)q_{t-1} + \delta a + \delta bp_t + \delta cy_t + \delta\varepsilon_t \tag{9.5}$$

The coefficients estimated are short-run price and income parameters. Long-run estimates are obtained by dividing each short-run coefficient by $\delta$, the partial adjustment parameter which is bounded between zero and one. This means all long-run effects must be larger than short-run effects.

### 9.2.3 State Adjustment Model

The state adjustment model (Houthakker and Taylor 1970) was developed to model both durable goods and habit formation. In contrast to the partial adjustment model, where we start with long-run demand, the state adjustment model starts with the short-run demand model:

$$q(t) = \theta + \alpha s(t) + \beta p(t) + \gamma y(t) \tag{9.6}$$

where $s(t)$ is the so-called state variable. For durable goods, this variable represents physical stocks; for nondurables, this variable represents stock of habits. For stock adjustment, we would expect the parameter $\alpha < 0$; for habit formation, we would expect $\alpha > 0$. The state variable is assumed to evolve according to the state equation:

$$\dot{s}(t) = \frac{ds}{dt} = q(t) - \delta s(t) \tag{9.7}$$

In general, the state variable, $s(t)$, is unobservable and can be eliminated by using both Eqs. (9.6) and (9.7) to obtain

$$\dot{q}(t) = \delta\theta + (\alpha - \delta)q(t) + \beta p(t) + \delta\beta\dot{p}(t) + \gamma y(t) + \delta\gamma\dot{y}(t) \tag{9.8}$$

In long-run equilibrium, $\dot{s}(t) = 0 \Rightarrow \dot{q}(t) = \dot{p}(t) = \dot{y}(t) = 0$, so from (9.8) we have

$$q^* = \frac{\delta\theta + \delta\beta p^* + \delta\gamma y^*}{(\delta - \alpha)} \tag{9.9}$$

provided $(\delta - \alpha) \neq 0$. When durability predominates, $\alpha < 0$, and long-run effects are smaller in absolute value than short-run effects; when habit formation predominates, $\alpha > 0$, and long-run effects are larger in absolute value than short-run effects.

For empirical estimation, the model needs to be converted to discrete time which necessitates an additional assumption be made about how the state variable changes over the discrete time interval. If it evolves linearly within each time interval, then Eqs. (9.6) and (9.7) are replaced by the equations (Phlips 1983, pp. 173–174):

$$q_t = \theta + \alpha\left(\frac{s_t + s_{t-1}}{2}\right) + \beta p_t + \gamma y_t$$

$$s_t - s_{t-1} = q_t - \delta\left(\frac{s_t + s_{t-1}}{2}\right)$$

Following the procedure before to eliminate the unobservable state variable, we obtain

$$q_t = A_0 + A_1 q_{t-1} + A_2 \Delta p_t + A_3 p_{t-1} + A_4 \Delta y_t + A_5 y_{t-1} + \varepsilon_t \tag{9.10}$$

where the $A$'s are functions of the underlying structural parameters. It can be shown that the structural parameters are overidentified, but just exactly identified if the following restriction holds:

$$\frac{A_2}{A_3} = \frac{(1 + \delta/2)}{\delta} = \frac{A_4}{A_5} \tag{9.11}$$

The model (9.10) subject to the nonlinear restriction, (9.11), may be estimated by nonlinear OLS. It is also likely that the error term is autocorrelated with a moving-average process of order one, i.e., MA(1), so the model should be estimated subject to that process. Because of presence of a lagged dependent variable, this will surely make estimation more difficult and the reader is referred to Fuller (1976, Chapter 9) for estimation of such a model.[1]

[1] Wohlgenant and Hahn (1982), in application of the state adjustment model to monthly demand for beef, pork, and chicken, approximate MA(1) process by second-order autoregressive process and then transform the model so that it is nonlinear in the $A$'s and autoregressive parameters, $\rho_1$ and $\rho_2$. The resulting model is estimated by nonlinear OLS.

## 9.3 Dynamic Models with Theoretical Foundations: Myopic Behavior

While the previous models are still useful in applied settings, particularly when one is interested only in modeling dynamic demand for an isolated commodity, attention has mostly focused on dynamic demand interrelationships. A number of issues have been raised theoretically about endogenous taste changes, which would occur if choices in the current period are based on choices in previous periods. A thorough discussion of the main issues is found in Gorman (1967) and in Phlips (1983). Gorman (1967) shows that, in general, a long-run preference indicator exists and can be thought of as an envelope to short-run preference indicators. A sufficient condition for existence of long-run utility is that the habit functions be independent of one another, which has not been a constraint in modeling taste changes to date. With respect to intertemporal behavior, consistency in choice and time preference require discounting future utility with a constant discount factor (Phlips 1983, Chapter XI).

The general approach to modeling taste changes is through specifying a utility function of the form $v(\boldsymbol{q}, \boldsymbol{s})$, which was presented in Chapter 2. Each function, $s_i$, depends on past consumption of the good in question. Thus, at time $t$, habit formation can be characterized as $s_{it} = f_i(q_{it-1}, q_{it-2}, \ldots)$. In continuous time, these functions are often specified according to (9.7), i.e., $\dot{s}(t) = q(t) - \delta s(t)$.

Based on Houthakker and Taylor's (1970) book, Phlips (1983) has generalized the functions, $\boldsymbol{s}$, to be state variables that could represent either stocks of durable goods or stocks of habits. Durability can refer to inventories held by consumers, even of somewhat perishable food items. Utility then is assumed to depend upon both consumption of goods purchased and consumed during the current period, and state variables corresponding to each commodity purchased.

Stigler and Becker (1977) explain habit formation as a consequence of learning through consuming. For example, if wine appreciation is the good demanded, then more wine appreciation can be produced through investment in wine appreciation, which likely would include "learning by doing" through the cumulative effects of earlier consumption. As shown in Chapter 2, we know that the comparative statics of change in the stock of habit formation are proportional to compensated price changes, Eq. (2.24):

$$d\boldsymbol{q} = \boldsymbol{K}\left(d\boldsymbol{P} - \lambda^{-1}\boldsymbol{V}d\boldsymbol{s}\right) + \boldsymbol{q}_y\left(dy - \boldsymbol{q}'d\boldsymbol{p}\right) \tag{9.12}$$

Therefore, we see that if, for simplicity, $\boldsymbol{V}$ is a diagonal matrix of effects of changes in $s_j$ on the effect of $mu_i$, then $\frac{\partial q_i}{\partial s_j} = -k_{ij}\lambda^{-1}v_{jj}$. Note that demand for good $i$ will depend on all $s_j$'s because of the fact that changes are proportional to the Slutsky substitution effects.

### 9.3.1 Dynamic Additive Quadratic Demand Model and Dynamic Linear Expenditure System

Houthakker and Taylor (1970) proposed a *dynamic Additive Quadratic Demand* (AQD) model and Phlips (1972) proposed a *dynamic Linear Expenditure System* (LES). The dynamic LES model has been more popular and is an extended form of Eq. (4.2):

$$p_i q_i = p_i \gamma_i + \beta_i \left( y - \sum\nolimits_{j=1}^{n} p_j \gamma_j \right) \tag{9.13}$$

$$\gamma_i = \theta_i + \alpha_i s_i \tag{9.14}$$

where the state variable, as before, is assumed to evolve according to the Eq. (9.7). The long-run demand functions corresponding to the short-run demand functions in (9.13) are

$$p_i q_i = p_i \gamma_i^* + \beta_i^* \left( y - \sum\nolimits_{j=1}^{n} p_j \gamma_j^* \right) \tag{9.15}$$

$$\gamma_i^* = \frac{\gamma_i \theta_i}{\delta_i - \alpha_i}, \ \beta_i^* = \frac{\delta_i \beta_i / (\delta_i - \alpha_i)}{\sum_j \delta_j \beta_j / (\delta_j - \alpha_j)}$$

As before, when $\alpha_i > 0$, the commodity is habit forming; when $\alpha_i < 0$, the commodity is durable.

For empirical analysis, the first-order conditions for utility maximization of the augmented Stone–Geary utility function are estimated. After making the transformation to discrete time as with the state adjustment model, the equations can be shown to have the following form:

$$q_t = K_{i0} + K_{i1} q_{it-1} + K_{i2} \frac{1}{\lambda_t p_{it}} + K_{i3} \frac{1}{\lambda_{t-1} p_{it-1}} \tag{9.16}$$

where the $K$'s are functions of the underlying structural parameters. After adding an error term to (9.16), the model is estimated, subject to the budget constraint: $y_t = \sum_j p_{jt} q_{jt}$. Estimation is somewhat complicated and involves iterating over different values of the marginal utility of income. Initial estimates of the $K$'s are used to generate a set of $\lambda_t$'s through the budget constraint, which in turn are used to estimate a new set of $K$'s through the demand model (9.16). A similar approach is used to estimate the dynamic additive quadratic demand model. In that case, the only difference is the form of the demand functions, which are the same as (9.16) with reciprocals of the price variables on the right-hand side, i.e., with $\lambda_t p_{it}$ and $\lambda_{t-1} p_{it-1}$ as price variables.

### 9.3.2 *Dynamic Models for Estimating Disaggregated Commodities*

One problem with the dynamic LES and dynamic AQD models is that both models are based on the restrictive assumption of additivity of the direct utility function. To alleviate this problem, researchers have focused on other more flexible functional forms, such as the *dynamic ITL* (Manser 1976) and the *dynamic AIDS model* (Blanciforti and Green 1983). One common specification is to make the intercepts depend upon lagged consumption

$$\alpha_i = \alpha_i^* + \alpha_i^{**} q_{it-1}$$

In the case of the dynamic AIDS model, we then have a set of equations from (4.21) modified as follows (Blanciforti and Green 1983):

$$\begin{aligned} w_{it} =&\alpha_i^* + \alpha_i^{**} q_{it-1} \\ &+\tau_i t + \sum_k \gamma_{ki} logp_{kt} \\ &+\beta_i \left[ \log y_t - \sum_i \alpha_i logp_{it} - \frac{1}{2} \left( \sum_j \sum_k \gamma_{jk} logp_j logp_k \right) \right] + \varepsilon_{it} \end{aligned} \tag{9.17}$$

subject to the restriction $\sum_i \alpha_i^{**} = 0$.

There are many other formulations of this type to flexible demand systems which will not be discussed here. The same approach has been taken to estimating inverse demand systems. For example, Holt and Goodwin (1997) develop an inverse dynamic AIDS model, which they show performs quite well for meat demand.

## 9.4 Dynamic Models with Theoretical Foundations: Intertemporal Behavior

In the previous section, myopic models of dynamic consumer behavior were presented. While these have served researchers well in empirical analysis, the assumption of myopic behavior is inconsistent with rational behavior of the consumer. A rational consumer will not only look to the past but also to perceived effects on marginal utility in the future. This section of the chapter presents intertemporal models of consumer behavior with emphasis on systems of consumer demand. To motivate the multivariate models, I start with the rational addition model of Becker et al. (1994).

### 9.4.1 Rational Addiction Model

It is sometimes necessary to have a model to account for the fact that consumers may anticipate expected future consequences of their current actions. Let $q_t$ be the quantity of the good consumed in period $t$, $y_t$ the consumption of a composite commodity, and $e_t$ the unmeasured life-cycle variables on utility. The consumer is assumed to maximize the present discounted value of future utility

$$\sum_{j=t}^{\infty} \beta^{j-t} v\left(y_j, q_j, q_{j-1}, e_j\right)$$

subject to

$$\sum_{j=t}^{\infty} \beta^{j-t} \left(y_j + p_j q_j\right) = A^{t-1}$$

$$q_{t-1} \qquad \text{(given)}$$

where $\beta$ is the one-period discount rate and $A^{t-1}$ is wealth at beginning of time $t$. The first-order conditions for utility maximization at time $t$ are as follows:

$$v_y(y_t, q_t, q_{t-1}, e_t) = \lambda \tag{9.18}$$

$$v_1(y_t, q_t, q_{t-1}, e_t) + \beta v_2(y_{t+1}, q_{t+1}, q_t, e_{t+1}) = \lambda p_t \tag{9.19}$$

where $\lambda$ is the marginal utility of wealth. Condition (9.18) says that the marginal utility of other goods equals the marginal utility of wealth, and condition (9.19) says that the marginal utility of current consumption plus discounted value of next period's marginal utility equals price times the marginal utility of wealth.

If the utility function is quadratic, then the first-order conditions in (9.18) and (9.19) are linear. After solving (9.18) for $y_t$ and $y_{t+1}$, and then eliminating these two variables from (9.19) we get

$$q_t = \theta q_{t-1} + \beta\theta q_{t+1} + \theta_1 p_t + \theta_2 e_t + \theta_3 e_{t+1} \tag{9.20}$$

The coefficient $\theta_1 < 0$ by the concavity of the utility function and $\theta > 0$ if the marginal utility of current consumption increases with increases in future consumption. (i.e., good is addictive). Equation (9.20) forms the basis for empirical analysis. The marginal utility of wealth, which is multiplied by price and is therefore embedded in $\theta_1$, will be constant with perfect certainty (Becker et al. 1994). Because of uncertainty, wealth can change and Becker et al. assume it is proxied by current income.

Note that ordinary least squares will yield inconsistent estimates because the variables $e_t$ and $e_{t+1}$ are correlated with $q_{t-1}$ and $q_{t+1}$. Therefore, past and future prices are logical instruments for lagged and future consumption. Estimates of the parameters of Eq. (9.20) can be used to derive price elasticities of demand. Short-run elasticities can be estimated directly from (9.20). Long-run elasticities can be computed by setting current quantity equal to lagged quantity and future quantity, and then solving for the effect of price on the long-run equilibrium quantity. The formula for the slope of long-run demand is

$$\frac{\partial q^*}{\partial p} = \frac{\theta_1}{1 - \theta - \beta\theta}$$

which will be larger in absolute value than the short-run slope, $\theta_1$, when $\theta > 0$. If $\theta < 0$, which would occur if durability is present, then long-run effects will be smaller than short-run effects in absolute value.

### 9.4.2 *Multivariate Rational Addiction (MRA) Model*

The rational addiction model of Becker et al. (1994) can be generalized to more than a single good. Bask and Meskerrson (2004), and Pierani and Tiezzi (2009) formulate and estimate models with two goods, tobacco and alcohol. Koksal and Wohlgenant (2016) extend the model to three goods: tobacco, alcohol consumed at home, and alcohol consumed in restaurants. None of these studies specifically utilize the restrictions implied by the theory or derive the dynamic properties of the model. Wohlgenant (2012) develops the theoretical and dynamic properties of the model for the general multivariate case. The consumer is assumed to maximize expected discounted future utility

$$E_t \sum_{j=t}^{\infty} \beta^{j-t} \left[ v\left(\boldsymbol{q}_j, \boldsymbol{q}_{j-1}\right) + \varphi\left(y_j\right) \right]$$

subject to

$$E_t \sum_{j=t}^{\infty} \beta^{j-t} \left( y_j + \boldsymbol{p}_j' \boldsymbol{q}_j \right) = A^{t-1}$$

$$q_{t-1} \qquad \text{(given)}$$

where all variables are defined as before except $E_t$, which is expectation given information at time $t$, $\boldsymbol{q}_j$ is a vector of quantities consumed, and $\boldsymbol{p}_j$ is the corresponding price vector. Consistent with the previous applications, I assume the composite good is additively separable from the goods in the separable branch that is modeled.[2]

#### 9.4.2.1 First-Order Conditions

The first-order conditions for utility maximization at time *t* are

$$E_t\left[\varphi'(y_t) - \lambda\right] = 0$$

$$E_t\left[\nabla_{\boldsymbol{q}_t} v\left(\boldsymbol{q}_t, \boldsymbol{q}_{t-1}\right) + \beta \nabla_{\boldsymbol{q}_t} v\left(\boldsymbol{q}_{t+1}, \boldsymbol{q}_t\right) - \lambda \boldsymbol{p}_t\right] = 0$$

where $\nabla_{\boldsymbol{q}_t}$ denotes the gradient vector with respect to the components of $\boldsymbol{q}_t$. As before, we assume a quadratic utility function, which implies

$$\boldsymbol{A} = \frac{\partial^2 v_t}{\partial \boldsymbol{q}_t \partial \boldsymbol{q}_t'} + \beta \frac{\partial^2 v_{t+1}}{\partial \boldsymbol{q}_t \partial \boldsymbol{q}_t'}$$

$$\boldsymbol{B} = \frac{\partial^2 v_t}{\partial \boldsymbol{q}_t \partial \boldsymbol{q}_{t-1}'}$$

#### 9.4.2.2 Euler Equations

The comparative statics of the first-order conditions can be expressed as

$$E_t\left[\boldsymbol{A}\boldsymbol{q}_t + \boldsymbol{B}\boldsymbol{q}_{t-1} + \beta \boldsymbol{B}\boldsymbol{q}_{t+1} - \lambda \boldsymbol{p}_t\right] = 0 \tag{9.21}$$

Assume $E_t \boldsymbol{q}_t = \boldsymbol{q}_t - \boldsymbol{u}_t$ and assume price is known so that Eq. (9.21) can be expressed as[3]

$$\boldsymbol{A}\boldsymbol{q}_t + \boldsymbol{B}\boldsymbol{q}_{t-1} + \beta \boldsymbol{B}\boldsymbol{q}_{t+1} - \lambda \boldsymbol{p}_t = \boldsymbol{A}\boldsymbol{\varepsilon}_t \tag{9.22}$$

or

---

[2]In Wohlgenant (2012), the composite good is included in the utility function as in Becker et al. (1994). For sake of convenience, it is treated as additively separable here. This is consistent with the two-stage budgeting process in Chapter 3. One could also make the function $\varphi(y_j)$ depend on lagged consumption of the composite good, but this would have no consequence for the problem at hand. For simplicity as well, I have not included the life-cycle variables as in Becker et al. (1994).

[3]While the consumer chooses quantities, he/she cannot know with certainty that the planned choice next period will be the actual choice, given that market prices and income are not known. Moreover, the analyst modeling consumer behavior does not know the consumer's next period choice. With rational expectations, it is thus logical to model $E_t \boldsymbol{q}_{t+1} = \boldsymbol{q}_{t+1} - \boldsymbol{u}_{t+1}$.

$$\boldsymbol{q}_t = -\boldsymbol{A}^{-1}\boldsymbol{B}\boldsymbol{q}_{t-1} - \beta\boldsymbol{A}^{-1}\boldsymbol{B}\boldsymbol{q}_{t+1} + \boldsymbol{A}^{-1}\lambda\boldsymbol{p}_t + \boldsymbol{\varepsilon}_t \tag{9.23}$$

provided $\boldsymbol{A}^{-1}$ exists and where $\boldsymbol{\varepsilon}_t = \boldsymbol{A}^{-1}(\boldsymbol{A}\boldsymbol{u}_t + \beta\boldsymbol{B}\boldsymbol{u}_{t+1})$.

#### 9.4.2.3 Theorem: Closed-Form Solution to Matrix Difference Equation

In Wohlgenant (2012), I assumed that the matrix $\boldsymbol{B}$ is diagonal, implying that the marginal utility of good $i$ is independent of quantity of good $j$, for $j$ not equal to $i$. We can relax this assumption by assuming only that $\boldsymbol{B}$ is a symmetric, positive definite matrix. This still implies that each marginal utility is positively correlated with itself for habit formation, but also allows for interdependencies among marginal utilities and lagged consumption of other goods. Whether $\boldsymbol{B}$ is diagonal or not, from (9.23) we see explicitly that quantity of any given good depends on lagged and future quantities of all goods, as well as prices of all goods. The matrix $\boldsymbol{A}$ is a strictly negative definite matrix so $\boldsymbol{A}^{-1}$ is also negative definite.

Generalizing Wohlgenant (2012) we have the following result:

**Theorem 4** The closed-form solution to the matrix difference Eq. (9.23) with $\boldsymbol{A}$ negative definite and $\boldsymbol{B}$ positive definite is

$$\boldsymbol{q}_t = \boldsymbol{Q}\boldsymbol{\Lambda}_1\boldsymbol{Q}^{-1}\boldsymbol{q}_{t-1} - \boldsymbol{Q}\sum\nolimits_{i=0}^{\infty}\boldsymbol{\Lambda}_2^{-(1+i)}\boldsymbol{Q}^{-1}\boldsymbol{B}^{-1}\beta^{-1}\lambda E_t\boldsymbol{p}_{t+i} + \boldsymbol{u}_t \tag{9.24}$$

where $\boldsymbol{\Lambda}_1$ and $\boldsymbol{\Lambda}_2$ are diagonal matrices of eigenvalues, $\boldsymbol{Q}$ is the orthogonal matrix that is used to diagonalize the matrix $-\boldsymbol{B}^{-1}\boldsymbol{A}$. The eigenvalues of $\boldsymbol{\Lambda}_1$ are all positive and less than one, while the eigenvalues of $\boldsymbol{\Lambda}_2$ are all positive and larger than one. See Appendix for proof.

#### 9.4.2.4 Formulas for Elasticities

The solution to the matrix difference equation shows that each quantity depends upon lagged quantities of all goods and discounted expected prices of all prices. The demand functions in the general form indicated by (9.24) can be used to estimate price elasticities of demand. The price derivatives for an expected temporary price change at time $t+i$ are:

$$\frac{\partial\boldsymbol{q}_t}{\partial E_t\boldsymbol{p}_{t+i}} = -\boldsymbol{Q}\boldsymbol{\Lambda}_2^{-(1+i)}\boldsymbol{Q}^{-1}\boldsymbol{B}^{-1}\beta^{-1}\lambda \tag{9.25}$$

For a permanent price change with past prices held content:

$$\frac{\partial\boldsymbol{q}_t}{\partial E_t\boldsymbol{p}_t} = -\sum\nolimits_{i=0}^{\infty}\boldsymbol{Q}\boldsymbol{\Lambda}_2^{-(1+i)}\boldsymbol{Q}^{-1}\boldsymbol{B}^{-1}\beta^{-1}\lambda = -\boldsymbol{Q}\left(\boldsymbol{I} - \boldsymbol{\Lambda}_2^{-1}\right)^{-1}\boldsymbol{Q}^{-1}\boldsymbol{B}^{-1}\beta^{-1}\lambda \tag{9.26}$$

Finally, the long-run price derivatives (permanent price change plus anticipated permanent price changes) are:

$$\frac{\partial \boldsymbol{q}_t}{\partial \boldsymbol{p}} = -\left(\boldsymbol{I} - \boldsymbol{Q}\boldsymbol{\Lambda}_1\boldsymbol{Q}^{-1}\right)^{-1}\boldsymbol{Q}\left(\boldsymbol{I} - \boldsymbol{\Lambda}_2^{-1}\right)^{-1}\boldsymbol{Q}^{-1}\boldsymbol{B}^{-1}\beta^{-1}\lambda \tag{9.27}$$

The advantage of the forms (9.25)–(9.27) is that one is able to compute elasticities based on whether the consumer's expectations for price change are transitory or permanent. Becker et al. (1994) illustrate the various types of elasticities for an increase in price of cigarettes.

## 9.5 Simple Non-Additive Preferences and Other Modeling Approaches

### 9.5.1 *SNAP Model*

Browning (1991) introduced the simple non-additive preferences (SNAP) model through an extended form of the AIDS model. This model is derived from the profit function

$$\pi\left(\boldsymbol{P}^t, \boldsymbol{P}^{t+1}, \ldots, \boldsymbol{P}^T, r\right) = \sum_{j=t}^{T-1} -\phi^j\left(\boldsymbol{P}^j, \boldsymbol{P}^{j+1}, r\right)$$

where $\boldsymbol{P}^t$ is a price vector of all goods at time $t$,$r$ is the price of utility (reciprocal of marginal utility of wealth), and $\phi^t\left(\boldsymbol{P}^t, \boldsymbol{P}^{t+1}, r\right)$ represents non-additive preferences at time $t$. Using Hotelling's theorem, Eq. (2.40), the intertemporal Frischian demand functions are

$$\boldsymbol{q}^t = \frac{\partial \phi^t\left(\boldsymbol{P}^t, \boldsymbol{P}^{t+1}, r\right)}{\partial \boldsymbol{P}^t} + \frac{\partial \phi^{t-1}\left(\boldsymbol{P}^{t-1}, \boldsymbol{P}^t, r\right)}{\partial \boldsymbol{P}^t} = \boldsymbol{g}^t\left(\boldsymbol{P}^{t-1}, \boldsymbol{P}^t, \boldsymbol{P}^{t+1}, r\right) \tag{9.28}$$

Imposing the intraperiod budget constraint we obtain

$$y_t = \sum_{i=1}^{n} p_i^t g_i^t\left(\boldsymbol{P}^{t-1}, \boldsymbol{P}^t, \boldsymbol{P}^{t+1}, r\right)$$

On the assumption that $y_t$ represents "normal" expenditures, in the sense it is an increasing function of wealth, then the marginal utility of expenditures ($r^{-1}$ will be a decreasing function of wealth and $y_t$ will be a strictly monotone function of $r$. Therefore, we can solve for $r$ and substitute into (9.28) to obtain the Marshallian demand functions:

$$\boldsymbol{q}^t = \boldsymbol{g}^t\left(\boldsymbol{P}^{t-1}, \boldsymbol{P}^t, \boldsymbol{P}^{t+1}, y_t\right) \tag{9.29}$$

So far the analysis has been entirely deterministic with perfect certainty. Incorporating uncertainty into the problem requires we replace $r$ with $r_t$ and define $\boldsymbol{P}^{t+1}$ as expected future prices. Moreover, we need to discount prices so both lagged and future prices are modified to account for discounting, i.e., lagged prices multiplied by $\beta^{-1}$ and future prices multiplied by $\beta$. We shall retain the same notation, however.

Browning (1991) uses an augmented form of the PIGLOG specification for intraperiod profit:

$$\phi^t\left(\boldsymbol{P}^t, \boldsymbol{P}^{t+1}, r\right) = -\left\{\log\left[\frac{r}{b\left(\boldsymbol{P}^t\right)}\right] - \log a\left(\boldsymbol{P}^t\right) - 1 + \log d\left(\boldsymbol{P}^{t-1}\right)\right\}\frac{r}{b\left(\boldsymbol{P}^t\right)} \tag{9.30}$$

where $d\left(\boldsymbol{P}^{t-1}\right)$ is homogenous of degree zero in prices. To obtain the demand functions, we use (9.28) and replace $r$ with $r_t$. We can also show that through use of the intraperiod budget constraint that

$$y_t = \frac{r_t}{b\left(\boldsymbol{P}^t\right)} \Rightarrow r_t = b\left(\boldsymbol{P}^t\right)y_t$$

The resulting demand functions are

$$w_{it} = \alpha_i + \sum_k \mu_{ki} logp_{kt} + \beta_i\left[\frac{y_t}{a\left(\boldsymbol{P}^t\right)}\right] + \beta_i\sum_k \theta_k logp_{kt-1}$$
$$-\theta_i E_t\left[\frac{b\left(\boldsymbol{P}^t\right)}{b\left(\boldsymbol{P}^{t+1}\right)}\right] + \varepsilon_{it} \tag{9.31}$$

Note that with $\theta_i = 0\forall i$, the model reduces to the AIDS model in (4.21). Thus, the AIDS model is nested within the SNAP model.

Prior to estimation, we must specify price expectations for future prices because they are generally unknown at time *t*. Browning (1991) invokes the rational expectations hypothesis

$$\left[\frac{b\left(\boldsymbol{P}^t\right)}{b\left(\boldsymbol{P}^{t+1}\right)}\right] = E_t\left[\frac{b\left(\boldsymbol{P}^t\right)}{b\left(\boldsymbol{P}^{t+1}\right)}\right] + u_t$$

When substituted back into (9.31), the model depends directly on the function of future prices as shown, but the error term is now $\varepsilon_{it} + \theta_i u_t$. We thus have the classic error-in-variables model. He chooses current and lagged prices, import prices, and time trends as instruments.

### 9.5.2 Spinnewyn Model

Another approach to modeling intertemporal demand is based on an insight by Spinnewyn (1981) that, under the assumption the consumer derives utility directly from stocks of consumer goods, one can transform any dynamic demand model into a static demand model with prices defined as user costs of the stocks. The consumer is assumed to maximize the intraperiod utility function

$$u = v(z_{1t}, z_{2t}, \ldots, z_{nt}) \tag{9.32}$$

subject to the intraperiod budget constraint

$$\sum_{i=1}^{n} \widehat{p}_{it} z_{it} = \widehat{y}_t \tag{9.33}$$

where

$$z_{it} = \sum_{\tau=0}^{\infty} \delta^{\tau} q_{it-\tau} = q_{it} + \delta_i z_{it-1} \tag{9.34}$$

and

$$\widehat{p}_{it} = p_{it} - \delta_i \beta p_{it+1} \tag{9.35}$$

Equation (9.32) defines the variables of choice as stocks. If $1 > \delta_i > 0$ the good is net durable and if $-1 < \delta_i < 0$, then habit formation prevails. Equation (9.35) is the user cost of the capital good. Maximizing (9.32) subject to (9.33) produces the demand functions $z_{it} = g_i(\widehat{y}_t, \widehat{p}_{1t}, \ldots, \widehat{p}_{nt})$ Substituting into Eq. (9.34) gives the final equations

$$q_{it} = g_i(\widehat{y}_t, \widehat{p}_{1t}, \ldots, \widehat{p}_{nt}) - \delta_i z_{it-1} \tag{9.36}$$

For a specific functional form, Eq. (9.36) can be estimated.[4] Paschardes (1982) and others use the AIDS model to specify and estimate the so-called *habits in durables* model:

$$w_{it} = \alpha_i + \beta_i[\log \widehat{y}_t - a(\widehat{\boldsymbol{p}}_t)] + \sum_{j=1}^{n} \gamma_{ij} \log \widehat{p}_{jt} - (p_{it}/y_t)\delta_i z_{it-1} \tag{9.37}$$

where $a(\widehat{\boldsymbol{p}}_t)$ is the quadratic log function, Eq. (4.17), defined in terms of the user cost variables rather than actual prices.

[4]The unobserved variable $z_{it-1}$ is calculated according to (9.34) with the initial value of $z_{it-1}$ set to $z_{i0} = q_{i0}/(1 - \delta_i)$.

The model is somewhat complicated to estimate, owing to the fact that the $z$ variables are constructed variables and estimation requires iteration over the $\delta_i$'s. Also, the user cost variable, Eq. (9.35), depends on expected future price. Past applications have assumed the consumer forms static expectations so that $\widehat{p}_{it} = p_{it}(1 - \delta_i\beta)$, but as I showed in the past chapter we could replace expected price with the actual price next period under the assumption that consumers form rational expectations. In general, though, the modeling approach is quite flexible and allows the researcher to apply two-stage budgeting. As an example, Zhen et al. (2011) use the model to estimate a system of nine sugar-sweetened beverages conditional on beverage expenditures, and a first-stage allocation equation relating beverage expenditures to an aggregate beverage price and aggregate household expenditures.

The Spinnewyn (1981) approach has implications for application of the multivariate rational addiction model. From the solution to the rational addiction problem, Eq. (9.24), define

$$\overline{\boldsymbol{q}}_t = \boldsymbol{q}_t - \boldsymbol{Q}\boldsymbol{\Lambda}_1\boldsymbol{Q}^{-1}\boldsymbol{q}_{t-1} \tag{9.38}$$

and

$$\overline{\boldsymbol{p}}_t = \boldsymbol{Q}\sum_{i=0}^{\infty}\boldsymbol{\Lambda}_2^{-i}\boldsymbol{Q}^{-1}\beta^{-1}E_t\boldsymbol{p}_{t+i} = \boldsymbol{Q}\sum_{i=0}^{\infty}\boldsymbol{\Lambda}_1^{i}\boldsymbol{Q}^{-1}E_t\boldsymbol{p}_{t+i} \tag{9.39}$$

where the last part of (9.39) results from the fact that $\beta^{-1}\boldsymbol{\Lambda}_2^{-1} = \boldsymbol{\Lambda}_1$ (Wohlgenant 2012). Browning (1991, Appendix A) shows that if preferences are defined over the adjusted quantities given by (9.38) ($\boldsymbol{H} = -\boldsymbol{Q}\boldsymbol{\Lambda}_1\boldsymbol{Q}^{-1}$ in Browning's notation), then the model is called the *short memory model* with prices defined precisely by (9.39). Therefore, Wohlgenant's model can be treated as a static model in the sense the consumer maximizes an additive intertemporal utility function with utility, $v(\overline{\boldsymbol{q}}_t)$, for each time period and budget constraint, $\overline{A}^t - \overline{A}^{t-1} = -\overline{p}_t'\overline{q}_t$.

### 9.5.3 Meghir and Weber Short Memory Model

A final model to discuss is one based on research by Meghir and Weber (1996). They estimate the short memory model by equating marginal utility per dollar spent on each good with marginal utility spent on a numeraire good. This produces general estimating equations of the form

$$\frac{mu_i(\boldsymbol{q}_t, \boldsymbol{q}_{t-1})}{p_{it}} + \beta\frac{mu_i(\boldsymbol{q}_{t+1}, \boldsymbol{q}_t)}{p_{it}} = \frac{mu_n(\boldsymbol{q}_t, \boldsymbol{q}_{t-1})}{p_{nt}} + \beta\frac{mu_n(\boldsymbol{q}_{t+1}, \boldsymbol{q}_t)}{p_{nt}}$$

when the $n^{\text{th}}$ good has been chosen as the numeraire. While the model eliminates the marginal utility of wealth, it can become difficult to estimate owing to the duplication of variables from equating the two marginal utilities, therefore inducing multicollinearity and making it difficult to identify and estimate the parameters of the marginal utility functions.

## 9.6 Empirical Application to Dynamic Demand for US Alcohol

### 9.6.1 Application of MRA Model to Alcohol Demand

In this section, I apply the multivariate rational addiction (MRA) model to demand for US alcoholic beverages: wine, beer, and spirits. These commodities are natural candidates for evaluating dynamic demand and, in particular, habit formation. I choose the MRA model because it is an extension of the single variable model proposed and applied to cigarette demand by Becker et al. (1994).

To be consistent with Becker et al., the MRA model, Eq. (9.23), needs to be modified to account for transitory, or short-run, changes in the marginal utility of wealth. As Becker et al point out, under perfect certainty, the rational consumer would keep $\lambda$ constant. With uncertainty, actual income will differ from expected or planned income and this may cause the consumer to adjust its expectation of wealth and therefore marginal utility of wealth. Thus, we use per capita personal consumption expenditures ($y_t$) as a proxy for the effect of uncertainty. The model to be estimated is

$$\boldsymbol{q}_t = \boldsymbol{a} + \boldsymbol{D}\boldsymbol{q}_{t-1} + \beta \boldsymbol{D}\boldsymbol{q}_{t+1} + \boldsymbol{C}\boldsymbol{p}_t + \boldsymbol{d} y_t + \boldsymbol{b}t + \boldsymbol{\varepsilon}_t \tag{9.40}$$

where $\boldsymbol{D} = -\boldsymbol{A}^{-1}\boldsymbol{B}, \boldsymbol{C} = \boldsymbol{A}^{-1}$ and $t$ is a linear time trend. As discussed previously, $\boldsymbol{C}$ is a negative semi-definite matrix.

The data set constructed consists of three commodities: (1) wine consumed at home, (2) beer consumed at home, and (3) spirits consumed at home.[5] The data for expenditures and price indices are quarterly, seasonally adjusted data from (https://apps.bea.gov/). The quantities are obtained by dividing expenditures by the price indices. Population data are from the Federal Reserve Bank at (https://fred.stlouisfed.org), and CPI data come from (https://www.bls.gov/data/). The time period covered is 1995Q1 through 2015Q4, a total of 84 observations. Table (9.1) reports the data used in estimation: spiritq, wineq, and beerq are per capita constant dollar expenditures for spirits, wine, and beer, respectively; spiritp, winep, and beerp are deflated

[5]Data covering at home and away from consumption are preferred, but only data by alcoholic beverage are available for only at home consumption.

**Table 9.1** Per Capita Constant Dollar Expenditures, Price Indices for Alcohol, and Per Capita Real Personal Consumption Expenditures, 1995Q1–2015Q4

| Date | spiritq | wineq | beerq | spiritp | winep | beerp | ppce |
|---|---|---|---|---|---|---|---|
| 1995Q1 | 55.88353 | 58.32045 | 174.341329 | 0.509324 | 0.52726 | 0.45922 | 12144.49 |
| 1995Q2 | 55.12561 | 51.00622 | 175.543309 | 0.507955 | 0.526555 | 0.456739 | 12187.71 |
| 1995Q3 | 55.17065 | 51.49585 | 176.891926 | 0.506703 | 0.525353 | 0.45416 | 12247 |
| 1995Q4 | 55.32256 | 51.82545 | 178.197141 | 0.504151 | 0.526311 | 0.452811 | 12281.76 |
| 1996Q1 | 56.57364 | 52.83976 | 180.765834 | 0.500817 | 0.528025 | 0.453966 | 12323.32 |
| 1996Q2 | 56.04869 | 53.21724 | 182.978604 | 0.497954 | 0.53007 | 0.453696 | 12397.04 |
| 1996Q3 | 55.58686 | 53.26523 | 182.995526 | 0.498233 | 0.532276 | 0.454584 | 12413.19 |
| 1996Q4 | 53.82097 | 52.69673 | 184.386716 | 0.496683 | 0.536055 | 0.450737 | 12449.09 |
| 1997Q1 | 54.12706 | 53.4903 | 188.496667 | 0.496231 | 0.539292 | 0.448359 | 12526.23 |
| 1997Q2 | 54.35182 | 53.27676 | 188.20302 | 0.497631 | 0.543019 | 0.44675 | 12549.38 |
| 1997Q3 | 54.51129 | 53.63129 | 191.049487 | 0.497624 | 0.544471 | 0.443588 | 12691.12 |
| 1997Q4 | 54.5818 | 53.93989 | 192.303248 | 0.498272 | 0.541082 | 0.439794 | 12774.17 |
| 1998Q1 | 55.94449 | 56.09762 | 191.290263 | 0.496414 | 0.539562 | 0.439191 | 12844.85 |
| 1998Q2 | 56.5574 | 58.19062 | 191.059771 | 0.496372 | 0.540732 | 0.438378 | 13015.95 |
| 1998Q3 | 57.75667 | 60.64139 | 191.201598 | 0.494611 | 0.537619 | 0.437703 | 13117.91 |
| 1998Q4 | 58.53279 | 62.73765 | 192.280826 | 0.496054 | 0.535449 | 0.438875 | 13239.97 |
| 1999Q1 | 58.33959 | 63.6825 | 193.251444 | 0.496202 | 0.535326 | 0.43982 | 13320.57 |
| 1999Q2 | 59.22982 | 65.24744 | 195.454779 | 0.495389 | 0.533613 | 0.439263 | 13450.76 |
| 1999Q3 | 59.16719 | 66.1088 | 196.904855 | 0.495861 | 0.533116 | 0.439007 | 13530.72 |
| 1999Q4 | 60.08455 | 68.57876 | 201.044962 | 0.497384 | 0.530406 | 0.439242 | 13667.86 |
| 2000Q1 | 60.33858 | 69.85823 | 201.230712 | 0.498824 | 0.527178 | 0.439471 | 13821.57 |
| 2000Q2 | 61.3824 | 72.54184 | 202.528572 | 0.49978 | 0.524921 | 0.439407 | 13874.4 |
| 2000Q3 | 62.55672 | 74.93523 | 204.042961 | 0.499017 | 0.521775 | 0.438387 | 13931.94 |
| 2000Q4 | 63.01336 | 76.57215 | 206.304314 | 0.497695 | 0.520233 | 0.437775 | 13992.58 |
| 2001Q1 | 63.06083 | 78.48878 | 204.323087 | 0.4983 | 0.513167 | 0.436094 | 13977.88 |
| 2001Q2 | 62.70403 | 80.34621 | 206.304432 | 0.499923 | 0.508583 | 0.43478 | 13945.96 |
| 2001Q3 | 62.39019 | 82.29746 | 201.172687 | 0.50338 | 0.50593 | 0.438251 | 13926.2 |
| 2001Q4 | 63.18622 | 84.97395 | 196.31634 | 0.507048 | 0.507318 | 0.44022 | 14117.72 |
| 2002Q1 | 63.47638 | 86.92532 | 195.9301 | 0.507703 | 0.507596 | 0.441065 | 14111.25 |
| 2002Q2 | 63.20671 | 88.06048 | 197.906576 | 0.505319 | 0.502751 | 0.441475 | 14148.65 |
| 2002Q3 | 62.61435 | 88.0216 | 196.816814 | 0.503782 | 0.501809 | 0.441421 | 14208.03 |
| 2002Q4 | 62.58246 | 87.97678 | 197.79118 | 0.500617 | 0.501928 | 0.440777 | 14236.55 |
| 2003Q1 | 63.24029 | 87.67833 | 195.509657 | 0.49563 | 0.496808 | 0.438913 | 14228.09 |
| 2003Q2 | 63.7625 | 86.86797 | 190.544263 | 0.49943 | 0.497835 | 0.440774 | 14383.19 |
| 2003Q3 | 65.72357 | 88.37809 | 190.800381 | 0.497551 | 0.494683 | 0.440555 | 14539.32 |

(continued)

**Table 9.1** (continued)

| Date | spiritq | wineq | beerq | spiritp | winep | beerp | ppce |
|---|---|---|---|---|---|---|---|
| 2003Q4 | 66.48153 | 89.82723 | 188.387444 | 0.499381 | 0.490036 | 0.444523 | 14614.5 |
| 2004Q1 | 67.10158 | 90.32105 | 188.165217 | 0.494413 | 0.48805 | 0.443894 | 14713.43 |
| 2004Q2 | 68.16978 | 91.47324 | 187.358452 | 0.492069 | 0.486032 | 0.446578 | 14757.95 |
| 2004Q3 | 68.51576 | 92.41483 | 186.232561 | 0.490736 | 0.481595 | 0.446193 | 14864.29 |
| 2004Q4 | 69.18112 | 92.79269 | 185.501101 | 0.487638 | 0.48082 | 0.444734 | 14956.03 |
| 2005Q1 | 69.60173 | 93.50104 | 184.977941 | 0.486935 | 0.478207 | 0.441755 | 15021.1 |
| 2005Q2 | 70.57265 | 93.92694 | 185.043089 | 0.483568 | 0.478064 | 0.438454 | 15147.78 |
| 2005Q3 | 71.60768 | 94.31549 | 185.912343 | 0.477625 | 0.475371 | 0.431673 | 15189.04 |
| 2005Q4 | 73.22506 | 96.40739 | 187.698385 | 0.475868 | 0.470969 | 0.428733 | 15173.23 |
| 2006Q1 | 74.84861 | 97.69185 | 189.284902 | 0.477308 | 0.473011 | 0.428117 | 15307.12 |
| 2006Q2 | 75.78068 | 98.03264 | 189.494457 | 0.473288 | 0.472502 | 0.426449 | 15335.18 |
| 2006Q3 | 76.74677 | 98.49107 | 189.085471 | 0.467124 | 0.468177 | 0.42317 | 15354.57 |
| 2006Q4 | 78.03278 | 99.48603 | 190.372645 | 0.469473 | 0.470807 | 0.425229 | 15501.07 |
| 2007Q1 | 79.33272 | 99.85869 | 189.26332 | 0.466652 | 0.470255 | 0.426661 | 15547.87 |
| 2007Q2 | 80.45206 | 100.5977 | 187.139347 | 0.46419 | 0.46675 | 0.429122 | 15492.41 |
| 2007Q3 | 80.61125 | 100.1114 | 184.828891 | 0.460832 | 0.46617 | 0.430237 | 15528.94 |
| 2007Q4 | 79.99506 | 99.11065 | 184.327364 | 0.456436 | 0.465291 | 0.425109 | 15496.37 |
| 2008Q1 | 78.75833 | 98.86412 | 180.50858 | 0.455507 | 0.463215 | 0.425798 | 15384.22 |
| 2008Q2 | 78.0727 | 98.83117 | 179.122483 | 0.454273 | 0.463269 | 0.422042 | 15334.29 |
| 2008Q3 | 78.09006 | 98.85886 | 177.785479 | 0.449162 | 0.461197 | 0.418558 | 15106.83 |
| 2008Q4 | 77.00183 | 97.51917 | 172.310657 | 0.461004 | 0.476463 | 0.437412 | 15051.91 |
| 2009Q1 | 76.0767 | 97.003 | 170.590333 | 0.467818 | 0.4824 | 0.443531 | 15000.68 |
| 2009Q2 | 75.0703 | 97.0092 | 169.038034 | 0.468195 | 0.478551 | 0.442843 | 14896.99 |
| 2009Q3 | 75.16327 | 97.56163 | 168.057327 | 0.465655 | 0.475681 | 0.443792 | 14940.06 |
| 2009Q4 | 75.4629 | 99.40581 | 169.704876 | 0.4653 | 0.471105 | 0.443077 | 14881.97 |
| 2010Q1 | 77.12653 | 102.5316 | 172.950004 | 0.46051 | 0.464872 | 0.441373 | 14952.98 |
| 2010Q2 | 77.59491 | 103.5413 | 172.504569 | 0.458694 | 0.463719 | 0.444248 | 15066.98 |
| 2010Q3 | 76.99026 | 103.9077 | 170.993645 | 0.459973 | 0.463029 | 0.446749 | 15125.25 |
| 2010Q4 | 77.59945 | 104.8547 | 170.839235 | 0.453616 | 0.459419 | 0.443775 | 15164.44 |
| 2011Q1 | 77.50844 | 105.7644 | 171.050198 | 0.449731 | 0.454983 | 0.439026 | 15175.35 |
| 2011Q2 | 77.21076 | 107.0044 | 169.502034 | 0.445588 | 0.447694 | 0.437502 | 15161.4 |
| 2011Q3 | 77.76918 | 109.3105 | 169.930799 | 0.442892 | 0.440821 | 0.434959 | 15165.9 |
| 2011Q4 | 78.09751 | 110.57 | 169.469096 | 0.440785 | 0.43779 | 0.435315 | 15148.6 |
| 2012Q1 | 79.65543 | 112.6245 | 170.383796 | 0.438763 | 0.43734 | 0.437554 | 15264.63 |
| 2012Q2 | 80.62469 | 113.9244 | 171.598713 | 0.436873 | 0.437738 | 0.436847 | 15267.12 |

(continued)

**Table 9.1** (continued)

| Date | spiritq | wineq | beerq | spiritp | winep | beerp | ppce |
|---|---|---|---|---|---|---|---|
| 2012Q3 | 79.3361 | 112.7546 | 169.275915 | 0.435096 | 0.435771 | 0.434983 | 15237.83 |
| 2012Q4 | 80.52676 | 113.8636 | 168.878879 | 0.4316 | 0.431466 | 0.432923 | 15261.4 |
| 2013Q1 | 80.28343 | 113.5582 | 167.296656 | 0.433325 | 0.431392 | 0.434551 | 15311.4 |
| 2013Q2 | 79.7073 | 112.0123 | 164.769004 | 0.435278 | 0.434748 | 0.437445 | 15327.23 |
| 2013Q3 | 80.67845 | 113.0122 | 165.87308 | 0.434222 | 0.433776 | 0.436674 | 15339.28 |
| 2013Q4 | 80.83968 | 114.9662 | 166.492777 | 0.4334 | 0.427553 | 0.437153 | 15447.08 |
| 2014Q1 | 81.34059 | 115.9521 | 166.922479 | 0.430407 | 0.424457 | 0.436162 | 15458.91 |
| 2014Q2 | 82.35445 | 117.4866 | 169.299956 | 0.42875 | 0.422536 | 0.43385 | 15594.04 |
| 2014Q3 | 82.78926 | 118.0367 | 170.635474 | 0.429349 | 0.424308 | 0.434313 | 15732.58 |
| 2014Q4 | 83.011 | 118.909 | 171.708762 | 0.432233 | 0.426192 | 0.435813 | 15911.04 |
| 2015Q1 | 84.09903 | 120.9575 | 174.036705 | 0.434352 | 0.426938 | 0.436974 | 16052.07 |
| 2015Q2 | 84.8152 | 122.2168 | 174.23805 | 0.430706 | 0.42254 | 0.435711 | 16123.42 |
| 2015Q3 | 85.9711 | 124.0582 | 174.916714 | 0.427605 | 0.419642 | 0.436766 | 16199.19 |
| 2015Q4 | 85.90836 | 123.9471 | 174.334392 | 0.427923 | 0.421289 | 0.43862 | 16227.82 |

price indices (1982–84 $=$ 1.0); and ppce is per capita deflated total consumption expenditures.

#### 9.6.1.1 GMM Results

The model was estimated by generalized method of moments (GMM). Initial estimation by 3SLS indicated presence of serial correlation.[6] This should be expected in light of the fact that we showed the error term, $\boldsymbol{\varepsilon}_t$, is likely to be autocorrelated (see Eq. 9.23). The GMM estimator is essentially a generalization of OLS, SUR, 2SLS, and 3SLS and allows different weighting functions of the residuals in estimation. While both GMM and 3SLS are consistent estimators, use of GMM allows us to account for serial correlation of a general order within and across equations to produce more efficient estimates of the parameters. Consistent standard errors of the parameters are obtained using the Newey–West estimator (Newey and West 1987). Use of this estimator requires selection of lag lengths and smoothness functions for the lag distributions of estimated residuals. I chose four lags and the Bartlett function for lag distributions. The instruments are all current, lagged, and one-period lead prices, per capita income, and the time trend. See, e.g., Greene (2003) for details on this estimator.

The results are presented in Table 9.2. These results are symmetry-constrained for both the matrices $\boldsymbol{C}$ and $\boldsymbol{D}$. As indicated above, theory indicates $\boldsymbol{C}$ is a symmetric,

[6]Because the instrumental variables used, $\boldsymbol{p}_t$, $\boldsymbol{p}_{t-1}$, $\boldsymbol{p}_{t+1}$, $y_t$, and $t$ are exogenous, the residuals from 3SLS are consistently estimated. Durbin–Watson statistics from these estimated models indicated serial correlation in all three equations.

**Table 9.2** Parameter Estimates of Dynamic Demand for Wine, Beer, and Spirits using GMM

| Parameter | Estimate | Approx Std Err | t Value | Approx Pr > \|t\| |
|---|---|---|---|---|
| $c_{12}$ | 5.015583 | 9.7073 | 0.52 | 0.6069 |
| $c_{21}$ | 5.015583 | 9.7073 | 0.52 | 0.6069 |
| $c_{13}$ | 37.02449 | 9.5551 | 3.87 | 0.0002 |
| $c_{31}$ | 37.02449 | 9.5551 | 3.87 | 0.0002 |
| $c_{23}$ | 10.56425 | 9.4403 | 1.12 | 0.2667 |
| $c_{32}$ | 10.56425 | 9.4403 | 1.12 | 0.2667 |
| $d_{12}$ | 0.019615 | 0.0110 | 1.78 | 0.0784 |
| $d_{21}$ | 0.019615 | 0.0110 | 1.78 | 0.0784 |
| $d_{13}$ | 0.067954 | 0.0168 | 4.04 | 0.0001 |
| $d_{31}$ | 0.067954 | 0.0168 | 4.04 | 0.0001 |
| $d_{23}$ | – 0.02073 | 0.0102 | – 2.04 | 0.0448 |
| $d_{32}$ | – 0.02073 | 0.0102 | – 2.04 | 0.0448 |
| $a_1$ | – 5.81184 | 5.8784 | – 0.99 | 0.3260 |
| $c_{11}$ | – 32.6376 | 12.6845 | – 2.57 | 0.0121 |
| $d_{11}$ | 0.457806 | 0.0181 | 25.31 | <.0001 |
| $d_1$ | – 0.00062 | 0.000330 | – 1.87 | 0.0649 |
| $b_1$ | 0.051224 | 0.0247 | 2.08 | 0.0412 |
| $a_2$ | 36.96773 | 8.9938 | 4.11 | <.0001 |
| $c_{22}$ | – 71.401 | 15.3629 | – 4.65 | <.0001 |
| $d_{22}$ | 0.462971 | 0.0186 | 24.89 | <.0001 |
| $d_2$ | 0.000186 | 0.000360 | 0.52 | 0.6063 |
| $b_2$ | – 0.04547 | 0.0232 | – 1.96 | 0.0540 |
| $a_3$ | 1.386329 | 5.5126 | 0.25 | 0.8021 |
| $c_{33}$ | – 55.6336 | 11.1089 | – 5.01 | <.0001 |
| $d_{33}$ | 0.46628 | 0.0338 | 13.80 | <.0001 |
| $d_3$ | 0.000569 | 0.000548 | 1.04 | 0.3029 |
| $b_3$ | – 0.12431 | 0.0242 | – 5.14 | <.0001 |

negative definite matrix. The restrictions were tested and we fail to reject with at a large p-value of 0.83. On the other hand, theory does not show $\boldsymbol{D}$ should be symmetric, but intuition may indicate so. Given symmetry on the price effects, symmetry was imposed and tested on $\boldsymbol{D}$ and was not rejected with a p-value of 0.07.[7] I have also restricted the coefficients on lagged and lead quantity variables with an assumed discount rate of 0.99, which corresponds to an annual continuously compounded interest rate of 5 percent. The reason for this is multicollinearity. The restrictions are

[7]We also fail to reject the test for overidentifying restrictions with a p-value of 0.9. This is often interpreted as a test of the validity of the model.

not rejected at conventional levels. Finally, the model was estimated using the GMM option with Proc Model using SAS software version 9.4. Commodities are wine (1), beer (2), and spirits (3).

Overall, the results conform to the theory. All own-price effects are significant. The eigenvalues of the matrix $\boldsymbol{C}$ were computed and all three were found to be negative, supporting the hypothesis that $\boldsymbol{C}$ is a negative definite matrix. All three beverages appear to be contemporary substitutes. The strongest substitution occurs between wine and spirits.

Many of the parameters of the matrix $\boldsymbol{D}$ are significant. Own lagged and lead quantities are highly significant and less than 0.5 in each case, as one would expect for stability of the difference equations. Also, we find all the cross-quantity effects are significant at p-values smaller than 0.1. The most significant cross-quantity effects are between wine and spirits, and between beer and spirits. Positive signs indicate intertemporal complementarity, while negative signs indicate intertemporal substitutability. Wine and spirits are intertemporal complements, while beer and spirits are intertemporal substitutes. Increases in wine consumption lead to increases in spirit demand over time, and vice versa. Increases in beer consumption lead to decreases in spirit demand over time, and vice versa. Finally, changes in the marginal utility of wealth through changes in income have little impact on demand for alcohol. Overall, the results indicate the importance of accounting for commodity interrelationships in a dynamic model in accordance with the MRA model.

I have calculated three types of elasticities from the estimated parameters. The first are short-run effects from a temporary, one-period, change in price, from Eq. (9.24). These own-price elasticities are relatively inelastic, with wine and beer most inelastic. All cross-price elasticities are positive, showing substitution. The elasticity of wine demand with respect to spirit price, and elasticity of spirit demand with respect to wine price are by far the largest. The second set of elasticities are for expected permanent price changes in the past, but where consumers only expect price change for the current period. These elasticities are obtained in an analogous fashion to the long-run elasticities obtained from myopic models, where the short-run elasticities are divided by one minus the coefficient on the lagged dependent variable. As shown, these elasticities are slightly less than twice the short-run elasticities, reflecting the fact that the own lagged quantity effects are all less than 0.5. The final set of elasticities are the long-run elasticities, where the consumer anticipates prices will continue to increase at the same rate forever, Eq. (9.26). The elasticities are all much larger (in absolute value). In fact, the own-price elasticities now suggest demand for wine and beer are elastic in the long run. On the other hand, demand for spirits is still inelastic and somewhat smaller than the long-run elasticity when only current prices are expected to change. Two of the cross-price elasticities change sign: the long-run elasticity of wine demand with respect to beer price, and the long-run elasticity of beer demand with respect to wine price. Now the relationships indicate complementary relationships, whereas for the short run and long run with only current price changes the relationships indicate substitutability. The short-run and long-run elasticities with temporary price change make sense and are in accordance with past studies (Gallet

2007). There are no published results to compare with long-run elasticities with perceived permanent price changes.

## Appendix: Proof of Theorem 4

Following Wohlgenant (2012), Eq. (9.21) can be written as a matrix polynomial in Lags as follows:

$$\left(\beta^{-1}\boldsymbol{I}L^2 + \beta^{-1}\boldsymbol{B}^{-1}\boldsymbol{A}L + \boldsymbol{I}\right)L^{-1}E_t\boldsymbol{q}_t = \lambda\beta^{-1}\boldsymbol{B}^{-1}E_t\boldsymbol{p}_t$$

Because $\boldsymbol{B}$ is a positive definite matrix, we know there exists an orthogonal matrix $\boldsymbol{P}$ such that $\boldsymbol{P}\boldsymbol{B}\boldsymbol{P}' = \boldsymbol{N}$, a diagonal matrix with all positive diagonal elements. Define $\boldsymbol{S} = \boldsymbol{N}^{0.5}\boldsymbol{P}$, where $\boldsymbol{N}^{0.5}$ is a diagonal matrix whose elements are positive square roots. Because $\boldsymbol{B} = \boldsymbol{P}'\boldsymbol{N}\boldsymbol{P} = \boldsymbol{S}'\boldsymbol{S}$, we see that $\boldsymbol{B}$ can be written as the product of two square root matrices. Because $-\boldsymbol{A}$ is a positive definite matrix, $-\boldsymbol{S}'^{-1}\boldsymbol{A}\boldsymbol{S}^{-1}$ is also positive definite. Therefore, there exists an orthogonal matrix $\boldsymbol{R}$ such that $-\boldsymbol{R}\boldsymbol{S}'^{-1}\boldsymbol{A}\boldsymbol{S}^{-1}\boldsymbol{R}' = \boldsymbol{M}$, a diagonal matrix whose diagonal elements are positive. Define $\boldsymbol{Q} = \boldsymbol{S}^{-1}\boldsymbol{R}'$, then $-\boldsymbol{Q}^{-1}\boldsymbol{B}^{-1}\boldsymbol{A}\boldsymbol{Q} = -\boldsymbol{R}\boldsymbol{S}'^{-1}\boldsymbol{A}\boldsymbol{S}^{-1}\boldsymbol{R}' = \boldsymbol{M}$. Thus, we have proved $-\boldsymbol{B}^{-1}\boldsymbol{A}$ is similar to $-\boldsymbol{A}$, implying it has the same positive roots. The rest of the steps are identical to Wohlgenant (2012), where we multiply both sides of the matrix polynomial by $\boldsymbol{Q}^{-1}$ and post-multiply by $\boldsymbol{Q}$ to obtain

$$\boldsymbol{Q}^{-1}\left(\beta^{-1}\boldsymbol{Q}L^2 - \beta^{-1}\boldsymbol{Q}\boldsymbol{M}L + \boldsymbol{Q}\right)\boldsymbol{Q}^{-1}L^{-1}E_t\boldsymbol{q}_t = \lambda\beta^{-1}\boldsymbol{Q}^{-1}\boldsymbol{B}^{-1}E_t\boldsymbol{p}_t \Rightarrow$$

$$\left(\beta^{-1}\boldsymbol{I}L^2 - \beta^{-1}\boldsymbol{M}L + \boldsymbol{I}\right)\boldsymbol{Q}^{-1}L^{-1}E_t\boldsymbol{q}_t = \lambda\beta^{-1}\boldsymbol{Q}^{-1}\boldsymbol{B}^{-1}E_t\boldsymbol{p}_t \Rightarrow$$

$$(\boldsymbol{I} - \boldsymbol{\Lambda}_1 L)(\boldsymbol{I} - \boldsymbol{\Lambda}_2 L)\boldsymbol{Q}^{-1}L^{-1}E_t\boldsymbol{q}_t = \lambda\beta^{-1}\boldsymbol{Q}^{-1}\boldsymbol{B}^{-1}E_t\boldsymbol{p}_t \Rightarrow$$

$$-\boldsymbol{\Lambda}_2 L\left(\boldsymbol{I} - \boldsymbol{\Lambda}_2^{-1}L^{-1}\right)(\boldsymbol{I} - \boldsymbol{\Lambda}_1 L)\boldsymbol{Q}^{-1}L^{-1}E_t\boldsymbol{q}_t = \lambda\beta^{-1}\boldsymbol{Q}^{-1}\boldsymbol{B}^{-1}E_t\boldsymbol{p}_t \Rightarrow$$

$$(\boldsymbol{I} - \boldsymbol{\Lambda}_1 L)\boldsymbol{Q}^{-1}E_t\boldsymbol{q}_t = -\left(\boldsymbol{I} - \boldsymbol{\Lambda}_2^{-1}L^{-1}\right)^{-1}\lambda\beta^{-1}\boldsymbol{\Lambda}_2^{-1}\boldsymbol{Q}^{-1}\boldsymbol{B}^{-1}E_t\boldsymbol{p}_t \Rightarrow$$

$$\left(\boldsymbol{I} - \boldsymbol{Q}\boldsymbol{\Lambda}_1\boldsymbol{Q}^{-1}L\right)E_t\boldsymbol{q}_t = -\boldsymbol{Q}\left(\boldsymbol{I} - \boldsymbol{\Lambda}_2^{-1}L^{-1}\right)^{-1}\lambda\beta^{-1}\boldsymbol{\Lambda}_2^{-1}\boldsymbol{Q}^{-1}\boldsymbol{B}^{-1}E_t\boldsymbol{p}_t$$

where we use the results that $\boldsymbol{M} = \boldsymbol{\Lambda}_1 + \boldsymbol{\Lambda}_2$ and $\boldsymbol{\Lambda}_1\boldsymbol{\Lambda}_2 = \beta^{-1}\boldsymbol{I}$. Wohlgenant (2012) shows that there are exactly $2n$ distinct positive roots such that $\lambda_{1i} < 1$ and $\lambda_{2i} = \beta^{-1}\lambda_{1i}^{-1} > 1$. After substituting $E_t\boldsymbol{q}_t = \boldsymbol{q}_t - \boldsymbol{u}_t$, we obtain the desired result. QED

## Problems

9.1 Derive the discrete version of the State Adjustment Model, Eq. (9.10), and show how the reduced-form coefficients, the $K_i$'s, are related to the underlying structural parameters. Show that Eq. (9.11) is the overidentifying restriction.

9.2 Derive Becker et al.'s (1994) rational addiction model. Discuss the issues in estimation of the model. How would you obtain short-run and long-run price elasticities of demand from this model? How do the elasticities change depending upon not only the length of time for adjustment to price changes but also the consumer's perception of how long the price change is expected to last?

9.3 Given the intraperiod profit function, Eq. (9.30), derive the SNAP model, Eq. (9.31). Discuss how expectations are modeled and how the model nests the AIDS model. Discuss why this model is highly restrictive regarding intertemporal substitution between individual goods.

9.4 Taxes on alcoholic beverages have favored wine and beer over spirits. The federal tax shares of alcohol price are approximately 4.6 percent for beer, 2.6 percent for wine, and 9.7 percent for spirits, respectively. Taxes are levied on a per gallon basis. Using the elasticities from the estimated MRA model in Table 9.3, estimate the effects on beer, wine, and spirits consumption from

**Table 9.3** Elasticities of Dynamic Demand for Wine, Beer, and Spirits

**SR Elasticities**

| | Price | | |
|---|---|---|---|
| Good | Wine | Beer | Spirits |
| Wine | -0.17705 | 0.024672 | 0.196763 |
| Beer | 0.013248 | -0.17102 | 0.027337 |
| Spirits | 0.256659 | 0.066407 | -0.37782 |

**LR Elasticities (Temporary Price Change)**

| | Price | | |
|---|---|---|---|
| Good | Wine | Beer | Spirits |
| Wine | -0.28054 | 0.037848 | 0.299712 |
| Beer | 0.013359 | -0.3174 | 0.065221 |
| Spirits | 0.429584 | 0.161278 | -0.65937 |

**LR Elasticities (Permanent Price Change)**

| | Price | | |
|---|---|---|---|
| Good | Wine | Beer | Spirits |
| Wine | -1.32431 | -1.95538 | 2.601441 |
| Beer | -0.3062 | -2.67486 | 1.070148 |
| Spirits | 0.77431 | 0.145974 | -0.47241 |

increasing the tax rates for beer and wine by 30 percent, but leaving the tax rate for spirits the same. How do the short-run and long-run effects (for permanent price change) differ?

## References


Almon, S. "The Distributed Lag Between Capital Appropriations and Expenditures." *Econometrica* 33(1965): 178–196.

Bask, M., and M. Melkersson. "Rationally Addicted to Drinking and Smoking?" *Applied Economics* 36(2004): 373–386.

Becker, G.S., M. Grossman, and K.M. Murphy. "An Empirical Analysis of Cigarette Addiction." *The American Economic Review* 84(1994): 396–418.

Blanciforti, L., and R Green. "An Almost Ideal Demand System Incorporating Habits: An Analysis of Expenditures on Food and Aggregate Commodity Groups." *The Review of Economics and Statistics* 65(3)(1983): 511–515.

Browning, M. "A Simple Nonadditive Preference Structure for Models of Household Behavior over Time." *Journal of Political Economy* 99(1991): 607–637.

Fuller, W.A. *Introduction to Statistical Time Series*. New York: Wiley, 1976.

Gallet, C.A. "The Demand for Alcohol: A Meta-Analysis of Elasticities." *Australian Journal of Agricultural and Resource Economics* 51(2007): 121–135.

Gorman, W.M. "Tastes, Habits and Choices." *International Economic Review* 8(1967): 218–222.

Greene, W.H. *Econometric Analysis*. Upper Saddle River, NJ: Pearson Education, Inc., 2003.

Holt, M.T., and B.K. Goodwin. "Generalized Habit Formulation in an Inverse Almost Ideal Demand System: An Application to Meat Expenditures in the U.S." *Empirical Economics* 22(1997): 293–320.

Houthakker, H.S., and L.D. Taylor. *Consumer Demand in the United States: Analyses and Projections*. 2nd Ed. Cambridge, MA: Harvard University Press, 1970.

Jorgenson, D.W. "Rational Distributed Lag." *Econometrica* 34(1966): 135–149.

Koksal, A., and Michael Wohlgenant. "How Do Smoking Bans in Restaurants Affect Restaurant and at Home Alcohol Consumption? *Empirical Economics* 50(2016): 1193–1213.

Manser, M. "Elasticities of Demand for Food: An Analysis Using Functions Allowing for Habit Formation." *Southern Economic Journal* (1976): 879–891.

Meghir, C., and G. Weber. "Intertemporal Nonseparability or Borrowing Restrictions? A Disaggregate Analysis Using a U.S. Consumption Panel." *Econometrica* 64(1996): 1151–1181.

Nerlove, M. *Distributed Lags and Demand Analysis*. Agricultural Handbook No. 141, U.S. Department of Agriculture, Washington, 1958.

Newey, K.N., and K.D. West. "A Simple Positive-Definite Heteroskedasticity and Autocorrelation Consistent Covariance Matrix." *Econometrica* 55(1987): 703–708.

Phlips, L. "A Dynamic Version of the Linear Expenditure Model." *The Review of Economics and Statistics* 54(1972): 450–458.

Phlips, L. *Applied Consumption Analysis*. Amsterdam: North-Holland Publishing Co., 1983.

Pierani, P., and S. Tiezzi. "Addiction and Interaction Between Alcohol and Tobacco Consumption." *Empirical Economics* 37(2009): 1–23.

Spinnewyn, F. "Rational Habit Formation." *European Economic Review* 15(1981): 91–109.

Stigler, G.J., and G.S. Becker. "De Gustibus Non Est Disputandum." *The American Economic Review* 67(1977): 76-90.

Wohlgenant, M.K. "The Multivariate Rational Addiction Model." *Theoretical Economics Letters* 2(2012): 459–464.

Wohlgenant, Michael K., and William F. Hahn. "Dynamic Adjustment in Monthly Consumer Demands for Meats." *American Journal of Agricultural Economics* 64(1982): 553–557.

Zhen, Chen, Michael K. Wohlgenant, Shawn Karns, and Philip Kaufman. "Habit Formation and Demand for Sugar-Sweetened Beverages." *American Journal of Agricultural Economics* 93(2011): 175–193.

# Chapter 10
# Dynamic Models of the Firm

## 10.1 Introduction

Just as dynamic models of consumer demand can be important in applied demand analysis, so can dynamic models of the firm applied to market intermediary behavior. An important input that we have ignored so far is capital. This input is inherently dynamic because it is a stock at a point in time that may be changed through investment decisions. Different models applicable to modeling capital, with special reference to agricultural models, are presented and discussed in this chapter. A second source of dynamics is adjustment costs in changing rate of change of raw material purchases. Because of contracting and other costs associated with purchasing raw materials, firms may incur adjustment costs that add to the normal costs of agricultural processing. Finally, inventories can be a source of dynamic adjustment of the firm. We have discussed a model in Chapter 8 that leads to lagged adjustment in retail prices and marketing margins. I discuss some ways in which this model can be modified and extended for other applications.

## 10.2 Investment Models of the Firm

We need to expand the production function of the firm to account for capital as an input. The assumption is made that a given capital stock provides a flow of services to the firm that, when combined with materials and labor services, leads to production of a given flow of output. Lucas (1976b) also suggested that the firm make the production function depend on the rate of investment in capital to account for the fact that resources are necessary to acquire new capital inputs, or disinvest in capital. Thus, for given labor, capital, and material inputs, more capital inputs can be acquired by sacrificing current output and more investment can be attained



M. K. Wohlgenant, *Market Interrelationships and Applied Demand Analysis*,
Palgrave Studies in Agricultural Economics and Food Policy,
https://doi.org/10.1007/978-3-030-73144-1_10

only through sacrificing increasing amounts of other inputs. Thus, we can define the production function as follows:

$$q = f\left(k, l, m, \dot{k}\right) \tag{10.1}$$

where $\dot{k}$ is the rate of *net investment* of capital.[1] As before, labor, capital, and materials are assumed to exhibit diminishing marginal returns; net investment also exhibits diminishing returns but the sign of its partial derivatives are $\frac{\partial f}{\partial \dot{k}} < 0$ and $\frac{\partial^2 f}{\partial \dot{k}^2} > 0$. The production function is assumed to be strictly concave in all inputs. Defining $u$ as *gross investment* of capital, capital is assumed to accumulate according to the well-known declining balance method:

$$\dot{k} = u - \delta k, k(0) = k_0 \tag{10.2}$$

where $\delta$ is the fixed rate of depreciation.

Given these specifications and defining prices for output, investment, labor, and materials as $p$, $v$, $w$, and $r$ respectively, and letting $i$ denote the interest rate, the firm maximizes the present discounted value of future net returns[2]

$$V(0) = \int_0^{\infty} e^{-it}\left[pf\left(k, l, m, \dot{k}\right) - vu - wl - rm\right]dt \tag{10.3}$$

subject to (10.2).

Following previous applications (e.g., Lopez 1985), we can solve problem in two steps. First, solve for the variable factors to obtain the restricted profit function, $\pi\left(p, w, r, k, \dot{k}\right) = \max_{l,m}\left[pf\left(k, l, m, \dot{k}\right) - wl - rm\right]$. Second, using (10.2), substitute back into (10.3) to obtain:

$$V(0) = \int_0^{\infty} e^{-it}[\pi(p, w, r, k, u - \delta k) - vu]dt$$

### *10.2.1 Current-Value Hamiltonian and Necessary and Sufficient Conditions for Value Maximization*

The current value Hamiltonian associated with this maximization problem is

$$H(u, k) = \pi(p, w, r, k, u - \delta k) - vu + \lambda(u - \delta k) \tag{10.4}$$

---

[1] Lucas (1976b) defines the production function with respect to *gross investment* as opposed to *net investment*. Subsequent applications are almost exclusively in terms of net investment.

[2] To simplify notation, the time dependence of all variables has been suppressed.

where $\lambda$ is the co-state variable associated with the equation of motion, Eq. (10.2). Assuming an interior solution, the necessary conditions for present value maximization are as follows (e.g., Arrow and Kurz 1970, Chapter 3):

$$\frac{\partial H(u,k)}{\partial u} = \frac{\partial \pi(p,w,r,k,u-\delta k)}{\partial u} - v + \lambda = 0 \tag{10.5}$$

$$\frac{\partial H(u,k)}{\partial k} = \frac{\partial \pi(p,w,r,k,u-\delta k)}{\partial k} - \frac{\partial \pi(p,w,r,k,u-\delta k)}{\partial \dot{k}}\delta - \lambda\delta = -\dot{\lambda} + i\lambda \tag{10.6}$$

$$\frac{\partial H(u,k)}{\partial \lambda} = \dot{k} - u + \delta k = 0 \tag{10.7}$$

$$k(0) = k_0 \text{ and } \lim_{t\to\infty} e^{-it}\lambda = 0 \tag{10.8}$$

When $H(u,k)$ is concave in $u$ and $k$, conditions (10.5)–(10.8) are both necessary and sufficient conditions for present value maximization (Arrow and Kurz 1970, Chapter 3).

### 10.2.2 Solution for Optimal Capital Accumulation

Assume the firm believes unit cost of investment, $v$, as well as other prices, will be constant over the planning horizon. Substituting (10.5) into (10.6), and totally differentiating the resulting single equation we obtain:

$$\pi_{\dot{k}\dot{k}}\ddot{k} + \pi_{k\dot{k}}\dot{k} = \pi_k + i\pi_{\dot{k}} - (i+\delta)v \tag{10.9}$$

where subscripts denote first-order and second-order partial derivatives. The steady-state solution to (10.9) is

$$\pi_k\big(k = k^*, \dot{k} = 0\big) + i\pi_{\dot{k}}\big(k = k^*, \dot{k} = 0\big) = (i+\delta)v \tag{10.10}$$

Linearize (10.9) around the steady-state solution:

$$\pi_{\dot{k}\dot{k}}\ddot{k} + \big(\pi_{k\dot{k}} - \pi_{k\dot{k}} - i\pi_{kk}\big)\dot{k} - \big(\pi_{\dot{k}\dot{k}} + i\pi_{k\dot{k}}\big)\big(k - k^*\big) = 0 \tag{10.11}$$

where $k^*$ is the solution to (10.10). The second-order homogenous differential equation from (10.11) has the form, $a\lambda^2 + b\lambda + c = 0$, which has solutions: $\lambda = \frac{-b\pm\sqrt{b^2-4ac}}{2a}$. Selecting the smallest root, the solution to the differential equation, Eq. (10.11), at time $t = 0$ is:

$$\dot{k} = \lambda\big(k - k^*\big) \tag{10.12}$$

where

$$\lambda = \frac{i - \sqrt{i^2 + 4\left(\frac{\pi_{kk}}{\pi_{\dot{k}\dot{k}}}\right)}^{0.5}}{2}$$

when we assume that $\pi_{k\dot{k}} = \pi_{\dot{k}k} = 0$ (see Lopez 1985).

Equation (10.12) looks like the partial adjustment model, Eq. (9.4), for consumer demand behavior, where now the long-run equilibrium stock of capital is the target that is adjusted slowly over time. It is clear that the adjustment coefficient, $\lambda$, is required to be less than zero by the requirement for stability of the differential equation. It can be inferred that the ratio, $\frac{\pi_{kk}}{\pi_{\dot{k}\dot{k}}} < 1 + i$, in order for the equation to be stable and $\lambda < 0$. The major difference with the partial adjustment model is that $\lambda$ is not a constant, even when the second-order partial derivatives of the profit function are constants. It depends on the (real) interest rate, and it can easily be verified that $\frac{\partial \lambda}{\partial i} < 0$.

### 10.2.3 Complete Model with Short-Run Output and Variable Factors

A complete model of market intermediary behavior can now be specified. Applying Hotelling's theorem to the short run, restricted profit function, $\pi\left(p, w, r, k, \dot{k}\right)$ yields the short-run supply and demand functions for the raw material and labor demand:

$$q\left(p, r, w, k, \dot{k}\right) = \frac{\partial \pi\left(p, w, r, k, \dot{k}\right)}{\partial p} \tag{10.13}$$

$$m\left(p, r, w, k, \dot{k}\right) = -\frac{\partial \pi\left(p, w, r, k, \dot{k}\right)}{\partial r} \tag{10.14}$$

$$l\left(p, r, w, k, \dot{k}\right) = -\frac{\partial \pi\left(p, w, r, k, \dot{k}\right)}{\partial w} \tag{10.15}$$

Add to this the investment demand function from Eq. (10.12) above

$$\dot{k} = \left(\frac{i - \sqrt{i^2 + 4\left(\frac{\pi_{kk}}{\pi_{\dot{k}\dot{k}}}\right)}^{0.5}}{2}\right)\left(k - k^*\right) \tag{10.16}$$

where $k^*$ is the long-run level of capital determined by Eq. (10.9).

Lopez (1985) shows that closed-form solutions for these equations can be obtained for the normalized quadratic profit function. This functional form for given real interest rate delivers linear relationships for the non-normalized subset of Eqs. (10.13)–(10.16). In other words, prices are relative to a numeraire good, say the material, farm input. Then those equations are linear in parameters. Differentiating the normalized profit equation with respect to the normalized price yields a function that is quadratic in normalized prices, the capital stock, and the rate of change in the capital stock. Replacing time derivatives by first differences and the actual capital stock by its beginning-of-the-period level leads to the set of equations that can be applied to discrete time-series data. Lopez (1985) applies the model to Canadian food processing and finds complete consistency with the underlying theory. The significance of the model is that the short-run demand for the variable inputs, including demand for the farm input, are linked to capital through both the level of capital at the beginning of the period and net investment during the time period.

## 10.3 Morrison-Paul Imperfect Competitive Model

Morrison (1988) and Morrison-Paul (2000, 2001) have extended the profit function approach above to one incorporating imperfect competition in the output market and market for raw materials. Instead of the profit function, she starts with the conditional cost function

$$C = C\left(q, \boldsymbol{w}, m, k, \dot{k}\right) = \min_{\boldsymbol{l}}\left[\boldsymbol{w}'\boldsymbol{l} : q = f\left(\boldsymbol{l}, m, k, \dot{k}\right)\right] \tag{10.17}$$

where is a vector of variable factor prices. The input demand function for raw materials is obtained as (e.g., Samuelson 1952–53)

$$-\frac{\partial C\left(q, w, m, k, \dot{k}\right)}{\partial m} = r + m\frac{\partial r}{\partial m} = r\left(1 + \frac{\phi}{\varepsilon_m}\right) \tag{10.18}$$

where the left-hand side is the marginal benefit to the firm of increasing raw material purchases, and the right-hand side is marginal factor cost (cf., equation 8.13). Likewise, we can obtain the output price-marginal cost relationship through differentiation of (10.17):

$$\frac{\partial C\left(q, w, m, k, \dot{k}\right)}{\partial q} = p + q\frac{\partial p}{\partial q} = p\left(1 + \frac{\theta}{e}\right) \tag{10.19}$$

Marginal cost of producing output equals marginal revenue (cf. equation 8.12). The net investment equation for capital is the Euler equation, similar to (10.9):

$$C_{\dot{k}\dot{k}}\ddot{k} + C_{k\dot{k}}\dot{k} + iC_{\dot{k}} = C_k + (i + \delta)v \tag{10.20}$$

This equation also could be derived directly as the first-order condition for the autonomous calculus of variations problem (see, e.g., Kamien and Schwartz 1981). Finally, we have the variable factor input demand functions through application of Shephard's lemma to (10.17):

$$\frac{\partial C\left(q, \boldsymbol{w}, m, k, \dot{k}\right)}{\partial w_i} = l_i\left(q, \boldsymbol{w}, m, k, \dot{k}\right) \tag{10.21}$$

Morrison (1988) and Morrison-Paul (2000, 2001) have successfully applied this model in various forms to the US meatpacking and beefpacking industries. In addition, she develops scale measures to evaluate the relative importance of scale economies to market power. There is little evidence of market power, especially in the markets for livestock, and scale economies offset any reduction in welfare due to market power.

## 10.4 Multivariate Models of Investment

So far we have only allowed for one quasi-fixed input capital. Past research (Holt et al. 1960; Nadiri and Rosen 1969; Pindyck and Rotemberg 1983) has also shown labor is often quasi-fixed. Most significantly, researchers have shown interrelated adjustment costs occur between capital and labor (Nadiri and Rosen 1969; Pindyck and Rotemberg 1983). Hiring resources, whether labor hours, capital services, or raw materials, all can entail resources. Thus, a production function like (10.1) augmented to include other factors would take the form: $q = f(\boldsymbol{u}, \boldsymbol{x}, \dot{\boldsymbol{x}})$, where $\boldsymbol{u}$ is a vector of variable factors with relative price vector $\boldsymbol{w}$ and $x$ is a vector of quasi-fixed factors with relative price vector of net investments $\boldsymbol{v}$.[3] The restricted profit function is $\pi(\boldsymbol{w}, \boldsymbol{x}, \dot{\boldsymbol{x}}) = \min_{l}[\boldsymbol{w}'\boldsymbol{u} : q = f(\boldsymbol{u}, \boldsymbol{x}, \dot{\boldsymbol{x}})]$. Lucas (1967a), Treadway (1971), and Mortenson (1973) show that the solution to the intertemporal problem, in the neighborhood of the stationary equilibrium, is

$$\dot{x} = \boldsymbol{M}\left(\boldsymbol{x} - \boldsymbol{x}^*\right) \tag{10.22}$$

where is the vector of stationary levels of the quasi-fixed variables, . The matrix is the matrix of adjustment parameters. In general, the properties of this matrix are unknown but if it is symmetric, then it has all real, negative, and distinct roots (see Mortenson 1973, Theorem 1).

McLaren and Cooper (1980) show that the optimal value function has the form, $\boldsymbol{V}(\boldsymbol{x}, \boldsymbol{w}, \boldsymbol{v}, i)$, is concave in $x$, and convex in $w$ and $v$ . Let the solutions (10.22) be expressed as $\dot{\boldsymbol{x}} = \phi(\boldsymbol{x}, \boldsymbol{w}, \boldsymbol{v}, i)$. They show that if $\boldsymbol{V}(\boldsymbol{x}, \boldsymbol{w}, \boldsymbol{v}, i)$ is twice-differentiable, then the solutions for the quasi-fixed input demands and variable factor demands are as follows:

[3]Factor prices are prices relative to output price.

$$\phi(\boldsymbol{x}, \boldsymbol{w}, \boldsymbol{v}, i) = i(V_{\boldsymbol{v}\boldsymbol{x}'} - \boldsymbol{I})V_v \tag{10.23}$$

$$\boldsymbol{l}(\boldsymbol{x}, \boldsymbol{w}, \boldsymbol{v}, i) = -iV_{\boldsymbol{w}} + iV_{\boldsymbol{w}\boldsymbol{x}'}(V_{\boldsymbol{v}\boldsymbol{x}'} - \boldsymbol{I})V_v \tag{10.24}$$

Therefore, we have intertemporal duality relationships that can be used to derive closed-form solutions for all the inputs for an arbitrary value function that satisfies the regularity requirements indicated by McLaren and Cooper (1980).

## 10.5 Dynamic Inventory Behavior

In this section, I present a dynamic model incorporating inventories. As discussed in Chapter 8, inventories are an important component of market intermediary and processor behavior, especially in the short run. The model discussed is useful for estimating market intermediary and processor behavior in commodity markets, especially agricultural markets. Except for highly perishable goods, inventories are held and used to smooth costs and production in response to uncertainty in demand and raw material prices.

The model proposed is in the spirit of the linear-quadratic models, of which there is a rather large literature beginning with the classic book by Holt et al. (1960). Modeling the objective function as quadratic and the constraints as linear has proved to be adequate and useful in many past applications. An important reason for this functional form specification is that it delivers linear difference equations, for which solutions are readily available. With a few exceptions, inventory costs are modeled as quadratic functions of the deviation of inventory from its target level, which is given as a linear function of sales, as shown by Eq. (8.32) in Chapter 8. Depending upon the application, the model would also include a quadratic cost function of output, a quadratic cost function of inventories, and quadratic functions of changes in output and/or inventories to reflect adjustment costs. Rising marginal costs of production and inventories account for capacity restrictions. Adjustment costs of changing output could result from hiring/firing and/or capital investment decisions. Adjustment costs of changing inventories could result from costs of changing storage capacity. Eichenbaum (1989) has shown it is important to include prices of inputs in the model. These costs are part of production costs.

### *10.5.1 Linear-Quadratic Model with Rising Marginal Costs of Production and Inventories and Adjustment Costs*

The most general model of inventory behavior consists of the intraperiod profit function (see, e.g., Bivin 2005):

$$\begin{aligned}\pi_t =& p_t x_t - 0.5c_1(h_t - gx_t)^2 \\ &-(v_1 r_t + v_2 w_t)q_t - 0.5c_2(q_t)^2 \\ &-0.5c_3(h_t)^2 - 0.5c_4(\Delta h_t)^2 - 0.5c_4(\Delta q_t)^2\end{aligned} \tag{10.25}$$

where $p_t$ is output price, $x_t$ is sales, $h_t$ is end-of-the-period inventory, $c_t = v_1 r_t + v_2 w_t$, $r_t$israw material price, and $w_t$is index of processing costs, and $q_t$ is production. The first cost function is inventory costs[4]; the second cost function, $c_t q_t + 0.5c_2(q_t)^2$, represents production costs derived from minimizing input costs subject to the production function, which is approximated by a quadratic function.[5] As inventory capacity is approached, marginal cost of inventories would be expected to rise; hence the third cost function as a squared function of $h_t$. The last two cost functions are adjustment cost functions for change in inventories and change in rate of output.

The firm is assumed to maximize the expected present discounted value of profit subject to the inventory constraint, $h_t = h_{t-1} + q_t - x_t$. Substituting for $q_t = \Delta h_t + x_t$ in Eq. (10.25), the optimization problem is

$$\max_{\{x_t, h_t\}} V_t = \sum_{j=0}^{\infty} \beta^j E_t \begin{bmatrix} p_{t+j}x_{t+j} - 0.5c_1\left(h_{t+j} - gx_{t+j}\right)^2 \\ -c_{t+j}\left(\Delta h_{t+j} + x_{t+j}\right) \\ -0.5c_2\left(\Delta h_{t+j} + x_{t+j}\right)^2 \\ -0.5c_3\left(h_{t+j}\right)^2 - 0.5c_4\left(\Delta h_{t+j}\right)^2 \\ -0.5c_5\left(\Delta h_{t+j} - \Delta h_{t-1+j} + \Delta x_{t+j}\right)^2 \end{bmatrix} \tag{10.26}$$

## 10.5.2 First-Order Conditions from Maximizing Expected Present Discounted Value of Net Returns

The first-order conditions at time $t$ are as follows:

$$\frac{\partial V_t}{\partial x_t} = E_t \begin{bmatrix} p_t + gc_1(h_t - gx_t) - c_t - c_2(\Delta h_t + x_t) \\ -c_5(\Delta h_t - \Delta h_{t-1} + \Delta x_t) + \beta c_5(\Delta h_{t+1} - \Delta h_t + \Delta x_{t+1}) \end{bmatrix} = 0 \tag{10.27}$$

[4]To simplify the notation, the constant $g_0$ has been omitted. It has no consequence for the final equation derived.

[5]All the terms in the quadratic function are not included (e.g., squared input prices), because they do not show up in the optimization results.

$$\frac{\partial V_t}{\partial h_t} = E_t \left[ \begin{array}{r} -c_1(h_t - gx_t) - c_t + \beta c_{t+1} - c_2(\Delta h_t + x_t) \\ +\beta c_2(\Delta h_{t+1} + x_{t+1}) - c_3(h_t) - c_4(\Delta h_t) + \beta c_4(\Delta h_{t+1}) \\ -c_5(\Delta h_t - \Delta h_{t-1} + \Delta x_t) + 2\beta c_5(\Delta h_{t+1} - \Delta h_t + \Delta x_{t+1}) \\ -\beta^2 c_5(\Delta h_{t+2} - \Delta h_{t+1} + \Delta x_{t+2}) \end{array} \right] = 0 \tag{10.28}$$

$$E_t h_{t-1} = h_{t-1} \text{ and } \lim_{j\to\infty} \beta^j E_t h_{t+j} = 0 \tag{10.29}$$

Equation (10.27) equates expected price with expected marginal costs of sales. Equation (10.28) equates marginal costs of holding inventories, $E_t[c_1(h_t - gy_t) + c_3(h_t)]$, with the marginal benefits of holding inventories. The marginal benefits consist of expected reductions in input costs, expected reductions in marginal production costs, and expected reductions in inventory costs from holding more inventories. These two motives for inventory holding are called "cost-smoothing" and "production-smoothing" (Eichenbaum 1989). Higher expected input costs, larger marginal production and inventory costs, and larger changes in inventories and production next period compared to the current period encourage the firm to increase inventories. Additional motives for holding inventories are reflected in the second term in Eq. (10.26), which balances the cost of holding inventories with depletion costs of stockouts (Holt et al. 1960, Chapter 11). Equation (10.29) gives the initial and transversality conditions.

### 10.5.3 Solution for Optimal Inventory Holding

In keeping with past studies (e.g., Blanchard 1983; Eichenbaum 1989; Biven 2005), I assume the firm makes decisions in two steps. It first determines its optimal inventory policy at time $t$, taking sales as exogenous, and then determines its sales decision via Eq. (10.27). Collecting terms on lag and lead values of $h_t$, Eq. (10.28) can be written as follows:

$$\begin{aligned} &E_t \left\{ \begin{array}{r} -\beta^2 c_5 h_{t+2} + \beta[c_2 + c_4 + 2(1+\beta)c_5]h_{t+1} \\ +\left[c_1 + (1+\beta)c_2 + c_3 + (1+\beta)c_4 + \left(1 + 4\beta - \beta^2\right)c_5\right]h_t \\ +[c_2 + c_4 + 2(1+\beta)c_5]h_{t-1} - c_5 h_{t-2} \end{array} \right\} \\ &= -E_t \left[ \begin{array}{r} c_1 g x_t + c_2(\beta x_{t+1} - x_t) - c_5\left(\beta^2 \Delta x_{t+2} - 2\beta \Delta x_{t+1} + \Delta x_t\right) \\ +v_1(\beta r_{t+1} - r_t) + v_2(\beta w_{t+1} - w_t) \end{array} \right] \end{aligned} \tag{10.30}$$

This fourth-order Euler equation has a closed-form solution that, in general, expresses end-of-period inventories as a function of inventories in periods $t-1$ and $t-2$, and present discounted values of future sales and input prices. Instead of presenting the full solution here, I refer the reader to Blanchard (1983) for details.

Instead, I will present in more detail the case I believe is more common when adjustment costs of the rate of output are zero. To tell if the more general model is needed, one can always estimate the reduced-form equation of distributed lags in inventories, sales, and factor prices and test for the significance of second-order lags in inventories.

The reduced model which we shall analyze in more detail is obtained by setting the coefficient $c_5 = 0$. The Euler equation (10.30) can be expressed as follows:

$$E_t \left\{ \begin{array}{r} \beta(c_2 + c_4)h_{t+1} \\ +[c_1 + (1+\beta)c_2 + c_3 + (1+\beta)c_4]h_t \\ +(c_2 + c_4)h_{t-1} \end{array} \right\} = -E_t \left[ \begin{array}{r} c_1 g x_t + c_2(\beta x_{t+1} - x_t) \\ +v_1(\beta r_{t+1} - r_t) + v_2(\beta w_{t+1} - w_t) \end{array} \right]$$

*or*

$$E_t \left\{ \begin{array}{r} \beta^{-1}L^2 \\ -\beta^{-1}(c_2 + c_4)^{-1} \\ [c_1 + (1+\beta)c_2 + c_3 + (1+\beta)c_4]L + 1 \end{array} \right\} L^{-1}h_t = -\beta^{-1}(c_2 + c_4)^{-1} E_t \left[ \begin{array}{r} c_1 g x_t + c_2(\beta x_{t+1} - x_t) \\ +v_1(\beta r_{t+1} - r_t) + v_2(\beta w_{t+1} - w_t) \end{array} \right] \tag{10.31}$$

The second-order polynomial in lag operators on the left-hand side of (10.31) can be factored into the product $(1 - \lambda_1)(1 - \lambda_2)$, where $\lambda_1 + \lambda_2 = \beta^{-1}\varphi, \varphi = (c_2 + c_4)^{-1}[c_1 + (1+\beta)c_2 + c_3 + (1+\beta)c_4]$, and $\lambda_1\lambda_2 = \beta^{-1}$. The roots of the polynomial on the left-hand side of (10.31) are: $\lambda_1, \lambda_2 = \frac{\beta^{-1}\varphi \pm (\beta^{-2}\varphi^2 - 4\beta^{-1})^{0.5}}{2\beta^{-1}}$. Because $\varphi > 0$, both roots are real and distinct implying $\beta^{-2}\varphi^2 - 4\beta^{-1} > 0$. Let $\lambda_1$ be the smaller root which is less than one, then $\lambda_2 = \beta^{-1}\lambda_1^{-1} > 1$. We can also show that $(1 - \lambda_2 L) = -\lambda_2 L\left(1 - \lambda_2^{-1}L^{-1}\right)$. Therefore, letting $E_t z_t = (c_2 + c_4)^{-1}E_t\left[c_1 g x_t + c_2(\beta x_{t+1} - x_t) + v_1(\beta r_{t+1} - r_t) + v_2(\beta w_{t+1} - w_t)\right]$, Eq. (10.31) can be written as

$$\lambda_2 L\left(1 - \lambda_2^{-1}L^{-1}\right)(1 - \lambda_1 L)E_t h_t = \beta^{-1}E_t z_t \Rightarrow$$

$$(1 - \lambda_1 L)E_t h_t = \lambda_2^{-1}\left(1 - \lambda_2^{-1}L^{-1}\right)^{-1}\beta^{-1}E_t z_t \Rightarrow$$

$$E_t h_t = \lambda_1 h_{t-1} + \lambda_1\left(1 - \beta\lambda_1 L^{-1}\right)^{-1}E_t z_t$$

upon using the initial condition in (10.29) and $\lambda_1\lambda_2 = \beta^{-1}$. Therefore, after substituting for $E_t z_t$ the solution is

$$h_t = \lambda_1 h_{t-1} + \sum_{j=0}^{\infty} \beta^j \lambda_1^{j+1} (c_2 + c_4)^{-1} E_t \left[ \begin{array}{r} c_1 g x_{t+j} + c_2(\beta x_{t+1+j} - x_{t+j}) \\ +v_1(\beta r_{t+1+j} - r_{t+j}) + v_2(\beta w_{t+1+j} - w_{t+j}) \end{array} \right] + u_{ht} \tag{10.32}$$

where $u_{ht} = -(x_t - E_t x_t)$ because of the fact that $h_t = E_t h_t - (x_t - E_t x_t)$. When the subjective expectations are equal to the actual market expectations (i.e., rational expectations), this error term will be distributed randomly with zero mean and constant variance.

A notable feature of the form of the inventory equation is that expected factor prices only enter as discounted expected changes from one time period to the next. These, according to (10.26) represent a portion of the speculative motive for holding inventories—a pecuniary gain from buying inputs now rather than later. The same is true with a portion of expected sales, $E_t(\beta x_{t+1+j} - x_{t+j})$, showing the gain from stocking up now to sell more next time period when demand is higher. Expected sales, $E_t x_{t+j}$ also enter separately to reflect the deeper buffer stock and transaction motives for holding inventories.

The influence of the cost parameters on inventory decisions are explicitly shown in Eq. (10.32). Among other things, the solution imposes no sign restrictions on $c_2$, the slope of the marginal cost of production function. This coefficient may be negative so long as the marginal costs of changing inventories as reflected in the sign of $c_4$ are positive. This means the model can accommodate increasing returns to scale within a limited range. This is important because of studies that show long-run average cost curves declining over the range of output.

### 10.5.4 Comparative Statics of Parameter Changes

As can be seen, expected end-of-period inventories depend upon beginning-of-period inventories, expected discounted value of future costs, and expected discounted value of future sales. Because $\beta^{-1}\varphi = \lambda_1 + \lambda_2 = \lambda_1 + \beta^{-1}\lambda_1^{-1}$ it is straightforward to see how $\lambda_1$ change as each of the cost parameters and discount rate change. The marginal effects of changes in these parameters on $\lambda_1$ can be shown to equal:

$$\frac{\partial \lambda_1}{\partial c_1} = \frac{\partial \lambda_1}{\partial c_3} = \beta^{-1}\left(1 - \frac{\lambda_2}{\lambda_1}\right)^{-1} (c_2 + c_4)^{-1} < 0 \tag{10.33}$$

$$\frac{\partial \lambda_1}{\partial c_2} = \frac{\partial \lambda_1}{\partial c_4} = -\beta^{-1}\left(1 - \frac{\lambda_2}{\lambda_1}\right)^{-1} (c_2 + c_4)^{-1}[\psi + (1 + \beta)] > 0 \tag{10.34}$$

$$\frac{\partial \lambda_1}{\partial \beta} = \left(1 + \beta^{-2}\lambda_1^{-1}\right)\left(1 - \frac{\lambda_2}{\lambda_1}\right)^{-1} < 0 \tag{10.35}$$

Let $h_t^* = \frac{\lambda_1}{(1-\lambda_1)} \sum_{j=0}^{\infty} \beta^j \lambda_1^j (c_2 + c_4)^{-1} E_t\left[c_1 g x_{t+j} + c_2\left(\beta x_{t+1+j} - x_{t+j}\right)\right.$ $\left.+ v_1\left(\beta r_{t+a1+j} - r_{t+j}\right) + v_2\left(\beta w_{t+1+j} - w_{t+j}\right)\right]$, then Eq. (10.32) can be written as follows:

$$h_t - h_{t-1} = (1 - \lambda_1)\left(h_t^* - h_{t-1}\right) + u_{ht} \tag{10.36}$$

The form of this equation, while the same as the partial adjustment model, shows explicitly the dependence of the speed of adjustment to equilibrium on the cost and discount parameters. The above derivatives indicate how the speed of adjustment will change as these parameters change relative to one another. Increases in the cost parameters associated with marginal cost of inventory holding ($c_1$ and $c_3$) will cause the speed of adjustment to increase (Eq. 10.33). On the other hand, increases in the cost parameter associated with a rising marginal cost of production ($c_2$) and cost of changing inventories ($c_4$) will decrease the speed of adjustment to equilibrium (Eq. 10.34). The effect of an increase in the discount rate (or decrease in the interest rate) will lead to an increase in speed of adjustment (Eq. 10.35).

### *10.5.5 Expectations Formation*

Note that the form of the solution (10.32) indicates that all future conditional expectations of sales and factor prices affect the current inventory decisions. Therefore, a critical component of the model is how expectations are modeled.

There are four basic types of expectations models: (a) static, (b) extrapolative, (c) adaptive, and (d) rational. Static expectations were discussed previously as expectations that assume the current value will prevail in the next time period, e.g., $E_t x_t = x_{t-1}$. Extrapolative expectations (Goodwin 1947) extend static expectations to include modification of the static forecast with error based on direction of change from the previous period, e.g., $E_t x_t = x_{t-1} + \delta(x_{t-1} - x_{t-2})$. Adaptive expectations extend the extrapolative model further by saying the difference in *forecast* between two time periods is proportional to the forecast error in the previous time period, e.g., $x_t^* = x_{t-1}^* + \delta\left(x_{t-1} - x_{t-1}^*\right)$ where the star superscript denotes expectation. Nerlove and Bessler (2001, p. 169) refer to $x_t^*$ as a "normal" expected variable. The solution to the adaptive expectations model is $x_t^* = \delta \sum_{i=0}^{t} (1 - \delta)^i x_{t-1-i}$.

The last expectations model is rational expectations. Rational expectations say that the subjective expectation of the economic agent equals the expectation of the market outcome of the variable being forecast. There are two types of rational expectations: full rational expectations (FRE) and quasi-rational expectations (QRE). FRE, first illustrated by Muth (1961), are expectations that know not only the processes generating the stochastic processes itself but the economic model itself. This degree of knowledge is often criticized as being too complete and ignores the costs and benefits of acquiring information. In contrast, QRE uses only the past history of the variable being forecast in forming expectations. This model can be obtained by applying time-series techniques to determine the best forecasting model, given past data on the forecast variable (Nerlove and Bessler 2001, pp. 173–176).

The first three types of expectations models, (a)–(c), are all special cases of the general time-series model. The general form of the time-series model is the autoregressive integrated moving-average (ARIMA) form (Box and Jenkins 1970, Chapter 4):

$$\phi(L)\nabla^d z_t = \theta(L)\varepsilon_t$$

where $\phi(L) = 1 - \phi_1 L - \ldots - \phi_p L^p$ is a *p-th* order autoregressive process, $\nabla^d$ represents first differencing of order *d*, $\theta(L) = 1 - \theta_1 L - \ldots - \theta_p L^q$ is a *q-th* order moving-average process, $z_t$ is the variable being forecast, and $\varepsilon_t$ is an i.i.d. error term. The general form is represented as ARIMA (p,d,q) and $z_t$ is often represented as a deviation from a constant, say $\mu$.

The static expectations model (a) can be represented as an ARIMA (0,1,0) process or random walk model, $z_t = z_{t-1} + \varepsilon_t$. This can also be modeled as a random walk with drift by including an intercept in the model. The extrapolative model (b) can be represented as an ARIMA (1,1,0) model, $z_t = z_{t-1} + \phi_1(z_{t-1} - z_{t-2}) + \varepsilon_t$. The third case of adaptive expectations (c) can be represented as an ARIMA (0,1,1) model, $z_t = z_{t-1} + \varepsilon_t - \theta_1\varepsilon_{t-1}$.

A notable feature of all these expectations models is that they describe processes that are non-stationary, hence all the variables are first-differenced first. It is also notable that most economic time series have unit roots, so such models are often consistent with time series behavior of economic variables. Chow (1989) shows that the adaptive expectations model, or equivalently the ARIMA (0,1,1) model, performs as well or better than rational expectations models in describing some financial variables. Thus, the expectations models (a)–(c) are not necessarily inferior to expectations based on rational expectations. It is important to keep in mind that expectations are fundamentally subjective. However, to expect subjective expectations to converge to objective, market expectations is not unreasonable, given enough time and experience by economic agents.

### 10.5.6 Form of the Structural Inventory Behavioral Equation

It should be clear then that the final form of the inventory Eq. (10.32) depends crucially on the type of expectations models used for the exogenous variables. I shall assume at the outset that wages are expected to be the same over the planning horizon, i.e., $E_t w_{t+j} = w_t$. In light of the empirical regularity that most economic time series are I(1), I shall assume that economic agents make expectations based on the most recent value of the exogenous variable and a distributed lag of past changes in the exogenous variables. In other words, I approximate the exogenous variables as ARIMA models as autoregressive models in first differences. So long as the autoregressive process is convergent, the model can approximate a model with an arbitrary mixed autoregressive and moving-average order process (Box and Jenkins 1970, Chapter 4).

Let $\boldsymbol{e}_1'$ be a row vector with a 1 in the first position and zeros elsewhere. Also let $\boldsymbol{A} = \begin{bmatrix} a_1 & a_2 & a_n \\ 1 & 0 & 0 \\ 0 & 1 & 0 \end{bmatrix}$. Then sales expectations can be written as $E_t x_{t+j} = x_{t-1} + \boldsymbol{e}_1'\boldsymbol{A}\left(\boldsymbol{I} + \boldsymbol{A} + \boldsymbol{A}^2 + \ldots \boldsymbol{A}^j\right)\Delta\boldsymbol{X}_{t-1} = x_{t-1} + \boldsymbol{e}_1'\boldsymbol{A}(\boldsymbol{I} - \boldsymbol{A})^{-1}\left(\boldsymbol{I} - \boldsymbol{A}^j\right)\Delta\boldsymbol{X}_{t-1}$, where $\Delta\boldsymbol{X}_{t-1} = \left(\Delta x_{t-1,}, \Delta x_{t-2,}, \ldots \Delta x_{t-1-n,}\right)'$. Also, we have for $E_t r_{t+j} = r_t + \boldsymbol{e}_1'\boldsymbol{B}(\boldsymbol{I} - \boldsymbol{B})^{-1}\left(\boldsymbol{I} - \boldsymbol{B}^j\right)\Delta\boldsymbol{r}_t$ where $\boldsymbol{B} = \begin{bmatrix} b_1 & b_2 & b_n \\ 1 & 0 & 0 \\ 0 & 1 & 0 \end{bmatrix}$. Obviously, the order of the lagged changes in exogenous variables is arbitrary and either exogenous variable can have a different lag length. Empirically, such lag lengths could be determined by applying Box–Jenkins type time series analyses to determine the form of QRE models.[6]

Given the above notation, the solution to (10.32) incorporating expectations can be shown to be

$$
\begin{aligned}
h_t &= \lambda_1 h_{t-1} + \lambda_1 \frac{[c_1 g + c_2(\beta - 1)]}{(c_2 + c_4)(1 - \beta\lambda_1)} x_{t-1} \\
&+ \lambda_1 \frac{v_1(\beta - 1)}{(c_2 + c_4)(1 - \beta\lambda_1)} r_t + \lambda_1 \frac{v_2(\beta - 1)}{(c_2 + c_4)(1 - \beta\lambda_1)} w_t \\
&+ \lambda_1 \frac{\boldsymbol{e}_1'\boldsymbol{A}(\boldsymbol{I} - \boldsymbol{A})^{-1} \left\{ \begin{array}{r} [c_1 g + c_2(\beta - 1)]\boldsymbol{I} \\ -[c_1 g\boldsymbol{I} - c_2(\boldsymbol{I} - \beta\boldsymbol{A})](\boldsymbol{I} - \beta\lambda_1\boldsymbol{A})^{-1} \end{array} \right\}}{(c_2 + c_4)} \Delta\boldsymbol{X}_{t-1} \\
&+ \lambda_1 \frac{\left\{ \begin{array}{c} v_1(\beta - 1)\boldsymbol{e}_1'\boldsymbol{B}(\boldsymbol{I} - \boldsymbol{B})^{-1} \\ [(\beta - 1)\boldsymbol{I} + (\boldsymbol{I} - \beta\boldsymbol{B})](\boldsymbol{I} - \beta\lambda_1\boldsymbol{B})^{-1} \end{array} \right\}}{(c_2 + c_4)} \Delta\boldsymbol{r}_t + u_{ht} \qquad (10.37)
\end{aligned}
$$

Aside from the terms involving $x_{t-1}$, $r_t$, and $w_t$, this is a rather complicated expression. While estimable with respect to the underlying cost and autoregressive parameters of the expectation models, one could opt to estimate the reduced-form model:

[6]In the general case, where the sum of coefficients on all lagged variables, $(\sum a_i)$, does not sum to one, as in the case of I(1) time series, the sales expectation model can be shown to equal $E_t x_{t+j} = \left(\sum a_i\right)^j x_{t-1} + \left(\sum a_i\right)^j \boldsymbol{e}_1'\boldsymbol{A}\iota\left(\boldsymbol{I} + \frac{1}{\sum a_i}\boldsymbol{A} + \frac{1}{(\sum a_i)^2}\boldsymbol{A}^2 + \ldots \frac{1}{(\sum a_i)^j}\boldsymbol{A}^j\right)\Delta\boldsymbol{X}_{t-1} = \left(\sum a_i\right)^j x_{t-1} + \left(\sum a_i\right)^j \boldsymbol{e}_1'\boldsymbol{A}\iota\left(\boldsymbol{I} - \frac{1}{\sum a_i}\boldsymbol{A}\right)^{-1}\left(\boldsymbol{I} - \frac{1}{(\sum a_i)^j}\boldsymbol{A}^j\right)\Delta\boldsymbol{X}_{t-1}$, where $\Delta\boldsymbol{X}_{t-1} = \left(\Delta x_{t-1,}, \Delta x_{t-2,}, \ldots \Delta x_{t-1-n,}\right)'$ as before and $\iota = (1, 1, \ldots, 1)'$. The price expectations model would have a similar form.

$$h_t = \lambda_1(h_{t-1} + \pi_1 x_{t-1} + \pi_2 r_t + \pi_3 w_t) + \boldsymbol{\gamma}_1' \Delta \boldsymbol{X}_{t-1} + \boldsymbol{\gamma}_2' \Delta \boldsymbol{r}_t + u_{ht} \quad (10.38)$$

or

$$\begin{aligned}\Delta h_t = &- (1-\lambda_1)\begin{pmatrix} h_{t-1} - \dfrac{\lambda_1}{(1-\lambda_1)}\pi_1 x_{t-1} \\ -\dfrac{\lambda_1}{(1-\lambda_1)}\pi_2 r_{t-1} - \dfrac{\lambda_1}{(1-\lambda_1)}\pi_3 w_{t-1} \end{pmatrix} \\ &+ \boldsymbol{\gamma}_1' \Delta \boldsymbol{X}_{t-1} + \left[\boldsymbol{\gamma}_2' + \lambda_1 \pi_2 \boldsymbol{e}_1'\right] \boldsymbol{B} \Delta \boldsymbol{r}_{t-1} \\ &+ \left\{u_{ht} + \left[\boldsymbol{\gamma}_2' + \lambda_1 \pi_2 \boldsymbol{e}_1'\right] \boldsymbol{u}_{rt} + \lambda_1 \pi_3 u_{wt}\right\} \end{aligned} \quad (10.39)$$

where $\boldsymbol{u}_{rt}$ is the vector of error terms associated with $\Delta \boldsymbol{r}_t = \boldsymbol{B}\Delta \boldsymbol{r}_{t-1} + \boldsymbol{u}_{rt}$ and $u_{wt}$ is the error term associated with $\Delta w_t = u_{wt}$. One may view (10.39) as an error-correction model (ECM), where $h_{t-1}$ is co-integrated with $x_{t-1}$, $r_{t-1}$, and $w_{t-1}$. The first-difference terms are included to adjust the error term for correlation with $x_{t-1}$ and $r_{t-1}$. On this interpretation, the parameters on $\Delta \boldsymbol{X}_{t-1}$ and $\Delta \boldsymbol{r}_t$ are treated as additional parameters, and optimal estimation of the parameters of the inventory model does not depend upon these parameters, even when they are functionally related to the cost function parameters (Phillips 1991). As can be seen by comparing (10.37) with (10.38), the reduced-form coefficients on $x_{t-1}$, $r_t$, and $w_t$ show the long-run effects of expectations of these exogenous variables on inventories. Banergee and Mizon (2006) extend the co-integration framework with linear-quadratic inventory models to higher order of integration in exogenous variables.

Under certain conditions, the underlying cost coefficients may be identified and estimated. We know first of all that $\lambda_1 + \lambda_2 = \lambda_1 + \beta^{-1}\lambda_1^{-1} = \beta^{-1}\varphi = \beta^{-1}(c_2 + c_4)^{-1}[c_1 + (1+\beta)c_2 + c_3 + (1+\beta)c_4]$. Also, the reduced-form coefficients associated with $x_{t-1}$ and $r_{t-1}$ are $\pi_1 = \frac{[c_1 g + c_2(\beta-1)]}{(c_2+c_4)(1-\beta\lambda_1)}$ and $\pi_2 = \frac{v_1(\beta-1)}{(c_2+c_4)(1-\beta\lambda_1)}$. The cost coefficients are only determined relative to $(c_2 + c_4)$. The expression for the sum of the roots can be written as $\beta^{-1}\varphi = \beta^{-1}\left[(c_2+c_4)^{-1}c_1 + (1+\beta) + (c_2+c_4)^{-1}c_3\right]$. With an estimate of $\varphi$ and assuming a value for $\beta$, we could determine the value for the sum $(c_2+c_4)^{-1}c_1 + (c_2+c_4)^{-1}c_3$. Note that the overall expression $\varphi$ is the reciprocal of the second-order derivatives of adjustment cost $(c_2 + c_4)$ to the discounted sum of these cost parameters and the sum of the second-order derivatives of inventory costs, $\beta(c_2 + c_4) + c_1 + c_3$. With estimates of $\pi_1$ and $\pi_2$, we could determine the relationship between $c_1$ and $c_2$, but it would depend upon the unknown parameters $g$ and $v_1$. Further information would be required to estimate individual cost parameters. If we had estimates of $g$ and $v_1$ and assumed a value for $c_3$, we could obtain estimates of $c_1$ and $c_2$ relative to $c_4$. One could estimate the full model (10.39) and estimate three out of four of the cost function parameters relative to the fourth assuming values for $\beta$, $g$, and $v_1$. (see, e.g., Bivin 2005).

Whichever form the model is estimated, Eq. (10.37), (10.38), or (10.39), it should be estimated jointly with the AR models for $x_t$ and $r_t$:

$$\Delta x_t = \sum\nolimits_{i=1}^{n} a_i \Delta x_{t-i} + u_{xt} \tag{10.40}$$

$$\Delta r_t = \sum\nolimits_{i=1}^{n} b_i \Delta r_{t-i} + u_{rt} \tag{10.41}$$

Intercepts could be included in (10.40) and (10.41) to account for non-stochastic trends.

### 10.5.7 Relationship of Linear-Quadratic Inventory Model to Flexible Accelerator

It is useful to compare the linear-quadratic inventory model we have derived with Lovell's (1961) classic flexible accelerator model. The flexible accelerator model has the form:

$$h_t - h_{t-1} = \delta\left(h_t^d - h_{t-1}\right) + \varepsilon_{ht} \tag{10.42}$$

where $h_t^d$ is the desired equilibrium level of inventories. This has the same form as the partial adjustment model and under a wide variety of circumstances can be shown to be observationally equivalent to the linear-quadratic model. For example if $h_t^d$ is a linear function of lagged sales, raw material price, and wage rate, it would be equivalent to (10.39) aside from the first-difference terms in sales and raw material prices. This model can be derived from a firm optimization problem where the firm minimizes the current period sum of inventory costs, $0.5c_h\left(h_t - h_t^d\right)^2$ and costs of changing inventories, $0.5c_{\Delta h}(\Delta h_t)^2$. The resulting first-order conditions can be rearranged to produce (10.42) where $\delta = \frac{c_h}{c_h + c_{\Delta h}}$. Thus, slow adjustment to equilibrium can be attributed to large costs of changing inventories, a feature that is consistent with the variance of output being larger than the variance of sales. Bivin (2005) shows the flexible accelerator model yields superior forecasts in a number of industries, compared to the traditional linear-quadratic model. What his results underscore is the importance of including costs of changing inventories in the model, which the model I develop here includes.

### 10.5.8 Optimal Sales/Price Decisions

Equation (10.38) is only one component of the market model of a market intermediary processor holding inventories. The model must also contain relationships for sales/ price decisions and input decisions, especially for raw materials. In Eq. (10.27), we have an equation regarding sales decisions of the firm. We assume price-taking behavior but we could just as easily assume imperfectly competitive behavior and replace (expected) price with marginal revenue, $p_t\left(1+\frac{\theta}{e}\right)_t$, in accordance with Eq. (8.28). Assume that the markup, $\mu_t^{-1} = \left(1+\frac{\theta}{e}\right)_t^{-1}$ is a constant, i.e., $\mu_t^{-1} = \mu^{-1}$. Equation (10.27), assuming $c_5 = 0$ and substituting from (10.38), can be shown to equal:

$$p_t = \mu^{-1}\begin{bmatrix} \pi_4 r_t + \pi_5 w_t + \pi_6 h_{t-1} \\ +\pi_7 E_t x_t + \pi_8 x_{t-1} + \boldsymbol{\delta}_1' \Delta \boldsymbol{X}_{t-1} + \boldsymbol{\delta}_2' \Delta \boldsymbol{r}_t + u_{ht} \end{bmatrix} + u_{pt} \tag{10.43}$$

where $\pi_4 = v_1 - (c_1 g - c_2)\pi_2$, $\pi_5 = v_2 - (c_1 g - c_2)\pi_3$, $\pi_6 = -[c_1 g \lambda_1 + c_2(1-\lambda_1)]$, $\pi_7 = c_1 g^2 + c_2$, $\pi_8 = -(c_1 g - c_2)\lambda_1 \pi_1$, $\boldsymbol{\delta}_1' = -(c_1 g - c_2)\boldsymbol{\gamma}_1'$, and $\boldsymbol{\delta}_2' = -(c_1 g - c_2)\boldsymbol{\gamma}_2'$.

As can be seen, this price equation depends on unobserved expected sales. With perfect competitive price-taking behavior, expected sales would equal expected market demand. Equation (10.43) would then equal

$$p_t = \pi_4 r_t + \pi_5 w_t + \pi_6 h_{t-1} + \pi_7 x_t + \pi_8 x_{t-1} + \boldsymbol{\delta}_1' \Delta \boldsymbol{X}_{t-1} + \boldsymbol{\delta}_2' \Delta \boldsymbol{r}_t + \left(\pi_7 u_{dt} + u_{pt}\right) \tag{10.44}$$

where $u_{dt}$ is the error term associated with the market demand function:

$$x_t = -dp_t + z_t + u_{dt} \tag{10.45}$$

Both price and quantity demanded are jointly determined by the (inverse) supply function (10.44) and the market demand function (10.45).

If the (representative) firm is imperfectly competitive, i.e., a price searcher, demand will likely not be known when it sets price. If it knows the demand structure (10.45), its expectation of market demand would equal $E_t x_t = -dE_t p_t + E_t z_t$. If the firm is not a monopolist, it will have to form expectations of other firms' prices and demand curve shifters. Given the cost of information, it may decide just to form expectations on past sales in which case (10.43) would become

$$p_t = \mu^{-1}\begin{bmatrix} \pi_4 r_t + \pi_5 w_t + \pi_6 h_{t-1} \\ +(\pi_7 + \pi_8) x_{t-1} + \left(\pi_7 \boldsymbol{e}_1' + \boldsymbol{\delta}_1'\right) \Delta \boldsymbol{X}_{t-1} + \boldsymbol{\delta}_2' \Delta \boldsymbol{r}_t + u_{ht} \end{bmatrix} + u_{pt} \tag{10.46}$$

Other somewhat more sophisticated models are available but that would take us into the area of dynamic oligopoly. At the time of this writing, there does not seem to be any single model that stands out. Every commodity and industry structure will be different so it is best to leave up selection of a price equation to each application. The two specifications indicated here, (10.44) and (10.46), would seem to be applicable in a large number of cases.

### 10.5.9 Input Decisions and Derived Demand

Input demand functions are determined by applying Shephard's lemma to the expected production cost function, $E_t c_q(q_t, r_t, w_t) = E_t\left[0.5c_2(q_t)^2 + 0.5v_{11}(r_t)^2 + 0.5v_{22}(w_t)^2 + v_{12}r_t w_t + v_1 r_t q_t + v_2 w_t q_t\right]$:

$$m_t = v_{11}r_t + v_{12}w_t + v_1 E_t q_t + u_{mt}$$

$l_t = v_{12}r_t + v_{22}w_t + v_2 E_t q_t + u_{lt}$ Substituting for expected output using (10.38) and the identity $E_t q_t = E_t h_t - h_{t-1} + E_t x_t$ gives[7]:

$$\begin{aligned} m_t = {} & (v_{11} + v_1\lambda_1\pi_2)r_t + (v_{12} + v_1\lambda_1\pi_3)w_t - v_1(1-\lambda_1)h_{t-1} \\ & + v_1\lambda_1\pi_1 x_{t-1} + v_1 E_t x_t + v_1\boldsymbol{\gamma}_1'\Delta\boldsymbol{X}_{t-1} + v_1\boldsymbol{\gamma}_2'\Delta\boldsymbol{r}_t + u_{mt} \end{aligned} \tag{10.47}$$

$$\begin{aligned} l_t = {} & (v_{12} + v_2\lambda_1\pi_3)r_t + (v_{22} + v_2\lambda_1\pi_3)w_t \\ & - v_2(1-\lambda_1)h_{t-1} + v_2\lambda_1\pi_1 x_{t-1} + v_2 E_t x_t + v_2\boldsymbol{\gamma}_1'\Delta\boldsymbol{X}_{t-1} + v_2\boldsymbol{\gamma}_2'\Delta\boldsymbol{r}_t + u_{lt} \end{aligned} \tag{10.48}$$

Like the price equation, these input demand equations depend on the unobserved expected sales. With price-taking behavior, input demand decisions would be determined jointly with output supply, Eq. (10.44), and market demand for the output, Eq. (10.45). In the case of imperfect competition, the firm may use an AR process to forecast current sales as discussed above for the price equation.

As an example of application of the dynamic processor behavioral model, Wohlgenant (1982) estimated a set of factor demand functions for grapes, production of wine, and output prices of wine for the California wine industry. Three different types of grapes are used in producing wine so a system of inverse demand functions was estimated showing beginning inventories, lagged sales two periods, and an index of wine processing costs were all statistically significant determinants of prices, in addition to the quantities of different grapes used in processing wine. Wine production and wine price equations were also estimated and found to be consistent with the theory, again with highly significant inventory and lagged sales variables.[8]

---

[7]One might be tempted to replace $E_t q_t$ with $q_t$, but this would produce a model with classical errors-in-variables problem. Both Pope and Just (1996) and Moschini (2001) recognize this problem and recommend substituting for market determined relationship as done here.

[8]Because this study was conducted before the methodology put forth here, it was based on the same methodology of Lopez (1985) where expectations were assumed to be static. Also, the expected demand function was modeled as a function of the firm's price, expected industry price, and expected

### 10.5.10 Overall Process of Market Equilibrium

Market equilibrium occurs where $h_t = h_{t-1} + q_t - x_t$. For the competitive case, output price and quantity are jointly determined. Inventories are determined through Eq. (10.38) and output is determined by the identity. Raw material input prices are jointly determined with input demand (10.47), input supply, output supply (10.44), and market demand (10.45). The model could be modified to include trade, so that the market-clearing condition would instead be $(exp_t - imp_t) = h_t - h_{t-1} + q_t - d_t$, where $imp_t$ and $exp_t$ are imports and exports, respectively, and $d_t$ is domestic consumption (imports plus consumption of domestic production). In this case, a separate behavioral equation may be required for net exports.[9] It is also the case that market demand is now more appropriately defined as $d_t$, where $x_t = d_t + (exp_t - imp_t)$. Thus, the market demand relationship (10.45) should be modified as follows: $x_t = -dp_t + z_t + (exp_t - imp_t)$.

Suppose there is an increase in consumer demand. The initial effect, assuming the change is unanticipated, is for inventories to decrease. If the market is competitive, both output price and raw material price will increase. Because of inventories and expectations based on past market behavior, inventories will then increase the following time period. Subsequent adjustments will occur in output and raw material prices and quantity of output and quantity of the raw material (due to supply response) until a new equilibrium is achieved, assuming the system is stable.

## 10.6 Other Empirically Based Approaches to Modeling Dynamics

In this chapter, and indeed in the whole book, the focus has been on conceptual models to estimate market interrelationships both horizontally and vertically. In recent decades, focus has been on empirical time-series models, almost to the exclusion of theoretical developments, except possibly in the area of models of imperfect competition. I find this regrettable because the models discussed here seem fundamental to our understanding of markets.

There are other empirical approaches to modeling systems of factor demands (and consumer demand) in the literature. Anderson and Blundell (1983) proposed that one estimate systems of demand functions with an error-correction model (ECM). Attfield (1997) proposed estimating a system of co-integrating demand systems within a triangular ECM framework (TECM). This approach is implemented by

---

industry demand. Thus, there were two demand shift variables, expected price modeled as lagged price, and expected industry demand modeled as lagged wine shipments for periods t-1 and t-2.

[9]See Labys (1973) for an extensive discussion of commodity models with inventory and trade variables.

adding first differences in the exogenous variables to the right-hand side of the equation to account for unit roots. I have already discussed how such approaches can be integrated with the linear-quadratic inventory model.

Mark et al. (2005) proposed estimating systems of co-integrating demand functions using a dynamic SUR estimator. This approach is actually more firmly grounded in theory. Note that the final form solution to (10.32) will depend upon all future and past exogenous variables. If we can approximate these effects by a finite number of lags and leads in first differences, then we can estimate a model that allows us to estimate the long-run, or steady-state, solution. Such an approach is useful when there are unit roots present, when there are difficulties modeling different sources of dynamics, and when there are simultaneous equation issues. This approach was applied by Wohlgenant (2010) to estimating a system of input demand functions for hogs from different market sources (spot, contract, company-owned) and production of pork. This approach was found to be extremely helpful in obtaining estimates of steady-state relationships estimated with weekly data.

**Problems**

10.1 What is the effect of changes in raw material price on raw material demand, Eq. (10.14), in both the short run and long run when complete capital adjustment occurs?

10.2 Derive the specifications for quasi-fixed capital, variable factor demand for raw materials, and variable factor demand for labor for a quadratic value function, using the formulas in Eqs. (10.23) and (10.24). Let the wage rate be the numeraire price.

10.3 Consider Eq. (10.32) where only future expected sales and lagged inventories affect current inventories. Define $x_{t+j} = \rho x_{t+j-1} + v_{t+j}$, where $v_{t+j}$ is independently identically distributed (i.i.d.). Derive the final form of Eq. (10.32) using this expectations model. With the value of $\rho$ defining the degree of persistence in changes in sales, contrast the effects of permanent change ($\rho = 1$) with purely transitory changes ($\rho = 0$).

10.4 Assuming perfect competition, use Eq. (10.47) to derive the short-run and long-run price elasticities of demand for the raw material input. Note that $E_t x_t$ is an unobservable variable. With price-taking behavior, this quantity is determined jointly with output price through Eqs. (10.44) and (10.45).

## References

Anderson, G., and R. Blundell. "Testing Restrictions in a Flexible Dynamic System: An Application to Consumers' Expenditures in Canada." *Review of Economic Studies* 50(1983): 397–410.

Arrow, K., and M. Kurz. *Public Investment, the Rate of Return, and Optimal Fiscal Policy*. Baltimore: Johns Hopkins Press, 1970.

Bivin, D.G. "Gauging the Performance of the Linear-Quadratic Inventory Model." *Applied Economics* 37(2005): 1215–1231.

Blanchard, O.J. "The Production and Inventory Behavior of the American Automobile Industry." *Journal of Political Economy* 91(1983): 365–400.
Box, G.E.P., and G.M. Jenkins. *Time Series Analysis: Forecasting and Control*. San Francisco: Holden-Day, Inc., 1970.
Chow, G.C. "Rational Versus Adaptive Expectations in Present Value Models." *The Review of Economics and Statistics* 71(1989): 376–384.
Eichenbaum, M. "Some Empirical Evidence on the Production Level and Production Cost Models of Inventory Investment." *The American Economic Review* 79(1989): 853–864.
Goodwin, R.M. "Dynamic Coupling with Expecial Reference to Markets having Production Lags." *Econometrica* 15(1947): 181–204.
Holt, C., F. Modigliani, J. Muth, and H. Simon. *Planning Production, Inventories, and Work Force*. Englewood Cliffs, N.J.: Prentice Hall, 1960.
Kamien, M.I., and N.L. Schwartz. *Dynamic Optimization: The Calculus of Variations and Optimal Control in Economics and Management*. New York: Elsevier North Holland, Inc., 1981.
Labys, W.C. *Dynamic Commodity Models: Specification, Estimation, and Simulation*. Lexington, MA: D.C. Heath and Co., 1973.
Lopez, R. "Supply Response and Investment in the Canadian Food Processing Industry." *American Journal of Agricultural Economics* 67(1985): 40–48.
Lovell, M.C. "Manufacturers' Inventories, Sales Expectations, and the Acceleration Principle." *Econometrica* 29(1961): 293–314.
Lucas, R.E. "Optimal Investment Policy and the Flexible Accelerator." *International Economic Review* 8(1967a): 78–85.
Lucas, R.E. "Adjustment Costs and the Theory of Supply." *Journal of Political Economy* 75(1976b): 321–334.
Mark, N.C., M. Ogaki, and K. Sul. "Dynamic Seemingly Unrelated Cointegrating Regressions." *Review of Economic Studies* 72(2005): 797–820.
McLaren, K.R., and R.J. Cooper. "Intertemporal Duality: Application to Theory of the Firm." *Econometrica* 48(1980): 1755–1762.
Morrison, C.J. "Quasi-fixed Inputs in US and Japanese Manufacturing: A Generalized Leontief Restricted Cost Function Approach." *The Review of Economics & Statistics* 70(1988): 275–287.
Morrison-Paul, C.J. "Market and Cost Structure in the US Beef Packing Industry." *American Journal of Agricultural Economics* 83(2001): 64–76.
Mortenson, D.T. "Generalized Adjustment Costs and Dynamic Factor Demand Theory." *Econometrica* 41(1973): 657–665.
Moschini, G. "Production Risk and the Estimation of Ex-Ante Cost Functions." *Journal of Econometrics* 100(2001): 357–380.
Muth, J.F. "Rational Expectations and the Theory of Price Movements." *Econometrica* 29(1961): 299–305.
Nadiri, M.I., and S. Rosen. "Interrelated Factor Demand Functions." *American Economic Review* 59(1969): 457–471.
Nerlove, M., and D.A. Bessler. "Expectations, Information and Dynamics." In B.L. Gardner and G.C. Rausser (eds.) *Handbook of Agricultural Economics*, Vol. 1A, pp. 155–206. Amsterdam: Elsevier Science B.V., 2001, Chapter 17.
Phillips, P.C.B. "Optimal Inference in Cointegrated Systems." *Econometrica* 59(1991): 283–306.
Pindyck, R.S., and J.J. Rotemberg. "Dynamic Factor Demands and the Effect of Energy Price Effects." *The American Economic Review* 73(1983): 1066–1079.
Pope, R.D., and R.E. Just. "Empirical Implementation of Ex-Ante Cost Functions. *Journal of Econometrics* 72(1996): 231–249.
Treadway, A. "The Rational Multivariate Flexible Accelerator." *Econometrica* 39(1971): 329–347.
Wohlgenant, Michael K. "Inventory Adjustment and Dynamic Winery Behavior." *American Journal of Agricultural Economics* 64(1982): 222–231. (Erratum: 64(1982): 546.).
Wohlgenant, Michael K. "Modeling the Effects of Restricting Packer-Owned Livestock in the U.S. Swine Industry." *American Journal of Agricultural Economics* 92(2010): 654–666.

# References


Allen, R.G.D. *Mathematical Analysis for Economists*. London: Macmillan & Co., 1938.

Allen, R.G.D., and A.L. Bowley. *Family Expenditures: A Study of Its Variations*. London: P.S. King & Sons, 1935.

Almon, S. "The Distributed Lag Between Capital Appropriations and Expenditures." *Econometrica* 33(1965): 178–196.

Alston, J.A., and G.M. Scobie. "Distribution of Research Gains in Multistage Production Systems: Comment." *American Journal of Agricultural Economics* 65(1983): 353–356.

Amemyia, T. *Advanced Econometrics*. Cambridge, MA: Harvard University Press, 1985.

Anderson, R.W. "Some Theory of Inverse Demand for Applied Demand Analysis." *European Economic Review* 14(1980): 281–290.

Anderson, G., and R. Blundell. "Testing Restrictions in a Flexible Dynamic System: An Application to Consumers' Expenditures in Canada." *Review of Economic Studies* 50(1983): 397–410.

Appelbaum, E. "Testing Price Taking Behavior." *Journal of Econometrics* 9(1979): 283–294.

Appelbaum, E. "The Estimation of the Degree of Oligopoly Power." *Journal of Econometrics* 19(1982): 287–299.

Arrow, K., and M. Kurz. *Public Investment, the Rate of Return, and Optimal Fiscal Policy*. Baltimore: Johns Hopkins Press, 1970.

Asche, F., and C.R. Wessells. "On Price Indices in the Almost Ideal Demand System." *American Journal of Agricultural Economics* 79(1997): 1182–1185.

Azzam, Azzeddine M. "Asymmetry and Rigidity in Farm-Retail Price Transmission." *American Journal of Agricultural Economics* 81(3)(1999): 525–533.

Banergee, A., and P. Mizon. "A Re-interpretation of the Linear Quadratic Model When Inventories and Sales are Polynomially Cointegrated." *Journal of Applied Econometrics* 21(2006): 1249–1264.

Banks, J., R. Blundell, and A. Lewbel. "Quadratic Engel Curves and Consumer Demand." *The Review of Economics and Statistics* 79(1997): 527–539.

Barnett, W.A. "Theoretical Foundations of the Rotterdam Model." *Review of Economic Studies* 46(1978): 109–130.

Barnett, W.A. "The Miniflex Laurent Translog Flexible Functional Form." *Journal of Econometrics* 30(1985): 33–44.

Barnett, W.A., and A. Jonas. "The Muntz-Szatz Demand System: An Application of a Globally Behaved Series Expansion." *Economics Letters* 11(1983): 337–342.

Barnett, W.A., and A. Serlitis. "Consumer Preferences and Demand Systems." *Journal of Econometrics* 147(2008): 210–224.







M. K. Wohlgenant, *Market Interrelationships and Applied Demand Analysis*, Palgrave Studies in Agricultural Economics and Food Policy, https://doi.org/10.1007/978-3-030-73144-1

Barnett, W.A., and O. Seck. "Rotterdam Model Versus Almost Ideal Demand System: Will the Best Specfication Please Stand Up?" *Journal of Applied Econometrics* 23(2008): 795–824.
Barten, A.P. "Consumer Demand Functions under Conditions of Almost Additive Preferences." *Econometrica* 32(1964): 1–38.
Barten, A.P. "Evidence on the Slutsky Conditions for Demand Equations." *The Review of Economics & Statistics* 49(1967): 77–84.
Barten, A.P. "Maximum Likelihood Estimation of a Complete Demand Systems." *European Economic Review* 1(1969): 7–73.
Barten, A.P. "The Systems of Demand Functions Approach: A Review." *Econometrica* 45(1977): 23-51.
Barten, A.P. "Consumer Allocation Models: Choice of Functional Forms." *Empirical Economics* 18(1993): 129–158.
Barten, A.P., and L.J. Betandorf. "Price Formation of Fish: An Application of an Inverse Demand System." *European Economic Review* 33(1989): 1509–1515.
Barten, A.P., and E. Geyskens. "The Negativity Condition in Consumer Demand." *European Economic Review* 6(1975): 227–260.
Barten, A.P., and S.J. Turnovsky. "Some Aspects of the Aggregation Problem for Aggregate Demand Systems." *International Economic Review* 7(1966): 231–259.
Bask, M., and M. Melkersson. "Rationally Addicted to Drinking and Smoking?" *Applied Economics* 36(2004): 373–386.
Baumol, W.J. "Contestable Markets: An Uprising in the Theory of Industry Structure." *The American Economic Review* 72(1982): 1–15.
Becker, G.S., M. Grossman, and K.M. Murphy. "An Empirical Analysis of Cigarette Addiction." *The American Economic Review* 84(1994): 396–418.
Berndt, E.R., and M.S. Khaled. "Parametric Productivity Measurement and Choice Among Flexible Functional Forms." *Journal of Political Economy* 87(1979): 1220–1245.
Berndt, E.R., and N.E. Savin. "Estimation and Hypothesis Testing in Singular Systems with Autoregressive Disturbances." *Econometrica* 43(1975): 937–957.
Berry, S.L. "Estimating Discrete Choice Models of Product Differentiation." *The Rand Journal of Economics* 25(1994): 242–262.
Bieri, J., and Alain de Janvry. *Empirical Analysis of Demand under Consumer Budgeting.* University of California, Giannini Foundation Monograph No. 30, Calif. Agric. Exp. Sta., Berkeley, CA, 1972.
Bivin, D.G. "Gauging the Performance of the Linear-Quadratic Inventory Model." *Applied Economics* 37(2005): 1215–1231.
Blackorby, C., and R.R. Russell. "Will the Real Elasticity of Substitution Please Stand Up? *The American Economic Review* 79(1989): 882–888.
Blackorby, C., D. Primont, and B.R. Russell. *Duality, Separability, and Functional Structure.* New York: North Holland Publishing Co., 1978.
Blanchard, O.J. "The Production and Inventory Behavior of the American Automobile Industry." *Journal of Political Economy* 91(1983): 365–400.
Blanciforti, L., and R. Green. "An Almost Ideal Demand System Incorporating Habits: An Analysis of Expenditures on Food and Aggregate Commodity Groups." *The Review of Economics and Statistics* 65(1983): 511–515.
Blundell, R., and C. Meghir. "Bivariate Alternatives to the Tobit Model." *Journal of Econometrics* 34(1987): 179–200.
Bollino, C.A. "GAIDS: A Generalized Version of the Almost Ideal Demand System." *Economics Letters* 23(1987): 199–202.
Box, G.E.P., and G.M. Jenkins. *Time Series Analysis: Forecasting and Control.* San Francisco: Holden-Day, Inc., 1970.
Brandow, G.E. *Interrelations Among Demands for Farm Products and Implications for Control of Market Supply.* Pennsylvania Agric. Exp. Sta. Bul. 680, University Park, PA, 1961.

Braulke, M. "The Firm in Short-Run Equilibrium: Comment." *The American Economic Review* 74(1984): 750–753.

Braulke, M. "On the Comparative Statics of a Competitive Industry." *The American Economic Review* 77(1987): 479–485.

Brennan, M.J. "The Supply of Storage." *The American Economic Review* 48(1958): 50-72.

Breshnahan, T.F. "The Oligopoly Solution is Identified." *Economics Letters* 10(1982): 87–92.

Breshnahan, T.F. "Empirical Studies of Industries with Market Power." In R. Schmalansee and R. Willig (eds.) *Handbook of Industrial Organization*, Vol. II, pp. 1011–1057. Amsterdam: Elsevier Science Publishers B V., 1989.

Brester, Gary W., and Michael K. Wohlgenant. "Correcting for Measurement Error in Food Demand Estimation." *The Review of Economics and Statistics* 75(1993): 352–356.

Brown, M., and D. Heien. "The S-Branch Utility: A Generalization of the Linear Expenditure System." *Econometrica* 40(1972): 737–747.

Browning, M. "A Simple Nonadditive Preference Structure for Models of Household Behavior over Time." *Journal of Political Economy* 99(1991): 607–637.

Buccola, S.T. "Material and Value-Adding Inputs in Manufacturing Enterprises." *Journal of Productivity Analysis* 13(2000): 231–247.

Carpentier, Alan, and Herve' Guyomard. "Unconditional Elasticities in Two-Stage Demand Systems: An Approximate Solution." *American Journal of Agricultural Economics* 83(2001): 222–229.

Chalfant, J.A. "A Globally Flexible, Almost Ideal Demand System." *Journal of Business and Economics Statistics* 5(1987): 233–242.

Chan, T.Y. "Estimating a Continuous Hedonic-Choice Model with an Application to Demand for Soft Drinks." *Rand Journal of Economics* 37(2006): 466–482.

Chavas,J-P., and T.L. Cox. "On Market Equilibrium Analysis." *American Journal of Agricultural Economics* 79(1997): 500–513.

Choi, Hee-Jung, Michael K. Wohlgenant, and Xiaoyong Zheng. "Household Level Welfare Effects of Organic Milk Introduction." *American Journal of Agricultural Economics* 45(2013): 1009–1028.

Chow, G.C. "Rational Versus Adaptive Expectations in Present Value Models." *The Review of Economics and Statistics* 71(1989): 376–384.

Christensen, L.R., D.W. Jorgenson, and L.J. Lau. "Transcendental Logarithmic Utility Functions." *The American Economic Review* 65 (1975): 367–382.

Christensen, L.R., and M.F. Manser. "Estimating U.S. Consumer Preferences for Meats with a Flexible Utility Function." *Journal of Econometrics* 5(1977): 37-53.

Clements, K.W. "Price Elasticities of Demand are Minus One-Half." *Economics Letters* 99(2008): 490–493.

Clements, K.W., and G. Gao. "Quality, Quantity, Spending, and Prices." *European Economic Review* 56(2012): 1376–1391.

Clements, K.W., and J. Si. "Diet Diversity, Engel's Law, and the Quality of Food Consumption." *American Journal of Agricultural Economics* 100(2017): 1–22.

Clements, K.W., and L.W. Johnson. "The Demand for Beer, Wine, and Spirits: A Systemwide Analysis." *Journal of Business* 56(1983): 273-304.

Cornes, R. *Duality and Modern Economics*. New York, NY: Cambridge University Press, 1992.

Cooper, R.J., and K.R. McLaren. "An Empirically Oriented Demand System with Improved Regularity Properties." *Canadian Journal of Economics* 25(1992): 652–657.

Cox, T. "An Analysis of Price Effects in Cross-Section Demand." Ph.D. Thesis, Texas A&M University, 1984.

Cox, T., and M.K. Wohlgenant. "Prices and Quality Effects in Cross-Sectional Demand Analysis." *American Journal of Agricultural Economics* 68(1986): 908-919.

Cowling, K., and A.J. Raynor. "Price, Quality, and Market Share." *Journal of Political Economy* 78(1970): 1292–1309.

Cramer, J.S. "Interaction of Income and Price in Consumer Demand." *International Economic Review* 14(1973): 351–363.

Dagenais, M.G. "The Use of Incomplete Observations in Multiple Regression Analysis." *Journal of Econometrics* 1(1973): 317–328.

Davidson, R., and J.G. MacKinnon. *Estimation and Inference in Econometrics*. New York: Oxford University Press, 1993.

Davis, G.C., N. Lin, and C.R. Shumway. "Aggregation Without Separability: Tests of the American and Mexican Agricultural Data." *American Journal of Agricultural Economics* 82(2000): 214–230.

Davis, G. C., and M. K. Wohlgenant. "Demand Elasticities from a Discrete Choice Model: The Natural Christmas Tree Market." *American Journal of Agricultural Economics* 75(1993): 730–738.

Deaton, A. "Panel Data from Time Series of Cross Sections." *Journal of Econometrics* 30(1985): 109–126.

Deaton, A. "Demand Analysis." In Z. Griliches and M.D. Intriligator (eds.) *Handbook of Econometrics*, Vol. 3, pp. 1769–1843. Amsterdam: Elsevier Science, 1986.

Deaton, A. "Estimation of Own- and Cross-Price Elasticities from Household Survey Data." *Journal of Econometrics* 36(1987): 7–30.

Deaton, A. "Quality, Quantity, and Spatial Variation of Price." *The American Economic Review* 78(1988): 418–430.

Deaton, A. "Price Elasticities from Survey Data: Extensions and Indonesian Results." *Journal of Econometrics* 44(1990): 281–309.

Deaton, A.S., and J. Muellbauer. "An Almost Ideal Demand System." *The American Economic Review* 70(1980a): 312-326.

Deaton, A.S., and J. Muellbauer. *Economics and Consumer Behavior*. Cambridge: Cambridge University Press, 1980b.

Dickey, D.A., and W.A. Fuller. "Distributions of the Estimators for Autoregressive Time Series with Unit Roots." *Journal of the American Statistical Association* 74(1979): 427–431.

Diewert, W.E. "An Application of the Shephard Duality Theorem: A Generalized Leontief Production Function." *Journal of Political Economy* 79(1971): 481–507.

Diewert, W.E. "Applications of Duality Theory." In M.D. Intriligator and D.A. Kendrick (eds.) *Frontiers of Quantitative Economics*. Amsterdam: North-Holland Publishing Co., 1974.

Diewert, W.E. "Duality Approaches to Microeconomic Theory." The Economic Series, Technical Report No. 281, Institute for Mathematical Studies in the Social Sciences, Stanford University, 1978.

Diewert, W.E. "The Comparative Statics of Long-Run Equilibrium." *Canadian Journal of Economics* 14(1981): 78–92.

Diewert, W.E., and T.J. Wales. "A Normalized Quadratic Semiflexible Functional Form." *Journal of Econometrics* 37(1988): 327–342.

Dong, D., J.S. Shonkwiler, and O.A. Capps, Jr. "Estimation of Demand Functions using Household Data: The Problem Revisited." *American Journal of Agricultural Economics* 80(1998): 466–473.

Eichenbaum, M. "Some Empirical Evidence on the Production Level and Production Cost Models of Inventory Investment." *The American Economic Review* 79(1989): 853–864.

Fackler, P.F., and B.K. Goodwin. "Spatial Price Analysis." In B.L. Gardner and G.C. Rausser (eds.) *Handbook of Agricultural Economics,* Vol. 1b, , pp. 971–1026. Amsterdam: Elsevier Science B.V., 2001, Chapter 17.

Fama, E.F. and A.B. Laffler. "The Number of Firms and Competition." *The American Economic Review* 62(1972): 670–674.

Freebairn, J.W. "Farm and Retail Food Prices." *Review of Marketing and Agricultural Economics* 52(1984): 71–90.

Friedman, M. *Price Theory*. Chicago: Aldine Publishing Co., 1976.

Frisch, R.A. "A Complete Scheme for Computing All Direct and Cross Demand Elasticities." *Econometrica* 27(1959): 177-196.

Fuller, W.A. *Introduction to Statistical Time Series.* New York: Wiley, 1976.
Gallant, A.R. "On the Bias in Flexible Functional Forms and Essentially Unbiased Form: The Fourier Flexible Form." *Journal of Econometrics* 15(1981): 211-245.
Gallant, A.R. *Nonlinear Statistical Models.* New York: Wiley, 1987.
Gallet, C.A. "The Demand for Alcohol: A Meta-Analysis of Elasticities." *Australian Journal of Agricultural and Resource Economics* 51(2007): 121–135.
Gardner, B. "The Farm-Retail Price Spread in a Competitive Food Industry." *American Journal of Agricultural Economics* 57(1975): 399-409.
George, P.S., and G.A. King. *Consumer Demand for Food Commodities in the United State with Projections for 1980.* Giannini Foundation Monograph No. 26, California Agricultural Experiment Station, Berkeley, CA, 1971.
Goldman, S.M., and H. Uzawa. "A Note on Separability in Demand Analysis." *Econometrica* 32(1964): 1-38.
Goodwin, R.M. "Dynamic Coupling with Expecial Reference to Markets having Production Lags." *Econometrica* 15(1947): 181-204.
Goodwin, B.K., and G.W. Brester. "Structural Change in Factor Demand Relationships in the U.S. Food and Kindred Products Industry." *American Journal of Agricultural Economics* 77(1995): 69-79.
Gorman, W.M. "Separable Utility and Aggregation." *Econometrica* 27(1959): 469-481.
Gorman, W.M. "Tastes, Habits and Choices." *International Economic Review* 8(1967): 218-222.
Green, H.A.J. *Aggregation in Economics Analysis: An Introductory Survey.* Princeton, NJ: Princeton University Press, 1964.
Green, R., and J.M. Alston. "Elasticities in AIDS Models." *American Journal of Agricultural Economics* 72(1990): 442-445.
Green, R., and J.M. Alston. "Elasticities in AIDS Models: A Clarification and Extension." *American Journal of Agricultural Economics* 73(1991): 874-875.
Greene, W.H. *Econometric Analysis.* Upper Saddle River, NJ: Pearson Education, Inc., 2003.
Griffith, G.R. "Sydney Meat Marketing Margins: An Econometric Analysis." *Review of Marketing and Agricultural Economics* 43(1974): 223-239.
Gourieroux, C., and A. Monfort. "On the Problem of Missing Data in Linear Models." *Review of Economic Studies* 48(1981): 579-86.
Gulseven, O., and M. Wohlgenant. "A Quality Based Approach to Estimating Quantitative Elasticities for Differentiated Products: An application to Retail Milk Demand." *Quality & Quantity* 49(2015): 2077-2096.
Hadley, G. *Linear Algebra.* Reading, MA: Addison-Wesley Publishing Company, Inc., 1961.
Hausman, J.A. "Specification Tests in Econometrics." *Econometrica* 46(1978): 1251-1271.
Hausman, J.A., G.K. Leonard, and J.D. Zona. "Competitive Analysis with Differenciated Products." *Annales d'Économie et de Statistique* (1994): 160–180.
Hausman, J.A., and W.E. Taylor. "Panel Data and Unobservable Individual Effects." *Econometrica* 49(1981): 1377-1398.
Heien, D.M. "Markup Pricing in a Dynamic Model of the Food Industry." *American Journal of Agricultural Economics* 62(1980): 10-18.
Heien, D.M., and C.R. Wessells. "Demand Systems Estimation with Microdata: A Censored Regression Approach." *Journal of Business & Economic Statistics* 8(1990): 365-381.
Heiner, R.A. "Theory of the Firm in 'Short-Run' Industry Equilibrium." *The American Economic Review* 82(1982): 555-562.
Heiner, R.A. "Theory of the Firm in Short-Run Industry Equilibrium: Further Comment." *American Economic Review* 74(1984): 754.
Hicks, J.R. *The Theory of Wages.* New York: St. Martin's Press, 1957.
Hoang, L.V. "Estimation of Food Demand with Survey Data from Vietnam," DEPOCEN Working Paper Series No. 2009/12, Center for Agricultural Policy, Institute of Policy and Strategy for Agriculture and Rural Development, Vietnam, 2009.

Hoderlein, S., and S. Mihaleva. "Increasing the Price Variation in a Cross Section." *Journal of Econometrics* 147(2008): 316-325.

Holloway, G.J. "The Farm-Retail Price Spread in an Imperfectly Competitive Food Industry." *American Journal of Agricultural Economics* 73(1991): 979-989.

Holt, M.T., and B.K. Goodwin. "Generalized Habit Formulation in an Inverse Almost Ideal Demand System: An Application to Meat Expenditures in the U.S." *Empirical Economics* 22(1997): 293-320.

Holt, C., F. Modigliani, J. Muth, and H. Simon. *Planning Production, Inventories, and Work Force.* Englewood Cliffs, N.J.: Prentice Hall, 1960.

Houck, J.P. "An Approach to Specifying and Estimating Nonreversible Functions." *American Journal of Agricultural Economics* 15(1977): 570-572.

Houthakker, H.S. "Compensated Changes in Quantities and Qualities Consumed." *Review of Economic Studies* 19(1952-53): 155-164.

Houthakker, H.S. "Additive Preferences." *Econometrica* 28(1960): 244-257.

Houthakker, H.S., and L.D. Taylor. *Consumer Demand in the United States: Analyses and Projections.* 2nd Ed. Cambridge, MA: Harvard University Press, 1970.

Huang, K.S. *A Complete System of U.S. Demand for Food.* USDA Technical Bulletin No. 1821, Washington, 1993.

Jorgenson, D.W. "Rational Distributed Lag." *Econometrica* 34(1966): 135-149.

Just, R.E., and W.S. Chern. "Tomatoes, Technology, and Oligopsony." *Bell Journal of Economics* 11(1980): 584-602.

Kamien, M.I., and N.L. Schwartz. *Dynamic Optimization: The Calculus of Variations and Optimal Control in Economics and Management.* New York: Elsevier North Holland, Inc., 1981.

Keller, W.J., and J. Van Driel. "Differential Consumer Demand Systems." *European Economic Review* 27(1985): 375-390.

Kinnucan, H.W., and O.D. Forker. "Asymmetry in Farm-Retail Price Transmission for Major Dairy Products." *American Journal of Agricultural Economics* 69(1987): 285-292.

Koksal, A., and Michael Wohlgenant. "How Do Smoking Bans in Restaurants Affect Restaurant and at Home Alcohol Consumption? *Empirical Economics* 50(2016): 1193-1213.

Labys, W.C. *Dynamic Commodity Models: Specification, Estimation, and Simulation.* Lexington, MA: D.C. Heath and Co., 1973.

LaFrance, J.T., and W. M. Hanemann. "The Dual Structure of Incomplete Demand Systems." *American Journal of Agricultural Economics* 71(1989): 262-274.

Lamm, R.M., and P.C. Westcott. "The Effect of Changing Input Costs on Food Prices." *American Journal of Agricultural Economics* 63(1981): 187-196.

Lau, L.J. "On Identifying the Degree of Competitiveness from Industry Price and Output Data." *Economics Letters* 10(1982): 93-99.

Lee, L.F. "Simultaneous Equations Models with Discrete and Censored Variables." In C.F. Manski and D. McFadden (eds.) *Structural Analysis of Discrete Data with Econometric Applications*, pp. 346-364. Cambridge, MA: MIT Press, 1981.

Lewbel, A. "Identification and Estimation of Equivalence Scales under Weak Separability." *The Review of Economic Studies* 56(1989): 311-316.

Lewbel, A. "Aggregation Without Separability: A Generalized Composite Commodity Theorem." *The American Economic Review* 86(1996): 524-543.

Lewbel, A., and K. Pendakur. "Tricks with Hicks: The EASI Demand System." *The American Economic Review* 99(2009): 827-863.

Liviathan, N. "The Marginalist Principle in a Discrete Production Model under Uncertain Demand." *Quarterly Journal of Economics* 85(1971): 684–709.

Leontief, W. "Introduction to a Theory of the Internal Structure of Functional Forms." *Econometrica* 15(1947): 361-373.

Lopez, R. "Supply Response and Investment in the Canadian Food Processing Industry." *American Journal of Agricultural Economics* 67(1985): 40-48.

Lovell, M.C. "Manufacturers' Inventories, Sales Expectations, and the Acceleration Principle." *Econometrica* 29(1961): 293-314.

Lucas, R.E. "Optimal Investment Policy and the Flexible Accelerator." *International Economic Review* 8(1967a): 78-85.

Lucas, R.E. "Adjustment Costs and the Theory of Supply." *Journal of Political Economy* 75(1976b): 321-334.

Manser, M. "Elasticities of Demand for Food: An Analysis Using Functions Allowing for Habit Formation." *Southern Economic Journal* (1976): 879-891.

Mark, N.C., M. Ogaki, and K. Sul. "Dynamic Seemingly Unrelated Cointegrating Regressions." *Review of Economic Studies* 72(2005): 797-820.

Marshall, A. *Principles of Economics*. New York: MacMillan Co. Ltd., Inc., 1920.

McLaren, K.R., and R.J. Cooper. "Intertemporal Duality: Application to Theory of the Firm." *Econometrica* 48(1980): 1755-1762.

Meghir, C., and G. Weber. "Intertemporal Nonseparability or Borrowing Restrictions? A Disaggregate Analysis Using a U.S. Consumption Panel." *Econometrica* 64(1996): 1151-1181.

Miedema, A.K. "The Retail-Farm Price Ratio, the Farmer's Share and Technical Change." *American Journal of Agricultural Economics* 58(1976): 750-756.

Meyerhoefer, C.D., C.K. Ranney, and D.E. Sahn. "Consistent Estimation of Censored Demand Systems Using Panel Data." *American Journal of Agricultural Economics* 87(2005): 660–672.

Mills, E.S. "Uncertainty and Price Theory." *Quarterly Journal of Economics* 73(1959): 116-130.

Morrison, C.J. "Quasi-fixed Inputs in US and Japanese Manufacturing: A Generalized Leontief Restricted Cost Function Approach." *The Review of Economics & Statistics* 70(1988): 275-287.

Morrison-Paul, C.J. *Cost Economies and Market Power in US Meat Packing*. Giannini Foundation Monograph No. 44, California Agricultural Experiment Station, Berkeley, CA, 1971.

Morrison-Paul, C.J. "Market and Cost Structure in the US Beef Packing Industry." *American Journal of Agricultural Economics* 83(2001): 64-76.

Mortenson, D.T. "Generalized Adjustment Costs and Dynamic Factor Demand Theory." *Econometrica* 41(1973): 657-665.

Mosak, J.L. "Interrelations of Production, Price, and Derived Demand." *Journal of Political Economy* 46(1938): 761-787.

Moschini, G. "Units of Measurement and the Stone Index in Demand Systems Estimation." *American Journal of Agricultural Economics* 77(1995): 63-68.

Moschini, G. The Semiflexible Almost Ideal Demand System." *European Economic Review* 42(1998): 349-364.

Moschini, G. "Production Risk and the Estimation of Ex-Ante Cost Functions." *Journal of Econometrics* 100(2001): 357-380.

Moschini, G., D. Moro, and R.D. Green. "Maintaining and Testing Separability in Demand Systems." *American Journal of Agricultural Economics* 76(1994): 61-73.

Mundlak, Y., and H. Huang. "International Comparisons of Cattle Cycles." *American Journal of Agricultural Economics* 78(1996): 855-868.

Murphy, K.M., and R.H. Topel. "Estimation and Inference in Two-Step Econometric Models." *Journal of Business & Economics Statistics* 3(1985): 370-379.

Murray, B.C. "Measuring Oligopsony Power with Shadow Prices: U.S. Markets for Pulpwood and Sawlogs." *The Review of Economics and Statistics* 77(1995): 486-498.

Muth, J.F. "Rational Expectations and the Theory of Price Movements." *Econometrica* 29(1961): 299-305.

Muth, M.K., and M.K. Wohlgenant. "A Test for Market Power Using Marginal Input and Output Prices with Application to the U.S. Beef Processing Industries." *American Journal of Agricultural Economics* 81(1999a): 638-643.

Muth, M. K., and M. K. Wohlgenant. "Measuring the Degree of Oligopsony Power in the Beef Packing Industry in the Absence of Marketing Input Quantity Data." *Journal of Agricultural and Resource Economics* 24(1999b): 299-312.

Nadiri, M.I., and S. Rosen. "Interrelated Factor Demand Functions." *American Economic Review* 59(1969): 457-471.

Nelson, J.A. "Quality Variation and Quantity Aggregation in Consumer Demand for Food." *American Journal of Agricultural Economics* 73(1991): 1204-1212.

Nerlove, M. *Distributed Lags and Demand Analysis*. Agricultural Handbook No. 141, U.S. Department of Agriculture, Washington, 1958.

Nerlove, M., and D.A. Bessler. "Expectations, Information and Dynamics." In B.L. Gardner and G.C. Rausser (eds.) *Handbook of Agricultural Economics*, Vol. 1A, pp. 155–206. Amsterdam: Elsevier Science B.V., 2001, Chapter 17.

Newey, K.N., and K.D. West. "A Simple Positive-Definite Heteroskedasticity and Autocorrelation Consistent Covariance Matrix." *Econometrica* 55(1987): 703–708.

Neves, P. "Analysis of Consumer Demand in Portugal, 1958–1981." Memorie de Maitrise en Sciences Economiques, Louvain-la-Neuve, France: University Catholiqque de Louvrain, 1987.

Okrent, A. and J.M. Alston. *Demand for Food in the United States: A Review of Literature, Evaluation of Previous Estimates, and Presentation of New Estimates*. University of California, Giannini Foundation Monograph No. 48, California Agricultural Experiment Station, Berkeley, CA, 2011.

Panzar, J.C., and R.D. Willig. "On the Comparative Statics of a Competitive Industry with Inframarginal Firms." *The American Economic Review* 68(1978): 474–478.

Parish, R.M. "Price Leveling and Averaging." *Farm Economist* 11(1967): 187–198.

Paschardes, P. "Myopic and Forward Looking Behavior in a Dynamic Demand System." *International Economic Review* 27(1986): 387–397.

Peeters, H.M.M. "The (Mis-)Specification of Production Costs in Production Smoothing Models." *Economics Letters* 57(1997): 69–77.

Pelzman, S. "Prices Rise Faster Than They Fall." *Journal of Political Economy* 108(2000): 466–502.

Penske, S., M. Slade, and C. Brett. "Spatial Price Competition: A Semiparametric Approach." *Econometrica* 70(2002): 1111–1155.

Phillips, P.C.B. "Optimal Inference in Cointegrated Systems." *Econometrica* 59(1991): 283–306.

Phlips, L. "A Dynamic Version of the Linear Expenditure Model." *The Review of Economics and Statistics* 54(1972): 450–458.

Phlips, L. *Applied Consumption Analysis*. Amsterdam: North-Holland Publishing Co., 1983.

Pierani, P., and S. Tiezzi. "Addiction and Interaction Between Alcohol and Tobacco Consumption." *Empirical Economics* 37(2009): 1–23.

Piggott, N.E. "The Nested PIGLOG Model: An Application to U.S. Food Demand." *American Journal of Agricultural Economics* 85(2003): 1–15.

Pindyck, R.S., and J.J. Rotemberg. "Dynamic Factor Demands and the Effect of Energy Price Effects." *The American Economic Review* 73(1983): 1066–1079.

Pollack, R.A. "Conditional Demand Functions and the Implications of Separable Utility." *Southern Economic Journal* 37(1970): 423-433.

Pollack, R.A., and T.J. Wales. *Demand System Specification and Estimation*. New York: Oxford University Press, 1992.

Pope, R.D., and R.E. Just. "Empirical Implementation of Ex-Ante Cost Functions. *Journal of Econometrics* 72(1996): 231–249.

Prais, S.J., and H.S. Houtkakker. *The Analysis of Family Budgets*. Cambridge: Cambridge University Press, 1955.

Pudney, S.E. "An Empirical Model of Approximating the Separable Structure of Consumer Preferences." *Review of Economic Studies* 48(1981): 561–577.

Puhani, P.A. "The Heckman Correction for Sample Selection and Its Critique." *Journal of Economic Surveys* 14(2000): 53–67.

Reed, A.J., Reed, A. J., H. Elitzak, and M. K. Wohlgenant. *Retail-Farm Price Margins and Consumer Product Diversity*. USDA Technical Bulletin No. 1899, Washington DC, 2002.

Reed, A.J., and J.W. Levedahl, and C. Hallahn. "The Generalized Composite Commodity Theorem and Food Demand Estimation." *American Journal of Agricultural Economics* 87(2005): 28–37.

Roberts, J.M. "Testing Oligopolistic Behavior." *International Journal of Industrial Organization* 2(1984): 367–383.

Samuelson, P. "Prices of Factors and Goods in General Equilibrium." *Review of Economic Studies* 21(1953–1954): 1–20.

Schroeter, J.R. "Estimating the Degree of Market Power in the Beef Industry." *The Review of Economics and Statistics* 70(1988): 158–162.

Shonkwiler, J.S., and S.T. Yen. "Two-Step Estimation of a Censored Demand System." *American Journal of Agricultural Economics* 81(1999): 972–982.

Silberberg, E. *The Structure of Economics: A Mathematical Analysis*. New York: McGraw Hill Publishing Co., 1990.

Spinnewyn, F. "Rational Habit Formation." *European Economic Review* 15(1981): 91–109.

Sproule, R. "A Systematic Analysis of the Links Amongst the Marshallian, Hicksian, and Frischian Demand Functions: A Note." *Economics Letters* 121(2013): 555–557.

Srivastava, P., K.R. McLaren, M. Wohlgenant, and X. Zhao. "Disaggregated Econometric Analysis of Consumer Demand Response by Alcoholic Beverage Types." *The Australian Journal of Agricultural and Resource Economics* 59(2014): 412–432.

Stigler, G.J., and G.S. Becker. "De Gustibus Non Est Disputandum." *The American Economic Review* 67(1977): 76-90.

Stone, R. "Linear Expenditure Systems and Demand Analysis: An Application to the Pattern of British Demand." *The Economic Journal* 64(1954): 511-527.

Strotz, R.H. "The Empirical Implications of a Utility Tree." *Econometrica* 25(1957): 269–280.

Sumner, D.A. "Measurement of Monopoly: An Application to the Cigarette Industry." *Journal of Political Economy* 89(1981): 1010–1019.

Tchetchick, A., A. Fleischer, and I. Finkelshtain. "Differentiation and Synergies in Rural Tourism: Estimation and Simulation of the Israeli Market." *American Journal of Agricultural Economics* 90(2008): 553–570.

Theil, H. "Qualities, Prices, and Budget Enquiries." *Review of Economic Studies* 19(1952–53): 129–147.

Theil, H. *Principles of Econometrics*. New York: Wiley, 1971.

Theil, H. *Theory and Measurement of Consumer Demand*, Vol. I. Chicago: University of Chicago Press, 1975/1976.

Theil, H. *The System-Wide Approach to Microeconomics*. Chicago: The University of Chicago Press, 1980.

Tomek, W.G., and K.L. Robinson. *Agricultural Product Prices*. Ithaca: Cornell University Press, 1981.

Treadway, A. "The Rational Multivariate Flexible Accelerator." *Econometrica* 39(1971): 329–347.

Varian, H.R. *Microeconomic Analysis*. New York: W.W. Norton & Co., 1992.

Verbeek, M., and T. Nijman. "Can Cohort Data be Treated as Genuine Panel Data?" *Empirical Economics* 17(1992): 9–23.

Vernon, J.M., and D.A. Graham. "Profitability of Monopolization by Vertical Integration." *Journal of Political Economy* 79(1971): 924–925.

Wales, T.J., and A.D. Woodland. "Estimating Consumer Demand Systems with Binding Non-Negativity Constraints." *Journal of Econometrics* 21(1983): 263–285.

Walters, A.A. "Marginal Productivity and Probability Distributions of Factor Services." *The Economic Journal* 70(1960): 325–330.

Ward, R.W. "Asymmetry in Retail, Wholesale, and Shipping Point Pricing for Fresh Vegetables." *American Journal of Agricultural Economics* 64(1982): 205–212.

Waugh, F.V. *Demand and Price Analysis* USDA Technical Bulletin No. 1216, Washington, D.C., 1964.

Wegge, L.L. "Constrained Indirect Least Squares Estimators." *Econometrica* 46(1978): 435–449.

Weiss, Y., and S. Sharir. "A Composite Good Theorem for Simple Sum Aggregates." *Econometrica* 46(1978): 1499–1501.

White, H. "Using Least Squares to Approximate Unknown Regression Functions." *International Economic Review* 21(1980): 149–170.

Wilde, J. "Estimating Multiple Equation Hybrid Models with Endogenous Dummy Regressors." *Statistica Neerlandica* 58(2004): 296–312.

Wohlgenant, Michael K. "Inventory Adjustment and Dynamic Winery Behavior." *American Journal of Agricultural Economics* 64(1982): 222–231 (Erratum: 64(1982): 546.).

Wohlgenant, Michael K. "Conceptual and Functional Form Issues in Estimating Demand Elasticities for Food." *American Journal of Agricultural Economics* 66(1984): 211–215.

Wohlgenant, Michael K. "Competitive Storage, Rational Expectations, and Short-Run Food Price Determination." *American Journal of Agricultural Economics* 67(1985): 739–748.

Wohlgenant, Michael K. "Demand for Farm Output in a Complete System of Demand Functions." *American Journal of Agricultural Economics* 71 (1989): 241–252.

Wohlgenant, Michael K. "Distribution of Gains from Research and Promotion in Multi-Stage Production Systems: The Case of the U.S. Beef and Pork Industries." *American Journal of Agricultural Economics* 75(1993): 642–651. (Errata: 75(1993): 1072.)

Wohlgenant, Michael K. "Marketing Margins: Empirical Analysis." In B.L. Gardner and G.C. Rausser (eds.) *Handbook of Agricultural Economics*, Vol. 1B, pp. 934–970. Amsterdam: Elsevier Science B.V., 2001, Chapter 16.

Wohlgenant, Michael K. "Modeling the Effects of Restricting Packer-Owned Livestock in the U.S. Swine Industry." *American Journal of Agricultural Economics* 92(2010): 654–666.

Wohlgenant, Michael K. "Consumer Demand and Welfare in Equilibrium Displacement Models." In Lusk, J., J. Roosen, and J. Shogren (eds.) *Handbook on the Economics of Food Consumption and Policy*. London: Oxford University Press, 2011, Chapter 11.

Wohlgenant, Michael K. "The Multivariate Rational Addiction Model." *Theoretical Economics Letters* 2(2012): 459–464.

Wohlgenant, Michael K. "Competition in the U.S. Meat Industry." *Annual Review of Resource Economics* 5(1013): 1–12.

Wohlgenant, Michael K. "Market Middlemen and Determinants of the Price Spread Under Competition." *Theoretical Economics Letters* 4(2014): 834–838.

Wohlgenant, Michael K., and William F. Hahn. "Dynamic Adjustment in Monthly Consumer Demands for Meats." *American Journal of Agricultural Economics* 64(1982): 553–557.

Wohlgenant, M.K., and J.D. Mullen. "Modeling the Farm-Retail Price Spread for Beef." *Western Journal of Agricultural Economics* 12(1987): 119-125.

Wohlgenant, M.K., and R.C. Haidacher. *Retail to Farm Demand Linkages of a Complete System of Demand Functions*, USDA Technical Bulletion No. 1775, Washington, 1989.

Wooldridge, J.M. *Econometric Analysis of Cross Section and Panel Data*. Cambridge, MA: The MIT Press, 2010.

Yen, S.T., and B-W Lin. "A Sample-Selection Approach to Systems of Demand Functions." *American Journal of Agricultural Economics* 88(2006): 742–749.

Zhen, Chen, Michael K. Wohlgenant, Shawn Karns, and Philip Kaufman. "Habit Formation and Demand for Sugar-Sweetened Beverages." *American Journal of Agricultural Economics* 93(2011): 175–193.

Zhen, Chen, Eric A. Finkelstein, James M. Nonnemaker, Shawn A. Karns and Jessica E. Todd. "Predicting the Effects of Sugar-Sweetened Beverage Taxes on Food and Beverage Demand in a Large Demand System." *American Journal of Agricultural Economics* 96(2014): 1–25.

# Index




M. K. Wohlgenant, *Market Interrelationships and Applied Demand Analysis*, Palgrave Studies in Agricultural Economics and Food Policy,
https://doi.org/10.1007/978-3-030-73144-1

## N



## O



## P



## Q

GPSR Compliance
The European Union's (EU) General Product Safety Regulation (GPSR) is a set of rules that requires consumer products to be safe and our obligations to ensure this.

If you have any concerns about our products, you can contact us on

ProductSafety@springernature.com

In case Publisher is established outside the EU, the EU authorized representative is:

Springer Nature Customer Service Center GmbH
Europaplatz 3
69115 Heidelberg, Germany

www.ingramcontent.com/pod-product-compliance
Ingram Content Group UK Ltd.
Pitfield, Milton Keynes, MK11 3LW, UK
UKHW022137040925
462575UK00021B/387
* 9 7 8 3 0 3 0 7 3 1 4 3 4 *